SUPREME COURTS AND JUDICIAL LAW-MAKING:
CONSTITUTIONAL TRIBUNALS AND CONSTITUTIONAL REVIEW

By the same author

1. Judicial Review in the English-Speaking World, (1st ed., 1956; 4th ed., 1969).
2. *Föderalismus und Bundesverfassungsrecht*, (1962).
3. Constitutionalism in Germany and the Federal Constitutional Court, (1962).
4. Comparative Federalism. States' Rights and National Power, (1st ed., 1962; 2nd ed., 1965).
5. "Peaceful Coexistence" and Soviet-Western International Law, (1964).
6. Federal Constitution-Making for a Multi-National World, (1966).
7. International Law and World Revolution, (1967).
8. *Conflit idéologique et Ordre public mondial*, (1970).
9. The Illegal Diversion of Aircraft and International Law, (1975).
10. The International Law of *Détente*. Arms Control, European Security, and East-West Cooperation, (1978).
11. The World Court and the Contemporary International Law-Making Process, (1979).
12. Quebec and the Constitution, 1960–1978, (1979).
13. Conflict and Compromise. International Law and World Order in a Revolutionary Age, (1981).
14. Constitution-Making. Principles, Process, Practice, (1981).
15. Canada and the Constitution, 1979–1982. Patriation and the Charter of Rights, (1982).
16. United Nations Law-Making. Cultural and Ideological Relativism and International Law Making for an Era of Transition, (1984).

SUPREME COURTS AND JUDICIAL LAW-MAKING: CONSTITUTIONAL TRIBUNALS AND CONSTITUTIONAL REVIEW

by

Edward McWhinney

Queen's Counsel, Barrister and Solicitor
Professor of International Law & Relations,
Simon Fraser University, Vancouver
Membre de l'Institut de Droit International
Member of the Permanent Court of Arbitration

1986 **MARTINUS NIJHOFF PUBLISHERS**
a member of the KLUWER ACADEMIC PUBLISHERS GROUP
DORDRECHT / BOSTON / LANCASTER

Distributors

for the United States and Canada: Kluwer Academic Publishers, 190 Old Derby Street, Hingham, MA 02043, USA
for the UK and Ireland: Kluwer Academic Publishers, MTP Press Limited, Falcon House, Queen Square, Lancaster LA1 1RN, UK
for all other countries: Kluwer Academic Publishers Group, Distribution Center, P.O. Box 322, 3300 AH Dordrecht, The Netherlands

Library of Congress Cataloging in Publication Data

```
McWhinney, Edward.
   Supreme courts and judicial law-making.

   Includes index.
   1. Judicial review.  2. Judge-made law.
3. Constitutional courts.  4. Courts of last resort.
I. Title.
K3367.M39  1985      347'.035              85-15241
ISBN 90-247-3203-4    342.735
```


ISBN 90-247-3203-4

FOREWORD

All of the tribunals discussed in the present volume are known to me, as to their decisions and also their internal organisation and practice, from research and study and also personal contact, over a number of years – in most cases extending over two or three decades – albeit with the occasional interruption which does not, however, seem to involve any break in the development of the jurisprudence. I have taught in most of the countries concerned, either as a Visiting Professor or as a Special Lecturer, have been a governmental consultant or adviser in some cases, and have also had the advantage of personal friendship and frequent exchange of letters with some of the key judges concerned.

The choice of particular legal systems, national and international, for purposes of comparative law study, must always be somewhat arbitrary. There are always certain obvious choices involving the major political and legal systems, and comparative law study will always be most persuasive, as to its main hypotheses or conclusions, when these derive from a certain plurality of sources, in political-ideological and also legal-systemic terms. Certainly, the empirical validity or weight of such conclusions is strengthened when they rest not merely on abstract research of Court decisions, as published, but also on some direct, first-hand, experiential exposure to the actual processes of decision-making.

One must always apply a certain caveat as to the conclusions from comparative law, going to the 'receivability', from one legal system to another, of the particular experience of any one country, based as it must be upon its own particular societal facts – the background, ethnic-cultural, political, social, and economic conditions – which inevitably condition and limit the positive law and its development in action. Without a substantial identity in such underlying societal facts, the attempt at transfer from one society to another of the special legal institutions and processes and also substantive rules developed is likely to prove a purely mechanical exercise in legal eclecticism, without too much lasting quality. And yet the same political, social, and economic problems do tend to recur in very many different societies at the same level of industrial development and to be presented to the tribunals for final arbitrament, legal or political-legal. It is, in this sense, no surprise to find that the newly-established Constitutional Court of post-Franco Spain should be called on to rule, in its first year, on the merits of 'regionalisation' on ethnic-cultural, linguistic considerations or on the permissibility, in community terms, of voluntary interruption of pregnancy. Different communities at the same level of political and economic development turn out to have the same sorts of community problems and interests-conflicts, though they may not always resolve them in precisely the same way, the basic community values being different. The attractions of comparative law study, and of benefiting from someone else's often trial-and-error experience and perhaps avoiding their mistakes, are thus clear at the present day in an increasingly interdependent and interrelated World Community of states of frequently vastly different ethnic-cultural and ideological bases. The lessons of comparative law, provided that they be not viewed as inexorable historical laws graven, once and for all and beyond hope of redemption and recall, on tablets of stone, have an understandable relevance and attractiveness in contemporary terms. We are all, in measure, sociologists of law today, and comparative sociological jurisprudence thereby becomes the prime intellectual method for inducing general propositions or rules for the establishment and organisation of constitutional tribunals, for regulating their internal procedures and decision-making practice, and even for shaping or influencing their ultimate interests-balancing and conflicts-resolution on the great political and economic *causes célèbres* of our modern, post-industrial society, whether Western, or Western-derived or Western influenced.

Some of the comparative, intersystemic constitutional-legal arguments advanced in the present study were tested in public lectures or seminars held in December, 1983, in New Delhi, under the auspices, variously, of the Indian Law Institute, the Indian Society of International Law, and the Faculty of Law, University of Delhi; and in June, 1984, in Tokyo, under the auspices of the Institute of Comparative Law in Japan, of Chuo University. The general propositions as to specialist constitutional tribunals were also put forward, in January, 1984, in a brief prepared at the invitation of the Law Commission of India, New Delhi, and presented to the Commission at that time.

The Social Sciences and Humanities Research Council of Canada generously assisted in the detailed, field research work involved in the preparation of the volume. These researches were completed, in considerable measure, while the author was serving as University Research Professor at Simon Fraser University. I am indebted to Dean Robert Brown and the administration of Simon Fraser University for their kind support and encouragement throughout the project, and also to Elsie Trott of

Simon Fraser University who typed all the manuscript for publication.

Responsibility for opinions expressed in the completed work remains that of the author alone, and not of any of the persons or institutions mentioned in it, nor of any of the Universities or academies or governmental or international organisations with which the author has been associated, in various ways, over the years.

English Bay   Edward McWhinney
Burnaby Mountain,
Vancouver

TABLE OF CONTENTS

INTRODUCTION

CONSTITUTIONAL REVIEW AND JUDICIAL REVIEW

In an earlier study, *Judicial Review in the English-Speaking World* (1st edition, 1956; 4th edition, 1969), I examined the interaction of the judiciary with the coordinate, executive-administrative and legislative arms of government, through the judicial testing of laws and of executive-administrative decrees and orders by reference to postulated 'higher law' grounds. That examination was made in the general context of the Anglo-Saxon, Common Law countries, and also of those countries that had 'received' Anglo-Saxon, Common Law constitutional institutions, procedures, and principles through the historical accident of past Imperial association – specifically, the United States, Great Britain, and the Commonwealth Countries (Canada, Australia, India, Pakistan, South Africa) formerly linked to Great Britain and British law as part of the old British colonial Empire of yesteryear. It did not matter, for these purposes, that some of the countries concerned had written constitutional charters and sometimes also entrenched constitutional bills of rights and some, like Great Britain, did not. The method was empirical and the emphasis, in Legal Realist tradition, was on what the judges actually did in their deciding of cases and only secondarily on the particular legal formulae – contained in constitutional charter or statutory text, or rationalised in terms of an inherent 'spirit of the laws' – by which the judges justified their decisions, in the official Opinions written in support thereof. The key question at the time *Judicial Review* was first published in 1956 – at least, the key question outside the United States – concerned the nature of the judicial process and the *rôle* of the judges in the deciding of cases. What Judge Jerome Frank and the Legal Realists called the 'basic myth',[1] – that judges do not make law, was then predominant and it was rooted in the positivistic conception of the judicial office as purely mechanical, value-neutral, non-discretionary in character. This led on to the further conception of purely neutral rules of construction which judges could, and did, use to reach conclusions from which extraneous, policy elements had been carefully excised in advance. A good deal of the thrust, then, of *Judicial Review* had to be in the empirical demonstration, through field studies in a number of countries sharing the same, or very much of the same, legal traditions and experience, that judges had, indeed, more or less consciously shaped constitutional and general legal development in the process of decision-making; and that judicial policy preferences had operated in the interstices of their decisions on great political, social and economic issues, sometimes avowedly but more often in terms of what Mr. Justice Oliver Wendell Holmes, Jr., of the United States Supreme Court had once described as 'inarticulate major premises'.[2] So much of the intellectual energies in the legal 'great debate' of that era had to be devoted, of necessity, to dispelling the 'basic myth', that too little attention was given, even in the United States, to the even more basic question for a liberal-democratic polity of the legitimacy, in constitutional terms, of such judicial policy-making, covert as it so largely was at the time, and to the related technical question of its efficiency in scientific-legal terms in comparison to other, more open forms of community policy-making in the modern state. Some part of these other questions was necessarily dealt with, and answered at the time, at least in part, in the battle in American Supreme Court jurisprudence of the era between the proponents of judicial activism, who rallied round the great liberal Justices, Hugo Black and William O. Douglas, of the post-1937, 'Roosevelt' Supreme Court; and those who advocated judicial self-restraint on issues of political, social and economic choice, who were associated in particular with Mr. Justice Felix Frankfurter (also a Roosevelt appointment to the Court, and representing that other intellectual stream of American constitutional liberalism, and claiming, like Black and Douglas and their disciples, a spiritual heritage flowing directly from Holmes and Brandeis).

The key question in *Judicial Review* today has to do, not with the 'basic myth'; for there will be few, today, who will try to deny the empirical record of judicial law-making or who will themselves want to give it up. Our prime concern, today, is rather with its constitutional legitimacy and with ways of rendering it 'responsible' and relating it to contemporary constitutional conceptions of popular sovereignty. This points the way to comparisons of institutions and processes for selection of judges and the rules regulating their tenure and behaviour, in different constitutional systems; and to the main trends in constitutional reform and constitution-making, in these areas, in modern times. There is also need for study of the key features of internal Court organisation, and of practice as to decision-making and opinion-writing, and of *rôle* of the Chief Justice and the collegial character and functioning of different tribunals. All this goes, of course, to the technical refinement of the judicial policy-making function and its perfectioning in social science terms, which is the necessary follow-up to the question of the constitutional legitimacy today of such expanded, law-making *rôle* for the judiciary, once this latter question has been properly posed and answered in affirmative terms.

In my survey of the English-speaking, Common Law or Common Law-derived or influenced, constitutional World, I used the term Judicial Review as the generic term or classification for the *rôle* played by Supreme Courts, in constitutional matters, in regard to the other, coordinate, executive and legislative, arms of government. In a later work, treating of cognate, West German experience, *Constitutionalism in Germany and the Federal Constitutional Court* (1962), I saw no reason for not using the same term, Judicial Review, in describing Court practice in applying constitutional norms to scrutinise executive and legislative action, this although it was to be employed in the special context of a Continental European, Civil Law-based constitutional system, albeit one heavily influenced, in its post-World War II phase at least, by 'received' American constitutional ideas as to institutions and processes and substantive legal principles too. The phenomenon of 'reception' from one legal system to another, across differences of language and culture and legal-systemic organisation and experience, is not new of course;[3] and sometimes, as with the Meiji 'reception' in Japan from 1867 onwards,[4] it has been widespread and fundamental, where elsewhere, in comparison, it may have been a purely mechanical eclecticism that has never taken firm root and so has disappeared. A successful 'reception', as in West Germany and in Japan after World War II, will normally involve the institutions or processes borrowed from another country taking on a new and autonomous existence of their own as the new, 'foreign' elements are blended or absorbed into the older, domestic legal system and modified or even transformed in the process. The 'received' institutions and processes may even end up being more successful politically, and better functioning in technical, scientific-legal terms, than the original models abroad from which they were taken in the first place, as, it may be suggested, is true with some of the post-World War II borrowings of distinctive United States institutions and processes. Such a situation is not to be regretted in any way, but rather to be welcomed and profited from, in turn. Why should not parent, donor country take advantage of the opportunity of study, in the context of another legal system than its own, the trial-and-error testing of particular institutions and processes whose vitality may seem to be flagging at home and in need of new inspiration and a new course?

In taking note of the 'reception' of the American system of judicial review, – its special legal institutions, processes, and thought-ways – in other countries after World War II, one recognises, of course, the presence in those other countries, in many cases, of indigenous precursors for judicial review that are rooted in those countries' own special, indigenous constitutional and general legal history. American scholars specialised in their own constitutional system and comparing it, for historical research purposes, with Japanese or West German post-War constitutionalism, have tended to stress the separateness and distinctness, in terms of historical origins, of the Japanese and West German systems of Court control of constitutionality. A distinction is sought to be advanced between an American-style *judicial* review posited upon a Supreme Court of general jurisdiction determining concrete case/controversies against a detailed fact record – in effect, a fact-oriented decision upon the rights and duties of different parties in active and direct conflict with each other; and a Continental European-style *constitutional* review, applied by a specialised constitutional court in the case of abstract controversies between different units (executive and legislature, for example) or different levels (central and regional administrations, for example) of government, about their respective rights and duties under the constitution, and never, in any circumstances, implying the authority of a Court to nullify legislation or legislative action on constitutional grounds. This distinction between a postulated American system of Court review of the concrete application of executive-legislative acts in individual cases (*das richterliche Prüfungsrecht*) and a postulated European system of Court arbitration of intra-governmental conflicts *in abstracto* (*die Staatsgerichtsbarkeit*)[5] has a certain historical validity, at least, in its second part as a purported summation of the range and extent of that embryonic form of Court-based constitutional scrutiny or control exercised, after World War I, by the *Verfassungsgerichtshof* under Kelsen's Austrian Constitution of 1920; or even the authority possessed by the *Staatsgerichtshof* under Preuss' celebrated but ill-fated (German Republican) Weimar Constitution of 1919.[6] Viewed, however, even as constitutional ideal-types or models for purposes of juridical classification they have their limitations, granted the empirical record in modern times of the 'reception' and exchange and borrowing of constitutional institutions, processes, and ideas from one legal system to another, and their mutual interaction; and also granted the extent to which functionalism in constitutional law will tend to produce similar institutional and processual responses to the same type of community problems occurring in different legal systems at the same time, even without any direct interaction between them. The Anglo-Saxon, Common Law or Common Law-derived, Supreme Court of general jurisdiction is tending, by sheer pressure of the quantity of Court business and the relative social importance of the different categories of business, to become, more and more, a *de facto* special constitutional tribunal, paralleling Continental European, Civil Law, models. And while the Anglo-Saxon, Common Law or Common

Law-derived Supreme Court might traditionally eschew intervening as to certain claimed exercises of executive-based prerogative powers or to control the legislature in its internal working and usages (for example, in electoral matters), the once quite large category of non-justiciable 'political questions' which amounted to a very real gap in the Courts' constitutional jurisdiction, has been progressively whittled away, to the point of disappearance, in modern times. Intra-governmental, inter-institutional conflicts are, quite definitely today, part of the normal business of Supreme Courts' constitutional jurisdiction, whether those Courts be *de jure* or *de facto* constitutional courts; and all such Courts rule, today, on the interpretation of the application of executive and legislative acts and decrees in concrete cases, and on individual citizens' complaints of violation of their constitutional rights. In an interdependent World made up of mutually interacting states, with a large degree of intellectual and cultural exchange and cross-fertilisation between them, the principles of Court structure and organisation and internal ordering and practice tend increasingly to approximate. I see no good reason, therefore, for maintaining, as an operational classification today, any distinction between *constitutional* review and *judicial* review; though study of the particular origins of Court scrutiny and control of constitutionality in the different countries and also detailed analysis of the actual constitutional charter or statutory-based definition of such jurisdiction may be necessary to establish whether it is comprehensive and applicable in principle, therefore, to all constitutional situations, or whether it is simply a series of specific categories of constitutional jurisdiction (as in West Germany, for example) and therefore capable of having gaps in it.

We shall use constitutional review and judicial review more or less interchangeably as to present-day constitutional jurisdiction of Courts, recognising, however, the possibility always that such review of constitutionality might be exercised by someone other than a judge or Court *stricto sensu,* as with the *Conseil constitutionnel* under the Fifth French Republican Constitution of 1958,[7] for example; and recognising also the tendency, even within constitutional courts, as such, to deemphasise strictly professional judicial training in the ground rules governing selection of the Court's members, in favour of a more general liberal learning in law or actual experience in the practice of constitutional government in its various executive and legislative branches, national and regional. Such a development, manifest in the post-World War II statutory provisions as to recruitment of Court members and also in the preferred patterns of executive-legislative selection for constitutional courts, seems logical enough, granted the new emphasis on, and public acceptance of, judicial policy-making and judicial legislation on constitutional questions. If the judge is to be a law-maker in the same very real sense as other community policy-makers, executive and legislative, why not choose the political man or woman-of-affairs, or the legal philosopher, quite as much as the more narrowly technical legal professional, (whether practising lawyer, as in Common Law countries or permanent, career civil servant, as in Civil Law countries).

NOTES

1. Jerome Frank, *Law and the Modern Mind* (1930), p. 20. And see generally Thurman Arnold, 'Judge Jerome Frank', 24 *University of Chicago Law Review* 633 (1957); Edmond Cahn, 'Jerome Frank's Fact-Skepticism and our future', 66 *Yale Law Journal* 824 (1957); E. McWhinney, 'Judge Jerome Frank and Legal Realism: an appraisal', 3 *New York Law Forum* 113 (1957); E. McWhinney, 'A Legal Realist and a Humanist: cross-currents in the legal philosophy of Judge Jerome Frank', 33 *Indiana Law Journal* 111 (1958).
2. *Lochner* v. *New York,* 198 U.S. 45 (1905), (Holmes J., dissenting).
3. A.F. Schnitzer, 'Ist massive Rezeption fremden Rechts gerechtfertigt?', in *Problèmes Contemporains de Droit Comparé,* vol. 1 (Naojiro Sugiyama, ed.) (1962), p. 115.
4. R.H. Minear, *Japanese Tradition and Western Law. Emperor, State, and Law in the Thought of Hozumi Yatsuka* (1970), p. 31 *et seq.,* p. 143 *et seq.*
5. E. Friesenhahn, 'Die Verfassungsgerichtsbarkeit in der Bundesrepublik Deutschland', *Verfassungsgerichtsbarkeit in der Gegenwart. Länderberichte und Rechtsvergleichung (H. Mosler, ed.) (1962), p. 89 et seq.*; H. Laufer, *Verfassungsgerichtsbarkeit und politischer Prozess* (1968), p. 7 *et seq.*; E. McWhinney, *Constitutionalism in Germany and the Federal Constitutional Court* (1962), p. 17 *et seq.*; Donald P. Kommers, *Judicial Politics in West Germany: a study of the Federal Constitutional Court* (1976), p. 30 *et seq.*
6. H. Grund, *'Preussenschlag' und Staatsgerichtshof im Jahre 1932* (1976).
7. L. Favoreu and L. Philip, *Le Conseil constitutionnel* (1978); F. Luchaire, *Le Conseil constitutionnel* (1980).

CHAPTER I

CONSTITUTIONAL REVIEW AND CONSTITUTIONAL JURISDICTION

1. CONTEMPORARY POPULARITY OF CONSTITUTIONAL REVIEW

Court-based testing and ultimately control, on 'higher law' constitutional grounds, of executive and legislative action, is one of the more striking trends in constitutionalism and in constitution-making of the post-World War II era. The institution of specialised constitutional courts, either created specially and in terms for the purpose of exercising constitutional review, or else developing *ad hoc,* through constitutional custom and convention (practice) in pragmatic, experiential response to the same perceived constitutional needs, is the most visible expression of that trend.

Part of the explanation for the popularity of an institutionalised system of court-based constitutional review after 1945 has to do with the major political facts-of-life of international relations of that time. The collapse of so many states in military defeat and supervening military occupation in the period 1939 to 1945 brought intense intellectual soul-searching and the belief that, among other things, the erstwhile national constitutional systems must have been at fault and contributing factors to the disasters that had just been lived through. This brought, in its turn, a conclusion that one must try to break new constitutional ground to ensure that history would not repeat itself, and that one should reach out, therefore, for new constitutional models in place of more traditional historical stereotypes. The politically dominant *rôle* played by the United States in the military victory of 1944-5 and the liberation of Europe and South-East Asia meant an enormous post-War prestige and popularity for distinctively American legal institutions and processes, like judicial review of the constitution, which were widely credited with the evident success of the American constitutional polity and way of life. The United States which had also, in terms of its own constitutional folk-lore, successfully emancipated itself, a century and a half earlier, by a form of War of national liberation against its old Imperial power, happened to be very well placed, after 1945, in the first wave of decolonisation and independence in response to the 'new' International Law principle of self-determination of peoples, to serve as a constitutional drafting paradigm or model for the new class of indigenous constitution-makers about to take over from their former Imperial powers and charged with the mandate of adopting a national constitutional charter in national constituent assembly.

Beyond that, the recently defeated Axis powers, subjected as they were to the further humiliation of prolonged military occupation by the victorious Allies and anxious to spare themselves that national indignity as soon as possible, were encouraged to replace their pre-War constitutional systems which were considered, rightly or wrongly at the time, to have hastened the onset of authoritarian, Fascist-style governments and thus to have contributed their share of the ultimate War guilt that was attributed, too loosely, at the time, to the defeated Axis powers alone. The desire, understandable enough, to move from the constitutionally old, with its historically discredited associations, to the constitutionally new, was assisted also by the increasing comprehension that the Western Allies, then increasingly preoccupied by the emerging Soviet-Western tensions within the temporary wartime Alliance against Fascism and the onset of the Cold War, would be more readily encouraged to terminate their military occupation and to restore sovereignty to defeated Germany and Japan, if only they could be satisfied that they were turning over power again to newly-cleansed, democratic constitutional systems. What better way of demonstrating, in concrete terms, the turning of a constitutional new leaf than by absorbing, in measure, American constitutional experience and adopting, in terms, special American constitutional institutions and processes and also, to the extent possible, constitutional thought-ways and values!

The times were thus especially favourable, after 1945, for a widespread 'reception' and borrowing abroad from distinctive American constitutionalism. The times were also especially ripe for constitution-making in general. What we may call, after the great protagonist of historical evolution of law in the early 19th century debate over the proposed codification of the German civil law, von Savigny's axiom, operated to full advantage. In his debate with the rationalist Thibaut, von Savigny had argued,[1] – successfully, from the political viewpoint, as it turned out, for it delayed the civil law project until the end of the century – that not all periods in a nation's historical development are propitious for codification or acts of generalised law-making; and that it is very difficult, if not impossible, to proceed in the absence of a general national understanding or consensus on the goals and directions of society and its legal institutions and processes. The correlative of that proposition, of course, is that when the times are ripe, because of widespread community consensus, then one should act, and act quickly, in order to profit from that normally fleeting period. The experience of a number of countries that have tried, in the late 1960s and the 1970s and early 1980s, to make fundamental revisions of constitutional systems that were already a going concern – Japan, Switzerland, West Germany, Canada, for example – is that it is extraordinarily difficult in normal times to succeed with such projects of constitutional novation, even if, as in the case of West Germany, it involved a project of renewal of a charter itself adopted in an earlier (post-1945) period of societal consensus. Manifestly, that national unity as to goals and directions of society and their best institutional implementation exists most easily in periods of public euphoria following on some crisis or similar national event – a great military victory or even defeat, a social and economic revolution – which provides a rallying of political forces in support of change and the legitimation of a new political-constitutional system. The period immediately after the Allied invasion and liberation of German-occupied Europe, in 1944-5, was just such a time, for the popular enthusiasm for change and a break with a constitutional *ancien régime* was there. But it was necessary to seize the short-lived moment in history and to act with dispatch, as General de Gaulle discovered to his cost. Too many delays and compromises made in response to surviving political forces from yesterday blunted the constitutional idealism inherited from the French wartime Resistance Movement and produced, in the end, after de Gaulle's retirement from the political scene, a new, Fourth French Republic not very unlike the old, Third Republic – the Government of the Assemblies – that it was supposed to have displaced in favour of strong executive leadership at the centre.

2. 'RECEPTION' OF FOREIGN LEGAL INSTITUTIONS AND IDEAS

It was a period, after 1945, as we have noted, especially favourable to the 'reception' of foreign legal experience in general, and of American legal experience in particular. The cataclysmic military and political events of World War II brought, on the part of those who survived, a new, strongly idealistic outlook reflected in the new sense of internationalism and 'One World' and the desire to break down the autarchic national frontiers that had so restrained and controlled the free circulation of people and goods and services and ideas in the years leading up to the outbreak of hostilities in 1939. Part of the new internationalism and the new idealism found an outlet in the new United Nations organisation founded at San Francisco in 1945 in anticipation, and as part, of the post-World War II political-military settlement and accommodation among the victorious allies, and not yet rent by incipient Cold War, East-West conflicts. But part of it was also realised in the avid study and pursuit of outside ideas and learning that had been, in so many cases, arbitrarily cut off during the years of foreign military conquest and occupation. The American social scientist, Harold Lasswell, best described the situation in the early post-War years, in a metaphor linking the 'Americanisation' of World culture, including constitutional-legal culture, to earlier historical process, in the Dark Ages, when scholars from all over Europe flocked to the Northern Italian Universities in search of learning and enlightenment. The highly ambitious, imaginative, and in the very largest sense idealistic, American Government programmes, post-War, for bringing foreign students to the great American Universities and their graduate schools and law schools, by way of the Fulbright Scholarships or State Department leadership awards, meant that the post-War generation of political and intellectual leaders of very many countries, including the defeated Axis powers, were exposed to the best of American constitutional-governmental teachers and their ideas in their period of greatest optimism and confidence in the future. The influence of that post-War 'reception' of American constitutional-governmental ideas was immediate and direct, and it was pervasive. It is manifest even in the case of those countries that had experienced neither the agony of military defeat and foreign occupation, nor (for those countries among the victorious allies) the shattering of their economic wealth and well-being through the strains of the War effort and the difficult readjustment to post-War conditions. Countries like Canada that had, in the pre-War years, directed their best and brightest graduate and professional students to Great Britain, were carried along in the post-War enthusiasm for things American by the new availability of research and study awards in the United States; and we can trace a strong 'Americanisation' of their constitutional thought-ways and practice, and eventually the Court jurisprudence, from that time onwards. In some cases, as in Canada and the Commonwealth, and as also in Germany, there were already existing precedents or historically-based patterns of practices, or at least constitutional precursors, for Court-based constitutional review. The Commonwealth Countries' historical experience with the old Imperial, Privy Council, sitting in its Judicial Committee as the highest appellate tribunal of the old British colonial Empire and its successor Commonwealth, provided an example of Court-based control of statutes and of executive-legislative acts and executive administration generally, that was related to compatibility or otherwise with the Imperially-enacted constitutional charters of those countries. It was an experience deriving its validity, ultimately, from the Austinian, pyramidal, Roman Law-style conceptions of legal sovereignty current in British Imperial legal thinking: the British Parliament at Westminster was sovereign; the Commonwealth and colonial constitutional charters were enacted by way of its statutes and therefore amounted to a form of delegated, limited law-making authority which could always legally be revoked by the parent, Imperial power and which must be constrained at all times, within the charter-stipulated limits. The Privy Council acted as an instrument of Empire and Imperial unity in exercising, in effect, a form of constitutional review over Commonwealth and colonial laws. But it was never acknowledged, as such, and its philosophical underpinnings were never explored nor its legitimation in constitutional terms. To have done so would no doubt have exposed it as an institutionalised practice very similar to that judicial review practised, from the opening of the 19th century onwards, by the United States Supreme Court: and that would have run counter to the venerable Dicey, the *doyen* of English constitutionalists', rejection of American constitutional examples and influence. As late as 1907, the presiding officer of the Privy Council, the Lord Chancellor, Lord Halsbury,[2] had questioned, in response to counsel's argument, the very notion that there could be such a thing as an 'unconstitutional' act of a Commonwealth or colonial legislature, once assented to by the Crown. The Lord Chancellor's remark reflects, of course, the un-speculative, un-theoretical approach traditionally applied by British judges to the nature of their office and the judicial process generally. It might not seem to matter too much, remembering the Legal Realists' precept of concentrating on what the judges actually do, as distinct from what they say they are doing. The Privy Council was, of course, throughout its modern history, exercising an American-style judicial review of constitutionality. But the lack of frank and open recognition and even self-awareness on the part of the judges of what was being done, immensely complicated the subsequent, *post*-Privy Council experience of Commonwealth Supreme Courts once they were sitting as final appellate tribunals in their own right with the cutting, post-World War II, of the last Imperial, British judicial and legal links. It meant a fusion, or confusion, of the empirical fact of Court-based review and control of constitutionality with what the American Legal Realists had described as the 'basic legal Myth', that judges do not make law;[3] and, long after the disappearance of that basic Myth in the United States and in American constitutional jurisprudence, immensely complicated the process, in the Commonwealth Countries, of rendering such judicial review more rational and scientific and, in the end, legitimate in constitutional-governmental terms. It meant, in particular, extra intellectual strains and extra intellectual ambivalence when what was involved, in the post-World War II operation and practice of judicial review of the constitution was, in effect, a double 'reception': a British, Imperial 'reception', derived from Privy Council practice, where the fact of judicial policy-making was never avowed or conceded in terms, and where social and economic ideas must operate, simply, as 'inarticulate major premises' to decision much on the basis on which the great Mr. Justice Oliver Wendell Holmes had excoriated the conservative, 'Old Court' majority on the United States Supreme Court in the period from after the Civil War to the 'Court Revolution' of 1937; and an American 'reception', in which ideas of judicial legislation and of the *rôle* and responsibility of the judges in legal innovation and change for the future were canvassed openly and debated on their substantive merits.

Professor Tripathi acknowledges the two distinct channels for reception of judicial review in post-World War II, post-decolonisation and independence, India under the republican constitution adopted by the national constituent assembly in 1949:[4] the first, through the medium of the very cautious and limited, belated British experiment in partial devolution of law-making authority in India, in terms of a British Imperial statute, the Government of India Act of 1935, which provided, somewhat on the earlier Imperial-made models of the Canadian and Australian constitutional charters, for various lists of law-making competences for federal and regional authorities and even a concurrent list, with the implication of Court-based regulation or arbitrament of any disputes or disagreement as to respective law-making competences. The second channel, of course, was United States experience, as filtered through the eyes of the Indian national constitution-makers and their expert advisers: Sir Benegal Rau, who was constitutional adviser to the Indian Constituent Assembly, made a five-week visit to the United States in late 1947, and talked with Chief Justice Vinson and Justices Frankfurter, Burton and Murphy of the then current bench of the Supreme Court, and also met the great former Chief Justice, Charles Evans Hughes.[5] Several influential members of the Constituent Assembly – Sir Alladi Krishnaswamy Ayyar, Governor Munshi, and Dr. Ambedkar – all of them lawyers of high standing, had some acquaintance with American constitutional ideas and made conscious openings to them. The interesting thing, nevertheless, is that the new republican constitution did not, in terms, entrench judicial review when it might so easily, as a contemporary charter, have opted to do so; and that the early benches of the Indian Supreme Court, with notable exceptions only like Mr. Justice Fazl Ali,[6] preferred to opt for an English, positivist, 'logical', strict and literal approach to interpretation of the new charter and its imperative principles, and to eschew, altogether, the more free-wheeling, legislative, policy-making approach favoured by the United States Supreme Court majority since the 'Court Revolution' of 1937. The contradiction in the double 'reception' noted by Professor Tripathi and its practical resolution in favour of judicial orthodoxy, English-style, confirms that the more pervasive form of legal 'reception' is one conditioned in legal education and professional training over a considerable period of years – in this case, imposed by the accidents of past British Imperial conquest and the Imperial attention to formation of an English Common Law-influenced, indigenous legal *élite* in India; where, by comparison, the latter-day opening of the windows to American legal ideas had hardly had enough time to persuade and control the top-level political and legal decision-making classes.

In West Germany, the introduction of the principle of constitutional review, through the agency of a specialised federal constitutional court, under the Bonn Constitution of 1949, was heavily influenced by the prestige of American constitutional institutions and values post-War after the constitutional debacle of the collapse of the Weimar Republic in 1933 and the twelve succeeding years of the National Socialist authoritarian *régime.* The interest of the members of the emerging Bonn leadership who had managed to survive the Nazi era in politically untainted form was in studying what had gone wrong with the institutions and processes of the Weimar Republic and in trying to ensure, by substantial constitutional checks and balances if needed, that the transfer of power, under and through the constitution itself, to political extremists who did not themselves respect democratic constitutionalism, could be avoided or prevented in the future. The distinguished German-American constitutinalist, Carl Friedrich, has noted in this regard the new concern with constitutionally entrenched human rights, but the correlative concern to limit these so that opponents of constitutionalism could not misuse them to their own ends.[7] The institutionalising of judicial review of constitutionality in a special constitutional court was a logical enough expression of these two, somewhat antinomic approaches to constitutional freedom, and it had the further advantage of some earlier, intrinsically German, historical-legal roots. The notion of court specialisation – here specialisation in the form of a constitutional court – has general Continental European Civil Law-based associations; but it is often forgotten that in the twilight hours of the Weimar Republic, the then highest court, the *Staatsgerichtshof,* had tried to ride out the political storm in its ruling on the constitutionality of the federal President's invocation of constitutional emergency powers in order to suspend the duly elected government of the largest regional government, Prussia and to replace it by a federally-named administrator. The imperfections of that Court-decision, rendered a scant six months before the Nazi take-over, reflect as much the practical political limits to judicial power as the constitutional novelty, in German terms at that time, – July, 1932 – of any Court-based assertion of judicial control over constitutionality of executive action.[8] But the precedent was well-known to those political leaders actively engaged, in the post-War period, in elaborating the Bonn constitutional charter in anticipation of the three Western Occupation Powers' return of full legal sovereignty to a rump West Germany; and their desire was to strengthen judicial control of constitutionality, and certainly not to abandon it because of any shortcomings in its actual practice in the extreme constitutional crisis of 1932. The successful introduction and consolidation of Court-based constitutional review under the Bonn constitution of 1949 was helped materially by the direct personal exposure of several strong judicial personalities of the early Bonn years, to American and foreign constitutional experience. Rudolf Katz, who was one of the key political leaders in the transition to the Bonn constitutional system, as Justice Minister for Schleswig-Holstein from 1947 to 1950, member of the Parliamentary Council in 1948-9, and member of the *Bundesrat* in 1949-50 and Chairman of its Legal Committee, had spent the Nazi period in the United States, with lectureships at Columbia University and at the New School in New York, and he was elected to the first bench of the new Federal Constitutional Court in 1951, and named Vice-President of the Court and president of its Second Senate. His colleague, Gerhard Leibholz, had been forced from his Chair in Göttingen in 1935 and had then moved to Oxford University, being by that time established as one of the great comparative constitutionalists of the era,[9] and he was also, in the post-War, Bonn era, elected to the first bench of the new Federal Constitutional Court with a seat in its Second Senate. These two distinguished jurists, together with their colleague Hans Rupp, who had been formed before the War at Harvard, provided an effective bridge of practical, first-hand knowledge and experience between American constitutionalism and the emerging new, Bonn Constitution-based, judicial review of constitutionality.

In the case of post-War Japan, the strong influence of American constitutional thinking and practice, through their spokesmen in the American Military Occupation command, is apparent throughout the 1946 constitutional charter. The 'reception' of American legal ideas and processes was, indeed, the second major 'reception' for Japanese law, following upon that earlier studying and borrowing from foreign, and especially Continental European and Imperial German law, represented most strikingly in the first modern constitution of Japan – the Constitution of the Empire of Japan of 1889, which is always associated with the Emperor Meiji and his programme of modernisation and industrialisation of Japanese society. The Imperial German society from which the Meiji constitution borrowed so heavily[10] achieved its ideals of constitutionalism much more through the principle of *Rechtsstaat* and the constitutional self-restraint of executive and legislative power, than through any notion of institutionally-based checks and balances in general or judicial supremacy in relation to the other, coordinate areas of government. That would have to wait, in the case of Germany, as we have noted, until the Weimar Republic of 1919 when it appeared in embryonic judicial-institutional form, and, much more, until the adoption of the Bonn constitutional system in 1949. The Japanese constitution-makers of 1949 would have had an intellectually more interesting task if the challenge had been to graft American-style judicial review on to the earlier, 'received' Imperial German institutions and processes, and if they could have permitted themselves to benefit, in the case of the 'received' German legal element, from the trial-and-error political testing of institutions from the Bismarckian era, through Weimar, on to the Hitler era and its abrupt ending in 1945. Such a sustained, intellectual exercise was hardly possible, politically, in the Japan of 1946, and so it was a relatively uncomplicated, and a comprehensive, 'reception' of American constitutionalism that occurred then, under hardly concealed American pressures.[11] If it had all taken place only a few years later, after the adoption of the Bonn Constitution of 1949 under the same difficult circumstances of foreign military occupation and the need of the local political leadership to conciliate and persuade the foreign powers concerned as a condition of restoration of sovereignty, then one might have had the much more modern, constitutionally rationalised and streamlined, version of Court-based control of constitutionality that the German constituent forces were able to achieve in their Herrenchiemsee convention – American judicial review as it might have been if newly and imaginatively restated in the light of a century and a half of developments since *Marbury* v. *Madison* in 1803,[12] rather than the more traditional, classical version in fact introduced in Japan after 1946.

3. CHARACTER AND CATEGORIES OF CONSTITUTIONAL REVIEW

It is a feature of virtually all modern systems of constitutional review that they avoid defining, in terms, just what it is, in the constitutional charter itself. Perhaps this is in deference to the oldest of constitutions, the United States Constitution, and its certain style leadership for purposes of constitutional drafting. The power of judicial review is neither expressed in the American Constitution itself nor apparently intended, historically, by the Founding Fathers of the charter of 1787: it was something asserted by a great early Chief Justice, Marshall, as part of the inherent logic of the constitutional system, and not effectively challenged, politically, throughout his long term of Chief Justice, by the end of which the party politically contestable origins of judicial review had largely been forgotten and the practice itself might be said to have become accepted or ingrained through constitutional custom. Article III of the U.S. Constitution speaks only of 'vesting' the judicial power in one Supreme Court and in such inferior courts as the federal legislature (Congress) might establish from time to time, and then goes on to list the federal court jurisdiction.

The Japanese Constitution of 1946 follows closely on the American model. The 'whole judicial power' is vested in a Supreme Court and in such inferior courts as are established by law (Article 76); with the Supreme Court declared as 'the court of last resort with power to determine the constitutionality of any law, order, regulation, or official act' (Article 81). (The legally somewhat more categorical language of the original draft constitution, prepared by the Supreme Command of the Allied Powers, to the effect that a judgment of the Supreme Court on constitutionality of any law, order, regulation or official act, in all cases arising under Chapter III of the Constitution (Rights and Duties of the People) was 'final', and subject to being set aside only by a two-thirds vote of all the members of the Diet (legislature) (SCAP Original Draft Constitution, Article 73), was dropped in favour of the legally more imprecise and open-ended formulation, just quoted, of Article 81 of the final constitution of 1946.)[13]

The most comprehensive statement of Court-based jurisdiction in constitutional review is set out in the Basic Law (constitutional charter) of West Germany, adopted in 1949. It is contained in Chapter IX on the Administration of Justice which opens, innocuously enough, with the declaration that 'judicial power shall be vested in the judges', and exercised by the Federal Constitutional Court and other federal courts provided for in the constitutional charter, and by the courts of the *Länder* (Provinces) (Article 92). But there follows Article 92 on the competence of the Federal Constitutional Court which proceeds, then, to list the constitutional jurisdiction *in extenso*. From Article 92, and also the Statute on the Federal Constitutional Court enacted pursuant to it, and, finally, a few additional Articles of the constitutional charter, we may establish the following categories of constitutional review which the Court is empowered to decide: –[14]

(a) *Conflict processes:*
   Federal Government institutional conflicts (Organstreitigkeiten)
   (Constitution/Article 93(1)1); Court Statute/Article 13(5))

These are constitutional disputes, within the federal Government, involving the highest institutions or organs of the federal Government – the federal head-of-State, (President), the federal Government (Chancellor and Cabinet), the federal upper House (*Bundesrat*), the federal lower House (*Bundestag*), and even elements or units of them such as, for example, a political party within the federal lower House (*Bundestag*). In other constitutional systems, these disputes, since they are between coordinate institutions of the same level of government, might often be considered, on ordinary constitutional separation of powers grounds, to be beyond the jurisdiction of the courts in view of their duty of mutual deference and constitutional self-restraint *vis-à-vis* those other, coordinate, institutions; but the West German constitutional charter establishes the matter beyond argument.

(b) *Objective processes:*
   Abstract Norm control (Abstrakte Normen Kontrolle)
   (Constitution/Article 93(1)2); Court Statute/Article 13(11))

What is involved, here, are differences of opinion or doubts on the formal and material compatibility of federal law, or of *Land* (Provincial) law, with the Constitution, or on the compatibility of *Land* law with other, federal law. The constitutional process before the Federal Constitutional Court is initiated by the federal Government, or a *Land* Government, or by one-third of the members of the federal lower House (*Bundestag*). The abstract norm control jurisdiction does not require a formal adversary proceeding in any strict legal sense or an actual case/controversy.

(c) *Objective processes:*
   Concrete Norm control (Konkrete Normen Kontrolle)
   (Constitution/Article 100(1); Court Statute/Article 13(11))

In contradistinction to the Abstract Norm control jurisdiction, Concrete Norm control can only be exercised in relation to an actual case/controvery. If, during the ocurse of a lawsuit before it, a court considers as unconstitutional any statute the validity of which is relevant to its decision, then it must stay the proceedings and obtain a decision from the Federal Constitutional Court on compatibility with the Constitution. This applies both to situations of conflicts between *Land* (Provincial) law and the constitution, and also to conflicts between *Land* law and federal law. Further, if, in the course of litigation, doubts exist whether a rule of Public International Law is an integral part of federal law and whether such rule creates rights and duties for the individual (in terms of Constitution Article 25, which declares the general rules of International Law to be part of federal law), the court concerned must obtain a decision from the Federal Constitutional Court (Constitution, Article 100(2)). The initiative to certify the constitutional question before the Federal Constitutional Court lies solely within the discretion of the court concerned and not of the actual parties; though once the constitutional question has been so raised, the highest federal organs (and, in the case of impugned *Land* (Provincial) law the *Land* Government concerned) are entitled legally to enter the case, with private parties in the court below also permitted to be heard (Court Statute, Article 82).

(d) *Individual Constitutional Complaints (Verfassungsbeschwerde)*
    (Constitution/Article 93(1)4a; Court Statute/Article 90)

Any person who considers that his constitutional basic rights generally, or certain specific rights – the right to political resistance (Constitution Art. 20(4)), the right to equality of political status (Constitution Art. 33), and procedural due process guarantees (Constitution Arts. 101, 103, 104) – have been violated by public authority, may approach the Federal Constitutional Court through a specially streamlined process (the constitutional complaint), though the complainant must normally first have exhausted the lesser, non-constitutional legal remedies. (Court Statute, Article 90(2)).

(e) *Federal-Provincial (Bund-Länder) conflicts*
    (Constitution/Article 93(1)3 and 4, Article 84(4); Court
    Statute/Article 13(7) and (8))

What is involved here are classical 'federal' disputes – differences of opinion on the rights and duties of the federation and the *Länder* (Provinces), particularly in the execution of federal law by the *Länder* and in the exercise of federal oversight of laws; plus other disputes involving public law, between the federation and the *Länder,* between different *Länder* or within a *Land.*

(f) *Uniformity of Court interpretation of the Constitution (Sicherung*
    einheitlicher verfassungsgerichtlicher Auslegung)
    (Constitution/Article 100(3); Court Statute/Article 85)

If the constitutional court of a *Land,* in interpreting the constitution, wants to deviate from a decision of the Federal Constitutional Court or the constitutional court of another *Land,* it must first obtain the decision of the Federal Constitutional Court.

(g) *Electoral Supervision (Wahlprüfung)*
   (Constitution/Article 41; Court Statute/Articles 13(3), 48)

While the scrutiny of elections, including the decision on whether or not a Member has lost his seat, is the responsibility of the federal lower House (*Bundestag*), an appeal from the House lies to the Federal Constitutional Court.

(h) *Impeachment of the Federal President (Präsidentenanklage)*
   (Constitution/Article 61; Court Statute/Articles 13(4), 49)

Either the federal lower House (*Bundestag*) or the federal upper House (*Bundesrat*) may impeach the federal President for wilful violation of the constitution or any other federal law, the introduction of an impeachment proposal requiring the support of at least one quarter of the members of the House concerned, and its legal initiation requiring a two-thirds majority vote of the House concerned, with the actual decision on the substantive issue then to be made by the Federal Constitutional Court.

(i) *Removal of federal judges (Richteranklage)*
   (Constitution/Article 98(2) and (5); Court Statute/Articles 13(9), 58)

The Federal Constitutional Court may decide by a two-thirds majority, on the request of the federal lower House (*Bundestag*), to transfer or remove any federal judge on the ground of infringement of the principles of the constitution, and may also exercise jurisdiction over the impeachment of *Land* (Provincial) judges.

(j) *Unconstitutionality of Political Parties*
   (Verfassungswidrigkeit der Parteien (Constitution/Article 21(1) and (2); Court Statute/Articles 13(2), 43)

The Federal Constitutional Court has jurisdiction to decide on the question of the unconstitutionality of political parties in the light of the constitutionally postulated principles of the free democratic basic order and the safeguarding of the existence of the federal republic.

(k) *Guarantee of communal (Municipal) self-government*
   (Gewährleistung der Kommunalen Selbstverwaltung)
   Constitution/Articles 28(2), 94(1)b; Court Statute/Article 91)

Communal (Municipal) governments within the *Länder* (Provinces) are constitutionally guaranteed the right to regulate on their own responsibility all the affairs of the local community 'within the limits set by law', with the right of constitutional complaint (*Verfassungsbeschwerde*) to the Federal Constitutional Court where no redress under *Land* law is available.

The catalogue of Federal Constitutional Court jurisdictional categories is exhaustive, by any comparative law standards. Yet as two of the most distinguished commentators on the Bonn constitutional charter and its Court-based interpretation, – Leibholz and Rinck, themselves Justices of the Federal Constitutional Court, – point out, the definition of the Court's jurisdiction *in extenso* is unaccompanied in the Bonn constitutional charter itself by any general clause on constitutional judicial review. The instances in which the Federal Constitutional Court can be invoked being indicated, rather, in particular cases, it does not follow that every constitutional conflict can be brought to the Court by any interested party. In spite of the constitutional charter's strong build-up of judicial review, therefore, not every objectively grounded constitutional law obligation involves a legal claim pursuable before the Federal Constitutional Court, or any other courts for that matter, on the part of some person or institution. One must indeed examine in each case whether the constitutional law principle invoked is founded either in a legal relationship with reciprocal rights and duties attaching to it or in one of the political, civil, electoral or procedural rights that are protected, in terms, under Article 93(1)4a of the constitutional charter and Article 90 of the Court Statute. Only then can someone who is injured in his rights make a motion in Court as to a constitutional conflict, or institute the constitutional complaint (*Verfassungsbeschwerde*) process. Leibholz and Rinck point out that the cases in which the objective processes of the Court – *abstract* norm control, and *concrete* norm control, as set out above – can be brought forward are very narrowly defined.[15] The limitations of the objective processes for protection of the constitution are that they serve solely the examination of legal norms by the measure of the constitutional charter, but not, however, the direct protection of a legal demand of the person making the motion to the Court. As Leibholz and Rinck suggest, the competence to bring an abstract norm control process into play serves solely to create a processual right. Another West German scholar, Laufer, in also taking note of the absence of special emphasis, in terms, on constitutional judicial review in the constitutional charter itself, refers in passing to the many complaints, from academic legal scholars and political figures, to the institutional preeminence in fact emerging for the Federal Constitutional Court. [16] Some of the critics, academic and other, belonged to the right of the political spectrum and had in the past been attracted to popular sovereignty-based; government-by-Assembly notions of constitutional government; and it is not perhaps surprising to find them signalling the constitutional *rôle* of the Federal Constitutional Court, variously, as a 'disturbing factor in the political order', a move from the Rule-of-Law state (*Rechtsstaat*) to the judicial or justice state (*Justizstaat*), a 'judicialising of politics', or even a 'politicising of justice'. [17] Criticisms such as these, widely offered and distributed as they were at the time of the Herrenchiemsee convention which so largely contributed to the evolution of constitutional judicial review in the Bonn constitutional charter help to explain why, in the most modern of constitutional charter statements of constitutional review jurisdiction, and the one most drawing on American constitutional example in a progressive, generic, and evolutionary way, the logical next step of accompanying the listing of the Constitutional Court jurisdiction *in extenso* by an umbrella-style, general establishment of constitutional review competence, is not taken.

4. ABSTRACT AND CONCRETE CONSTITUTIONAL REVIEW: CASE/CONTROVERSY AND ADVISORY OPINION

It is a truism of Anglo-Saxon Common Law constitutionalism – American, and American-influenced at least – that the effective exercise of constitutional judicial review requires a genuine adversary proceeding, the existence of a case or controversy *inter partes,* in order to ensure a concrete factual record on the basis of which the Court concerned can render its judgment. There is a correlative insistence that it is a misuse or abuse of the judicial function to render judgment on a purely abstract or hypothetical question unaccompanied by a specific fact-setting. It is the rare final court today – the International Court of Justice at The Hague, the Supreme Court of Canada – that is authorised, under its statutes, to render Advisory Opinions on legal questions not directly arising from concrete case/controversies. The International Court is empowered under the United Nations Charter (Article 96) and its own Court Statute (Articles 65-68) to give Advisory Opinions on any legal question referred to it by the U.N. General Assembly or Security Council or by other U.N. organs and specialised agencies authorised by the General Assembly. The Supreme Court of Canada renders its Advisory Opinions on reference from the Canadian Government. The West German Federal Constitutional Court, which had the power under Article 97 of the Court Statute, as first drafted, to render Advisory Opinions (*Rechtsgutachten*) on the joint motion of the federal lower House (*Bundestag*), the federal Upper House (*Bundesrat*), and the federal Government, or on the sole motion of the federal President, had its fingers badly burned in the European Defence Community controversy over the constitutionality of the newly sovereign state of West Germany's integration in the then projected military organisation of the six Continental Western European states, paralleling in military terms the economic union of the same six states in the European Coal and Steel Community. The internal, West German political debate over the issue was complicated by the memory of the still-recent Nuremburg Tribunal indictments against the former Nazi leaders on the count of making 'aggressive War'; and the Bonn constitutional charter, in recognition no doubt of the Allied Military Occupation powers' Manichaean conception of Germany's war guilt, contained absolutely no provision for a governmental law-making competence over military matters generally, or even military defence. As in the case of post-War Japan, a constitutional amendment would have been legally desirable to put the matter beyond question; but it seemed politically impossible, at the time, to produce the two-thirds majority in both Houses of the federal legislature that was constitutionally necessary to secure such an amendment, for this would have required bi-partisan, Government and Opposition consensus. We will discuss, at a later stage, the substantive merits of the constitutional argument over compatibility or otherwise of the European Defence Community project with the Bonn Charter; and we will also look, in another context, at the special Court organisational, processual elements of the West German Federal Constitutional Court that permitted the two different chambers (Senates) of the Court to be seised with the same issue, in the same year, on the respective motions of the rival political forces, and that also permitted the *plenum* or full Court, uniting both Senates *en banc,* to be approached by way of Advisory Opinion on the very same substantive question.[18] In the political reaction against the game of musical chairs that the rival political personalities and parties now seemed to be playing with the three different divisions of the Court, the federal President, who had initiated the request for Advisory Opinion to the *plenum* jurisdiction of the Court, withdrew that request six months after launching it.[19] The latter-day, informed academic and professional legal reaction to the whole affair, with its embarrassments, potential and actual, for the Court, was to decide that the Court's power to render Advisory Opinions had contributed to its political problems; and to go on from that to conclude that Advisory Opinions, though authorised by the law as it then stood, were alien to the judicial function and should be abolished, which in fact was done in the general revision and reform of the Court Statute in 1956 which repealed the Article 97-based Advisory Opinion power. That conclusion, in retrospect, seems rather hasty and not fully reasoned: an alternative solution, rooted in sound procedural principles, might have been to adopt rules preventing more than one jurisdiction of the Court from being seised with the same issue at the same time, and establishing temporal priority or jurisdictional preeminence in such cases. The dividing line between the power to render an Advisory Opinion (*Rechtsgutachten*) on a defined constitutional question (*eine bestimmte verfassungsrechtliche Frage*) under the old Article 97 of the Court Statute, now amended, and that Abstract Norm Control jurisdiction established under Article 93(1)2 of the constitution and Article 13(11) of the Court Statute is not clear: the distinction is certainly not of a substantive law character, and each involves, in the end, an abstract, un-fact-oriented ruling in the absence, in each case, of the detailed factual record provided by a case/controversy proceeding. The distinction, if any, has to be found in the relatively casual element of the processual, adjectival law origins of the two different suits.

Among other final tribunals, as we have noted, the Advisory Opinion jurisdiction tends neither to exist, in terms, in the constitutional charter nor to be tolerated as a developed judicial practice for expanding and facilitating the court's power. Courts like the United States Supreme Court might, – the constitution itself being silent on the point – have sensibly softened the rigidities of the case/controversy requirement under Article III of the Constitution to permit rulings on abstract norm issues referred to them by one or other of the coordinate, executive and legislative arms of government. But the opportunity was passed up in the early years of the Court when it was still fashioning its own future course of action, including the institution of judicial review itself. And, in more recent times, the back-door approach to Advisory Opinions by way of the attempt to test abstract norms of constitutionality – somewhat on the basis of the contemporary West German abstract norm control, but with the difference that it would have been at the initiative, not of governmental authorities, but of a private citizen, was firmly rejected by the Supreme Court, on the stated ground of insufficiency of constitutional 'interest' to have *locus standi* and so raise the constitutional issue. The post-World War II Japanese Supreme Court, in 1952, in the *Suzuki* case,[20] followed the strict American rule in limiting itself to the decision of constitutional issues arising in concrete legal disputes between specific parties.

Other Supreme Courts in other countries, while rendering lip-service to the American doctrine of constitutional 'interest' as the basis for being allowed to test constitutionality, have so watered down the content and extent of the minimum 'interest' required as to have sanctioned, *de facto,* a form of abstract norm control jurisdiction. This seems true, for example, of the Canadian Supreme Court where the judicial approach to constitutional *locus standi* is extremely facultative, even though the Court is one of the rare final tribunals to have, also, an express constitutional Reference or Advisory Opinion jurisdiction. It may be argued, of course, that the United States Supreme Court, in modern times, faces the sociological reality that, constitutional litigation being costly, it must normally be financed by special interest or lobbying groups (civil libertarian and race relations groups here included); and the sheer range and number of cases available from which to choose the most favourable one for purposes of future litigation confers a selective, 'ideal-type' character on the one finally chosen to take to Court that is, with difficulty, reconcilable with the classic case/controversy approach.

Of course, tribunals like the International Court of Justice whose regular *inter partes* jurisdiction is severely hemmed in, in practice, by the requirement that the only legal parties, – states, – should consent to its jurisdiction before being compelled to submit to it – a jurisdictional requirement only partly ameliorated by the practice of many states of making a general consent to jurisdiction in advance of cases, usually on a basis of reciprocity with other states – have found in the coordinate, Advisory Opinion jurisdiction the potential for escape from the current dilemma of too few effective state consents to jurisdiction and hence no work agenda. It may be added that the Advisory Opinion approach to Court jurisdiction does not seem to have made too much difference, in practical terms, to the content and character of the litigation coming before the International Court, – to its relative degree of philosophical abstraction or concrete detail; and that may say something for the nature and character of judicial review when it is exercised at the final court level. If anything, in the case of the International Court, issues like *Namibia* (*South West Africa*) have seemed to acquire much more of an empirical base when presented by the Reference route,[21] than when originally raised *inter partes* through opposing litigant-states;[22] though that again may simply acknowledge the greater technical sophistication and legal comprehensiveness of the legal briefs when prepared by the official, World Community intervenors enjoined, under the United Nations Charter and the Court Statute, when the Advisory Opinion jurisdiction is invoked.

5. CONSTITUTIONAL REVIEW: JUDICIAL AND NON-JUDICIAL

It is assumed, usually without examination, that constitutional review must be exercised, and can only be exercised, by a court. That is to yield too much to the authority of the United States experience of judicial review of the constitution, effectively exercised over the years by the federal Supreme Court. Those countries that, after World War II, 'received' American constitutional ideas and institutions as part of their general constitutional renewal, either created special constitutional courts modelled on the United States Supreme Court as a *de facto* specialised public law tribunal, or else grafted American constitutional practices on to their existing institutions thereby transforming them in the process of continuing reception. But the approach through the courts, – special constitutional courts or courts of general jurisdiction – is not the only way to exercise constitutional review. Countries like France, with their inheritance from the Revolutionary era of the suspicion and mistrust of the royal judges of the *ancien Régime,* had shewn no temptation, in the spate of constitution-making at the end of the 18th century and throughout the 19th century up to the inauguration of the Third Republic, to experiment with American-style constitutional checks-and-balances or with the American institution of judicial review. The projects of the 'Resistance' and the Free French forces, after the Liberation in 1944, were ambitious enough, in their attempt to correct the perceived errors of the Third Republic and its constitutional-institutional contributions to the military and political collapse of 1940, to have broken away from purely French precedents and models. But the initial idealism and commitment to fundamental constitutional renewal was lost in the compromises and delays of 1944-5, and after General de Gaulle's withdrawal from the post-War government and the constituent process generally, a new constitution emerged in 1946 for the new Fourth Republic that seemed not too very different from the constitutional system of the Third Republic that it had replaced. One minor constitutional innovation was to be a *Comité constitutionnel,* but that early, tentative venture in constitutional review hardly operated in practice. Instead, the Gaullist-inspired constitution of the Fifth Republic, of 1958, went several steps beyond and created its own *Conseil constitutionnel,* with a number of constitutional review functions and powers listed in the constitutional charter. These include the supervision of the election of the President of the Republic, including investigation of objections (Article 58); deciding on the regularity of elections of Deputies and Senators, and supervising the conduct of referenda (Articles 59, 60). The Constitution also provides that *organic* laws (changes of the constitutional charter) *must,* before their promulgation, be submitted to the *Conseil constitutionnel* which pronounces, then, on their conformity with the constitution (Article 61). On the other hand, ordinary laws will only reach the *Conseil* on the voluntary initiative of the President of the Republic, the Prime Minister, or the presiding officer of either House of the legislature (Article 61). A constitutional amendment effected in 1974 considerably enlarged the practical scope of this last provision as to *Conseil* review of ordinary laws, by providing that any sixty Deputies or any sixty Senators could also bring the issue of conformity to the constitution of such ordinary laws before the *Conseil constitutionnel,* [23] and this provision has been actively availed of since that time in a number of issues involving controversial policy decisions by the executive – issues of public morality as well as social and economic decisions. We shall examine some of these determinations by the *Conseil constitutionnel* at a later stage, when specific areas of community policy-making are studied comparatively. Suffice it to note, now, that the consequences of a ruling by the *Conseil constitutionnel* are not dissimilar to those of a ruling by a constitutional court: a provision declared unconstitutional may not be promulgated or applied, while decisions of the *Conseil constitutionnel* are not subject to appeal and are binding on public authorities and on all administrative and judicial authorities (Article 62). Yet the *Conseil's* nine members, who are appointed, one third each, by the President of the Republic, the President of the lower House of the legislature, and the President of the Senate, for a term of years, and to whom are added, as *ex officio* life members, former Persidents of the Republic, are not required to be lawyers, no conditions as to age or professional competence being specified either in the constitution or in the Ordinance of 7 November 1958 constituting its organic law. In fact, for the most part, the members have tended to vary between outstanding political personalities with an early formation and education in law, and outstanding professional jurists. The mix, an interesting balance in itself, approaches that in some of the more consciously legislating constitutional courts of today, the West German Federal Constitutional Court and the United States Supreme Court, and recalls some of the promises by the French Socialist and left-of-centre parties, before their successful Presidential election campaign of 1981, to transfer the functions of the *Conseil* to a constitutional Supreme Court whose jurisdictional character would be clearly affirmed. This would have a certain constitutional logic in itself, perhaps, but it would be a considerable step beyond the more limited, original Gaullist constitutional design of 1958 which was to establish a new equilibrium between legislative and executive institutions and to correct that supremacy of the legislature that had so dominated French constitutional practice after 1870 and weakened executive authority under both the Third and Fourth Republics.

NOTES

1. F.K. von Savigny, *Vom Beruf unserer Zeit für Gesetzgebung und Rechtswissenschaft* (1814); Julius Stone, *The Province and Function of Law* (1946), p. 421; Julius Stone, *Social Dimensions of Law and Justice* (1966), p. 86; E. McWhinney, *Constitution-Making. Principles, Process, Practice* (1981), p. 14 *et seq.*
2. *Webb* v. *Outrim* [1907] A.C. 81 (P.C.); *Survey of British Commonwealth Affairs* (W.K. Hancock, ed.) (1937), p. 566.
3. Jerome Frank, *Law and the Modern Mind* (1930), p. 20.
4. P.K. Tripathi, 'Perspectives on the American Constitutional Influence on the Constitution of India', in *Constitutionalism in Asia. Asian Views of the American Influence* (L.W. Beer, ed.) (1979), p. 59, pp. 62-63.
5. *Ibid.,* p. 67.
6. *Gopalan* v. *State of Madras,* A.I.R. 1950 S.C. 27 (Fazl Ali J., dissenting opinion).
7. Carl J. Friedrich, 'The Political Theory of New Democratic Constitutions', 12 *Review of Politics* 217 (1950); Heinz Laufer, *Verfassungsgerichtsbarkeit und politischer Prozess* (1968), p. 19 *et seq.*
8. H. Grund, *'Preussenschlag' und Staatsgerichtshof im Jahre 1932* (1976); Laufer, *op. cit.,* p. 267 *et seq.*
9. Gerhard Leibholz, *Die Gleichheit vor dem Gesetz. Eine Studie auf rechtsvergleichender und rechtsphilosophischer Grundlage* (1925); Leibholz, *Das Wesen der Repräsentation unter besonderer Berücksichtigung des Repräsentativsystems* (1929); Leibholz, *Die Auflösung der liberalen Demokratie in Deutschland und das autoritäre Staatsbild* (1933).
10. R.H. Minear, *Japanese Tradition and Western Law. Emperor, State, and Law in the Thought of Hozumi Yatsuka* (1970), p. 31 *et seq.*
11. John M. Maki, *Government and Politics in Japan. The Road to Democracy* (1962), p. 33 *et seq.*; H. Fukui, 'Twenty years of revisionism', in *The Constitution of Japan. Its First Twenty Years, 1947-67* (Dan Fenno Henderson, ed.) (1968), p. 41 *et seq.*; Nobushige Ukai, 'The significance of the reception of American constitutional institutions and ideas in Japan', in *Constitutionalism in Asia* (L.W. Beer, ed.) (1979), p. 114 *et seq.*
12. 1 Cranch 937 (1803).
13. Hideo Wada, 'The Supreme Court of Japan as Adjudicating Agency and its functions', 23 *Jahrbuch des öffentlichen Rechts der Gegenwart* 537, 539 (1974); Hideo Wada and Hiroshi Itoh, 'A comparative overview of the Japanese Supreme Court', 28 *Jahrbuch des öffentlichen Rechts der Gegenwart* 689, 690 (1979).
14. E. Friesenhahn, 'Die Verfassungsgerichtsbarkeit in der Bundesrepublik Deutschland', *Verfassungsgerichtsbarkeit in der Gegenwart. Länderberichte und Rechtsvergleichung* (H. Mosler, ed.) (1962), p. 89 *et seq.*; G. Leibholz and H.J. Rinck, *Grundgesetz für die Bundesrepublik Deutschland* (4th ed., 1971), p. 686 *et seq.*; H. Lechner, *Bundesverfassungsgerichtsgesetz* (1954), p. 49; H. Lechner, *Gesetz zür Änderung des Gesetzes über das Bundesverfassungsgericht* (1957); Wiltraut Rupp v. Brünneck, 'Admonitory Functions of Constitutional Courts', 20 *American Journal of Comparative Law* 387, 388 (1972).
15. Leibholz and Rinck, *op. cit.,* p. 687.
16. Laufer, *op. cit.,* pp. 22-23.
17. *Ibid.*
18. Decision of 30 July 1952, 1 B Verf GE 396 (1952) (First Senate); decision of 9 December 1952, 2 B Verf GE 79 (1953) (*plenum*); decision of 7 March 1953, 2 B Verf GE 143 (1953) (Second Senate). And see generally E. McWhinney, *Constitutionalism in Germany and the Federal Constitutional Court* (1962), p. 34 *et seq.*
19. Withdrawal of the Presidential request to the *plenum* for Advisory Opinion is formally noted in the decision of the Second Senate of 7 March 1953, 2 B Verf GE 143, at 147 (1953).

20. Decision of 8 October 1952 (Supreme Court (Grand Bench)); *Court and Constitution in Japan. Selected Supreme Court Decisions, 1948-60* (J. M. Maki, ed.; transl. Ikeda Masaaki, *et al.*) (1964), p. 362.
21. I.C.J. Reports 1971, p. 16.
22. I.C.J. Reports 1966, p. 6.
23. L. Favoreu and L. Philip, *Le Conseil constitutionnel* (1978), p. 80 *et seq.*; F. Luchaire, *Le Conseil constitutionnel* (1980), pp. 29-30.

CHAPTER II

CONSTITUTIONAL COURTS: STRUCTURE, ORGANISATION, INTERNAL PRACTICE

1. COURT ORGANISATION: CIVIL LAW AND COMMON LAW APPROACHES

The differences in Civil Law and Common Law basic approaches to Court organisation may be identified, most easily, in terms of three principles more generally applied in the Continental European Civil Law countries, – collegiality, anonymity, specialisation.

(a) *Collegiality*

The first of these principles, collegiality, involves the Court's functioning as a group for purposes of decision-making, and also of opinion-writing in rationalisation or restatement of the grounds of the Court's final decision. Mr. Justice Felix Frankfurter of the United States Supreme Court, in a tacit rebuke perhaps to some of his more outspoken and publicly debating judicial colleagues, referred to Court decision-making as an orchestral work, rather than a series of individual, solo performances.[1] That is true, no doubt, as an ideal of all plural, multi-member tribunals, Common Law as well as Civil-Law; but among Common Law tribunals only the old Imperial, Briitsh, Privy Council, sitting as final appellate tribunal for the British colonial Empire and British Commonwealth overseas,[2] in the Imperial heyday, really functioned in true collegial fashion in the sense of trying to reach decision through committee-of-the-whole, with designated judicial *rapporteur* and one single decision and single Court opinion in support thereof. In the case of the Privy Council, its unique (for Common Law purposes) collegial character was determined by the historical legal fiction, dating from its original, mediaeval antecedents and preserved after its statutory reconstitution in 1833 as an instrument of Empire, that it was not a Court *stricto sensu* but a committee of the Crown that existed to give advice to the Crown – which advice, *ex hypothesi,* had to be rendered in a single voice, thereby necessitating a full collegiality in the processes of arriving at decisions and also of rendering them in written form. We know in fact today, as ordinary, Legal Realist-style, empirical examination of the actual record of Privy Council decisions in modern times would clearly have indicated, that the Privy Council, as a tribunal whose membership was often casually selected and in any case subject to frequent change, tended to be strongly influenced by those particular judges serving on it with any degree of permanence over a period of years, and hence with the opportunity and interest to develop some sort of continuing, coherent and consistent judicial philosophy. This was certainly true of the great Scottish legal philosopher, Lord Watson, who dominated those Boards of the Privy Council on which he served as *rapporteur* around the close of the 19th century, and even truer perhaps of his intellectual *protégé* and disciple, Lord Haldane,[3] a philospher in his own right and sometime reformist War Minister in the Asquith Cabinet just before World War I. Lord Haldane, as a brilliant politician and a brilliant jurist, contributed his own particular, idiosyncratic policy viewpoints – strongly liberal and pluralistic in philosophic viewpoint – wherever he sat in constitutional cases, and without any necessary regard to the text of the legal documents, constitutional charter or statute as the case may be – that he might happen to be charged to interpret. We also know, today, that one of the great political *causes célèbres* of the Privy Council's history of judicial review – the Canada *Labour Conventions* decision of 1937[4] – was rendered by a divided Court, with a single vote, 4-to-3, majority,[5] in spite of the surface unanimity and harmony of the recorded judgment and the rather bland, single Court opinion, signed by the official *rapporteur,* that accompanied it. Such strong differences of judicial opinion are perhaps inevitable when what is involved in decision-making are issues of high policy in law – of political judgment or philosophical-ideological preference, if you wish. It was not, however, until 1966, long after its jurisdiction in relation to the Overseas Empire had become reduced almost to the vanishing point, and swept away in the tide of decolonisation and independence, that the Privy Council was finally authorised to break its surface collegiality and to render dissenting opinions.[6] Such dissenting opinions, and specially concurring opinions too, are, of course, the stuff of Common Law-based tribunals in general, and especially of the United States Supreme Court and those other, *de jure* or *de facto* constitutional tribunals that have accepted it as their preferred model. It is not so, of course, with Civil Law-based tribujnals, where the unbroken collegial *facade* of decision-making is maintained. When, therefore, after the philosophic strains of attempting to reach, and to maintain in public, a collegial-style judicial consensus on the larger issues of social and economic policy coming before it, had become too great, the West German Federal Constitutional Court decided to allow some public expression of the internal disagreements as a contribution to intellectual clarity in its decisions and opinions, the example borrowed from was that of the United States Supreme Court, rather than its own or other Civil Law experience which of course pointed the other way. Even so, because of the pervasive, still-continuing influence of the Civil Law and Civil Law historical thought-ways in post-World War II West German constitutional practice, the recourse to special, dissenting opinions occurred belatedly and gingerly, being neither very common nor exercised with other than a prudent judicial self-restraint as to language and styling. By contrast, the International Court of Justice, as a tribunal which draws on both Civil Law and Common Law traditions and experience for its Court internal organisation and practice has, from the beginning, allowed special opinions – dissenting and concurring – and its judges have exercised this option freely and, at times, enthusiastically. So much so that, in the period of judicial activism that followed on the judicial elections of 1966 and the increasing penetration of the Court's ranks by Third World jurists who were not inhibited by the traditionalist, 'law-as-logic' conceptions of the judicial office espoused by the judges from the older, Western countries who had dominated the Court's early years, the plethora of special judicial opinions sometimes meant great difficulty in ascertaining what exactly the Court majority had decided – in classical, Common Law terms, just what was the *ratio decidendi* or lowest common denominator of agreement among the majority judges. After several major *causes célèbres* of the 1970s – *Nuclear Tests*[7] and *Western Sahara*,[8] for example – that were characterised by very many, long, sometimes pejorative, special opinions – the Court, functioning collegially in its administrative arm, attempted to correct the drift to judicial Byzantinism and to return, somewhat, to more conventional Civil Law patterns through amendments in the Court's rules to give the Court, as a collectivity, some more control over its judges' practice. But the strains on abstract, *a priori* concepts of judicial collegiality presented by a constitutional review jurisdiction today are amply evidenced in the post-World War II practice of the main constitutional tribunals: the Supreme Court of Japan, in spite of its Civil Law antecedents; the Supreme Court of India in spite of its acquaintance with, and prior historical subjection to, the old Imperial, British, Privy Council; and the Supreme Court of Canada – all have preferred the American, plural opinion-writing approach. An attempt, in the early 1950s, by the then Chief Justice of Canada, to have the Supreme Court of Canada 'follow the Privy Council practice' and issue only a single, *per curiam* opinion in each case,[9] was quickly dismissed as a judicial aberration, a step backward in legal history, and, in any case, an unnecessary restraint on the dialectical unfolding of the nation's constitutionalism for the future.

(b) *Anonymity*

Collegiality, as a principle of Court organisation, shades off into the principle of anonymity, – of the Court as a whole, and of the judges individually. The Continental European, Civil Law-derived practice when the Court's collegial decision is rendered *per curiam,* on behalf of the whole, without even the *rapporteur* or *rapporteurs* identified, is the most complete safeguard of judicial anonymity and guarantee of collective responsibility of the individual judges, broken only by the recent innovations, as with the West German Federal Constitutional Court, where individual judicial dissents are recorded and dissenting opinions published over the names of their authors. The International Court of Justice, as already noted, with twin, Civil Law and Common Law legal traditions, permits the filing of individual opinions, dissenting and also special (concurring) and even what are now called declarations – this in addition to the official Opinion of the Court which is signed by the President of the Court or the next most senior judge in the majority, if the President is not among them. The President or other judge signing the official Opinion of the Court is not, however, necessarily, or even usually, the *rapporteur* who will be designated from among the majority judges according to the Court's Rules. On purely stylistic grounds, and occasionally even on philosophical grounds, it will be evident from time to time, particularly in the great political *causes célèbres,* that more than one (anonymous) judge has contributed to a majority Opinion of the International Court of Justice; or that it has had joint authors; or that it is a composite of several different opinions each with different individual authors. With the old Imperial Privy Council, the *rapporteur* was always expressly identified by name, and where these were strong judicial personalities the *per curiam* opinion was invariably evident as their own, solo work, the deference to collegiality and collegial participation in decision-making and opinion-writing being nominal at best. With other, less wilful judges as *rapporteurs,* the Privy Council's *per curiam* opinions, particularly in the great political *causes célèbres* begin to acquire a quality of cloudiness in formulation or non-sequential reasoning that seems only partly attributable to the intellectual qualities of the *rapporteur* concerned and much more to policy disagreements and fractionalism within a tribunal bound, perforce, to the collegial obligation of a publicly unanimous decision and a single Court opinion. With the other final tribunals surveyed, – Japan, India, Canada, – where dissenting and specially concurring opinions are fully permitted, on the United States Supreme Court model, the relative public anonymity of the judges, in comparison to contemporary American judges, seems attributable to a number of different factors, in combination or separately: persistence of what the American Legal Realists called the basic judicial myth, that the judicial function is a purely mechanical, logical one, and that judges do not make law in their decisions; the absence of an informed tradition of Court-tolerated public criticism – even irreverent, pejorative criticism – of Court decisions, on the part of the legal establishment (Law Faculties and Law Reviews) and the information media at large; and, finally, the absence of any public, participatory-democracy *rôle* in the judicial appointment processes, corresponding to the legislative (Senate) ratification of executive (Presidential) nominations to the Court in the case of the United States Supreme Court, or even the federal legislative (*Bundestag, Bundesrat*) election of judges in the case of the West German Federal Constitutional Court. The still-persisting anonymity of the judges of final tribunals, other than the United States Supreme Court, seems certain to disappear, however, as more instrumental theories of the judicial process and of the judicial *rôle* in constitutional review gain strength outside the United States, and particularly as the contribution of the judicial special Opinion, dissenting or specially concurring, to a continuing, dialectical process of law-making, is fully appreciated.

(c) *Specialisation*

Specialisation, as a principle of Court establishment, has already been discussed. The notion of final tribunals specialised by subject matter is typically Continental European Civil Law in origins. France has the *Cour de Cassation* as the apex of the pyramid of Civil Law tribunals; the *Conseil d'Etat* as the specialised Administrative Law tribunal, the *Tribunal des Conflits* whose *raison d'être* is to decide and allocate jurisdictional conflicts or denials of jurisdictions as between the private law and public (administrative) law jurisdictions; and now the *Conseil constitutionnel,* specialised for constitutional law questions and with a quasi-judicial character. West Germany has half a dozen Supreme Courts, specialised, variously, by private law, administrative law, finance law and other jurisdictions and including, of course, the special constitutional court (*Bundesverfassungsgericht*). Other, Common Law-based tribunals, though developed, in accord with Common Law doctrine and philosophy as to Court organisation, as tribunals of general, comprehensive appellate jurisdiction, extending to all branches of the law, whatever their subject matter, have, through the sheer weight of the record and the number of cases coming to them on appellate review and in original jurisdiction in some instances, been compelled to adopt drastic measures to limit their work load and have chosen, like the United States Supreme Court, to allow themselves to develop into *de facto* special constitutional courts, to the exclusion of other business – this, presumably, because constitutional law is deemed by the judges to be more important than other matters, or found by them to be intellectually more challenging and interesting. We speak, now, of specialisation, in internal court organisation, in terms of the establishment of special boards or panels (Senates) of the Court, specialised in jurisdictional terms either by subject matter or even in the geographical or party-origins of litigation. Such purely internal Court specialisation, through creation of a plural-Senate system within the Court, can occur even within a Court that is already specialised by subject matter under constitutional or statutory rules setting it up in the first place. The West German special constitutional court, from the beginning, has been divided into two Senates that are further specialised, *inter se,* as to subject matter, within the Court's larger constitutional mandate. Such a division, within an already specialised tribunal, may sometimes seem rather arbitrary or artificial in view of the necessary intellectual overlap between the different branches of the one specialty; but it is not too difficult to maintain either as an *a priori* jurisdictional arrangement or in working practice. The few real problems in West Germany have stemmed from such matters as a rapidly developing imbalance in the actual work load division as between the two Senates, – something that could be cured, easily and quickly if need be, and that was in fact cured, by making fresh allocations of *a priori* jurisdictional categories in order to even out the number of cases heard by each of the Senates. [10] Potentially more serious, however, in the case of a plural-Senate system within a Court is the temptation to litigants to try to derive casual political profit from the fact of such internal Court division: in the complex European Defence Community litigation of 1952, rival political forces within the new Bonn republic attempted to further their own political interests by invoking, severally, the jurisdiction of the two Senates of the Federal Constitutional Court – the First Senate and the Second Senate, known, respectively, according to their supposed political-ideological colouration at that time, as the 'red' Senate and the 'black' Senate. [11] Such patent abuses of Court processes, with resulting threat to the public integrity of the Court and its reputation for independence from passing political causes, can be countered, easily enough if needed, by having provision for arbitration and mandatory allocation of jurisdiction where more than one division of a Court is seized with the same basic issue at the same time: the full Court, or *plenum,* is obviously best suited to make just such a determination of jurisdictional priority as between different divisions of the Court, or even to decide such cases, on the merits, on its own motion. Ordinary principles of judicial self-restraint, sensibly applied by the judges themselves, can help and may in fact be more than enough to resolve the dilemma, as happened in fact with the European Defence Community litigation in

West Germany when both Senates of the Court, and also the full Court, or *plenum,* cooperated in a remarkable demonstration of collegial solidarity by, variously, ruling the issue to be legally 'premature' denying standing to sue, and, in the case of the *plenum,* ruling that its own decision, in Advisory Opinion jurisdiction, should be binding on both Senates. Thus may jurisdictional gaps or contradictions, which might otherwise be profited from by rival litigants to no particular public interest or advantage, be cured by ordinary judicial common-sense pragmatically applied in the public interest. If it be an interest of the state that there be an end to litigation, it is also a public interest, – which Courts should themselves recognise perhaps more fully, – that litigation not be permitted too easily simply because ingenious litigants can discover unexpected loop-holes in the jurisdictional system and rules.

In the case of basically Common Law tribunals like the old, Imperial Privy Council, panel system operated *de facto,* through the fact of constitution of the board of the tribunal to sit on any case by decision *ad hoc* of the Lord Chancellor of the day. Past patterns of practice as to constitution of such boards of the Privy Council indicate a remarkable element of consistency and regularity in the actual choosing of the judges, the same judicial names tending to recur, year after year, for the same general categories of cases and being determined either by technical-legal background, or by expressed personal preference (as with Watson and Haldane's known predilection for constitutional cases from Canada) or by original casual accident of choice. With other Common Law-based systems such as the Supreme Courts of the United States and Canada, the Court operates always as a full Court or *plenum;* though with the Supreme Court of Canada still functioning as a general, all-purposes, appellate review tribunal, the creation within the Court of special panels, specialised by subject matter, for such questions as the Quebec private law *droit civil,* has sometimes been advanced as a reform proposal, designed either to reduce the full Court's work load, or to produce better technical standards of judicial workmanship on the (by Common Law standards) rather esoteric Quebec law, or to give the psychological appearance of rendering full justice to French-Canadian nationalism.

With the Supreme Court of India, successive increases in the Court's numbers from an original eight judges in 1950, through stages, to a total of eighteen judges in 1978, were made, apparently on the initiative of the various Chief Justices on the argument that the Court's work load was unduly heavy – something that was hardly contestable, on the facts, and that an increase in numbers would permit an effective sharing of the cases among the judges and so control the problem. This last point may seem doubtful: why, for example, not consider other possible remedies for the work load problem, for example, as with other Court systems in other countries, the conferring of a discretionary power on the Supreme Court to pick and choose among the very many, often repetitive, law-and-fact complexes, coming before it on motion, and to exercise its decision in favour of acceptance or rejection of jurisdiction on the basis of the relative importance, novelty, and freedom from irrelevant factors of the particular cases concerned? Once you advance beyond a certain point in numbers of judges on a tribunal, collegial decision-making may become difficult, if not impossible, and compel adoption of a panel system. The Supreme Court of India today rarely sits as a full Court or *plenum,* having preferred a panel system, except for a few political *causes célèbres.* This does, of course, give a certain power to the Chief Justice to influence or determine the long-range trends in the Court's jurisprudence, granted that the Chief Justice determines the composition of the different panels. An American student of the Court noted, with wry humour, that one of the Court's great dissenting Justices, Subba Rao, always found himself with the Court majority after his promotion from ordinary Justice to Chief Justice; for it was, of course, Chief Justice Subba Rao himself who then composed the Court panels, and there was absolutely no need for him to dissent thereafter.[12] In 1982, Prime Minister Gandhi instituted a two-bench system, with a constitutional bench and another, general bench, and with only the constitutional bench thenceforward eligible to decide constitutional cases.

The Supreme Court of Japan, perhaps also by reason of its size, fifteen judges, utilises a panel system involving three separate divisions, each of five judges, the so-called Petty Benches, with the full Court of fifteen judges (the Grand Bench) required for any case involving a constitutional question, or requiring a change in established precedents. The Supreme Court of Japan is, of course, a tribunal of general jurisdictiion, extending to the civil law and criminal law as well as constitutional law proper, though it is limited to appellate review (except for some strictly defined original jurisdiction) and its review over the civil law and criminal law is, for practical purposes, confined to constitutional law issues or those touching the authority of precedents.

The International Court of Justice, which had always functioned as a full Court, with its full complement of judges, began experimenting, in the 1970s, with the idea of limited-in-numbers, special chambers. The reason for this interest in the chamber system was not any desire to lighten the Court's existing work-load, for its docket, for numbers of reasons that need not concern us immediately, had by then dwindled away almost to the vanishing point. Rather, it was intended to encourage reluctant states, who were already parties to the Court's jurisdiction, to submit their differences to the Court for decision, by giving them some part in the actual determination of the composition of the smaller chambers –

'of three or more judges as the Court may determine', according to Article 26 of the Court Statute – that could then be instituted. There had been objections voiced, *sotto voce,* in several Western European foreign ministries, after *North Sea Continental Shelf* in 1969,[13] (a case involving West Germany, The Netherlands, and Denmark), to the active participation in the full Court's ruling and opinion-writing, by judges from states outside the Continental Western European special legal community involved. The three states, party to *North Sea Continental Shelf* litigation, belonged to that older group of Western European states that had so largely contributed to the evolution of 'classical' International Law and, specifically, to the institutionalisation of the principle of international adjudication with the establishment of the International Court's predecessor, the old Permanent Court of International Justice, in 1920. Their objection to the non-passive *rôle* chosen by judicial 'strangers' to their own Western European special legal community dispute, is understandable politically, if quite unacceptable in legal terms. The proposed new special chamber system, with its positive openings to the preferences or idiosyncrasies of choice of the state litigants concerned, might serve to reassure, in particular, older, Western countries concerned both by the growing tendency in the World Community to question or reject 'classical' International Law as Eurocentrist[14] in basic philosophy and orientation, and also by the increasing politicisation of the processes of election to the Court and the threatened emergence of a new Third World majority within the Court's judicial ranks in place of the Western dominance of yesteryear. Great Britain and France, for example, two erstwhile champions of the principle of judicial settlement in international disputes had shewn a tendency to keep their own *inter partes* disputes away from the International Court's jurisdiction and to submit them to special arbitration tribunals whose membership would be a matter for their own joint selection and nothing more. Unfortunately, in the first case selected for invocation of the special chamber system within the International Court, the full bench of the Court chose to interpret the Court's own revised Rules of Court as conceding to the parties' not merely control over the numbers of judges to make up the special chamber concerned, but even the right to determine the actual membership. This seems a distortion of the language of Article 17 of the Court's revised Rules of Court, although it has been suggested by an ex-President of the Court that that was in fact the intention of the drafters, the then judges of the Court, when the revision of the Rules was being made in the 1970s in response, *inter alia,* to the reluctance of so many states to go to the Court at all. Still, according to normal rules of interpretation, Civil Law and Common Law, a mere inchoate intention, even if adequately evidenced (which is not, indeed, beyond contest), cannot prevail over clear and unambiguous statutory language, as here.

Beyond that, the more substantial objection would appear to be that it is completely inconsonant with the character of a Court, as a supposedly neutral body above and beyond the parties' ability to control, that the parties should be able, in effect, to put their own people on the Court. The decision by the full bench of the Internatinal Court, approving the constitution of the special chamber in *Delimitation of the Maritime Boundary in the Gulf of Maine Area,* in 1982, [15] defers absolutely to the wishes of the two state parties concerned as to the numbers and membership of the special chamber. It is accompanied, however, by two dissenting opinions [16] and a special declaration [17] which, it is respectfully submitted, indicate much more attention than the majority opinion to the basic question of the nature and character of a Court and the compatibility therewith of the new special chamber system. These strongly-expressed judicial doubts, plus certain other, political flaws in the actual process used for constituting the Court – the actual selections were rushed through and approved by the Court, with an ill-disguised haste, a few days only before the full Court itself was to be reconstituted following on the regular triennial elections of the Autumn of 1981 – suggest that the special chamber, as such, may be approached with more political caution, in the future, by the full Court. The Court's revised Rules of Court would benefit from reexamination and rewriting, to make assurance doubly sure and avoid future exercises in political gamesmanship by the parties at the expense of the Court. What is thrown into question, however, is the particular process by which any such special chamber is now constituted within the International Court, not the notion of a special limited-in-numbers chamber, panel, or Senate of a Court, as such. In the case of the International Court, the formal authority of a judgment by a special chamber is declared, by Article 27 of the Court Statute, to be 'considered as rendered by the Court'; though Article 59 of the Court Statute somewhat cuts down on the sweep of that proposition, in Common Law terms at least, by declaring that a decision of the Court 'has no binding force except between the parties and in respect of that particular case'.

In the *Gulf of Maine* case, the two parties, the United States and Canada, after initially deferring to the wishes of the then President of the Court, Sir Humphrey Waldock, to constitute a fully neutral panel of judges not involving nationals of either party, changed their mind, after Sir Humphrey's sudden death, and insisted on the inclusion of their own national judges (their regular national judge of the Court, for the U.S., and an *ad hoc* judge for Canada). With the two national judges predictably cancelling each other out, this would mean that the case would be decided, effectively, by a panel of three judges only – as it turned out, and in accordance with the dictates of the parties as accepted by the full 15-member Court in constituting the 5-member special chamber – an

Italian, a West German, and a French judge. The classical Western, Euro-centrist character and image of the special chamber and of the proceeding as a whole which involved possible intellectual openings both to the New International Economic Order and the new Equity, was reinforced by the parties' choice of counsel – though counsel represented a number of different nationalities, all were from the same Western European-North American ethnocultural grouping, with one of the state parties, (somewhat disingenuously), taking pains to include in its team of advocates one Italian, one West German, and one French lawyer, in the possible belief that this might better persuade the judges of those three nationalities. Bearing in mind the recurring attacks on the International Court, – after the political disaster of its 8-to-7 decision in *South West Africa. Second Phase* in 1966 [17a] – that it was a Western, 'white man's' tribunal, dispensing a Western, 'white man's' international law, it would seem a matter of ordinary political prudence or self-defence for the 15-member *plenum* of the Court, in voting to constitute such special chambers in the future, (and whether or not it should decide to defer to the dictates of the parties as to actual choice of judges), to insist, nevertheless, on a panel that is more fully 'representative' in inter-systemic terms, (legal and political). This could mean at least one judge from the Third World in any such 5-member special chamber created in the future, and perhaps also one judge from the Socialist bloc and one from the West. Having two national judges included in such 5-member special chambers would seem an unnecessary, extra political burden for such 5-member special chambers to have to carry, granted the limited numbers; and no doubt the 15-member *plenum* of the Court could insist on their exclusion in the case of future special chambers. If the actual state parties did not like it, they could always resort to an *inter partes* arbitration for their dispute, giving up, thereby, the vicarious prestige attaching to a Court decision, as such. The International Court itself, though clearly in need of business in recent years, is surely not in such desperate straits as to have to surrender its inherent right, *qua* Court, to determine composition of its own tribunal and chambers, by ceding to the parties the actual choice of judges. There are certainly other useful ways for promoting expansion of the Court's work-load: encouraging the U.N. General Assembly to request Advisory Opinions, under Article 96(1) of the Charter, 'on any legal question'; relaxing the Court's own procedural, adjectival law pre-conditions to the making of rulings, as in *Nicaragua v. U.S., Provisional Measures,* in May, 1984. [17b] In September, 1983, the Governments of Upper Volta and of Mali, two francophonic African states, concluded a Special Agreement, (notified to the International Court the following month) submitting to a special chamber of the Court, to be constituted in accordance with Article 26(2) of the Court Statute, the issue of delimitation and demarcation of their common territorial frontier inherited from the French Imperial era, the settlement, according to the terms of the Special Agreement, to be – 'based in particular on respect for the principle of the intangibility of frontiers inherited from colonisation'. [17c]

2. JUDICIAL NUMBERS: OPTIMUM SIZE OF A COURT

We have already touched on the problem of numbers in connection with the discussion of Court organisation, and the issue of creation of special chambers, panels, or Senates within a full Court, either in the design of reducing the overall work-load by sharing the number of cases between different divisions of the Court, or else for purposes of allowing judicial specialisation by subject matter (private law, criminal law, constitutional law, as the case may be). In some instances, as with the Supreme Court of India, the establishment of a panel system may seem like an attempt to bolt the door after the horse has bolted – to overcome practical problems resulting from a purported reform, by increase in numbers, adopted too quickly and before other, alternative controls had been fully explored. Final tribunals, for the most part today, range between 9 and 15 members. The United States Supreme Court has nine judges, and since it sits *en banc* the nine will normally be present except for reasons of illness or personal disqualification from serving in a particular case. But it was not always so, the Court, under its first Chief Justice, John Jay, having only six members, the increase over the years being justified on the argument that more judges could turn out more work. The proposition seems arguable, though in fact it was used in relation to the Supreme Court of Canada to justify expanding it, also, to a present nine members. It seems accepted, as a truism involving final Courts, that at a certain point any increase in numbers becomes counter-productive and impedes effective decision-making. What is to be the norm, then, for useful collegial operatin? If the United States and Canadian Supreme Courts, each of which operates *en banc*, as a full Court, are now nine judges, the West German constitutional court, which was originally established with two separate Senates, each with its own clearly defined jurisdiction, started out with twenty-four judges, but was subsequently, by deliberate design, reduced to sixteen judges. Since the two Senates are distinct from each other, and of coordinate authority, and since the *plenum* or full Court hardly functions today, with the disappearance of its original Advisory Opinion jurisdiction with the Court reforms of 1956, it is better to think of the West German Court, for purposes of our present consideration of the relation of judicial numbers to collegiality in decision-making, as two separate tribunals, originally of twelve judges apiece but now, by trial-

and-error experience, reduced to eight judges apiece.

The Supreme Court of Japan, as already noted, consists of fifteen judges, but the Court sits in three separate divisions (Petty Benches) each of five judges, except for constitutional cases in which it sits *en banc* (as a Grand Bench). The quorum of the Court, *en banc,* is nine judges, but it is stipulated that a majority of eight judges is needed to declare a law unconstitutional. The Supreme Court of India, rising over the years from its establishment, in 1950, from eight judges, in stages to eleven judges, then fourteen judges, and finally, with the Court reform of 1978, to eighteen judges, has operated with a divisional system, with four or more panels, giving however, as we have already seen, a very considerable discretion to the Chief Justice to influence the historical course of jurisprudence with his power to determine the composition of panels. Prime Minister Gandhi's institution of a two-bench system in 1982, with only the constitutional bench competent to decide constitutional cases, would bring the largest of the Courts surveyed more in line with all the others in terms of working numbers. The International Court of Justice, with its fifteen judges, who may be supplemented, in the case of states party to litigation who do not already have one of their own nationals on the Court, by the nomination of *ad hoc* (national) judges, increasing judicial numbers, thereby, to sixteen or seventeen, is by far the largest of the tribunals surveyed, in terms of working practice. (In the rare cases, in great political *causes célèbres* such as *Golak Nath* in 1967[18] and *Kesavananda Bharati* in 1973,[19] when the Indian Supreme Court, at the direction of the Chief Justice, sat *en banc,* its membership was fourteen judges, and the decisions were rendered by 6-to-5 and 7-to-6 votes, respectively). If we went only on the public record of the International Court, we would perhaps assume, too easily, that its larger numbers fully account for what, in West German legal circles, has been called judicial Byzantinism; an evident lack of full consultation and cooperation among the judges in their approach to decision-making; a failure to coordinate and discipline different intellectual viewpoints to the point of producing a single, well-reasoned statement of the majority consensus, such as it might happen to be, as a rationalisation of the majority grounds of decision or *ratio decidendi* in any case; a noticeable lack of self-restraint or mutual deference, at times, producing dissenting or special (concurring) opinions that have an unpleasantly perjorative quality. The proliferation of dissenting and special (concurring) opinions in some of the great political *causes célèbres* of the 1960s and 1970s is only partly a reflection of the difficulties of judicial policy choice in an era of transition and rapid change in which 'classical' International Law is under challenge by the new political forces in the World Community. There are special difficulties of internal organisation with a tribunal like the International Court which has its seat in a city, like The Hague, in which most of its members do not choose to reside; and these are compounded where, as with the Court, its President (Chief Justice) is, in terms of the Court's own Statute (Article 21), elected only for a term of years – three years, and where almost unbroken custom over the years dictates that he be not a candidate for reelection to that post. Lack of any degree of permanence in the post of Court President, beyond the stipulated three year term, ensures lack of continuity of administration and practice as to decision-making and the effective absence of any overall leadership as to policy development and philosophic orientation in law. These weaknesses in internal organisation, inherent in the Court's statutory arrangements and its actual practice, – including the developing custom of rotating the Presidency among the different main political-ideological blocs or ethnic-cultural groupings in the World Community – compound the problems created by swollen judicial numbers, a dualist (Civil Law and Common Law) legal systemic base, and the two official Court languages (French and English) in both of which not all of the judges will be able to work effectively. Collegial decision-making, and even a collegial approach to opinion-writing and rationalisation of the grounds of the Court's decision in any case, become very difficult under these circumstances.

When the Gaullist constitution-makers of the Fifth Republic made their tentative steps towards institutionalising constitutional review, in 1958, they decided, without any particular difficulty or hesitation, on a tribunal of nine members, supplemented only by a special category of 'members by legal right' which is limited to former Presidents of the Republic and has hardly operated to date. By a sort of common consensus among constitutionalists, in various, widely differing legal systems, the norm seems to have emerged that a final tribunal should be composed of eight or nine members. If less than that, the thought seems to be, the work load will be too heavy for the individual judges; if more than that, they will cease to function effectively as a collegial body. As between a total of eight or nine members, the Common Law reasoning seems to be that eight might involve the disadvantage of an even-split vote in fiercely contested causes, where nine would always yield a majority. That argument fails to take full account of the fact that, because of illness, disqualification, or other casual factors, a full bench of nine judges will not always be present to decide cases; and in any case the problem of a potential, even-split vote is more psychological than real, since a Court's rules can always be made to stipulate clearly, on an *a priori* basis, what should be the result in such case – preservation of the decision of a Court below that is being appealed from, maintenance of the constitutionality of a statute or executive decree or ruling whose validity is being impugned.

3. JUDICIAL OPINION-WRITING: DISSENTING AND CONCURRING OPINIONS

The dissenting opinion has occupied a place of honour, in American jurisprudence, since the era of Holmes and Brandeis when their dissents to the 'Old Court', *laissez-faire* majority on the United States Supreme Court became, in effect, appeals to the future, foreshadowing eventual distinguishings or reversals of the majority opinions with the pressure of public opinion and the impact of later changes in Court personnel through the deaths or retirements of the more conservative judges and their replacement by more liberal and open-minded jurists. The romantic conception of the judicial dissenter, following Holmes' great dissent in the *Lochner* case in 1905,[20] was assisted by a certain confusion or ambiguity in Holmes' reputation for posterity: was he objecting to the substantive (social and economic *laissez-faire*) values of the 'Old Court' majority opinions and seeking to replace those values by a newer, more social democratic orientation; or was the thrust of the Holmes' opinions, as his disciple and later Supreme Court Justice, Felix Frankfurter, always contended, the technically more sophisticated argument, with its deference to separation of powers notions, that the judges had no business in introducing their own conceptions of policy, of whatever nature, in substitution for those of legislative majorities? With the general expansion and 'reception', abroad, of American constitutional ideas and processes, the tendency to borrow from or adopt, also, the American conception of the affirmative *rôle* of the judicial dissenter was very strong also. The old Imperial, Privy Council did not, until long after its jurisdiction in relation to the former colonial Empire had, for all practical purposes, disappeared into history, concede the right to its members to indicate the fact of individual disagreement with the Court judgment or, *a fortiori,* to file a reasoned dissent thereto. But neither the Canadian nor the Indian Supreme Court has had any problem in indicating the final judicial vote in any case and also the fact of individual judicial disagreements with the judgment; and dissenting and specially concurring opinions were both permitted and also freely exercised. The Supreme Court of Japan, in its post-World War II phase, chose to follow its American model and to allow recording of dissents and also publication of individual judicial opinions in support thereof.

With the West German Federal Constitutional Court, Civil Law principles as to judicial anonymity and collegial solidarity were still very strong at the outset. The Court statute, as enacted in 1951, prescribed only that the Court should decide its cases in 'secret deliberation' (s. 30(1)). One early commentator, Lechner,[21] concluded from this and the fact of the silence of the law-makers in the Statute itself expressly and in terms to permit individual judicial opinions (*Sondervoten*) in the Anglo-

Saxon Common Law sense, that the law-makers clearly intended to continue historically-based German court practice against such individual opinions. During the drafting of the Court statute, in fact, a proposal had been made to give judges in a voting minority in any case the right to indicate that fact and the reasons for their disagreement with the majority vote and its reasoning. It was here that the phrase judicial Byzantinism emerged, the proposal to allow publication of the actual Court vote and of minority as well as majority argument being rejected by a small margin on the score that it would encourage factionalism on the Court and judicial publicity-seeking. [22] On one early occasion, however, – the great political controversy over the proposed West German adherence to the proposed new European Defence Community, in 1952, accompanied as that was by complex procedural-law manoeuvring with the Court being approached by the rival political forces in each of its two Senates, and by the federal President in its *plenum* or full Court jurisdiction, – the unusual event occurred, in the *plenum,* of an official noting of the actual judicial vote in the Advisory Opinion (*Rechtsgutachten*) proceedings instituted by the federal President. In the first public break from the unanimity principle, it was recorded, in a *plenum* ruling that an Advisory Opinion determination by the *plenum* would be legally binding upon the two Senates of the Court, that this ruling had been agreed upon by a 20 to 2 vote, though no mention was made in the official reports as to the reasons for the judicial disagreement. [23] But one of the two dissenting judges, Dr. Geiger, shortly after the announcement of the official Court decision, released the text of his dissenting opinion for publication in a private (non-official) work, [24] the unprecedented character of such action being sought to be minimised on the argument that the *plenum* Advisory Opinion ruling was only a resolution (*Beschluss*), and not an actual decision (*Urteil*) and, hence, that the usual principles as to safeguarding the secrecy of Court votes should not apply. The argument in favour of allowing publication of dissenting and specially concurring judicial votes, with the names of the judges concerned being mentioned, had been part of the Social Democratic Party draft for the Court statute, and the debate over the principle continued in the 1960s, as it had begun in the 1950s, with the more traditional legal forces arguing that the revelation of the actual Court vote, in so far as it would break through the public facade of collegial unanimity, would undermine the Court's authority and also public confidence in its integrity. The countervailing arguments were that it would in fact improve working collegial relations within the Court, and contribute to the development of legal doctrine through exposing the alternative options in Court interpretation and thus allowing systematic canvassing and evaluation of their relative social value. In general the more progressive intellectual-legal forces and also those judges who had some sustained experience of Anglo-Saxon legal doctrine and practice and especially American constitutionalism – Gerhard Leibholz, Hans Rupp, and Friedrich Wilhelm Wagner, all of the Second Senate of the Court, with Judge Wagner serving as its chief judge and Vice-President of the Federal Constitutional Court as a whole – were publicly in favour of the change. The matter came to a head in the middle 1960s. Up to that time, the special vote (either concurring or dissenting) had been widely practised in both Senates of the Court, but their existence had simply been recorded in the secret archives of the Court. In 1966, in the *Der Spiegel* affair,[25] the First Senate of the Court published in its judgment not only the grounds for the declining of the process, for which four judges had voted, but also the views of the judges who had argued the other way and contended that a violation of constitutional rights was involved – though all this without giving the names of the judges on the two different sides. In the same year, 1966, the Second Senate of the Court had been much troubled by the Party Financing case,[26] and it was a matter of general public knowledge that the Second Senate had been deadlocked, four-to-four, on the substantive merits of the case and the federal Government's proposal to finance, through public funds, political parties' election expenses. The deadlock within the Second Senate was only broken, after some months, by a motion – politically contrived as it appeared at the time – to have Judge Leibholz disqualified from sitting in the case on the ground of 'interest', because of prior public expressions, as a University Professor, on the philosophical issue of state financing of political parties.[27] The Second Senate voted – again according to general public knowledge – four-to-three to disqualify Judge Leibholz, with Judge Leibholz himself abstaining from voting on his own case,[28] and then the rump, seven-member Second Senate, without Judge Leibholz, voted four-to-three to hold the federal Government statute for the state financing of political parties' election expenses, unconstitutional.[29] The whole unhappy affair within the Second Senate, however, demonstrated very clearly the dangers of secret Court proceedings, and the anxiety they can cause among the general public and also the legal profession at large as to the political integrity of the Court's internal processes, however unjustified such fears might be. There was, in fact, an almost unanimous reaction of indignation, in West German academic and scientific legal circles, over the Second Senate's final decisions in both cases – the disqualification of Judge Leibholz, and the invalidation, on the substantive merits, of public financing of political parties' election expenses.[30] Regrettable as may have been these two decisions of the Second Senate, the happy *dénouement* of the resulting debate within the West German legal establishment[31] was a change in the Court's ground rules so as to permit publication, with the decisions of either Senate, of any dissenting or concurring opinions and also the actual judicial vote. This right has existed since December, 1970, under s. 30(2) of the Court Statute, and in terms of Rules of Court adopted by the *plenum* of the Court in February, 1971, pursuant to the Court Statute; and it has been availed of from time to time since, though with perhaps more conscious self-restraint and modesty of usage than has been the case with the United States Supreme Court and other tribunals with much longer practice in the area.

In truth, the arguments for and against allowing dissenting and concurring votes within a collegial body like a Court, and of publishing the actual opinions in support of such votes, are closely linked to general theories of law and of the judicial process and of the *rôle* of the judge in what the United Nations Charter calls the 'progressive development'[32] of law. Once the older, positivistic theories of law are put to one side and the law-making potential of the judge recognised, then law itself becomes understood, not as a frozen cake of doctrine that jelled once and for all in some bygone era, but as a dynamic, dialectical process of continuing unfolding and development of legal principles and rules in accord with changing societal conditions and needs. These contemporary, more instrumental approaches to law, in place of the older, static, contemplative theories, require, as a correlative, the widest possible canvassing of alternative judicial policy constructs, if the dialectical legal process is to be carried on scientifically and usefully.

In the twilight era of the Imperial, Privy Council's jurisdiction as final appellate tribunal for Canada, and in fact shortly after the Canadian Parliament had itself legislated, in 1949, to abolish such Imperial jurisdiction, the then Chief Justice Rinfret of the Supreme Court of Canada proposed, in a seeming spirit of nostalgic salute to the Imperial practice now put aside, that the Supreme Court of Canada should 'follow the practice of the Privy Council' and henceforward issue only a single, *per curiam* opinion in each case.[33] But the Chief Justice's proposal received absolutely no support in Canadian legal circles, being viewed as a step backwards in time to the old, mechanical theories of law and the judicial process that were quite unsuited to the new, autonomous Canadian society then in full development, and so the Chief Justice's proposal lapsed very quickly. In contrast, the Canadian Supreme Court in modern times, and especially since its emancipation from the Privy Council's appellate jurisdiction, has moved, more and more, into an American-style practice as to decision-making, voting, and opinion-writing in justification or rationalisation of those decisions and votes. If anything, since the Canadian Supreme Court, for a number of different reasons – among these, a relatively rapid turn-over of Chief Justices, and an absence of strong tradition of self-discipline within the Court as to reconciling or compromising of philosophic differences among the individual judges, has tended to a proliferation, more and more, of special opinions, dissenting and concurring, with very little evidence of prior exchange of views or consultation among the judges concerned. The absence of the American system of an official Opinion of Court, in which the majority judges accept a common obligation to produce at least a lowest-common-denominator statement of the points of agreement among them, means that it is often difficult to establish the actual grounds of decision or *ratio decidendi* in a given case. On the other hand, the Canadian Supreme Court has generally been free of that more pejorative or personalised form of judicial dissent or special concurrence, in which opposing judicial viewpoints are excoriated, that has sometimes marred the work of the United States Supreme Court. The International Court of Justice began, in the 1970s, with the more explosive *causes célèbres* of contemporary international law and relations now reaching its docket, to be troubled by the occasional contentious note in individual special opinions, and so it took some measures, – tactfully and with a certain prudent economy of power, – to try to insert some safeguards into its Rules, so as to allow for possible screening in advance of actual publication of such special opinions. The matter is not free from doubt: too much in the way of advance controls would, of course, amount to a form of prior restraint on publication and so, in very large measure, defeat the very purpose of allowing publication of special opinions side by side with the official Opinion of Court. It is for this reason that the actual formulation in the Resolution concerning the Internal Judicial Practice of the Court (International Court of Justice, Rules of Court, Article 19), adopted on 12 April 1976, seems especially felicitous. Article 7 (ii) and (iv) of the Resolution requires the filing of the text of any separate or dissenting opinions within a fixed time-limit of publication of the first draft of the official Opinion of Court, and limits the making of further changes in such separate or dissenting opinions to responsive changes to alterations in the first draft of the official Opinion of Court, without attempting in any way to postulate or otherwise to spell out any Court sanctions that might be sought to be applied in case of abuse of the right to file such separate or dissenting opinions.

NOTES

1. An 'orchestral and not a solo opinion': Felix Frankfurter, *The Commerce Clause under Marshall, Taney, and Waite* (1937), p. 43.
2. E. McWhinney, 'The Privy Council as final appellate tribunal for the Overseas Empire', in *Judicial Review* (4th ed., 1969), p. 49.
3. As to Lord Watson, see Lord Haldane's own tribute: Haldane 'The Judicial Committee of the Privy Council', 1 *Cambridge Law Journal* 143, 150 (1923).

4. *Attorney-General for Canada* v. *Attorney-General for Ontario* [1937] A.C. 326 (P.C.).

5. See the *ex post facto* comments by Lord Wright, who had been a member of the Board of the Privy Council deciding the case, in 33 *Canadian Bar Review* 1123 (1955); and see the comments, 'Labour Conventions Case: Lord Wright's undisclosed dissent?', 34 *Canadian Bar Review* 114, 115, 243 (1956).

6. Judicial Committee (Dissenting Opinions) Order, 1966 (adopted 4 March 1966).

7. *Nuclear Tests (Australia* v. *France), Interim Protection, Order of 22 June 1973*, I.C.J. Reports 1973, p. 99; *Nuclear Tests (Australia* v. *France), Judgment of 20 December 1974*, I.C.J. Reports 1974, p. 253. And see generally E. McWhinney, *The World Court and the contemporary International Law-Making Process* (1979), p. 34.

8. *Western Sahara, Advisory Opinion*, I.C.J. Reports 1975, p. 12. And see generally E. McWhinney *The World Court and the contemporary International Law-Making Process* (1979), p. 65.

9. M. Bruce, 'The 1953 Mid-Winter Meeting of Council', 31 *Canadian Bar Review* 178, 181-182 (1953).

10. H. Laufer, *Verfassungsgerichtsbarkeit und politischer Prozess* (1968), pp. 170-171.

11. E. McWhinney, *Constitutionalism in Germany...* (1962), p. 34.

12. George H. Gadbois Jr., 'Supreme Court Decision Making', 10 *Banaras Law Journal* 1, 24 (1974).

13. I.C.J. Reports 1969, p. 3.

14. On Eurocentrism in law, compare René David's perceptive study, 'Existe-t-il un droit occidental?' in *XXth Century Comparative and Conflicts Law. Legal Essays in Honour of Hessel E. Yntema* (K. Nadelmann, A.T. Von Mehren, and J.N. Hazard, eds.) (1961), p. 56.

15. I.C.J. Reports 1982, p. 3.

16. By Judge Morozov, *ibid.,* p. 11; and by Judge El-Khani, *ibid.,* p. 12.

17. By Judge Oda, *ibid.,* p. 10.

17a. I.C.J. Reports 1966, p. 6.

17b. *Military and Paramilitary Activities in and against Nicaragua (Nicaragua* v. *U.S.A.) Provisional Measures, Order of 10 May 1984*, I.C.J. Reports 1984, p. 169.

17c. United Nations, N.Y., Press Release, ICJ/421, 2 November 1983; 22 *International Legal Materials*, 1252, 1253 (1983).

18. *I.C. Golak Nath* v. *State of Punjab*, A.I.R. *1967* S.C. 1643.

19. *Kesavananda Bharati* v. *State of Kerala*, A.I.R. *1973* S.C. 1461.

20. *Lochner* v. *New York*, 198 U.S. 45 (1905) (per Holmes J., dissenting). And see also Charles Aikin, 'The United States Supreme Court: The Judicial Dissent', 18 *Jahrbuch des öffentlichen Rechts der Gegenwart* 18 (1969).

21. Hans Lechner, *Bundesverfassungsgerichtsgesetz* (1954), pp. 173-174. And see also A.T. Von Mehren, *The Civil Law System* (1957), p. 834; K. Nadelmann, 'The Judicial Dissent: Publication v. Secrecy', 8 *American Journal of Comparative Law* 415, 427-428 (1959); E. McWhinney, 'Die Bedeutung des Sondervotums in der Verfassungsgerichtsbarkeit', [1961] *Juristenzeitung* (no. 21) 655.

22. A.T. Von Mehren, 'The Judicial Process: A comparative analysis', 5 *American Journal of Comparative Law* 197, 208-209 (1956).

23. 2 B Verf GE 79 (1953) (*plenum*).

24. See generally W. Geiger, *Der Kampf um den Wehrbeitrag* (1953); H. Lechner, *Bundesverfassungsgerichtsgesetz* (1954), p. 174. And see also Wolfgang Heyde, 'Dissenting Opinions in der deutschen Verfassungsgerichtsbarkeit', 19 *Jahrbuch des öffentlichen Rechts der Gegenwart* 201 (1970).

25. Decision of 5 August 1966, 20 B Verf GE 162 (1966) (First Senate). And see Donald P. Kommers, *Judicial Politics in West Germany* (1976), pp. 152-153.

26. For the judgment, as finally rendered after the 'disqualification' issue had been dis-

posed of, see Decision of 19 July 1966, 20 B Verf GE 56 (1966) (Second Senate).

27. For Judge Leibholz' paper, rendered as Professor, see G. Leibholz, 'Staat und Ver-
bände', in *Veröffentlichungen der Vereinigung der Deutschen Staatsrechtslehrer* (1967)
no. 24.

28. Decision of 2 March 1966, 20 B Verf GE 9 (1966) (Second Senate).

29. Decision of 19 July 1966, 20 B Verf GE 56 (1966) (Second Senate).

30. See, for example, E. Friesenhahn (former Judge of the Federal Constitutional Court),
'Anmerkung: Zur Ablehnung und Selbstablehnung eines Richters des Bundesverfas-
sungsgerichts wegen Besorgnis der Befangenheit', [1966] *Juristenzeitung* (no. 21) 704;
H. Laufer, 'Zur staatlichen Finanzierung der politischen Parteien', *Aus Politik zur
Zeitgeschichte* (no. 44, 1966), 2 November 1960; W. Sarstedt (President of the Senate
of the Federal Supreme Court (Civil Law)), [1966] *Juristenzeitung* (no. 21) 314.

31. H. Laufer, *Verfassungsgerichtsbarkeit und politischer Prozess* (1968), pp. 516-518.

32. United Nations Charter, Article 13 (1) (a).

33. M. Bruce, 31 *Canadian Bar Review* 178, 181-182 (1953).

CHAPTER III

CONSTITUTIONAL JUDGES: APPOINTMENT, TENURE, REMOVAL

1. JUDICIAL APPOINTMENT PROCESSES

The appointment processes vary widely from country to country, but there are some clear trends observable in the constitutional-legal machinery and processes governing such matters, related to several main factors: the relative age or contemporaneity in the adoption of such appointment processes, the degree of intellectual flexibility and openness to legal and societal change of those in charge of such processes, and finally, and principally perhaps, the degree of persistence today of the 'basic legal myth', described by the Legal Realists, that the judicial *rôle* is a purely mechanical one and that judges do not make law in their decisions. Where the basic legal myth remains dominant, the appointing processes will tend to have been assimilated to those for all other judges, involving an insistence on the possibility of judicial neutrality on great political, social and economic issues arising in cases coming before them and a refusal, therefore, to canvass openly the particular value-preferences or ideological orientation of candidates for high judicial office or to admit that as a matter for public examination and screening prior to appointment. Such a determinedly value-neutral approach to judicial appointments at the final Court level finds a certain *raison d'être* where the Courts concerned are, *de jure* anyway, tribunals of comprehensive, mixed or general appellate jurisdiction, and not specialised constitutional tribunals whether in law or in fact. It may be suggested, however, on the empirical record, that the judges inevitably turn up with individual value-preferences and particular ideological orientations, whether those facts are canvassed, in public, prior to their appointments or not; and that the public dissatisfaction and criticism may be the less when those intellectual attitudes are placed on the record, *a priori,* through public screening of judicial candidates, and not left to the shock of later discovery hidden in the interstices of great 'policy' decisions on law. The postulated democratic character of constitutional review today would seem to carry with it its own special imperatives as to judicial responsibility, if the principle of constitutional legitimacy is to extend to constitutional judges too, in addition to the executive and legislative arms of government.

The British-'received' or British-derived judicial appointment processes represent one extreme, in terms of conceding the maximum discretion to executive power in the selection and appointment of judges, free from the potentially politically embarrassing constitutional checks and balances provided by conceding a *rôle* in the appointing processes, also, to other coordinate constitutional institutions, like the legislature, or even the people. In Canada, appointments to the Supreme Court are made by the federal executive, *tout court*. No one else has any legal say in the matter, although various informal, and in any case legally non-binding, procedures have been announced from time to time to blunt public criticisms that the process is undemocratic in contemporary terms, or that it leads to unrepresentative appointments or to favouring of the executive's own political party. Some of these informal measures seem, however, either counter-productive (such as the prior consultation of the heads of the Bar Association of the Province or region concerned, such people being generally fairly conservative and non-innovatory in legal terms and likely, for this reason, to take a dim view of the intellectual front-runner of the Holmes or Brandeis variety who is so necessary to leaven the dullness of most final appellate tribunals); or else somewhat objectionable in constitutional due process terms (such as the secret screening by committees of civil servants of lists of potential candidates on moral and other grounds). The power of nomination to the highest judicial office is one of the great privileges and responsibilities of the constitutional executive; and while that power can be abused, such constitutional correctives as are needed are better applied openly where they can themselves be subjected to the democratic corrective of public debate and criticism. It seems foolish, in any case, to fetter the executive discretion as to appointment by secret consultations and discussions before secret professional gatherings; otherwise the dynamic, creative element inherent in judicial law-making is likely to be lost before the more traditional and orthodox, grey judicial candidates.

The Supreme Court of India, for inherited (British) reasons similar to those in Canada, is constituted through appointment by federal executive power alone, without any requirement of confirmation by, or even any practice of consultation with, the federal legislature or other coordinate arms of government. The Indian Constitution does, indeed, stipulate that, in the making of such appointments by the federal executive, there shall be a prior 'consultation with such of the Judges of the Supreme Court and of the High Courts in the States as the (federal) President may deem necessary for the purpose', and that in the case of the appointment of a Judge other than the Chief Justice of the Court, the Chief Justice shall always be consulted (Constitution, Article 124 (2)). Since the Chief Justice is himself, of course, appointed by the federal executive, and since there has been continuing, one-party control of the federal Government from Indian decolonisation and independence on to the present, (with the brief Janata Government interlude, in the late-1970s, excepted), this has presented no particular political problems for the federal Government and so the consultation with the Chief Justice did take place and, in some views, has been decisive.

The Constitution of Japan stipulates that the Judges of the Supreme Court, with the exception of the Chief Justice, are to be appointed by the Cabinet (Article 79). Although the Constitution provides that the Chief Justice is to be appointed by the Emperor (titular head-of-state), it declares, in the same breath, that such appointment is on the designation of the Cabinet (Article 6). It all amounts, in practice, to the same thing – legally unfettered executive appointment of Supreme Court Justices. The more interesting features of the Japanese executive appointment process are the various attempts to institutionalise, also, a process of executive consultation prior to making appointments to the Court. The first bench of the Supreme Court of Japan was appointed following on advice given by an Advisory Committee on the appointment of Judges, the Advisory Committee consisting of fifteen members – the Speaker of the lower House and the Speaker of the upper House of the Diet (legislature), four members elected from among all judges, one member elected from among the public prosecutors and the judges of the Administrative Court, four members elected from among practising lawyers, two professors of law nominated by the Prime Minister, and two other members nominated by the Prime Minister. The Advisory Committee reported back with thirty names – twice as many as the number of judicial seats to be filled, – and the actual Cabinet selections appear to have been made from that short list. The Advisory Committee was, however, abolished in 1948 on the argument that appointments to the Supreme Court were a matter, constitutionally, to be decided on the sole responsibility of the Cabinet, and that any such committee of outside advisers would tend to fetter what, in constitutional terms, was a free, discretionary, executive choice. An expert paper submitted to the Cabinet Commission on the Constitution (Takayanagi Commission)[1] by Hideo Tanaka in 1962,[2] noted various opinions expressed at that time in favour of reestablishment of such an Advisory Committee on appointments. Within the Takayanagi Commission itself the issue was raised in terms either of another, informal (and non-binding as to its recommendations) advisory committee, or else a screening or selection committee established in the constitutional charter itself – this latter suggestion on the argument of the need for independence from the Government of the day, and to eliminate partisan political considerations from the appointment process. The counter-arguments, within the Takayanagi Commission, were against any rigidifying of the appointment processes through their entrenchment in the Constitution, and the *de minimis* proposition that if it were felt necessary to control possible partisan political abuses by the Cabinet, then another purely advisory committee would be enough and it could always be created by ordinary legislation. In fact, the Cabinet seems to have been sensitive, in later years, to the views of the Chief Justice and incumbent Justices of the Supreme Court, at least where these have been strongly expressed and negative in regard to a proposed executive appointment: it is recorded that in 1971 and 1973, two successive executives, the Sato and Tanaka Governments, backed down in the face of strong objections by Chief Justice Ishida and other Supreme Court Justices against the choice of a particular Justice Ministry official, and appointed, instead, the Chief Justice's own preferences to two successive vacancies, – Justices Kishi and Yoshida.[3] This is hardly surprising, in comparative legal science, experiential terms. Legally unfettered executive discretionary powers tend to be exercised, very frequently, with moderation and upon consultation and advice.

The antonym to the executive appointment process of filling the highest judicial office is founded in those systems, contemporary and older, that bring in the other, coordinate, legislative arm of government in some way, either in terms of a federal legislature-based right of confirmation or rejection of executive nominations as in the United States, or of a federal legislature-based system of election of the judges as in West Germany. Under the United States Constitution, the federal upper House or Senate, itself, in modern times, a popularly elected body, must ratify, by majority vote, all Presidential nominations to the Supreme Court for them to be effective (U.S. Constitution, Article II (2) 2 – Presidential appointment 'by and with the Advice and Consent of the Senate'). Such Senate power of rejection has been exercised from time to time; and, perhaps more importantly, the very existence of that power and the practice of the Senate to hold public hearings to examine nominees to judicial office as to their technical legal qualifications and experience and also as to their general philosophy of law in the search for concealed value preferences, have compelled a certain Presidential executive self-restraint as to presenting candidates who are patently unqualified or otherwise unfit for high public office, and have sometimes induced such unhappy candidates to withdraw their names from consideration before the actual Senate vote on confirmation. Simple publicity as to a nominee and as to his or her legal and general background may indeed, as the recent experience under the Johnson and Nixon Presidencies demonstrated, be a sufficient sanction to compel certain standards in appointment without the need of any formal rejection by the legislature.

In the case of West Germany, the Judges of the Federal Constitutional Court are elected by the federal legislature. As stipulated by the Basic Law (Constitution) of 1949, (Article 94 (1)), one half of the members of the Court are elected by the federal lower House (*Bundestag*), itself a popular, elected body; and the other half by the federal upper House (*Bundesrat*), in fact a species of regional governmental council whose members are not elected but appointed by the various regional (*Länder*) Governments of the day. The bare bones of the constitutional stipulations were fleshed out in the Statute on the Federal Constitutional Court of 1951. Under the Court Statute, the *Bundestag* elects its quota of Judges for the Court, by a form of indirect election through a twelve-member committee of its own members who are themselves selected according to the proportionate strength of each political party in the *Bundestag,* with eight votes now required for purposes of election. (Court Statute, as amended, section 6 (1), (2) and (3)). Under the Court Statute, the *Bundesrat* elects its quota of Judges by a two-thirds majority vote, (Court Statute, as amended, section 7), voting as a whole and voting directly. The rules, with their effective division of the judicial seats among the two federal institutions, *Bundestag* and *Bundesrat,* functioning separately and independently as electoral colleges, and with the quite different voting formulae for each such electoral college, are rather complex. However, they operate in such a way as to produce a representative Court that reflects, more or less, the respective strengths of the different political parties in the *Bundestag* and in the different political administrations at the regional, *Länder* level.[4] Under the electoral system as it has been worked out in practice, and with the Federal Constitutional Court divided, internally, into its two distinct and autonomous Senates, each federal institution – *Bundestag* und *Bundesrat* – selects half the members of each of the two Senates. The electoral eligibility rules establish, in effect, two different categories of judges, with a special quota of judicial seats – under the original, 1951 Court Statute, four seats out of the then twelve seats in each Senate; and under the Court Statute, as now amended, three seats out of the present eight seats in each Senate – reserved for Judges who are already members of the highest federal Courts (the Federal Supreme Court, Federal Administrative Court, Federal Finance Court, Federal Labour Court, and Federal Social Court), (Court Statute, section 4 (1)). These particular Judges were elected with a term corresponding to the balance of the term remaining to them on their original federal Court (Court Statute, section 4 (1)), – that is, as professional, career civil servant judges, for a life term (until the normal, compulsory career civil service judicial retirement age of sixty-eight). The other, non-career civil service judges' elected places on the Federal Constitutional Court were for a precise and limited, term of years only. (The tenure rules as to the two categories of Judges on the Federal Constitutional Court were, in effect, assimilated in a further amendment to the Court Statute in 1970, so that, thereafter, all Judges of the Court would be elected for a term of years only, with a common, mandatory retirement age of sixty-eight, though without application to Judges already on the Court in 1970: the effect of these changes will be discussed, later, under the heading of judicial tenure.)

Another major tribunal to utilise the election system for the appointment of its Judges is the International Court of Justice. Under the Court Statute, the Court consists of fifteen Judges no two of whom may be nationals of the same state, (Court Statute, Article 3). The Judges are elected by the two Parliamentary organs of the United Nations, the General Assembly in which each member-state has a single vote; and the very much smaller, Security Council which is politically very heavily weighted to the post-World War II Big Powers (the United States, Great Britain, France, Soviet Union and China) with these five states being Permanent Members and the remaining ten members elected for two-year terms on a rotating basis. To be elected to the Court, absolute majorities of votes are required in both the General Assembly and the Security Council, though the Permanent Members' normal right of Veto in the Security Council does not apply (Court Statute, Article 10). The double majority requirement in the election processes for the International Court offsets the numerically superior political advantages once possessed by the Western bloc in the General Assembly and now enjoyed by the new Third World forces, and encourages political compromises and trading of votes in the elections. In the result, there has been a certain continuity and stability and conservatism in the actual operation of the electoral processes for the Court, in contrast to the marked impact of the new political forces in the World Community upon other United Nations institutions and arenas and special processes.

The *Conseil constitutionnel* established under the Gaullist Constitution of the Fifth French Republic in 1958 is, as we have noted, an institution taking on many of the elements of a specialised constitutional tribunal, even if not a Court *stricto sensu*. Even though the President of the Republic is given a general watch-dog *rôle* to ensure respect for the Constitution and the regular functioning of the public powers and the continuity of the State (Article 5), the constitution-makers of the Fifth Republic avoided the obvious step of according to the President the competence to designate all the members of the *Conseil constitutionnel*. The experience under the preceding Fourth Republic (1946-1958) with the somewhat amorphous and, at the close of that Republic, still somewhat unfulfilled *Comité constitutionnel,* in the entrusting of the power to nominate members to the two Houses of the legislature, was considered to have produced a highly politicised selection process. Instead, under the Fifth Republic, a new mode of designation of members was employed for the new *Conseil constitutionnel,* with the President of the Republic and the presiding officers (Presidents) of the two Houses of the legislature, the Senate and the National Assembly, each appointing three members. The three-way division of the appointment power, in this way, was thought more likely to introduce a certain philosophical balance into the *Conseil* and thus to increase its political authority, this likelihood being increased by the different terms of office and different electoral constituencies involved for each of the three appointing officers referred to. In fact, the long-time President of the Senate, Gaston Monnerville, who functioned as such for eleven years, was not especially sympathetic to President de Gaulle; and the Gaullist President of the National Assembly, Jacques Chaban-Delmas, who held that office for ten years, carried over into Giscard d'Estaing's term as President of the Republic and had been an unsuccessful contender against him for that office. The splitting up of the appointing power to the *Conseil* thus tended to operate a little in practice, as it had no doubt been intended to operate in theory, as a form of constitutional check and balance,[5] not dissimilar in result to the proportional representation-style, legislative election to the West German constitutional Court.

2. JUDICIAL TENURE: LIFE, OR TERM-OF-YEARS?

Linked to the issue of the nature of the judicial appointing processes and their representative character, if any, are questions of the length of the judicial term and whether it is to be for life and thus beyond effective political review, or else for a limited, term-of-years only and so subject to potential political control. The last question shades off into the larger debate over judicial independence, and the degree of constitutional responsibility before the other, coordinate institutions of community decision-making, – executive and legislature – that one wants to accord to the Courts in furtherance of the principle of constitutional legitimacy in the contemporary democratic state. There is, once again, an opposition, or at least fundamental antinomy, between 'classical', Anglo-Saxon Common Law conceptions and developing Continental European Civil Law-based constitutional practice. The Common Law and 'received' Common Law approach is to insist that it is a necessary element of judicial independence and protection from political or other pressures from coordinate, executive and legislative authority, to have the members of the final Courts appointed for life, as with the United States Supreme Court, or for life subject only to a mandatory retirement age applied to all judges uniformly, as with the Supreme Courts of Canada, India, and, finally, the Supreme Court of Japan under the post-War Constitution. Since judges of the U.S. Supreme Court are often appointed at a very young age, by Presidents anxious to promote and extend their own special constitutional philosophy and general political ideas over a considerable span of years, and since there is no normal legal control on U.S. Supreme Court judges' tenure other than their own sense of self-restraint and personal judgement of their own physical capacities and the continued relevance and timeliness of their own particular constitutional ideas, it will quite often happen that judges will serve for a very long period of time – more than thirty years, as with the early and great Chief Justice, John Marshall, or the great Oliver Wendell Holmes, Jr., who, though appointed at an advanced age (sixty-one), continued to sit into his nineties, or the crusading liberal judge, William O. Douglas, who was appointed by President Franklin Roosevelt at a very young age (forty). It is evident, in cases such as these, that the 'during good Behaviour' definition of judicial tenure established under the U.S. Constitution (Article III (1)), does indeed operate to shield the members of the Court from extra-judicial political and other pressures, and will certainly assist a long-range continuity in Court jurisprudence. But when it is considered that the incumbents of the two other institutions of U.S. Government directly charged with community policy-making functions, Congress and the Presidency, must present themselves for popular review and reaffirmation at reasonably frequent and precisely stipulated time intervals and that, in the case of the Presidency, there is a maximum time limit (two terms) expressly established under the 22nd Amendment to the Constitution, adopted in 1951, one may ask what the implications of life tenure for the judiciary are, today, in terms of the principle of constitutional legitimacy when judges insist, as they do so strongly in the case of the U.S. Supreme Court, that their decision-making *rôle* is, indeed, a community policy-making, legislative one. The problem is softened, perhaps, in the case of the other Courts referred to by the provision of a common, mandatory retirement age as an imposed, ceiling limit within the life tenure. In the case of the Canadian Supreme Court, the ceiling limit of seventy-five years, allied to an executive practice of not appointing judges near to that age, has ensured reasonably long periods of judicial service, even allowing for the fact that the Canadian judges are not normally named until they have reached a ripe age. The age limit was extended, by special legislation during World War II, in respect to the one judge, the long-serving Chief Justice Sir Lyman Duff, and the issue was at least raised in private, though not acted upon, in the case of the Court's great liberal judge of modern times, Ivan C. Rand, as he approached the mandatory retirement age of seventy-five in 1959. There is, indeed, a certain inherent arbitrariness in age limits applied uniformly to all persons in ways that ignore physical and intellectual idiosyncrasies: Rand, in the view of many, was intellectually more vigorous and *avant-garde* than all his younger contemporaries on the Court as he approached his compulsory departure, and the great Holmes (in a Court system without a compulsory retirement age) remained throughout his long career an intellectual innovator and judicial front-runner. One interesting question raised by the enactment of the constitutionally-entrenched bill of rights – the Canadian Charter of Rights and Freedoms – in 1982, is whether the compulsory retirement age for judges is compatible with the new constitutional guarantees against discriminations based, *inter alia,* on age (section 15 (1)).

The compulsory retirement age, in the case of the Supreme Courts of India and Japan, when it is both a fairly low age (sixty-five, as stipulated for the Supreme Court of India by the Constitution, Article 124 (2); seventy, as established for the Supreme Court of Japan by legislation enacted pursuant to the Constitution, Article 79), and also allied to a settled executive practice of choosing only 'mature' jurists who are usually equated with those in their late fifties or early sixties, has produced patterns of judicial tenure exactly the opposite of those on the United States Supreme Court, with fairly frequent and continuing changes in personnel and some obvious implications for the development of long-range trends in jurisprudence. The Japanese Supreme Court's record, up to mid-1984, reveals that 86 Justices had served on the Supreme Court, in its fifteen seats, in the thirty-seven years since the Court's establishment in 1947.[6] Professor Hayakawa has noted, as these statistics as to turnover of judges amply confirm, that the average age of a Japanese Supreme Court judge, on appointment, is sixty-one, which means, effectively, a non-renewable period of nine years' service as a judge.[7] With the Supreme Court of India, a tribunal whose membership was fixed at 8, at the time of the Court's establishment in 1950, (under section 124 (1) of the Constitution), and then increased to 11 in 1956, to 14 in 1960, and then 18 in 1978, some 70 judges had served on the Court in its first thirty years. This very high number is understandable enough if we consider that judges have not normally been appointed before their late fifties, and then must step down at sixty-five – a retirement age apparently dictated to the constitution-makers at the end of the 1940s, by their conviction that it was no less than reasonable for a country with a very hot climate. However that may be, it ensures, effectively, a judicial term, on average, of six or seven years.[8] There is obviously no ground for complaining, here, of any constitutionally in-built, entrenched quality of judicial obstructionism or delaying of social and economic policy decisions of the executive-legislative arms of government, though, as we shall see, there has been a remarkable degree of consistency and continuity in the Indian Supreme Court's jurisprudence, in spite of the remarkable frequency in turnover in its personnel.

With the other, Civil Law-based or influenced tribunals that we have surveyed, the legal ground rules as to judicial appointment and the emphasis on some form of representative, electoral process in the selection of judges, have usually been allied to a limited, term-of-years tenure, renewable or non-renewable as the case may be, and producing patterns of judicial service that, at the level of constitutional law-in-action, are not too different from those resulting under the rather different Common Law-based or influenced systems. The West German system, as we have already noted, had the two categories of judges on the Federal Constitutional Court, – those drawn from the professional, career civil service, judiciary who, once elected, held office for life (subject to the mandatory retirement age of sixty-eight applying to professional, career civil service judges), and the others, who were all chosen for eight-year terms and were eligible for re-election, and, indeed, repeated re-election if desired. This was all changed in 1970, with, in effect, the assimilation of the two categories of judges for purposes of their tenure: under the Statute on the Federal Constitutional Court, as amended in 1971, the term-of-years of judges is now fixed as twelve years, with, however, an automatic cut-off on reaching the age limit of the end of the sixty-eighth year, and with either re-election or later, fresh election of a judge positively excluded, (Section 4 (1), (2), and (3)). The Court, as we have noted, was, as originally constituted in 1951, a tribunal of 24 members, sitting in two separate and distinct panels or Senates of 12 judges apiece, and then was reduced, progressively, in 1956, to 20 members (with the two Senates each having 10 members), and, finally, reduced in 1962 to the present 16 members (with the two Senates each now having 8 members). In the first twenty years, from 1951 until the 1970 Court reform, 46 judges had been elected to the Court, (24 for the First Senate and 22 for the Second Senate), and elected in equal numbers by the two federal Houses (23 elected by the *Bundestag* and 23 by the *Bundesrat*).[9] Re-election of an incumbent judge was not merely not considered undesirable, but was viewed, rather, as almost an obligation in the case of a genuinely distinguished jurist: the great liberal jurist of the founding years of the Court, Gerhard Leibholz, though not popular in all political circles because of his occasionally outspoken views on constitutional issues, and the public identification of his championing of progressive legal ideas within the Second Senate of the Court, was consistently re-elected, and served throughout the first twenty years of the Court until 1971. The Court reform instituting, from 1971 onwards, the twelve-year, single, non-renewable term, has changed all that, of course. The original proposal for amendment of the Court Statute, as to tenure had accompanied the new twelve year-term for all judges with eligibility for re-election for at least one more such term; but this was dropped at the insistence of the Social Democratic groups who conditioned their support of the parallel, reform proposal, to permit publication of dissenting opinions, upon the cut-off after twelve years. This hardly seems too short in comparison to the constitutionally-stipulated four-year term for the federal lower House (*Bundestag*) (Article 39 (1)); and the five-year term for the federal President, which is accompanied by a right of re-election, once only, for a consecutive term and which has a minimum age requirement of forty years (Article 54 (1) and (2)). In fact, in terms of constitutional law-in-action, it is effectively much longer than the average judicial term served on either the Indian or the Japanese Supreme Courts, and it parallels that on the Canadian Supreme Court. The arbitrary feature would appear to be the automatic cut-off at sixty-eight, which hardly seems necessary with a limited, term-of-years appointment. It is also stated that a twelve-year term, without any constitutional possibility of removal, is now presenting certain professional career problems both for incumbent judges and also potential candidates for election to the Court. What can an ex-judge do, after retirement at the end of the twelve-year term, if he or she is still young? The consequence, it is said, is effectively to limit the range of candidates to those within striking distance of the mandatory retirement age of sixty-eight – those in their late fifties or early sixties, – and to discourage younger candidates still in mid-career stream.

With the French *Conseil constitutionnel,* the nine ordinary (appointed) members have a constitutionally-stipulated term of nine years, which is not renewable, the membership being replaced, as to one third, every three years, (Constitution, Article 56). The special, as-of-right members, – former Presidents of the Republic, – retain their membership for life (Article 56), but this provision has had little practical significance to date. Only ex-President Coty (of the Fourth Republic) participated at all actively, – from the formation of the *Conseil* in 1959 until his death in 1962; ex-President Auriol (of the Fourth Republic) took little part, and no part at all from 1960 until his death in 1966; ex-President de Gaulle took no part at all from his resignation in April, 1969, until his death in November, 1970; and President Pompidou died in office. With very few exceptions, the nine ordinary members have been quite advanced in age at the time of first appointment.[10] Georges Pompidou was only forty-eight when appointed by President de Gaulle in 1959, but normally those named have been in their sixties or seventies, with the occasional member named at eighty or more (as with former Senate President Monnerville in 1977). With the exception of special cases like the venerable jurist and Nobel Prize winner, René Cassin, first named in 1960 to fill a casual vacancy and then renamed in 1962 to a full nine-year term, the constitutionally-stipulated term of nine years has not been exceeded and there have been terms shorter than this on account of death, or resignation (M. Pompidou, for example, in 1962). Apart from the as-of-right, ex-Presidents of the Republic, category of members, there were 31 members in the first twenty years of the *Conseil's* history, almost half of these in the first six years. Since 1965, there has been a large degree of continuity and permanence in the *Conseil's* membership, created in considerable part by the continuity of Party occupancy of the Presidency and of Party majority control in the National Assembly, – two of the three institutions from which appointments are made and thereby accounting for two-thirds of the *Conseil* membership. This is one of the reasons why there has been, also, a certain intellectual discipline and consistency, and reasoned, philosophical development, in the *Conseil's* jurisprudence from the late 1960s onwards, leading on to the inevitable comparisons with the work of fully-fledged, *de facto* or *de jure,* constitutional courts of other countries.

The International Court of Justice reveals internal organisational features, present in both the West German Court and the French *Conseil,* as to tenure of its members. The fifteen judges are elected, as already noted, by a system of twin electoral colleges in the General Assembly and the Security Council, with a double majority (majority in each of these two institutions) required. The term of office is nine years, and the judges are eligible for re-election, without any legal bar to the number of times. A third of the Court is replaced every three years, thus opening the elections to the Court, in theory at least, to changing currents of opinion in the two main United Nations Parliamentary-style institutions. In spite of the absence of any legal bar to re-election on completion of the nine-year elected term, it does not often occur. This is partly a reflection of the normally advanced age of candidates whom states choose to present to the periodic elections, and partly a consequence of the political fact that the fifteen seats tend to be substantially allocated, in advance of the elections, on a 'regional' – sometimes ideological, sometimes geographical, sometimes legal-systemic, sometimes linguistic – basis, with resulting fierce competition, within each such recognised region, for the 'regional' seat concerned and the development, in consequence, of a species of tacit rules of the game as to periodic rotation within the region concerned.[11] Judge-President Guerrero of Panama of the old, pre-War, Permanent Court of International Justice, managed to survive, as Judge-President, the transition from that Court to election to the new, post-War International Court of Justice. Badawi of Egypt, Basdevant of France, Hackworth of the United States, and Winiarski of Poland, as judges elected to the inaugural bench of the new International Court of Justice in 1946, managed to secure re-election into the 1960s; but, since that time, it has been rare. Lachs of Poland, who managed, because of his general intellectual stature, to overcome an inchoate custom that regional seats (in this case, the second East European seat, other than the Soviet Union) should rotate among the states of the region concerned, and to succeed, directly, to his fellow-countryman, Winiarski, at the end of the latter's term in 1966, was re-elected in 1975, and then further re-elected in 1984 – again, no doubt because of his intellectual standing which had been augmented, with the U.N. General Assembly and Security Council electors, by a term as President of the Court and the reputation as a judicial innovator not afraid to break new legal ground, developed during his first nine-year term. But this experience is unlikely to be repeated very often in the future, even though two other incumbents, Judge (and President) Elias of Nigeria, and Judge Oda of Japan, were also re-elected in 1984.

Jiménez de Aréchaga, for example, equally a President of the Court and a distinguished legal scholar in his own right, ceded after only one term, though still young, to another Latin American candidate. The death toll among serving judges has also been high, so that special elections for the casual vacancies become a feature of the Court's system of renewal of its membership.

In truth, then, we are not too far from the norm of a single judicial term, that is not renewed, and that will last from seven to twelve years at the outside, that is to be observed in the case of most final Courts (the United States Supreme Court excepted, of course), either as a direct consequence of the constitutional rules as to judicial appointments and tenure, or else as a matter of constitutional law-in-action through the operation of settled executive-legislative attitudes and habits as to appointment on those same rules. It may be suggested, at this stage, that the norm of practice corresponds, increasingly, to a rule of reason in comparative legal science as to the desirable time limits for exercise of their mandate by individual judges, granted the increasing exercise by Courts today of a frankly and avowedly community policy-making, legislative *rôle*.

3. JUDICIAL INDEPENDENCE: JUDICIAL DISQUALIFICATION, REMOVAL FROM OFFICE

The rules and practice of judicial tenure, viewed from the larger perspective of comparative legal science, reveal the antinomy between the older, classical conception of the judicial office, with its insistence that the judicial *rôle* is a purely mechanical and non-discretionary one, that can be reduced to a matter of legal logic and the application of objective, neutral rules of construction, and the more contemporary view that judges do indeed participate in general community policy-making and exercise creative choices between contending social and economic interests in the great political *causes célèbres* coming before them. The consequences of these two rival conceptions of the judicial office, pursued to their logical conclusion, are quite different. The classical conception insists upon the principle of judicial independence and upon a necessary judicial immunity from adverse, politically pejorative criticism of the value content or the end-results, when applied, of Court decisions, and is prepared to enforce such judicial protection against public attacks by all the armoury of non-reviewable contempt powers, where necessary. The more contemporary approach, in embracing the notion of judicial legislation, – judicial law-making – as a good and proper exercise in the judicial process, must necessarily accept also the right of public criticism of judicial decisions, for their philosophical or ideological content quite as much, or more, as for their legal logic. The species of augmented constitutional legitimation that the election (direct or even indirect) of judges confers upon them in systems like that of the contemporary West German Federal Constitutional Court or of the International Court of Justice might be thought to relieve the judges from any political or constitutional obligation to explain or justify their policy positions and preferences – prior to election to the bench or thereafter; just as election or appointment, for a term of years only, necessarily blunts some of the arguments against judicial irresponsibility or political and constitutional non-answerability to the public. In the end, after a certain lapse of time, the judicial mandate will either end automatically or else it must be renewed by fresh election or appointment and so legitimated *de novo* in constitutional terms. There is, nevertheless, some confusion apparent today in the coexistence of the classical conception of judicial independence which emphasises complete detachment from the exigent here-and-now of party politics and policy choice on great political, social, and economic issues, and the more contemporary conception which emphasises judicial responsibility and judicial answerability for actual policy choices as a necessary correlative of the claim for judicial independence. The American system of judicial appointments to the Supreme Court involves the Presidential-executive nominee running the political gauntlet of public examination and then legal confirmation by Senate vote: the operation is highly political, the nominee will normally be recognisably political in background together with his or her high professional qualifications, for a vote on the Supreme Court is a vote, in the end, for or against particular acts of executive and legislative policy and administration. Yet judges of the U.S. Supreme Court still adopt the polite rule of disqualifying themselves, in advance of the hearing of a particular case, 'for interest', if they have, by any chance, worked on its file at some time or other in an earlier professional career as federal Attorney-General or federal Solicitor-General or as a high official in one of those departments. The rule seems legally anachronistic and unnecessary today, and to subtract a properly-held policy position, fully known at the time of appointment, from the Court-based resolution of an important community policy conflict. Yet one of the judges of the Canadian Supreme Court seems to have regarded the American precedent as a proper one to follow and so to disqualify himself from sitting on the Court's hearing on proposals for reform of the federal Senate, simply because he had, in an earlier professional capacity, prepared a technical position paper on the general issue for the Prime Minister's office. The gesture, if that was its motivation, does credit to the judge concerned, though it hardly seems warranted on the facts of Canadian Supreme Court decision-making today.

Within the West German Federal Constitutional Court, the issue erupted publicly with the Party Financing case of 1966[12] which raised issues of general constitutional and political theory that had been much debated in West German academic-legal circles. The issue was the federal Government's proposal, by legislation, to finance political parties' election expenses by a system of contributions from public funds, the public financing to extend to political parties represented in the federal legislature but excluding others. (This exclusion was in line with general principles of Bonn constitutionalism and West German electoral law, directed against 'splinter parties', in reaction to the fractionalism that had helped to end the Weimar Republic and excluding from participation in the allocation of seats in the federal legislature parties falling below 5 per cent of the overall national vote). The federal Government bill reflected the concept of the Political Parties' state (*Parteienstaat*), based on the operation and interaction of such organisms as the foundation of modern, representative, democratic government. The general principles had been developed by Dr. Gerhard Leibholz, then currently a judge of the Second Senate of the Federal Constitutional Court, in his career as a University Professor and writer extending back over forty years. The federal Government bill having been challenged before the Court by an un-Holy Alliance of left-wing and extreme right-wing, neo-Nazi political forces, it soon became known, publicly, that the Second Senate was deadlocked, 4-to-4, on the question of the constitutionality of the federal Government bill, after the oral argument had been completed. The extreme right-wing splinter party involved in the challenge before the Second Senate, moved, six months later, for the disqualification of Judge Leibholz; and the Second Senate (with Judge Leibholz abstaining from voting on the disqualification demand) then voted, 4-to-3, to exclude him;[13] and, thereafter, (without Judge Leibholz' presence to deadlock the

Court) voted 4-to-3 to reject the federal Government bill as unconstitutional. [14] The disqualification issue, in its political timing and staging, seemed politically contrived and artifical; and, understandably, the two single-vote-majority decisions of the Second Senate – to disqualify Judge Leibholz and then to invalidate an electoral law that was widely hailed, in academic-legal circles, as constitutionally progressive and forward-looking in the best democratic sense, – were almost unanimously condemned in the general intellectual debate that followed in West Germany. In the end, though he was, in a sense, the victim of both Court votes, Judge Leibholz gained a form of moral victory, long after the event: the Court Statute was amended in 1971 by the addition of a new paragraph to its provisions as to judicial disqualification, which specifically excluded as a ground of objection – 'the assertion of a scientific opinion on a legal question which can be significant for the process'. (Court Statute, section 18 (3) 2). The same amendment also excluded as a ground of objection to a judge – "the taking part in the law-making process' (Court Statute, section 18 (3) 1), this measure adding a certain touch of realism to the broader conceptions of legal disqualification on ground of past political 'interest', having regard to the fact that, increasingly, former members of the *Bundestag* and *Bundesrat* seemed likely to provide a highly talented and constitutionally wise and experienced recruitment pool for the Court's membership. The issue had not, however, finally been put to rest in West Germany. In a further case involving the emotionally and politically highly charged question of the so-called Basic Treaty on intra-German Relations, (*Grundlagenvertrag*) [15] which was at the core of Chancellor Brandt's *Ostpolitik,* the *Land* (state) of Bavaria, which had challenged the constitutionality of the Basic Treaty, attempted to remove a former member of the Free Democratic Party, (the coalition partner of Chancellor Brandt's Social Democratic Party) from the bench of the Second Senate hearing the case on the ground that the judge concerned, Judge Rottmann, had addressed a meeting of his Party on the international status of Berlin when the Basic Treaty case was pending. The Bavarian Government motion to exclude Judge Rottmann was rejected by the Second Senate; [16] but a further motion by the Bavarian Government to exclude Judge Rottmann, this time on the score of some correspondence he had written on the issue, succeeded. [17] The reasoning in the three judicial disqualification cases, taken together, seems not entirely satisfactory or well thought through, as if the Court itself has had difficulty in finding its way to a correct policy solution for a tribunal that, increasingly, is made up of jurists who are men-of-affairs, drawn from public life in its various contemporary manifestations – Cabinet posts, membership in the federal legislature, and even University Professorships which, in the Public Law field, increasingly demand the taking of public positions on controversial legislative projects or executive action.

No other final Court than the West German one seems to have had the agonising appraisal to make as to whether or not to disqualify a judge, against his own better judgment, not for any objective bias or 'interest' in the outcome of a particular case but because of general opinions expressed on major political, social and economic issues, either in a scientific, University or similar forum or else in the course of legislative debate and discussion as an elected member of a Parliamentary Assembly. The legal remedies of removal, (normally by Parliamentary vote) for judicial misconduct or misbehaviour, or the Mediaeval era-divided sanction of Impeachment of judges, seem wildly inappropriate since all are predicated, in modern times, on positive breaches of the law or similar legal or moral delinquency. Is there a case for attempting to revive, in modern times, that aspect of Mediaeval impeachment that involved the pursuit of Government officials, including judges, not merely for proven *criminal* misconduct in office but simply for alleged *political* misconduct – that is to say, conduct in one's official capacity that a majority of the legislature may happen to disapprove of on political grounds only, and not legal ones? This two-headed (*criminal* and *political*) aspect of the Impeachment offence, as received from Mediaeval times in latter-day constitutionalism, was manifest in the ultimately still-born attempts in the United States in 1973-4 to impeach President Nixon: *criminal* impeachment would require proof of criminal delinquency to base a legally correct bill of particulars, whereas *political* impeachment could presumably be adequately based in the simple political vote of the legislature, as had sufficed against Charles I's Ministers and those of his predecessors.[18] The ambiguity, legal and political, surrounding the whole matter was not resolved in 1973-4, President Nixon's resignation from office in 1974 terminating the constitutional debate while in full course. It may be suggested, however, that it would involve a complete reversal of latter-day understandings of the nature of the constitutional remedy of Impeachment and the ends to which it may legitimately be applied, to suggest its potential application as a means of removing judges from a Court merely because of the general philosophy of their constitutional decisions and a current legislature-based decision that they are out of touch with the general historical course and direction of society, as, for example, with the conservative, 'Old Court' majority on the United States Supreme Court in the 1930s. Is there a case, however, for some other, cognate remedy freed from Impeachment's antique historical associations? Some states within the United States federal system have experimented with a system of constitutional 'recall' of judges of their state courts on petition of a certain minimum number of voters. The post-War

Japanese Constitution of 1946, influenced by these ideas as filtered through the American Military Occupation officials, contained, both in the S.C.A.P. Original Draft, and also in the final text, as adopted, provision for the removal of Supreme Court judges by political, as distinct from legal means. After defining very precisely and in traditional, limited, way, the process for legal removal of judges by impeachment (Article 78), the Constitution went on to make the following express stipulation (Article 79):

'The appointment of the judges of the Supreme Court shall be reviewed by the people at the first general election of members of the House of Representatives following their appointment, and shall be reviewed again at the first general election of members of the House of Representatives after a lapse of ten years, and in the same manner thereafter.

'In cases mentioned in the foregoing paragraph, when the majority of the voters favours the dismissal of a judge, he shall be dismissed.

'Matters pertaining to review shall be prescribed by law.'

The provision is novel for a national constitution, and it was examined by the Cabinet Commission on the Constitution (Takayanagi Commission) in its survey of proposals for constitutional change in the early 1960s.[19] The expert paper on the Judiciary, prepared for the Takayanagi Commission in 1962 by Hideo Tanaka[20] related the Japanese innovation of popular review of the judiciary to the so-called Missouri Plan in several states of the United States, and he noted no judge had been dismissed by popular review, any votes for dismissal being usually under 10% of the total votes, and the largest figure reached being only 12.5%. It had, however, been suggested that the low percentage figures were due to the system of voting, voters having to check off the names of judges whom they wanted dismissed, with all those names remaining unchecked being presumed to be desired to be retained. Dr. Tanaka's paper identified the main constitutional antinomy involved in the system of popular review of the judges: on the one hand, the principle of the independence of the judiciary from political pressures of all kinds, including such popular review; and on the other hand the principle of popular sovereignty and the relating of the power of judicial review, ultimately, to the popular will. Within the Takayanagi Commission itself, a majority of the Commissioners concluded that the Japanese constitutional system of popular review of Supreme Court judges was improper and should be abolished: the main arguments cited against the popular review system were that the general public were not really competent to make value judgments on the fitness of judges, and that the existence of the system might tend to induce judges to be swayed by public opinion and so lose their independence. Some compromise reform proposals, designed to meet the argument of popular sovereignty, were in fact put forward within the Commission: more recourse to the system of judicial impeachment already established in the Constitution (Article 78), and the establishment of a limited (and presumably non-renewal) term-of-years for service by judges on the Supreme Court, of seven or ten years.[21] In the late 1960s, during the controversy surrounding the membership of some of the younger judiciary, in the lower courts, in the *Seihokyo* (Young Lawyers Association), an allegedly Communist-oriented organisation dedicated to defence of the 1946 Constitution against attempts to remove the Renunciation-of-War clause (Article 9), there were suggestions made that the Cabinet might consider using the judicial impeachment system against 'political' judges in the lower courts. Although these suggestions were rejected by the Supreme Court as a threat to judicial independence, the then Chief Justice Ishida made a strong public attack, on Constitution Day, 1970, on judicial radicals; and this produced, in its turn, an impeachment movement against Chief Justice Ishida himself.[22] This impeachment move sponsored a petition, signed by 2,208 lawyers, calling for the Chief Justice's resignation, being submitted to the Supreme Court, but the movement itself petered out without result; and any revival of the notion of a 'political', as distinct from 'criminal' impeachment process against Supreme Court judges seems most unlikely in the future. Except for proven, objectively grounded, misbehaviour, impeachment-style proceedings as a constitutional control over the judiciary seem out-of-step with all the main trends in democratic constitutionalism, as involving an excessive expenditure of community power in relation to the results to be achieved and too many threats to judicial independence. The more moderate constitutional control of limiting the judicial office to a term-of-years only, with or without right of renewal of the term, seems more in tune with contemporary constitutionalism and constitutional trends in it. The Canadian practice today of referring any complaint of alleged abuse of the judicial office to enquiry and examination by a 'committee of peers' – other judges of coordinate or higher rank – of the Canadian Judicial Council, an assembly of Canadian judges presided over by the Chief Justice of the federal Supreme Court, seems an attempt, in itself, to reach out for some more moderate control than the more drastic impeachment remedy (by majority vote of each of the two Houses of the federal Parliament, in terms of Section 99 (1) of the Constitution); though it could also, it seems, serve as a preparatory step in building the necessary psychological as well as legal base for a subsequent successful political-legislative vote on impeachment. In the Berger case in 1981-2, a Provincial Supreme Court judge and former one-man Royal Commission in charge of a politically high-profile, federal Government-appointed enquiry involving oil Pipeline development in Canada's northern territo-

64

ries and its effects on the natural environment and on Indian and Native (aboriginal) peoples' rights, publicly criticised the federal Government and the Provincial Governments for a political compromise deal made in late 1981 as to future constitutional changes which, in the judge's personal opinion, was made at the expense of Indian and Native rights. The judge had been a former social-democratic party leader at the Provincial level, and the public criticisms that he expressed received considerable public and political support. An official complaint was initiated before the Canadian Judicial Council by another judge, a member of the lower federal Court system, and the Council appointed a three-judge investigation committee which reported back with harsh criticism of Mr. Justice Berger's conduct. The full Judicial Council softened this to a reprimand, but after some further public criticisms of Mr. Justice Berger, following on release of the Judicial Council report, by the Chief Justice of the federal Supreme Court, the judge resigned from the Provincial Supreme Court. There were, of course, no binding constitutional stipulations covering the matter, other than the drastic impeachment provision already referred to, and no precedents in past Judicial Council practice that seemed relevant and that might carry enough legal authority to warrant a Judicial Council recommendation for escalation to impeachment. The affair, with its roots in the politically highly sensitive issue of Indian and Native (aboriginal) constitutional rights, had major political implications, and there were suggestions that the original complaint against the judge might have been inspired by the federal Government. In any case, the Berger case was widely debated in public; and the not inconsiderable number of political and legal spokesmen who rallied in support of the judge contended that the Judicial Council action should itself be viewed as constituting a denial of a constitutional right of the citizen who is a Supreme Court judge to speak out, according to his conscience, on issues of public interest and concern. The analogies to Judge Leibholz' intellectual position in the West German judicial controversy of the middle and late 1960s, are clear; and the final West German solution, as expressed in the Amendment to the Federal Constitutional Court Statute already referred to, represents an elegant intellectual attempt at balancing the two antinomic positions of judicial independence and judicial responsibility (including, here, judicial self-restraint).

NOTES

1. *Japan's Commission on the Constitution: The Final Report* (translated and edited by John M. Maki) (1980).
2. Hideo Tanaka, 'Chapter VI, Judiciary' (Position Paper), *Cabinet Commission on the Constitution (Japan)* (1962). And see also *Comments and Observations by Foreign Scho-*

lars on Problems concerning the Constitution of Japan, 1946 (Secretariat of the Commission on the Constitution, Tokyo) (1964), pp. 263-270.

3. *Asahi Shimbun,* 16 and 19 May 1973: cited in David J. Danelski, 'The Political Impact of the Japanese Supreme Court' (Paper, International Political Science Association, Congress (1973)). See also David J. Danelski, 'The Supreme Court of Japan: an exploratory study', in *Comparative Judicial Behaviour: Cross Cultural Studies in Political Decision-Making in the East and West* (Glendon Schubert and David J. Danelski, eds.) (1969), p. 127 *et seq.* And see generally *Justice in Japan* (Supreme Court of Japan) (1978).

4. See the detailed break-down of the practice as to judicial elections since the inauguration of the Court, in Heinz Laufer, *Verfassungsgerichtsbarkeit und politischer Prozess* (1968), pp. 206-253; Donald P. Kommers, *Judicial Politics in West Germany* (1976), pp. 113-149; Glenn N. Schram, 'The Recruitment of Judges for the West German Federal Courts', 21 *American Journal of Comparative Law* 691 (1973).

5. L. Favoreu and L. Philip, *Le Conseil constitutionnel* (1978), pp. 11-24.

6. *Justice in Japan* (Supreme Court of Japan) (1978).

7. Takeo Hayakawa, 'Age and the Judiciary in Japan', *Kobe University Law Journal* (1975); Takeo Hayakawa and John R. Schmidhauser, 'A comparative analysis of the internal procedures and customs of the Supreme Courts of Japan and the United States' (Paper, International Political Science Association, Congress (1979)).

8. George H. Gadbois Jr., 'Selection, Background Characteristics, and Voting Behaviour of Indian Supreme Court Judges, 1950-1959', in *Comparative Judicial Behaviour* (Glendon Schubert and David J. Danelski, eds.) (1969), p. 221 *et seq.;* Gadbois, 'Indian Supreme Court Judges. A portrait', 3 *Law and Society Review* 317 (1968); Gadbois, 'Supreme Court Decision Making', 10 *Banaras Law Journal* 1 (1974); Rajeev Dhavan and Alice Jacob, *Selection and Appointment of Supreme Court Judges. A Case Study* (1978); M. Chakraborty and S.N. Ray, 'Supreme Court Justices in India and the U.S.A.: a comparative study of background characteristics, 1969-1976', 13 *Journal of Constitutional and Parliamentary Studies* 1 (1979); M. Chakraborty, 'Chief Justices of the Supreme Court of India, 1950-1978', 17 *Political Science Review* (1978).

9. H. Laufer, *Verfassungsgerichtsbarkeit und politischer Prozess* (1968), p. 206 *et seq.;* D. P. Kommers, *Judicial Politics in West Germany* (1976), p. 90.

10. L. Favoreu and L. Philip, *Le Conseil constitutionnel* (1978), pp. 12-13.

11. *Documents on the International Court of Justice* (Shabtai Rosenne, ed.) (1974), pp. 327-334.

12. Decision of 19 July 1966, 20 B Verf GE 56 (1966) (Second Senate).

13. Decision of 2 March 1966, 20 B Verf GE 9 (1966) (Second Senate).

14. Decision of 19 July 1966, 20 B Verf GE 56 (1966) (Second Senate).

15. Decision of 31 July 1973, 36 B Verf GE 1 (1973) (Second Senate). And see Hans G. Rupp, 'Judicial Review of International Agreements: Federal Republic of Germany', 25 *American Journal of Comparative Law* 286, at 295 *et seq.* (1977); Hugo J. Hahn, 'Trends in the Jurisprudence of the German Federal Constitutional Court', 26 *American Journal of Comparative Law* 631, 633 (1978).

16. Decision of 29 May 1972, 35 B Verf GE 171 (1974) (Second Senate). And see D. P. Kommers, *Judicial Politics in West Germany* (1976) pp. 201-203.

17. Decision of 16 June 1973, 35 B Verf GE 246 (1974) (Second Senate). And see D. P. Kommers, *ibid.,* pp. 201-203.

18. E. McWhinney, 'Congress and the Presidency and the Impeachment Power', 7 *Indiana Law Review* 833 (1974); E. McWhinney, 'The English and the American Impeachment powers and the constitutional Separation of Powers', 24 *Jahrbuch des öffentlichen Rechts der Gegenwart* 577 (1975).

19. *Japan's Commission on the Constitution: The Final Report* (translated and edited by John M. Maki) (1980), pp. 324-326.

20. Hideo Tanaka, 'Chapter VI, Judiciary' (Position Paper), *Cabinet Commission on the Constitution (Japan)* (1962).

21. *Japan's Commission on the Constitution: The Final Report,* at p. 325. And see also *Comments and Observations by Foreign Scholars on Problems concerning the Constitution of Japan, 1946* (Secretariat of the Commission on the Constitution, Tokyo) (1964), pp. 268-269.

22. Hiroshi Itoh and L. W. Beer, 'Introduction', *The Constitutional Case Law of Japan. Selected Supreme Court Decisions, 1961-70* (Hiroshi Itoh and L. W. Beer, eds.) (1978), pp. 16-17.

CHAPTER IV

COURTS AS COLLEGIAL BODIES:
CHIEF JUSTICE AND ASSOCIATE JUSTICES

1. JUDICIAL PROFILE: PROFESSIONAL, INTELLECTUAL, REGIONAL FACTORS

Constitutional charters and the Court Statutes enacted pursuant to them rarely spell out, in deatil, the qualifications and criteria for judicial appointment, other than those applying to tenure (whether life, life subject to a certain mandatory retirement age, or a limited term-of-years). The stipulation of a minimum age for judicial appointment – for example, as under section 3 of the West German Federal Constitutional Court Statute, the completion of one's fortieth year – is the rarety, and in any case seems politically unnecessary or irrelevant, granted the conservative attitude, common to all main legal systems, of reserving the highest judicial appointments for fairly mature citizens, usually in their late fifties or even older. In the absence of too many formal, *a priori,* stipulations, constitutional and statutory, limiting the character and range of exercise of the judicial appointing power, there are, nevertheless, certain clear and discernible patterns, in the main legal systems, as to the actual exercise of such power, pointing to certain informal criteria or ground rules which, through continuing usage and respect, may come to acquire a certain conventional, customary base. On such criterion is the necessary deference to regionalism and political-geographical considerations. Under the Canadian Supreme Court statute, one third of the Justices of the Supreme Court (currently, three out of nine) must come from the Province of Quebec, – a stipulation whose original *raison d'être* was as much legal-systemic (in deference to the Quebec *droit civil*) as political-geographical, for a final Court whose jurisdiction was general and included, necessarily, appeals in private law matters, both Common Law and also Quebec *droit civil*). [1] Nevertheless, the statutory requirement had historically, and still has today, a certain basic political reality in its tacit recognition of the 'French fact' in Canadian federalism and the consequence that one third of the Court, in constitutional cases as well as all other matters, will come from Quebec. In a sense, it is a reflection, in measure, of the 'Deux Nations' conception of Canadian federalism, as founded on the coexistence fo two original, 'founding nations', French and English, and the political merits of their joint assent to fundamental constitutional and general legal change. Other federal systems, like the United States, have always understood the necessity for a wide, regional distribution of seats on the Supreme Court to avoid an excessive concentration on a few main centres – the national capital, and the 'establishment' legal corporations of the great commercial and industrial centres like New York. The Canadian deference to regionalism, while it is there, seems less free and uninhibited than the American practice: a custom (for it has no constitutional or statutory base) grew up, apparently out of regard for past religious quarrels between French, Roman Catholic Quebec, and English, Protestant, Ontario, the largest Province, of balancing the three Quebec judges on the Supreme Court by three from Ontario, leaving, of course, only three seats remaining for distribution among the other Provinces or main regions of the federal system. That practice, broken only briefly at the end of 1978 when one of the three normally Ontarian seats on the Court fell vacant and was filled by naming a judge from the Pacific coast Province of British Columbia (this with the private political acquiescence of the Premier of Ontario, but on condition that the third Ontario seat be restored at the next appropriate vacancy), seems unnecessarily limiting and confining as to the fulfilment of the obligation to make the best possible judicial appointments – deference to regionalism in effect codified and jelled in abstract, artificial categories and missing the flexibility and imagination present in United States practice. The International Court of Justice, by comparison, positively prohibits the election to its ranks of more than one judge from the same state (Court Statute, Article 3 (1)). The electoral system as the base for judicial selection, with the necessity of the double majority (Security Council, General Assembly), allows, it may be suggested, a very full opportunity for representation, within the Court's fifteen-judge membership, of all the World's main legal systems, linguistic and ethnic-cultural systems, and political-ideological groupings of states. The bitter criticisms of the Court, particularly after the narrow, one-vote majority ruling in *South West Africa. Second Phase,* in 1966,[2] that it was a 'white man's tribunal', or that it was politically dominated by the Western bloc countries, or (more subtly and more persuasively, in scientific-legal terms), that it remains today Eurocentrist in its internal habits and it processes and its judicial thought-ways, seem better directed not at the constitutional processes for election of judges to the Court but at the relative lack of political sophistication and experience on the part of the new, non-Western political majorities within the United Nations and their failure to maximise their full voting potential in the Court elections in recognition of the potential power *rôle* of the Court in fulfilment of the general United

Nations' mandate (under Article 13 (1) (a) of the U.N. Charter) for 'the progressive development of international law'. The changes in the composition of the Court, to bring its own membership more in line with the vastly expanded and now nearly universal United Nations' membership, have come only tardily, and the Court has lagged behind the other main U.N. institutions in terms of becoming 'representative', in ethnic-cultural as well as political-ideological terms. The Veto in the Security Council of the original, post-World War II, 'Big Five' (the United States, Great Britain, France, Soviet Union and China) does not legally apply in regard to World Court elections (Court statute, Article 10 (2)), yet candidates from four of these five states (China alone excepted) have been elected without fail since the constitution of the Court in 1946. There is evidently a conservative factor in the psychological approach of very many 'new' states to Court elections that causes them to respect traditional voting habits from past years, at the expense of Legal Realist-style recognition that the Court's *rôle* today has a high political content and quality, and a positive capacity for making the 'new' international law as distinct from merely mechanically restating the 'old'. The judicial candidates from the four 'Big Five' states referred to – residual and contestable as their political claims to Big Power status may seem, in several cases at least, today – have generally involved very good candidates, but their intellectual claims have not, nevertheless, seemed overwhelming to the point of excluding other, countervailing electoral policies such as the favouring of hitherto unrepresented or under-represented regions of the World for which intellectually well-qualified candidates are also present.

One of the more interesting questions in judicial selections, and one intimately related to general conceptions of the nature of the judicial process itself and the *rôle* of the judges in community policy-making prevailing within particular legal systems at any time, relates to the personal intellectual qualities one should look for in a judicial candidate, and the relative importance, for example, of prior judicial experience, or competence in appellate advocacy, or a background in legal scholarship, or direct testing in Ministerial office and the Parliamentary political arenas.

The issue of sex, – a latter-day constitutional concern, only, in most legal systems' practice as to judicial selection – has now been recognised, in the United States and in Canada, with the appointments of the first female judge on each country's Supreme Court. The West German Federal Constitutional Court[3] had a female judge from the outset of the Court, with the election of Judge Erna Scheffler to the First Senate in 1951, and her re-election to a term ending in 1963, when she was replaced by another female judge, Wiltraut Rupp-von Brünneck. Both the Bonn Constitution of 1949, and the Canadian Constitution as amended with the introduction of the Canadian Charter of Rights and Freedoms 1982, contain constitutional stipulations as to equality before the law, including express provisions as to sexual equality (Bonn Constitution, Article 3 (2); Canadian Charter of Rights and Freedoms (as adopted, 1982), sections 15 (1) and 28). None of the other tribunals surveyed seems to have accepted the imperative of female representation on final Courts; though this attitude, plus the extreme tardiness in appointment of the first woman to the United States and Canadian Supreme Courts seems attributable in some part to the relative paucity of strong female candidates in the much older age groups to which such judicial appointments are normally confined, in what has been a male-dominated legal profession in most countries until very recent years. No doubt, however, traditional male chauvinism among those in charge of the judicial appointing processes, has been a dominant influence, too, in denying Supreme Court appointments to women.

As to the balance between professional practice and scholarly training, and the relevance of prior judicial experience in lower jurisdictions or of the political experience gained in public life, we can note certain shifts in basic attitudes in the various countries. After tending to be dominated by the 'men of affairs' – people who had been directly involved in community policy-making as members of Congress or the Cabinet or as presidential advisers – in the Roosevelt era of Court appointments, with the occasional opening also to the legal scholar, United States Supreme Court judges began, also, to be promoted to the final Court from lower-level federal Courts, with their concrete record of performance in those lower courts as a factor to be examined and considered as relevant. The Roosevelt era is noteworthy, for our present purposes, in establishing the paradigm of the 'man of affairs' as constitutional judge – Hugo Black from the Senate, and Felix Frankfurter and William Douglas as law professors who also dabbled very largely in Presidential executive branch administration or Presidential advising.

With the West German Federal Constitutional Court, because American constitutional influences were very strong at the moment of its establishment in 1951, it was accepted from the beginning that a larger intellectual experience than technical legal training and legal practice (as judge, civil servant, or attorney) was desirable and necessary. When the original plans for a fluid system of judicial recruitment, within the Court, from a large pool of 24 judges to a system of panels with changing membership, gave way, in the final Court plan, to the system of two separate Senates, each with its own fixed personnel and clearly defined, and separate, jurisdiction, the first allocation of such jurisdiction, as between the two Senates, gave the First Senate what were considered as the more intrinsically 'legal' questions, those involving the interpretation and application of the constitutional Basic Rights (Articles 1-17); while the Second Senate received questions involving conflicts between the different organs of the federal Government (*Organstreitigkeiten*) and federal-Provincial conflicts (*Bund-Länder-Streitigkeiten*), which were dubbed the 'political' conflicts. A scientifically more exact designation might be to describe the First Senate as the Basic Rights Senate (*Grundrechtssenat*), and the Second Senate as the Law of the State, or Public Law, Senate (Staatsrechtssenat). However that may be, in the first elections in 1951, the First Senate was considered to have achieved a greater proportion of technical jurists and technical legal experience in its members, and the Second Senate rather more of the 'men of affairs', corresponding to the popular understanding of the principles of division of jurisdiction between the two Senates. But both Senates had, at least in popular terms, a certain identifiable political philosophy or ideological orientation: the First Senate, because of its supposed Social Democratic weighting, was known as the 'Red Senate', and the Second Senate, because of its supposed Christian Democratic weighting, as the 'Black Senate'. In retrospect, these particular, politically colourable appellations, seemed unwarranted or overdrawn, at least in terms of predicting the outcome or consequences of the respective Senates' decision in party terms; but they caused some passing public embarrassement in connection with the Court's handling of some of its early political *causes célèbres,* like the European Defence Community controversy.[4] Apart from the professional, career civil service judges whose election was required by the Court Statute (4 judges out of the 12 judges on each of the two Senates, under the 1951 Statute; 3 judges out of 8 judges on each of the two Senates, under the Statute as amended today), the remaining judges shew a wide range of political, civil service, and academic backgrounds. The first bench of the Court, as elected in 1951, included three of the most distinguished Professors of the day, – Leibholz and Friesenhahn in Public Law, and Konrad Zweigert in Private Law. This interesting mix of the technical, the political, and the academic, in terms of legal background and experience, has continued, in general, to this day. The break with the general Continental European Civil Law-based insistence on entry to the higher judiciary through an arduous system of career civil service recruitment and promotion after examination was clearly deliberate, and the success of such break complete.

With the Japanese Supreme Court, prior judicial experience, – usually considerable such experience, – seems to have been a major factor in appointment. It is suggested that service in several important and prestigeful judicial posts – as President of the Tokyo or some equivalent High Court – will normally lead to promotion to the Supreme Court; and the status quality attaching to graduation from the University of Tokyo Law

School has also been important. But the pre-War, Continental European Civil Law influences and the separation of the judicial and the practitioner elements in the legal profession, with the judiciary constituting a civil-service style cadre within the general profession, predominate in the Japanese legal system to an extent they no longer do, for example, in the original German legal system from which they were 'received' long ago.

With the Indian Supreme Court, to a quite surprising extent in comparison to other Common Law-influenced countries, the dominant criterion in appointment of judges seems to have been service on the High Courts of the various States, with up to ten years of such service prior to promotion. Such intermediate Court background establishes a judicial record from which technical and general intellectual competence as a lawyer can be assessed; but, having regard to the 'received' English Common Law system of precedent and hierarchical Court organisation, it might be thought to be discouraging to too much tendency to judicial innovation or experimentation in law, or to judicial law-making as a whole. An intermediate judge who experiments too freely with legal doctrine or who is too irreverent as to past precedents may as readily be considered, by his superiors in the Court system, to be 'unsound' as a judicial front-runner, and thus may lose the opportunity for promotion in a system in which, as we have already noted, the Chief Justice of the federal Supreme Court has claimed, and been accorded in fact, a decisive *rôle* in the recommendation to the federal executive of appointments to his Court.

The French *Conseil constitutionnel* being, as we have noted, a hybrid body perhaps on the way to becoming a constitutional court, has been able the more readily to justify openings to broader, 'policy' interests and experience, as distinct from technical-legal factors, among the members appointed to it. A survey of the first twenty years of the *Conseil's* experience[5] shewed 22 out of the 31 members appointed had connections with the legal World: 8 members of the *Conseil d'Etat* (Administrative Law Court), 2 judges of the *Cour de Cassation* (Civil Law Supreme Court), 5 attorneys, 1 legal adviser, 1 head of the legal division of a public enterprise, 4 law professors, and 1 professor of political science. Among the same group of 31 members and former members, 8 had their first degree in law, 2 the diploma of graduate studies in law, 6 the doctorate in law, and 4 the State examination qualification as teachers of law; while, in addition, there were 10 graduates of the *Ecole des Sciences politiques.* While the *Conseil* has sometimes been criticised for not having enough constitutional specialists within it, it is clear that the problem is one, really, of omnicompetence for its dossier of cases reveals issues not merely of constitutional law but of international law, budgetary law and fiscal law, criminal law, civil and commercial law, and administrative and parliamentary law.[6] In fact, three main categories of members, viewed in terms of background and experience prior to appointment, have emerged within the *Conseil:* the law professors; the former Parliamentarians and Cabinet Ministers; and the judges (of the *Conseil d'Etat* and the *Cour de Cassation,* as the case may be) and the practising attorneys. It is an interesting mix for cases which, as with the constitutional courts in the strict sense that we have looked at in other legal systems, are so often political-legal in character; and the balance between the three categories has largely been maintained with each three year-renewal of the *Conseil* from 1962 onwards.

As for the International Court, its Statute speaks of a 'body of independent judges... who possess the qualifications required in their respective countries for appointment to the highest judicial offices, or are jurisconsults of recognised competence in international law' (Article 2). The Court Statute also enjoins the electors (the General Assembly and Security Council) to 'bear in mind... that in the body as a whole the representation of the main forms of civilisation and of the principal legal systems of the world should be assured'. An earlier, more idealistic trend favouring the selection of 'jurisconsults' of high international reputation transcending their own national frontiers and legal systems, was manifest in the earlier period of the Court when it was more noticeably Eurocentrist in character, dominated, in terms of political numbers in its membership and also, in consequence, in its intellectual-legal attitudes and thought-ways and legal procedures, by the Western powers. The Court, in its earlier, pre-World War II, Permanent Court of International Justice manifestation, had seemed sometimes to function as a court of the Western and European-influenced 'special legal community', being largely ignored, in terms of its dispute settlement processes, by other legal systems. With the increasing changes in Court membership corresponding, a little belatedly perhaps, to the changes in United Nations membership and the general political balance of power within the U.N. General Assembly, and the increasing politicisation of the cases coming before it, the International Court is seen, increasingly, as an important arena for international law-making and for international problem-solving in general. In that situation, with national vital interests increasingly involved in the Court's rulings, even in cases not directly involving oneself, considerations of *Realpolitik* begin to take over, openly and avowedly, in the making of nominations and in the acutal voting on candidates for the Court. With the disappearing or muting of the concept of the inherent political neutrality of classical international law, and with political challenges to classical international law itself being made in the name of the 'new' international law, the jurisconsults who were supposed to be, and very often in fact were, above the battle, give way, as candidates for election to the Court, to the Foreign Ministry Legal Advisers, or the professors on long term retainer to those Ministries in that form of *dédoublement fonctionnel* rightly decried by Georges Scelle. The disappearance of the independent jurists of yesteryear is, in fact, one of the most notable evidences of the acceptance, at the international level, of the truth of the Legal Realists' basic thesis that judges do make law; and the legal professionals from the national Foreign Ministries or contractually bound to them are, as elected judges, manifestly most competent to determine and to implement their own particular national interest, in cases coming before the International Court.

2. THE CHIEF JUSTICE: APPOINTMENT, TERM, POWERS

A Supreme Court, as Mr. Justice Frankfurter reminded us,[7] is an orchestra and not a series of solo performances. The *rôle* of the Chief Justice or President, simply because he is, by protocol, the senior member of the Court, and, by law, the presiding officer with disposition over the Court's internal administration, can be crucial in determining the *rôle* of the Court as a whole and whether it functions as a team, with a sense of collegial responsibility for Court decision-making and Court opinion-writing in rationalisation of those decisions, or whether, in contrast, it is racked by internal discord and public dissonance. The crucial appointing power to the Court presidency is a compound, in practice, of constitutional charter and Court Statute-based rules and, even more, of developed custom which is itself a product of historical attitudes in a particular national legal system and in its legal *élite*.

The Chief Justice of the Unites States Supreme Court is appointed in the same manner as any ordinary, Associate Justice of the Court, – by federal Presidential nomination, confirmed by subsequent Senate vote. Once appointed, the Chief Justice holds office on the same basis as ordinary Justices, for life (or until he voluntarily steps down). In appointing a new Chief Justice when a vacancy arises in the office, the President may promote an Associate Justice already on the Court, or he may reach outside the Court. In the present century, the internal promotion route to the Supreme Court's Chief Justiceship has been used only twice: White, Associate Justice 1894-1910, and Chief Justice 1910-1920; and Harlan Stone, Associate Justice 1925-1941, and Chief Justice 1941-1946. Stone's immediate predecessor as Chief Justice, Charles Evans Hughes, had served as an Associate Justice from 1910 to 1916, but had then resigned to run as Republican candidate against President Woodrow Wilson in the Presidential elections of 1916, and after his narrow defeat he returned to private practice until his Chief Justiceship (1930-1941). In all the other cases – Taft, Vinson, Warren, Burger, – the President has maintained the older, settled custom of looking outside the Court, most probably because the post of Chief Justice is, by history and tradition in the United States, a very strong one, ever since the great fourth Chief Justice, John Marshall, who served from 1801 to 1835 and so largely shaped the office by his own strong character and administrative talents and capacity for leadership. A President, occupying his own office for a relatively short, and constitutionally limited, term of years, will normally wish to project his own contemporary image in the Court in the making of his own Court appointments, and there is no better place to bring such influence to bear than in the Chief Justice. It is also a fact, with a Court grown accustomed to accepting strong leadership, that such strong executive talents are not the normal quality of an Associate Justice who will have found his way to the Court for other reasons – intellectual distinction in law, distinguished record of prior judicial service at a lower court level and the like. Those of the Roosevelt-era 'men of affairs' who had served in key policy posts in the executive branch of Government, might have qualified, but strong personality factors and personality clashes with other, serving Associate Justices effectively, perhaps, nullified their claims, as with Associate Justice Robert H. Jackson's unsuccessful campaign to secure promotion to the Chief Justiceship in 1946 on Harlan Stone's death, the failure of which campaign Jackson seems to have blamed, variously, on his absence at the time in Nuremberg as American Chief Prosecutor at the War Crimes Trials and on opposition from his colleague, Associate Justice William O. Douglas. The emphasis on the executive *rôle* of the United States Supreme Court's Chief Justice suggests that the incumbent need not be, and perhaps should not be, the Court's pre-eminent intellect nor its most sparkling personality; and that he need not even be among its most intelligent members. Charles Evans Hughes was the rare exception of a man of a very great intelligence, conceded by all his colleagues, and of a dominating, if cold and reserved, personality, and also, at the same time, a superb administrator. His was a Court that included, in the earlier part of his term as Chief Justice, great jurists like Oliver Wendell Holmes, jr., Brandeis, and Cardozo, and at the close of the term the first of the brilliant Roosevelt 'New Deal' appointees, Black, Frankfurter, and Douglas; yet Hughes' intellect and his mastery of the cases and his control of Court organisation were respected by all.[8] It would not be unfair, however, to say of the other Chief Justices of the present century – White, Taft, Stone, Vinson, Warren, and Burger – that they were neither outstanding intellectually nor dominant in relation to their colleagues. Their claims to success as Chief Justice, and their capacity to leave their own philosophical imprint on the Court, and thus on Court and general constitutional history, would have to turn on other factors: the quieter virtues of patience and reasonableness, and the ability to promote compromises and to use the Court's rules as to assignment of opinion-writing, and thus actively to build majorities for a particular viewpoint in a Court of strong, competing, and often mutually hostile personalities. The Chief Justice's personality and leadership talent will also shew in the statistical evidence of the Court's record and its ability to dispose of its work-load in timely fashion. Hughes did all these things to perfection. An extra quality of judicial wisdom and the ability to impart moral leadership to one's colleagues, which is in no way dependent on one's intellect or technical mastery of past precedents, may also be there and it can gain from the office of Chief Justice, if it be wisely used. Perhaps, in this sense, from different, even directly opposing philosophical viewpoints – liberal activism in the one case, and conservatism in the other – Warren and his immediate successor Burger led their Courts. It is to be noted that, with the advantages, generally, of appointment from outside the Court and the life term of American judges (including Chief Justices), American Presidents are able, if they wish, to exercise a fairly long-range influence on the Court by their choice of Chief Justice.[9] Marshall, the fourth Chief Justice, as we have said, lasted for thirty-four years in the post and shaped it decisively for the future, in consequence; his successor, Taney, served for eighteen years, and thereafter terms of ten years or more are not uncommon right up to the present day. It is clearly a factor conducive to continuity and long-range predictability in a Court's work, and it contrasts sharply with almost every other major national jurisdiction where constitutional charter and Court statute will either stipulate the election for a term-of-years only or else historical practice and custom will enjoin the promotion of an incumbent associate judge, usually the next in line in terms of Court seniority and thus inevitably consigned to a fairly brief term in office, as Chief Justice.

The principle of promotion from within the Court's ranks, and promotion of the senior serving associate judge, has been applied, with varying degrees of absolutism, in the case of the Canadian, Indian, and Japanese Supreme Courts. It is not an absolute rule in regard to the Supreme Court of Canada, and it is somewhat complicated by another, 'bicultural' principle, flowing from 'deux Nations' (French and English) conceptions of Canadian federalism, of trying to alternate the Chief Justiceship between francophone, Civil Law jurists from Quebec and anglophone, Common Law jurists from the other Provinces. When, however, Chief Justice Laskin was promoted from within the Court, in late 1973, only three and a half years after his appointment as an Associate Justice in 1970, it meant vaulting over the heads of no less than five judges with much longer Court seniority, including the two, Conservative Party-appointed judges,

Martland and Ritchie, with Martland being the then senior serving judge. The promotion rule had never been an absolute rule in Canadian Supreme Court practice, though it had tended to be followed in more recent times. The gravamen of the offence to tradition, if tradition there indeed was, consisted in taking a relatively junior judge from within the Court's ranks and one known for his liberal, frequently dissenting opinions, ahead of legally more conservative and traditional, more senior colleagues. The Trudeau Government, in its choice of Chief Justice, had clearly moved closer towards a more American conception of the post, in common with the 'reception' of American ideas in many other areas of Canadian law in the post-War period; and had wanted to give a more liberal, innovatory stamp to Canadian law as developed by the Courts, in line with its own desired image as a liberal, reformist, Liberal Party government. It was simply convenient that a Chief Justice thought to meet these philosophical criteria was already available within the Court's ranks, and an extra advantage perhaps, in terms of policy continuity in the future, that the new Chief Justice could expect a fourteen year term in the post before mandatory retirement at age seventy-five. The jump over senior colleagues involved in the appointment caused considerable public debate at the time and, with its policy-political implications, may have contributed to a certain souring of relations within the Court manifested in the patterns of strong Court divisions and dissents in some of the great political *causes célèbres* of the end of the 1970s and the beginning of the 1980s. [10] When Chief Justice Laskin died in office in March, 1984, Prime Minister Trudeau promoted to Chief Justice the second most senior Associate Justice, Justice Dickson. It meant passing over the most senior serving judge, Justice Ritchie, who had, however, only another year to serve before reaching mandatory retirement at seventy-five. This qualified deference to seniority within the Court, in promoting from within to Chief Justice, meant, at the same time, ignoring the other tradition of alternating the Chief Justiceship between anglophone Common Lawyer (as Laskin was) and francophone Civil Lawyer. The most senior serving francophone, Justice Beetz, was, however, junior in terms of service to the ultimate appointment as Chief Justice, Justice Dickson, an anglophone Common Lawyer like Laskin; and the tradition of French-English alternation was, in any case, fairly recent, dating only from 1954. Before that time, only one of the first eight Chief Justices, from 1875 to 1954, had been a francophone.

Within the Supreme Court of India, even more than within its Canadian counterpart, the principle of the normal, automatic promotion of the most senior serving associate judge on the Supreme Court to the Chief Justiceship became well established. The Indian federal Government's acquiescence in such a custom seems attributable to several factors: first, inherited 'British' elements in the Indian judicial system and judicial though-ways, which insisted, against the increasing evidence of the facts of Indian constitutional law-in-action in the post-decolonisation era, that the judicial process was a neutral one and that judges in no sense made policy decisions, and that in any case the post of Chief Justice was no more than *primus inter partes* and therefore incapable of tilting the balance decisively in bitterly contested political *causes célèbres;* and, second, the very pragmatic argument, that an objective system of appointment based on automatic progression to the Chief Justiceship in strict accordance with seniority within the Court, would discourage internecine rivalries within the Court or judicial lobbying for personal advancement by 'playing to the gallery' in one's judicial votes and opinion-writing and thereby promote a more collegial attitude within the Court. In 1973, however, immediately after the *Kesavananda* decison,[11] a major political case in which the Court, by a 7-to-6 majority, overruled its earlier decision given by a 6-to-5 majority in the *Golak Nath* case in 1967,[12] Prime Minister Indira Gandhi suddenly changed the previous rules-of-the-game as to appointment of the Chief Justice followed in respect to the preceding six Chief Justices by naming, as successor to Chief Justice Sikri, Justice A.N. Ray. The political problem in all this, with the Prime Minister's obvious desire to break new ground constitutionally and to give the Court some more conscious and specific philosophical orientation for the future, much in the manner in which Presidents of the United States have been accustomed to utilise their constitutionally fully discretionary power as to choice of nominees, was that it involved Chief Justice Ray's superseding three colleagues who had more seniority of service within the Court. These three 'superseded' judges, – Shelat, Hegde, and Grover – promptly resigned in protest in the ensuing political storm, thereby inadvertently giving Prime Minister Gandhi a further and augmented opportunity to remake the Court in her own preferred philosophical orientation; and one of them, K.S. Hegde, subsequently had a successful political career, being elected Speaker (presiding officer) of the *Lok Sabha* (lower House) of the federal Parliament, in 1977, under the short-lived Janata Government which had replaced Madame Gandhi's Government.[13] Chief Justice Ray, who had served as an Associate Justice of the Supreme Court from 1969 until his promotion in 1973, resigned in 1977 on reaching the mandatory retirment age for all Justices of sixty-five;[14] and Prime Minister Gandhi once again, in her choice of the Chief Justice, superseded the most senior serving Justice on the Court, Justice Khanna, who had been the lone judicial dissenter, voting against the Gandhi Government position, in the key *Jabalpur* v. *Shukla* (Habeas Corpus) decision the previous year,[15] in favour of the second most senior serving Justice, Justice Beg. When Justice Beg himself

retired in 1978 on reaching the mandatory retirement age, the new Janata
Government reverted to the seniority principle and promoted Justice
Chandrachud, the most senior judge, to the Chief Justiceship. With a
fairly early mandatory retirement age of sixty-five, and all judges being
appointed only fairly late in life, it is apparent that any custom of promotion of Chief Justices within the Court from the ranks of the already
rather mature associate judges will ensure very, very short terms as Chief
Justice, and in fact this has been so with the term, on average, one or two
years only. From the appointment of the first Chief Justice of India,
Chief Justice Kania, in January, 1950, up to and including Justice Chandrachud's promotion to Chief Justice in February, 1978, there had been
no less than sixteen Chief Justices of India in the twenty-eight years,
several serving only a few months. Sarkar, appointed in 1966, served for
three and a half months, and Shah, appointed at the end of 1970, served
for only five weeks, and three others each served for less than a year;
Mahajan, 1954; Subha Rao, 1966-7; Wanchoo, 1967-8. The longest term
before Chief Justice Chandrachud's appointment in 1978, was that of
Sinha, appointed in late 1959, and serving just over four years. There is
hardly enough time for any Chief Justice, by the course of his own judicial votes and opinion-writing, to influence the Court's general philosophy. In fact, some Chief Justices, – Gajendragadkar, 1964-6, is a prime
example – have been judicial leaders, but that seems due more to their
general intellectual qualities than to vicarious prestige attaching to the
office of Chief Justice. On the other hand, the Chief Justice's legal power,
within the Supreme Court of India, to determine the composition of
Court panels, in a Court that utilises the multi-panel system for purposes
of its decision-making and also utilises panels with shifting judicial membership, enables the Chief Justice, if he so wishes, consciously to shape
the Court's decision in particular individual cases or even long-range in
particular categories of cases. It has been remarked, in this regard that
Justice Subha Rao who, on the empirical record of his votes as Associate
Justice, was the greatest dissenter in the Court's history, never found it
necessary to dissent after he was promoted to the Chief Justiceship; for,
of course, in that office, he himself composed the Court panels and there
was no need for him to dissent thereafter.[16] However, the happy accidents of age at time of first appointment to the Court and of judicial
retirements meant that, even with the application of the full seniority
principle and the naming of the most senior serving judge, the new Chief
Justice named in February, 1978, Chief Justice Chandrachud, should
have a seven-and-a-half year term in that post before reaching the mandatory retirement age of sixty-five in July, 1985, and thus the opportunity, if he so wished, to try to develop, through the collegial instruments of
Court conferences prior to decision and the actual opinion-writing, some

long-range jurisprudential trends[16a].

The Supreme Court of Japan, as a tribunal with a compulsory retirement age – seventy – and a tradition, also, of appointing to the Supreme Court only at a very mature age, developed, after its first three, post-War Chief Justices, a custom of promoting to the Chief Justiceship from within the Supreme Court's own ranks, according to seniority of service. It is not surprising, therefore, that the same factors already observed with the Supreme Court of India of a very rapid turn-over in Chief Justices and an average term of a few years only, are present in Japan too.[17] The first Chief Justice of the Court, Chief Justice Tadahiko Mibuchi, served from 1947 to 1950, and then was followed by Kotaro Tanaka who held office as Chief Justice for ten-and-a-half years, from 1950 to 1960, before being elected to the International Court of Justice as Japan's first post-World War II judge on that tribunal. Chief Justice Tanaka's successor, Kisaburo Yokota, also came from outside the Court and held office as Chief Justice until 1966. Thereafter, the Chief Justices were promoted from within the Court, almost invariably according to strict seniority within the Court, with terms sometimes of a little more than a year. From Chief Justice Tadahiko Mibuchi's appointment in 1947, up to mid-1984, and including Chief Justice Jiro Terada, who was promoted, from within the Court, to the Chief Justiceship in 1982, there had been in thirty-seven years, no less than ten Chief Justices of Japan, the first three being appointed from outside the Court and the last seven being promoted from within the Court from the ranks of the serving Associate Justices, and with the longest term of these seven being four years – Chief Justice Kazuto Ishida, from 1969 to 1973. The term as Chief Justice being constrained in time, and the Court itself sitting in Grand Bench (*en banc*) for constitutional questions, there is little opportunity for the Chief Justice to exercise a major influence on the Court's decision-making through his power in the Court administration, and in some senses the observable proliferation of the number of cases reaching the Court and relative failure of the Court to develop adequate screening controls to reduce this work-load flows from the weakness of the office of Chief Justice as compared with final Courts in other legal systems. The Japanese Supreme Court, not less than most other Courts, lacking a long-term, driving executive like Chief Justice John Marshall of the United States, in its early, founding era, has never managed to accord to the Chief Justice that dominant *rôle* in Court decision-making processes that a strong Chief Justice – as described by the greatest administrator among the U.S. Supreme Court Justices, Charles Evans Hughes, – can so effectively develop. Speaking first in the judicial conference at the beginning of the decision-making process, the Chief Justice, if he is intellectually capable and confident, effectively determines the legal issues to be resolved; and his control, also, of opinion-writing, if he is in the majority, determines, by the allocation of the task of writing the official Opinion of Court, the shape of that decision *qua* precedent for the legal profession and the law schools, and for constitutional-legal history. No other Chief Justice or Court President today seems to have inherited such formidable powers and authority from his predecessors. The Chief Justice of Japan, according to the Constitution, is appointed by the Emperor on the designation of the Cabinet (Article 6), where all the other Supreme Court judges are appointed by the Cabinet (Article 79); but, as a matter of constitutional law-in-action, there is nothing different in the two processes, the selections and appointments being made by the executive.

The West German Federal Constitutional Court, as already noted, has the two permanent Senates, each with fixed membership as constituted through the federal Parliament-based election system, and with separate, autonomous jurisdiction. With the two federal Houses, the *Bundestag* and the *Bundesrat*, functioning as electoral colleges, and each selecting half of the total number of judges on each Senate, (that is, four judges of the presently eight judge-membership for each Senate), and with what is, in effect, (though the actual selection systems are different for each House) a form of proportional representation of the relative strength of the different federal political parties occurring in the actual judicial selections, the Court Statute has codified the selection of the presiding officers of the two Senates so that the choice is effectively divided between the two federal Houses. According to the Court Statute, the *Bundestag* and *Bundesrat* are to select, in alternation, the President of the Court and his Deputy President, with the Deputy President selected from the Senate of which the President for the time being is not a member; and it was also provided that, for the first elections to the Court, in 1951, the *Bundestag* would select the President, the *Bundesrat* the Deputy President, (Court Statute, section 9 (1) and (2)). In effect, the Court President is the presiding officer of the one Senate, and the Deputy President the presiding officer of the other, and since the same rules as to election apply to the two presiding officers as to the ordinary judges (section 9 (3)), the party political balance which is the clear constitutional intent of the whole judicial electoral system is able to be maintained through the ordinary party political give-and-take.[18] For the first bench of the Court, in 1951, the *Bundestag* elected Dr. Hermann Höpker-Aschoff, a prominent pre-War political figure and opponent of the Nazi *régime,* who was a member of the *Bundestag* at the time of his election to the Court and a member of the Free Democratic Party, the party in political coalition with Chancellor Adenauer's Christian Democratic Party.[18a] The *Bundesrat* elected Dr. Rudolf Katz, also with a record of opposition to the Nazi *régime,* who was a member of the *Bundesrat* at the time of his election to the Court, but as a member of the federal opposition Social Democratic Party. Höpker-Aschoff, as President of the Court, became the presiding officer of the First Senate of the Court, until his death in 1954; while Katz, as Deputy President of the Court, became presiding officer of the Second Senate, and continued in that function, after re-election, until his death in 1961. When Höpker-Aschoff died, the succession to the presidency of the First Senate and the office of Court President remained with the federal Government coalition, passing to Josef Wintrich (Christian Democratic Party), a career judge; and after his death to Gebhard Müller, again a Christian Democrat leader and Minister-President (Premier) of the *Land* (Province) of Baden-Württemberg. After Katz' death, the succession to the presidency of the Second Senate and the office of Court Deputy President went to Friedrich Wilhelm Wagner, a member of the Social Democratic Party and member of the *Bundestag* at the time of his election. Müller gave way, as Court President and presiding officer of the First Senate, eventually to Benda, an active Christian Democratic Party politician, member of the *Bundestag* and federal Minister; while on the Second Senate, Wagner gave way to another Social Democrat, Seuffert. The informal, inter-Party understandings or rules-of-the-game, operating upon the judicial election system established in the Bonn constitutional charter of 1949 and the Court Statute, thus managed to continue through the political vicissitudes of the Christian Democratic and Free Democratic coalition government, the 'Grand Coalition' of Christian Democrats and Social Democrats, and the later Social Democratic government, its essence being the balance in political affiliations as between the presiding officers of the two Senates, and the relative sharing of the available judicial seats within the two Senates. The key characteristics are the acceptance of a necessary degree of politicisation of the judicial appointing processes themselves, and of a certain inter-party consensus as to the actual formation of the Court, – which reflect in measure the larger degree of all-party consensus as to the fundamentals of the West German polity as a whole.

The President of the French *Conseil constitutionnel* is named by the President of the Republic from among its members (Constitution, Article 56). It is not clear whether the President of the *Conseil* is limited to the nine appointed members, or whether he could also be named from among the by-legal-right members (former Presidents of the Republic); but the question has remained academic up to the present, as the choice has been limited to the nine appointed members. It is also not clear what the term of the President is, but it has been assumed that it is for nine years (the term of an appointed member which, under Article 56, is not renewable). In any case, it has not been felt necessary to try to withdraw the mandate of a *Conseil* President on change in the Presidency of the

Republic. President Mitterand waited, for example, until 1983, the expiry of the then incumbent President of the *Conseil,* Roger Frey's, normal nine-year mandate, before replacing him by his own choice, Daniel Mayer. The *Conseil* had had three Presidents – Noël, Palewski, and Frey – from its inception in 1959 until the appointment of M. Mayer in 1983, with the most visible of these, in public terms, perhaps being M. Frey, a *fidèle* of General de Gaulle like his predecessors, and an active politician prior to appointment.[19] M. Frey was generally given credit for the Constitutional Law of 29 October 1974, (amending Article 61 of the Constitution) which was adopted just after his naming as *Conseil* President, and which tried to reform the *Conseil* by enlarging access to its jurisdiction, through permitting a certain minimum number of members (60) of either House of the legislature, to seize it with a constitutional question. This measure was evidently designed to reinforce the means of constitutional control, by Opposition parties, of the government, and its adoption and utilisation has perhaps, more than anything else, changed the nature and character of the *Conseil* by leading it, more and more, into Constitutional Court-style determinations.

Finally, with the International Court of Justice, the Court Statute stipulates that the Court shall elect a President and Vice-President for three years, and that they may be re-elected (Article 21 (1)). Like very many United Nations institutions, however, the International Court has been subjected to strong political pressures for rotation of its scarce number of offices – the fifteen judgeships, and the Presidency and Vice-Presidency among these – among the increasingly large number of U.N. member-states. As we have already noted, with the seats effectively pre-empted, up to the present at least, by four of the Wartime 'Big Five' being excepted, there has been intensive competition for the remaining eleven judgeships, with regional accords and understandings and 'Gentleman's Agreements' among ideological, ethnic-cultural, linguistic, legal-systemic, and political-geographical blocs generally, often limiting highly qualified and experienced judges, who would normally wish to present themselves for re-election, to a single, nine-year judicial term. With the Presidency of the Court, these pressures have been even more extreme. Apart from the special case of the first President, J.G. Guerrero, of the new International Court of Justice that succeeded to the old Permanent Court of International Justice in 1946, who had been the last President of that old Permanent Court (from 1936 to 1946) and then continued on with the new Court for the one term, 1946 to 1949, no President of the International Court has served more than the single, three-year term.[20] The loss to the Court, in terms of continuity of administration and even of Court philosophy, is considerable, and it compounds the problems created by the frequent changes in judicial personnel caused by the retirement of one-

84

third of the Court's membership every three years under the staggered system of Court elections. The consequences are apparent in the proliferation of judicial opinion-writing, (dissenting and specially concurring), in addition to the official Opinion of Court, which often renders difficult the establishment of common grounds of decision (*ratio decidendi*) in any case. This, and the occasionally pejorative note creeping into the Court's public discussions, adds to the burden for the Court in a period of transition and rapid change in the World Community with competition and conflict as to ideology and basic values underlying law.

NOTES

1. *Canadian Jurisprudence. The Civil Law and Common Law in Canada* (E. McWhinney, ed.) (1958).
2. I.C.J. Reports 1966, p. 6.
3. 'Die Richter des Bundesverfassungsgerichts', in *Das Bundesverfassungsgericht* (Gebhard Müller, ed.) (1963), pp. 305-338.
4. Decision of 30 July 1952, 1 B Verf GE 396 (1952) (First Senate); decision of 9 December 1952, 2 B Verf GE 79 (1953) (*plenum*); decision of 7 March 1953, 2 B Verf GE 143 (1953) (Second Senate).
5. L. Favoreu and L. Philip, *Le Conseil constitutionnel* (1978), pp. 22-23.
6. *Ibid.*, p. 22.
7. F. Frankfurter, *The Commerce Clause under Marhsall, Taney, and Waite* (1937), p. 43.
8. See generally F. Frankfurter, 'The Administrative side of Chief Justice Hughes', 63 *Harvard Law Review* 1 (1949); E. McElwain, 'The Business of the Supreme Court as conducted by Chief Justice Hughes', 63 *Harvard Law Review* 5 (1949); *Of Law and Men. Papers and Addresses of Felix Frankfurter 1939-1956* (P. Elman, ed.) (1956), pp. 133, 139, 144.
9. Henry J. Abraham, *The Judicial Process* (1962), p. 47 *et seq.*
10. See, for example, *Reference re Resolution to Amend the Constitution* [1981], 1 S.C.R. 753. And see P.W. Hogg, 'Supremacy of the Canadian Charter of Rights and Freedoms', 61 *Canadian Bar Review* 69, 74 *et seq.* (1983); E. McWhinney, *Canada and the Constitution 1979-1982. Patriation and the Charter of Rights* (1982), p. 80 *et seq.*
11. *Kesavananda Bharati* v. *State of Kerala,* A.I.R. *1973* S.C. 1461.
12. *I.C. Golak Nath* v. *State of Punjab,* A.I.R. *1967* S.C. 1643.
13. Alice Jacob and Rajeev Dhavan, 'The Dissolution Case: Politics at the Bar of the Supreme Court', 19 *Journal of the Indian Law Institute* 355, 355 note 1 (1977). And see generally Rajeev Dhavan, *The Supreme Court of India. A Socio-Legal Analysis of its Juristic Techniques* (1977), ch. 1.
14. Henry J. Abraham, '"Merit" or "Seniority"? Reflections on the Politics of Recent Appointments to the Chief Justiceship in India', 16 *Journal of Commonwealth and Comparative Politics* 303 (1978).
15. *A.D.M. Jabalpur* v. *Shivkant Shukla,* A.I.R. *1976* S.C. 1207.
16. George H. Gadbois Jr., 'Supreme Court Decision Making', 10 *Banaras Law Journal* 1, 24 (1974); Anirud Prasad, 'Imprints of Marshallian Judicial Statesmanship on Indian Judiciary', 22 *Journal of the Indian Law Institute* 240 (1980).

16a. Chief Justice Chandrachud, in fact, served out his full term. When he reached the mandatory retirement age in July, 1985, the Government of Prime Minister Rajeev Gandhi applied the seniority rule and promoted the most senior serving judge on the Court, Justice Bhagwati, in his place as Chief Justice.

17. *Justice in Japan* (Supreme Court of Japan) (1978), pp. 1-3; John M. Maki, *Court and Constitution in Japan. Selected Supreme Court Decisions, 1948-60* (1964), pp. 425-432; Hiroshi Itoh and L. W. Beer, *The Constitutional Case Law of Japan. Selected Supreme Court Decisions, 1961-70* (1978), pp. 11, 251-253.

18. *Das Bundesverfassungsgericht* (Gebhard Müller, ed.) (1963), pp. 305-308; Heinz Laufer, *Verfassungsgerichtsbarkeit und politischer Prozess* (1968), pp. 206-253; Donald P. Kommers, *Judicial Politics in West Germany* (1976), pp. 113-149; E. McWhinney, *Constitutionalism in Germany and the Federal Constitutional Court* (1962), pp. 27-30.

18a. Theo Ritterspach, 'Hermann Höpker Aschoff. Der erste Präsident des Bundesverfassungsgerichts. 1883-1954', 32 *Jahrbuch des öffentlichen Rechts der Gegenwart (N.F.)* 55 (1983).

19. L. Favoreu and L. Philip, *Le Conseil constitutionnel (1978), pp. 19-20.*

20. *Documents on the International Court of Justice* (Shabtai Rosenne, ed.) (1974), pp. 327-334, 337-349. The post of President has, by now, developed its own customary rules as to rotation on a 'regional' basis among the members of the Court: thus, the most recent Presidents of the International Court have membered Lachs (Poland), Jiménez de Aréchaga (Uruguay), Waldock (Great Britain), Elias (Nigeria), and, currently, Nagendra Singh (India).

CHAPTER V

JUDICIAL PHILOSOPHY: CONSTITUTIONAL TEXT AND CONSTITUTIONAL CONSTRUCTION; JUDICIAL SELF-RESTRAINT AND JUDICIAL ACTIVISM

1. CONSTITUTIONAL TEXT: LAPIDARIAN TEXT OR DETAILED BLUEPRINT?

At the beginning, there is always the constitutional text, though it is important to remember that the text is not always, and will indeed rarely be, comprehensive and all-inclusive. Constitutional Charters, as such, derive from the Age of Reason: there are precursors in the mid-17th century English, Cromwellian instruments of government, but the golden age of constitutional charters dates from the end of the 18th century – the Constitution of the United States which remains the principal model for constitution-makers, even today, as the authoritative precedent to be followed with reverence, or departed from only for cause and on reasoned argument; and the various charters of the French Revolutionary and Napoleonic eras, which present a fascinating range of alternative options as to institutions, processes, substantive principles and their mutual interrelations and interactions, reflecting the different combinations of political forces that were dominant during that brief, twenty-five year span of brilliant constitutional experimentation, and the particular balances that those different political forces endeavoured to make with the changing social and economic interests around them. But the American and the French constitution-making of that era, at the end of the 18th and the beginning of the 19th centuries, even though revolutionary in stated design and in actual intent, did not represent in any sense a complete break with the past, but built, to a considerable extent, on existing law and existing patterns of decision-making. This large element of inherited, customary constitutional law will be present in any society, and is bound to continue, unless the constituent forces charged with producing a new charter are determined to make changes in these areas too, and are constitutionally sophisticated and resolute enough to know how to do it effectively – as new constitutional law-in-action, as well as being simply part of a new verbal prescription. Even then, as some of the experience with newly drafted constitutional charters, or recently adopted constitutional charters, demonstrates, it may involve great tenacity on the part of the constitution-makers and a determination to come back again and again, if need be, with the same constitutional project, to ensure that it can be carried through successfully against the last-ditch opposition of other institutionally-entrenched forces – the Supreme Courts, for example, as in the United States in the period of the 'Old Court' from right after the Civil War until the Court Revolution of 1937; or in India in the 1960s and early 1970s, when the judges seemed determined somehow or other to beat back Prime Minister Gandhi's social and economic reforms even when they were finally endowed with the 'Higher Law' status of legally-adopted Amendments to the Constitution.[1]

Normally, executive and legislative practice and executive-legislative relations generally, and for that matter judicial practice and the degree of mutual deference and mutual responsibility to be accorded as between judicial authority and the other two, coordinate arms of government, will not be spelled out in the constitutional charter, either because it was there before in customary constitutional law and there was not the time, at the moment of constitution-making, to try to spell it out in detail in the charter; or because the very efforts of reducing it to written form in the charter would tend to act as a brake on future development in an area of law, above all, that benefits from continuing evolution. Such matters as the ambit and scope of the powers of the other, coordinate institutions of government and the manner in which they are to be exercised, will normally have to be spelled out by contemporary courts in a contemporary political context, or else avoided altogether, by judicial self-denying ordinance, as a 'political question' more apt to be resolved by those other institutions themselves or else resolved by the people. In general, as to institutions, the constitutional charter will content itself with establishing the ground rules – how a particular organ of government is constituted, its membership, tenure, and mandate for decision-making; and the real stuff of the constitutional charter will lie in relations between the citizen and the state and the permissible limits of governmental power and of the processes by which it is exercised. Today, these particular fundamental constitutional dispositions will tend to be found set out in a constitutionally-entrenched Charter of Rights of the citizen, though in the case of older constitutional systems, and particularly those with a British, Common Law legal heritage, total or partial only, such principles will have to be found in the interstices of other (non-citizens' rights) constitutional dispositions, for example those purporting to distribute decision-making power on a geographical basis – as with those federal charters that seek to divide governmental power between a central authority and various forms of regional or local administrations.

One basic dilemma of constitution-making goes to the different, alternative styles of constitutional drafting and literary elaboration available at any time, each of them having its own special advantages and disadvantages. Should one try for a lapidarian text, short and succinct and with a sounding generality of utterance that lends itself to easy comprehension, as to its main thrust and direction, by the public and politicians alike, and that will not, because of its very generality of formulation, be likely to create too many unnecessary legal barriers to social change and so to act as a brake on community development in the future? Or should one, rather, seek for a detailed social blueprint that tries to spell everything out very precisely and at very great length if necessary, in such a way that administrators and also judges could not (perhaps, in the light of empirical experience, one would better say, should not) be able to defeat or divert its clear stipulations.[2] The first approach, manifestly, is that of the great Constitution of the United States of 1787, and, though there are the occasional odd contradictions of too much specificity on relatively minor and quickly dated points contained in it, it is one of the principal reasons advanced for its having lasted so long, until the present day, without any very considerable number or range of formal amendments. It is also the general way of the French constitution-makers of the Revolutionary era, and we may, hence, identify it as the classical approach to constitution-making, the classical text. At its best, as with the American charter and certain of the French Revolutionary texts – notably, the Declaration of the Rights of Man and the Citizen, of 1789, which was adopted by the Preambles of the 1946 (Fourth Republic) and the 1958 (Fifth Republic) Constitutions – it will be poetry as well as law, and capable very easily of making the jump from abstract law-in-books – an esoteric art-form reserved for and practised among professional lawyers – to community 'living law' in which, as the Emperor Napoleon set as the design for his great *Code civil,* the ordinary citizen can read the law in the evening, by candlelight, and understand his constitutional rights.

The second approach, somewhat pedantic or didactic in character, is to be found in those constitutional charters designed by Imperial Britain for her colonial Empire overseas in the 19th century, Victorian era, and later; and it is also to be found in many of the post-World War II, new national charters of the newly-independent, decolonised countries of Asia and Africa, whether these be charters conceived and drafted and bestowed, as going-away presents, by the former Imperial power, or else charters drafted by national constituent assemblies in their own right composed of political-legal *élites* educated and formed in the erstwhile Imperial country and so absorbing so very much of its special legal thought-ways and literary-legal habits and preferences. It is to be found, still further, in some of the new socialist charters of some of the Communist countries, European and non-European, usually accompanied by an extra, moralising element – the mandate for public education, after all

- that the old, Imperial, and the newer, post-Imperial, charters of the colonies, and former colonies, of the European trans-Oceanic states never really had.

The dilemma of specificity in these pedantic, didactic charters is that, in the pursuit of detailed exposition, they usually end up saying too much, and so become far too long and destined, inevitably, to a form of selective use and application, in which a few key sections will have to do all the work and everything else relegated to one side and quickly forgotten. Further, where they are specific they are often inconveniently and awkwardly so. Someone, at the moment of constitution-making, will have tried to jell, once and for all in permanent, constitutional form, the exigent here-and-now of some passing public fad or contemporary community pressure group preference. The American Constitution's Eighteenth (Prohibition) Amendment comes readily to mind in this context, although it happens to be one of the rare aberrations in a short and succinct, lapidarian charter that was able, in its historical origins and also its subsequent historical development, to remain happily free from moral cant or sermonising. On the whole this is not the stuff to seek to entrench in a constitutional charter, at least if one wants the charter to have a certain life of its own and term-of-years and not be overthrown in a new exercise in constititution-making or else by-passed and ignored altogether.

What emerges, with the short and succinct, lapidarian charters, is that in seeking to render the necessarily abstract and general propositions concrete and operational and, so to speak, to put flesh on the bones of the constitutional text, the authoritative decision-makers are compelled to reach out for ordering principles – jural postulates, as Roscoe Pound, founder of the North American School of Sociological Jurisprudence called them;[3] goal values as the social scientists in law, Lasswell and McDougal, prefer.[4] It parallels, and, at a certain point in time, meets the tendency, in the case of the larger, sprawling and prolix, didactic tests – where authoritative decision-makers do indeed take those texts seriously and try to render them as law-in-action – to reduce those charters to a few key syntheses, involving the critical issues of community social and economic choice for the future. Constitutional law as a process, on this view, involving a continuing flow of authoritative community decisions, finds its reality in the main contradictions or antinomies of contemporary society and in the actual community resolution of the conflicts involved in them. The actual constitutional text, on the same view, becomes secondary or marginal and rarely controlling or determinative of the community decision. This is why, in accord with the methods of comparative legal science, it has been possible to arrange and group the case law of the major legal systems of the World – in spite of the frequent, very great verbal differences in their respective constitutional texts – under a few key categories of subject matter, and then to analyse, comparatively, the responses of the various national Supreme Courts as exercises in the identification and application of community jural postulates to community social and economic problems of our time era.

2. RULES OF CONSTRUCTION: GRAMMATICAL, LOGICAL INTERPRETATION AND THE 'POLICY' APPROACH

(a) *A 'strict and complete legalism'*

The debate over rules of construction and differing judicial approaches to the task of interpreting constitutional charter or statute is one common to all legal systems.[5] The Anglo-Saxon, Common Law or Common Law-derived or influenced constitutional systems, speak of the 'ordinary meaning' of words, of strict and literal interpretation, of logical interpretation, and these are all part and parcel of the conception of the judicial function as being, in itself, a politically neutral *rôle,* capable of being reduced to a purely mechanical and objective one in which values and value-choice can play no part – what the Legal Realists derided as the basic legal myth. This species of approach to the judicial office is, perhaps, best summed up in the remarks of the then Chief Justice of Australia, Sir Owen Dixon, on the occasion of his being sworn in as Chief Justice in 1952, an opportunity which he used to administer a stern rebuke to those who had criticised his Court as being excessively 'legalistic':

> 'It is not sufficiently recognised that the Court's sole function is to interpret a constitutional description of power or restraint upon power and say whether a given measure falls on one side of a line consequently drawn or on the other, and that it has nothing to do with the merits or demerits of the measure. Such a function has led us all I think to believe that close adherence to legal reasoning is the only way to maintain the confidence of all parties in Federal conflicts. It may be that the Court is thought to be excessively legalistic. I should be sorry to think that it is anything else. There is no other safe guide to judicial decisions in great conflicts than a strict and complete legalism.'[6]

The problem with such an approach, as the Legal Realists were quick to point out in assorted national legal contexts, lay not in its formulation as an *idealtyp* of judicial behaviour, but in its concrete application, and the all too frequent gap between what the judges were saying that they were doing in exercise of their judicial function, and the actual record of judicial performance in concrete cases. Even in relation to Chief Justice Dixon's own Court, it might be suggested that while wearing the cloak of a strict and complete legalism the Court majority was reading particularist conceptions of social and economic philosophy – here *laissez-faire* liberalism – into sections of the Australian constitutional charter designed by its Founding Fathers with a quite limited historical intent of preventing imposition of customs and excise duties at regional, provincial boundaries within the federal system – the 'barbarism of borderism' as it was called at the time.[7] The philosophical joinder of issue, here, would be not with the particular social and economic values that Chief Justice Dixon's colleagues were reading into the Constitution, for we shall find parallel judicial action in a number of different countries with rather different constitutional texts; and that particular issue deserves debating on its merits – as a value question, involving choice of particular values among a number of competing values, and the defence of that ultimate choice in value terms. Rather, the joinder of issue, here, must be over the postulated nature of the judicial process and the judicial insistence that a maintenance of a 'strict and complete legalism', divorced from values and value considerations, is possible in judicial decision-making; and if and when that question has been answered affirmatively, a second question arises, inevitably, whether it is desirable as a statement of the limits of the permissible judicial *rôle* in decision-making on great political and social issues of the day. A still further question arises, then, according to our answers to the first two questions. Is the basic judicial myth, as the Legal Realists called it, that judges do not make law, something that arises as a result of the judges' own confusion and their inability or unwillingness to address themselves to the first two questions, or is it something that the judges consciously and deliberately help to maintain and extend themselves, lest public awareness of the potential policy-making character of judicial review should bring still further questions as to its democratic character today, and as to whether or not, therefore, the judicial appointment processes should not incorporate some form of election, direct or indirect, or some form of legislature-based confirmation or ratification of executive choices, to ensure some greater judicial responsibility, and hence legitimation, in contemporary constitutional terms? We may address ourselves, now, to these questions.

First, as to whether it is indeed possible for judges to maintain value-neutrality and a 'strict and complete legalism', so that that claim is more than just another academic-legal construction or *idealtyp* of judicial behaviour, most final tribunals will present a range of judicial attitudes and approaches in a continuum running from strict construction and scrupulous deference to past precedents, to a form of judicial 'free interpretation' where the rules of construction and the corpus of past decisions seem no more than a convenient point of departure for exercises in wide-ranging community policy-making. Among the strict constructionists, Sir Gerald Fitzmaurice, the long-time Legal Adviser to the British Foreign Ministry and Judge on the International Court of Justice throughout the 1960s, stands out because of his undoubted intellectual distinction and capacity for leadership among his peers and also because, in all his public statements, he embraced most enthusiastically the conception of the strictly legal, non-political character of membership on the Court and the obligation, therefore, of the Judge to divorce himself completely from policy considerations in his decisions. Sir Gerald is generally considered as the author of the majority, Opinion of Court in *South West Africa, Second Phase,* in 1966,[8] in which the Court by an 8-to-7 majority, achieved only with the second, tie-breaking vote of its President, the Australian judge, Sir Percy Spender, declined jurisdiction to rule on the continued legality, today, of the old League of Nations-created Mandate of the Republic of South Africa over South West Africa (Namibia). To achieve that particular result, in 1966, declining jurisdiction to rule on the merits, the Court majority had to distinguish an earlier, 1962, ruling,[9] in which, by an 8-to-7 vote, it had in fact already conceded *locus standi* to raise the issue to the two complaimant states, Ethiopia and Liberia, who then proceeded, in the subsequent hearings, to contest before the Court the compatibility with International Law of the white-minority-ruled Republic of South Africa's racially discriminatory, *Apartheid* programme which would, of course, apply by extension to its administration of Namibia. The distinction which the Court made, by a single vote difference, in 1966 to put aside its earlier, 1962 holding, was one that would have baffled the ingenuity of the medieval schoolmen who argued over such fine philosophical points as how many Angels could sit on the point of a needle; yet it was a distinction which Sir Gerald Fitzmaurice was not afraid to defend on technical legal grounds, against the angry charges, advanced at the time in the United Nations General Assembly and elsewhere, that the one-vote majority holding in 1966 was a racially-inspired decision rendered by a 'white man's tribunal'. There is no doubt that, whatever its merits in intrinsically legal terms, the 1966 Court holding was a disaster in political terms, creating suspicion and distrust of the Court among Third World countries and a crisis of political confidence from which it is only beginning to recover at this time. Fortunately for the Court in political terms, an opportunity for a *reprise* of the *South West Africa, Second Phase* ruling came very soon. In 1971, the Court, on Advisory Opinion reference from the United Nations Security Council, by overwhelming judicial majorities on the substantive issues (13 to 2, and 11 to 4 respectively), declared the Republic of South Africa Mandate to be at an end.[10] The Court invoked contemporary standards of civilisation to determine the meaning of the old League of Nations Mandates as a 'sacred trust of civilisation', with which, of course, any form of legally-sanctioned or tolerated discrimination on account of race or colour, would be in direct conflict. It was a form of progressive, generic interpretation, resting upon the notion of inter-temporal law and the relativism, in space and time, of particular legal rules and categories and the need, in consequence, for their continuing up-dating to meet new social conditions and demands. As such, it was an exercise in judicial creativity and judicial imagination that could only with extreme difficulty be reconciled with strict construction or the positivist approach to law generally. The majority Opinion of Court in *Namibia* in 1971, was accompanied by a strong Dissenting Opinion by Judge Fitzmaurice in which he adopted as his own the comments of the one-time American judge on the old Permanent Court of International Justice, Manley Hudson,[11] on the necessity for the Court to keep 'within the limits which characterise judicial action', – in short, for the Court to act 'not as an "academy of jurists" but as a responsible magistrature.'[12] It was, in retrospect, a last-ditch battle by Sir Gerald Fitzmaurice, for a cause already lost: after the angry public reaction to *South West Africa, Second Phase* in 1966, an increasing (and, in terms of United Nations constitutionalism, it might be argued, legitimate) politicisation of the election processes and the renewal, every three years, of a third of the Court's membership, brought significant changes in Court personnel and a Court majority increasingly committed to the notion of change in the old, 'classical' International Law to correspond to fundamental changes in the World Community as a whole. For the changes in Court membership, foreshadowed by the defeat in the Court elections of 1966, in the aftermath of the *South West Africa, Second Phase* decision, of the distinguished Australian jurist and long-time United Nations delegate, Sir Kenneth Bailey, who was strongly favoured to succeed his compatriot Sir Percy Spender, foreshadowed the disappearance of that old 'European family compact' image of the Court, dating from the old Permanent Court of International Justice era between the two World Wars, and the disappearance also of the European or European-leaning voting majority on the present Court from its establishment in 1946 onwards. With the changes in the membership of the Court went changes in its basic, collegial philosophy, for the new judges were much less concerned with the *status quo* and with the restatement of the 'classical' International Law, such as it might be, as with active participation in changing it.

(b) *Postitivism and Natural Law, and Policy Approaches to Law*

The antinomy between strict, logical interpretation and more consciously policy-oriented approaches to law is to be found represented in the continuum of judicial attitudes in all major legal systems. Even within Sir Gerald Fitzmaurice's own bench of the International Court of Justice and in the *locus classicus* in which he developed his particular, positivist approach to law as the official Opinion of Court, *South West Africa, Second Phase* in 1966, the Court majority was directly challenged by the then American member of the Court, Judge Jessup, who took judicial notice of the 'accumulation of expressions of condemnation of *Apartheid*' as 'proof of the pertinent contemporary international standard'.[13] Latter-day benches of the International Court have seen distinguished judicial innovators, who have not been afraid to break new legal ground, like Vice-President Ammoun and Judge (and sometime President of the Court) Manfred Lachs. Within national tribunals, the two approaches to the judicial process will manifest themselves under different names at times, but the fundamental opposition in the two points of view will be there: positivism and Natural Law, in both Common Law and Civil Law-derived systems; grammatical and logical interpretation, in contradistinction to purposive, teleological interpretation, following Gény's terminology, in the Civil Law and Civil Law-derived systems. In the earliest days of the new Republic of India, its new Supreme Court faced the problem of the compatibility with the new, Fundamental Rights sections of the constitution, of the system of Preventive Detention of political opponents inherited directly from the pre-independence, British Imperial *Raj*. In the *Gopalan* case, decided in 1950,[14] the key section, for present purposes, was the guarantee contained in Article 21 of the Consitution: 'No person shall be deprived of his life or personal liberty except according to procedure established by law'. It had been contended, in argument, by the Attorney-General, that the words 'procedure established by law' meant simply any procedure established or enacted by statute, an interpretation that the majority of the Supreme Court, with Justices Fazl Ali and Mahajan dissenting, readily accepted. Mr. Justice Fazl Ali, however, in his dissenting opinion, suggested that the expression 'procedure established by law' should be interpreted in a much wider sense as meaning what is understood in American constitutional law by 'procedural due process':

'... In America, the word "law" does not mean merely State-made law or law enacted by the State and does not exclude certain fundamental principles of justice which inhere in every civilised system of law and which are at the root of it.'[15]

Mr. Justice Fazl Ali went on from this to conclude that the expression 'procedure established by law' in Article 21 of the Constitution must include the 'principle that no person can be condemned without a hearing by an impartial tribunal, which is well-recognised in all modern civilised systems of law'[16] and which must therefore be regarded as part of the law of post-independence India. By contrast, the Court majority, as represented by Chief Justice Kania, rejected that interpretation, for, in the Chief Justice's crisply-worded opinion which insisted that the Fundamental Rights sections of the Constitution be

'read with their natural grammatical meaning' – 'No extrinsic aid is needed to interpret the words of Article 21, which, in my opinion are not ambiguous. Normally read, and without thinking of other Constitutions, the expression "procedure established by law" must mean procedure prescribed by the law of the State.'[17]

It is impossible to exaggerate the importance of this judicial debate over the basic approach of the Supreme Court to constitutional interpretation, coming so early as it did in the professional life of the new tribunal after the cutting of the last legal links with Imperial Britain, with the Imperial Privy Council (as final appellate tribunal of the old British Empire overseas), and *ex hypothesi* with British judicial practice and special legal thought-ways insofar as these might still be considered as automatically binding and controlling in the Indian Court system after decolonisation. The debate, with its majority resolution as expressed by Chief Justice Kania, set the general intellectual-philosophical tone for the Indian Supreme Court for the next several decades, in the deliberate rejection of the broader, purposive, policy approaches to law. When, a year later, in *Keshavan Madhava Menon* v. *The State of Bombay,*[18] the Supreme Court had to review a prosecution under the Indian Press (Emergency Powers) Act, adopted under the old Imperial British *Raj* in 1931 and still in force at the moment of Indian independence, it was argued that the British-made statute should now yield to Article 13 (1) of the new, post-independence Constitution which declared all such pre-independence laws to be void – 'insofar as they are inconsistent with the provisions of this Part [Part III of the Constitution, Fundamental Rights].' Mr. Justice Fazl Ali, dissenting once again, contended that a British-made, press censorship law should so fall before the new, post-independence Constitution, since incompatible with its quite explicit guarantees of freedom of speech and expression. On the other hand, the Court majority, represented this time by Mr. Justice Das, echoed Chief Justice Kania in the *Gopalan* case in rejecting what it characterised as an

'argument founded on what is claimed to be the spirit of the Constitution... always attractive for it has a powerful appeal to sentiment and emotion; but a Court of law has to gather the spirit of the Constitution from the language of the Constitution.... The Court should construe the language of Article 13 (1) according to the established rules of interpretation and arrive at its true meaning uninfluenced by any assumed spirit of the Constitution.'[19]

Some might suggest that the Court majority, in the first full flush of juridical decolonisation and independence from Imperial Britain, had managed to remain even more British than the British judges before them in their insistence upon maintaining 'natural grammatical meanings' and 'established rules of interpretation', this in spite of the intellectual challenge of charting out a new constitutional course for a new country freshly endowed with its own new constitutional charter and a host of inherited or accumulated political, social, and economic problems to resolve under it. In that context, the great Chief Justice John Marshall's admonition, pronounced in *McCulloch* v. *Maryland* in 1819, in the very early years of the new United States Supreme Court, that one must – 'never forget that it is a *constitution* we are expounding',[20] and not just any ordinary legislation, seems more apt and relevant. And as we shall also see, the later record of interpretation of the constitution by the Indian Supreme Court, particularly in the property cases where the Indian Government's social and economic planning measures were challenged before the Court, seems legally explicable and intellectually justifiable only on the basis of a particular 'spirit of the Constitution' that the Court majority judges insisted on reading into the constitutional charter and constitutional charter amendments, in spite of the constitutional texts involved and of the historical intentions behind them.

The liberal activist judges on the United States Supreme Court of the post-1937 era, particularly Justices Black and Douglas with their 'preferred position' approach to the Constitution's First Amendment Free Speech guarantee, would certainly have approved of Mr. Justice Fazl Ali's approach which seems to have been rendered without any direct contact with that position. Chief Justice Duff and Mr. Justice Cannon of the Canadian Supreme Court, in the late 1930s, without the official sanction and support of any constitutional Bill of Rights, postulated a Common Law constitutional freedom of the press in Canada in order to strike down highly repressive Provincial (Albertan) legislation directed against anti-government newspaper editorials and reporting;[21] though the only positive law support that could be found for such a freedom resided in the spirit of the Constitution and in vague phrases in the Preambular formulation to the Constitution.[22] A decade and a half later, in the 1950s, the great liberal judge, Mr. Justice Ivan Rand of the Canadian Supreme Court moved boldly to fill the gap in the Constitution created by the absence of any constitutional Charter of Rights, by developing his own special constitutional concept of the 'Rights of the Canadian citizen', which he interpreted as extending, variously, to freedom of movement, freedom of speech and the press, and freedom from arbitrary power, and which he used most vigorously and effectively to persuade successive Court majorities to strike down various Provincial laws and executive and administrative actions running counter to these postulated primary principles of constitutionalism.[23] We will note two interesting points from all this. First, the constitutional text itself, or even the absence of a constitutional text, is not paramount in the judicial behaviour examined: like-minded judges, in different countries, with often quite different constitutional-textual provisions, manage to reach very much the same results in their opinions. This suggests the existence of common principles of constitutionalism, transcending the historical accidents of particular national constitutional and Court systems; or, if you wish, a sort of *Jus Gentium*-based Natural Law, common to very many legal systems and shared by very many judges in spite of ethnic-cultural, legal-systemic, or national historical differences and in spite of the absence of direct personal contact or exchange of constitutional ideas in most cases. It also confirms that the strict construction/policy construction or positivism/Natural Law antinomy is one common to most legal systems, in spite of the best efforts of strong judicial personalities to impose a strict and complete legalism on their own courts. With the Civil Law or Civil Law-derived legal systems, because of the continued prevalence of strict Civil Law principles of collegiality and anonymity in Court practice, the actual decision-making processes still tend to remain concealed, and with that the character and also the very existence of divisions within the Court and the particular intellectual positions taken by particular judges or informal groupings of judges within the Court. Nevertheless, it has been possible to lift the veil from the otherwise arcane proceedings of tribunals like the West German Federal Constitutional Court. We know, for example, that the personal intellectual influence of Judge Gerhard Leibholz, the eminent constitutional scholar in his own right, was very great in the evolution of the Court's collective thinking, and hence of its jurisprudence, on the key constitutional princple of equality before the law and the Parties-state democracy, with important and immediate application in terms of the constitutional control of the fairness of elections and the equitable functioning of political parties as organs of government.[24] And we shall also see the beginnings of formation of philosophical wings in the Court, grouping judges who find, increasingly, that they share the same general values and, perhaps also, the same general sense of the movement and direction of history, transcending the relatively casual elements of procedural base and contending parties in particular litigation coming before the Court. This tendency, paralleling those already well established, over a period of many years, within the United States Supreme Court, with its relatively open and public processes of decision-making and opinion-writing, is confirmed and extended as the Federal Constitutional Court begins to use the power – acquired by formal amendment to the Court Statute after considerable debate within the Court itself and in public legal circles – to record, publicly, the actual Court vote, and also to publish together with the official Opinion of Court signed dissenting opinions.

3. COURTS QUA JUDICIAL INSTITUTIONS: JUDICIAL SELF-RESTRAINT AND JUDICIAL ACTIVISM

(a) *Judicial auto-limitation: the Brandeis formulae*

As the great liberal jurist, Mr. Justice Brandeis, noted in his concurring opinion in *Ashwander* v. *Tenneessee Valley Authority* in 1936:

> 'Considerations of propriety, as well as long-established practice, demand that we refrain from passing upon the constitutionality of an Act of Congress unless obliged to do so in the proper performance of our judicial function, when the question is raised by a party whose interests entitle him to raise it.'[25]

The argument is clear enough. A Supreme Court is no more than a coordinate institution of government, in no way superior to executive and legislative institutions with which it is linked in obligations of mutual respect and mutual deference. The theory and practice of judicial review have to be reconciled with more general and overriding constitutional checks and balances, a difficult enough situation when the Court's review of executive or legislative action brings it into direct political collision with those other, coordinate institutions. Mr. Justice Brandeis' approach, if not a complete and satisfying resolution of the dilemma of judicial policy-making, at least tries to minimise the opportunities for unnecessary political conflict between the Court and executive and legislative authority, by establishing ground rules for the Court's intervention in great community policy issues – rules of judicial auto-limitation which any Supreme Court will prudently seek to apply before rushing in where even Angels might fear to tread. After noting that the U.S. Supreme Court had, in the past, frequently called attention to the 'great gravity and delicacy' of its function in passing upon the validity of an act of Congress, Mr. Justice Brandeis then set out, *seriatim,* the rules which the Court has – 'developed, for its own governance in the cases confessedly within its jurisdiction, ... under which it has avoided passing upon a large part of all the constitutional questions pressed upon it for decision':[26]

> '1. The Court will not pass upon the constitutionality of legislation in a friendly, non-adversary, proceeding... "It never was the thought that, by means of a friendly suit, a party beaten in the legislature could transfer to the courts an inquiry as to the constitutionality of the legislative act." [footnote omitted]

'2. The Court will not "anticipate a question of constitutional law in advance of the necessity of deciding it"... "It is not the habit of the court to decide questions of a constitutional nature unless absolutely necessary to a decision of the case".

'3. The Court will not "formulate a rule of constitutional law broader than is required by the precise facts to which it is to be applied".

'4. The Court will not pass upon a constitutional question although properly presented by the record, if there is also present some other ground upon which the case may be disposed of.

'5. The Court will not pass upon the validity of a statute upon complaint of one who fails to show that he is injured by its operation.

'6. The Court will not pass upon the constitutionality of a statute at the instance of one who has availed himself of its benefits.

'7. When the validity of an act of Congress is drawn in question, and even if a serious doubt of constitutionality is raised, it is a cardinal principle that this Court will first ascertain whether a construction of the statute is fairly possible by which the question may be avoided.'

These are sensible principles and, sensibly applied, it might be suggested, they might have avoided in a number of legal systems the considerable political embarrassments caused to Supreme Courts when they ventured into great political *causes célèbres,* involving fiercely-contested issues of public morality or social and economic choice, in which the Court's presence was not required or necessary under the Court's own rules and which, in any case, might more easily have been left to the other, popularly-elected institutions of community policy-making. In the case of the United States Supreme Court, the Brandeis rules of judicial auto-limitation have been most rigorously applied in the almost ritualistic insistence of an actual case/controversy as the necessary base of constitutional jurisdiction, and on the continuing rejection of any notion of rendering Advisory Opinions although that proposal has never been current in modern history. We shall see that the Brandeis auto-limitation rules, technical in character as they are, shade off into the larger philosophical concept of judicial self-restraint which has implications not simply for the observance of strict procedural requirements as a condition to the Court's exercising jurisdiction, but for the Court's behaviour after it is properly seized of jurisdiction in relation to the range and sweep of its decision-making and even more of its opinion-writing in support of its decisions. The joinder of issue, here, becomes one between the proponents of a certain judicial modesty in relation to the other, popularly elected organs of government which thus have their own full mandate for community policy-making – judicial self-restraint, and the proponents of a determinedly interventionist *rôle* by the Court, relating either to the general principles or 'spirit' of the Constitution or to some postulated 'higher law' grounds extrinsic to the constitutional charter itself. It is a debate within a debate, for both groups – those who opt for judicial self-restraint and those who espouse judicial activism – operate within the agreed context of a policy-making approach to the judicial function. It is all a matter of degree – of relative emphasis upon procedural requirements as a condition of exercising jurisdiction, of relative respect for executive-legislative authority, and of relative tact in expressing one's own judicial point of view on policy in rendering decisions; but the differences have bitterly divided the United States Supreme Court, above all among its post-1937, Roosevelt-nominated judges, all of whom professed to the mantle of judicial liberalism. We shall examine the philosophical conflict within the U.S. Supreme Court between Mr. Justice Frankfurter as the most sophisticated and erudite and historically-documented exponent of self-restraint, and the two prime liberal activists with their crusading libertarian motivation, Justices Hugo Black and William O. Douglas.[27]

(b) Standing-to-sue and the constitutional 'interest' requirements

In the meantime, if the strictly preliminary, procedural aspect of judicial auto-limitation be considered, we find as to the various national Supreme Courts a continuum running from the U.S. Supreme Court's strict case/controversy approach, to the ultra-permissive Canadian Supreme Court which has so relaxed earlier rather severe standards for the minimum degree of 'interest' necessary for a petitioner to be granted standing-to-sue to raise general constitutional issues, as to permit, for example, an ex-judge of the lower Federal Court, already retired on reaching the mandatory retirement age of seventy-five, to challenge the constitutionality of the federal Official Languages Act, establishing French and English on a basis of parity in federal Government services, although the ex-judge concerned could shew no apparent damage or injury to himself;[28] and so as to permit, also, a middle-aged, male, ex-Provincial Cabinet Minister, not apparently in a condition to become pregnant himself, to challenge the constitutionality of those sections of federal statute law in effect permitting therapeutic abortions under certain controlled circumstances.[29] It is tempting to think of these gestures of the Canadian Supreme Court as a latter-day attempt to meet Dicey's constitutional ideal of the free-willing individual vindicating his or her constitutional rights by ordinary law suits in the ordinary law courts,[30] unrealistic as Dicey's ideal is today in an era of enormous costs in Supreme Court litigation which virtually confine it to governments, corporations, and trade unions, or to well-financed private pressure groups or political lobbying organisations. The criterion of 'interest' allowed by the Canadian Supreme Court in permitting bringing of suits would appear, however, to be so lax and open-ended as to make a field day for politically disgruntled, sectarian action groups that have lost out by the ordinary democratic political processes in the ordinary constitutional-governmental arenas, but are financially affluent enough to be able to launch a partisan, guerilla war before the Courts in a last-ditch delaying action to frustrate majority opinion.

The Supreme Court of Japan, very early in its new, post-War phase, chose the American, case-controversy based approach to contitutional jurisdiction, when in the *Suzuki* case in 1952[31] it refused to accept a petition asking it to declare the newly-established National Police Reserve as unconstitutional as violating Article 9 of the Constitution of 1946 (the so-called 'No-War' clause). The Japanase Court rejected various Continental European, Civil Law analogies which, it was argued, allowed it to decide whether or not there was a concrete legal dispute, the Court indicating that while it might rule on issues where specific injury to rights was contested, it could not exercise jurisdiction on issues presented in the abstract. In similar vein, the United States Supreme Court, in 1970, in *Massachussets* v. *Laird,*[31a] refused, by a 6-to-3 vote, to accept jurisdiction over a suit initiated by the legislature of the State of Massachusetts to determine the constitutionality of American participation in the Vietnam armed conflict in the absence of a formal declaration of War. Two members of the Court, Justices Harlan and Stewart, would have been prepared to hear argument on standing-to-sue and justiciability, while a third judge, Justice Douglas, filed a formal dissent contesting, in some detail, the majority's rejection of the suit on both points.[31b] The Massachusetts legislature's approach to the Court had occurred at the height of the internal political conflict, in the United States, over the merits of U.S. involvement in Vietnam and at a time of widespread American dissent and civil disobedience, as American bombing raids were expanded in North Vietnam and Cambodia invaded in the Spring of 1970 at the same time that the Nixon administration was contending that the Vietnam war was ending.

(c) *Making an ally of time: conscious judicial attrition*

The West German Federal Constitutional Court, having, at its outset, both an Advisory Opinion jurisdiction (later abolished), and also highly facultative provisions for the raising of constitutional issues by official (governmental-legislative) parties, also experimented very early with another tool of judicial auto-limitation – what we might call conscious judicial attrition. In the early years of the Bonn Republic, which had been created by the decision of the three Western Military Occupation powers to restore sovereignty to a rump West Germany created by uniting their three territorial zones of occupation, the issue of relations between West

Germany and the new East Germany created by the Soviet Government out of the former Soviet Military Occupation Zone was omnipresent for it touched, of necessity, all other issues, including the continuance of the present Bonn Constitution stated in its final Article (Article 146) to be provisional only pending achievement of a 'constitution adopted by a free decision of the German people', an objective also referred to in the final recital of the Preamble to the Bonn Charter. The federal government had, however, initiated before the Court in November, 1951, the question of the constitutionality of the West German Communist Party, the Bonn constitution-makers of 1949, with memories of the subverting of the Weimar Republic by totalitarian political parties operating within the legislative arenas, having included a specific Article on Political Parties (Article 21) which, in addition to setting out their affirmative obligations (free establishment, conformity of internal organisation to democratic principles, public accounting for sources of funds), also declared to be unconstitutional those Parties which – 'by reason of their aims or the behaviour of their adherents, seek to impair or abolish the free democratic basic order or to endanger the existence of the Federal Republic'. (Article 21 (2)). In a case arising at the same time as the Communist Party case and referable to the same section of the Bonn charter, the Federal Constitutional Court decided, within a matter of months, to rule as being unconstitutional an other (and neo-Nazi) political party, the Socialist Reich Party, and to order its immediate dissolution and also the vacation of all Parliamentary seats held by its members. [32] This case, like the Communist Party case, had been initiated by the federal government before the Court, and there were perhaps policy considerations of appearing to administer equal justice to the political extremists of the right and of the left that had induced the federal Government to move against both parties at the same time. On the other hand, in the case of the Communist Party, there were also strong policy arguments against rendering a decision prematurely before other major aspects of East-West relations – the projected European Defence Community, grouping the main Continental Western European countries, including West Germany – had been resolved or otherwise clarified. It was, above all, an issue of foreign policy with internal, municipal law consequences; and there were arguments to be made for not involving the Court in its solution, although once seized of the matter the Court could hardly refuse to decide since the Bonn charter stipulated, in quite categorical terms, that – 'the Federal Constitutional Court shall decide on the question of unconstitutionality'. (Article 21 (2)). What the Court did, instead, was to make an ally of time and adopt a policy of deliberately dragging its feet, and allowing the extra-judicial, political facts to achieve their own momentum. Finally, five years after the matter had been initiated before it, the Court gave its ruling in 1956, declaring the Communist Party to be unconstitutional – as it could hardly have avoided doing on the facts, in the light of its decision in the cognate case of the Socialist Reich Party. [33] Even then, it seems the Court might have been disposed to wait a little longer still; but four of the judges of its First Senate, which was seized with the matter, were due to retire or to present themselves for reelection in the Court election of 1956, and there were doubts as to the First Senate's continuity and its ability, in constitutional terms, to function beyond that date in regard to the case. By 1956, however, some of the more awkward political questions present in 1951 when the matter was first raised before the Court – the constitutionality, and also the political wisdom, of West Germany's participation in the proposed European Defence Community, as it was being pressured to do by the United States and other Western countries – had been solved by the movement of political events (here the collapse of the European Defence Community project), and East-West relations generally were calmer with the new Khrushchev *régime* in control in the Soviet Union. In short, the times were much calmer, and a particular judicial decision that might have been explosive if rendered as early as 1951, and that could hardly have been different if the Court's reputation for judicial integrity were to be maintained, could be handed down and received, in West Germany and outside, with a certain element of political equanimity.

(d) *Collegial solidarity on a plural-banc tribunal*

In its resolution of the European Defence Community controversy, already referred to, the West German Federal Constitutional Court also demonstrated, very early in its history, a certain skill in steering a course through dangerous political shoals and in not allowing itself to be drawn unnecessarily into political problems more sensibly belonging to the other, coordinate, executive and legislative arms of the federal government. What was involved was the political issue of the new West German state's integration into the proposed new European Defence Community, to link the six states of Continental Western Europe already associated in the new European Coal and Steel Community. It was a political issue because of its potential effects on the long-range goal of an All-German state, uniting West Germany and East Germany, to which all political parties were committed, the Adenauer Christian Democratic coalition Government supporting the E.D.C. project and the Opposition Social Democrats opposing and thus effectively denying the two-thirds majorities in both Houses of the federal legislature necessary to secure a constitutional amendment empowering West German participation in the project.[34] In the complicated party political manoeuvring which followed, rival political actors on the Bonn scene endeavoured to make use of the Federal Constitutional Court in its various jurisdictional capacities in order to give a constitutional sanction to their differing political objectives. In January, 1952, 145 Social Democratic members of the *Bundestag* (federal lower House) – amounting to the one-third of the *Bundestag* necessary to seize the Court with a constitutional issue[35] – petitioned the First Senate of the Court, the so-called 'Red Senate', with its supposedly Social Democratic-leaning judicial majority, for a declaration of the unconstitutionality of any West German participation in the E.D.C. project. But the First Senate refused to become embroiled in the issue, concluding, in a decision given at the end of July, 1952, that a ruling at this stage would be premature and that judicial review could only be available in respect to statutes which had been formally enacted by the legislature.[36] In the meantime, in June, 1952, the federal President, Dr. Heuss, a member of the Free Democratic party coalition partner of the Adenauer Government, asked the Federal Constitutional Court in its *plenum* or Full Court, uniting both Senates, to give an Advisory Opinion ruling on whether the E.D.C. treaties, so far as they authorised West German participation, were compatible with the Bonn constitution. In December, 1952, the Adenauer Government, in a petition filed on behalf of some two hundred members of the Government coalition in the *Bundestag,* now approached the Second Senate of the Court, the so-called 'Black Senate' with its supposedly pro-Government judicial majority, for a ruling that, in effect, the E.D.C. treaties could be adopted in the *Bundestag* by simple majority vote (without the necessity of proceeding *via* a constitutional amendment with the special two-thirds majorities required for them). The Adenauer Government had evidently concluded that if it would be bound to lose in the First Senate with its 'Red' political colouration, it would also be doomed to be outvoted in the *plenum* when the First and Second Senates ('Red' and 'Black') were put together; and that the most successful political course would be to approach the Second Second, the 'Black Senate', for an expectedly favourable ruling.

Such political games by the contending political forces in Bonn, attempting as they were to play one Court jurisdiction off against another, could seriously embarrass the Court before public opinion if the various rulings by the two Senates and of the *plenum* should happen to differ from each other in their conclusions and reasoning. But the various political actors in Bonn clearly underestimated the judges' intelligence and their sense of collective solidarity, and also their political sophistication and ability to react collegially to such a threat. Immediately after the Adenauer coalition petition to the Second Senate, the *plenum* ruled, by a 20 to 2 vote, that any decision by the *plenum* by way of Advisory Opinion would be legally binding on either Court Senate when considering an identical legal question in the future.[37] This was patently an indignant judicial response to such blatantly selective invocation of Court jurisdiction, and it had some immediate results. The federal President now withdrew his request to the *plenum* of the Court for an Advisory Opinion;[38] and then the Second Senate proceeded to reject the Adenauer coalition's petition, this on technical, procedural, adjectival law grounds, (based on a strict interpretation of the allocation of jurisdictional competence under the Court Statute and ultimately the constitution, which need not here concern us).[39] The most important thing was that, whatever personal views or preferences the individual judges might have had as to the E.D.C. project and West German participation, they had all, in a response as a collegial body to the necessities of efficient judicial administration, exercised judicial self-restraint and returned the controversy over the E.D.C. to the public political arenas for political resolution.

(e) *The time factor again: the issue is 'Moot'*

The International Court of Justice, in the *Nuclear Tests* litigation in the 1970s,[40] had an opportunity in substantive law terms to be on the side of the Angels. But the Court majority put it all aside in deference to procedural law requirements, and it was the liberal activist judges on the Court and the ones most open to the argument of policy considerations in law, who decided the Court in favour of judicial self-restraint. How did it all come about? At the opening of of the 1970s, when President Nixon had made his highly successful visits to Peking and Moscow, and when the Soviet Union and the United States were talking to each other and *Détente* was in full flower, certain new issues of International Law, previously subordinated to the paramount East-West peace and security issues, suddenly surfaced and became 'trendy'. The new International Law of Environment, involving postulated imperative principles of law as to protection of the Earth and its scarce natural resources, was one of these issues, and it gained a large popularity before Third World countries came to conclude that the main impetus came from post-industrial societies anxious to preserve other societies than themselves in their pristine, undeveloped state and unwilling to share any of the financial cost to the Third World countries involved in their foregoing or retarding industrialisation as a means of retaining forests, wild game reserves. All this was to come later, however. At the beginning of the 1970s, socialist administrations newly elected in Australia and New Zealand in replacement of long-time conservative governments, moved in the International Court to try to ban the French Government's holding of high altitude nuclear test explosions in the mid-South Pacific, this although the earlier conservative governments in those countries had cooperated, uncritically and indeed enthusiastically, in twenty years of British and United States nuclear test explosions in their own countries and in the South Pacific generally. Allowing for the legal principle of State continuity in the succession from conservative to socialist governments in the two countries concerned, it was surely a case for application of the old Equity principle that he who seeks Equity must come to Court with clean hands. However, the International Court, by a narrow majority, decided the preliminary and procedural issue in favour of the two complainant states, Australia and New Zealand, and voted to exercise jurisdiction. By the time the hearings on the substantive issue arrived, the French Government which, for technical-legal reasons relating to the original general French adherence to the Court, had denied the Court's jurisdiction and refused to be present in Court or to present direct legal argument, announced that it had completed its high altitude nuclear experiments in the South Pacific and would hold no more. This was the issue on which the International Court, by a 9 to 6 majority, finally decided the case. Taking judicial notice of high-level official statements – by the French President, Valéry Giscard d'Estaing, the French Foreign Minister, and the French Defence Minister – made in systematic and sustained and repeated fashion from 1974 onwards, the Court shewed flexibility and imagination in relation to the doctrine of estoppel, hitherto viewed, too narrowly, as restricted to limited, *inter partes* estoppel, and held that these unilateral declarations of intention by the French Government should be considered as legally binding.[41] That being so, there was no longer any concrete case/controversy or genuine adversary proceeding, and so the proceeding before the Court had become moot and the Court should not proceed further.[42] The decision is a striking affirmation of the principle that Courts should not act in vain, and that they are not there to deal with abstract, philosophical issues, not involving or no longer involving actual legal conflicts, at the mere whim of state litigants. The International Court has, of course, its own Advisory Opinion jurisdiction, in terms of the Court Statute (Article 65); and abstract issues not directly flowing from any case/controversy may certainly be raised there. But it is the organised World Community, through the United Nations, that initiates such requests to the International Court for Advisory Opinions; and the difference between the collectivity of U.N. member-states and casual State-litigants is clear. The Opinion of Court in *Nuclear Tests* is thought to be the work of Judge Manfred Lachs, and since, in terms of his general substantive law philosophy, Judge Lachs might normally have been considered as favourable to the abstract issue raised by the two litigants, Australia and New Zealand, it is clear that the Court was anxious, by its procedural ruling, to demonstrate that it was, indeed, (to borrow Judge Manley Hudson's words as earlier invoked by Sir Gerald Fitzmaurice) a 'responsible magistrature' and certainly not an 'academy of jurists' sitting merely to render opinions in the air.[43] After its own very conscious application of the rules of judicial self-restraint, in *Nuclear Tests* in 1974, the International Court, only a decade later, disposed very easily and elegantly – *sub silentio* – of a 'moot'-ness argument, in its preliminary decision of 10 May 1984 on the complaint filed by Nicaragua against the United States.[43a] The Nicaraguan Government had, on 9 April 1984, instituted proceedings in the International Court against the United States based upon the clandestine political-military operations then being mounted against it by the U.S. Central Intelligence Agency, involving, amongst other things, the laying of mines in Nicaraguan ports so as to interdict the passage of Nicaraguan and also foreign merchant ships. The U.S. Government had, in anticipation of the Nicaraguan approach to the International Court, already, on 6 April 1984, informed the United Nations that it was temporarily modifying its acceptance of the Compulsory Jurisdiction of the Court, in order to exclude Court jurisdiction over the United States in cases involving Central America, for the next two years.[43b] For purposes of its preliminary decision of 10 May 1984, the Court did not, according to its own past jurisprudence (including *Nuclear Tests. Interim Protection,* of 1973),[43c] need to resolve this jurisdictional question before proceeding, pending final judgment, to grant Provisional Measures of relief as requested by the Nicaraguan Government. These Provisional Measures, as now approved by the Court, included a Court order that – 'the United States of America should immediately cease and refrain from any active restricting, blocking or endangering access to or from Nicaraguan ports, and, in particular, the laying of mines' (by unanimous vote of the 15-member Court); and a further order that – 'the right to sovereignty and to political independence possessed by the Republic of Nicaragua... should be fully respected and should not in any way be jeopardised by any military or paramilitary activities which are prohibited by principles of International Law', (by 14-to-1 vote of the judges, the U.S. national judge, Judge Schwebel, dissenting). For purposes of this preliminary judgment, the Court did not yield to the U.S. Government contention that the whole affair had become moot, at least so far as the mining of Nicaraguan ports was concerned, in so far as the U.S. Central Intelligence Agency had, allegedly, by the time of the present process, already terminated such mining operations. In refusing to entertain any argument of 'moot'-ness, and in the very sweep of its ruling imposing Provisional Measures, the International Court, without doubt, reflected the widespread condemnation, in the World Community at large and even among the United States' political-military allies, over the clandestine U.S. Central Intelligence Agency operations against Nicaragua. Such U.S. Government actions seemed not merely patently illegal but, in their very excess, might be enough to outweigh the normal Court insistence, in the exercise of its *inter partes* jurisdiction, on an actual, ongoing controversy, so as to avoid the Court's ruling in vain on an issue already academic and by-passed by historical events. The Court, it seems, in the same spirit in which Chief Justice Sir Edward Coke had admonished James I some centuries earlier, was at pains to establish that even a King is under God and the Law and the lesson may be worth repeating even today.

This normal Court insistence on an actual, ongoing controversy as a precondition of decision-making, and the policy of prudent judicial self-restraint upon which it rests, were perhaps too easily overlooked by the Supreme Court of Canada when, at the end of 1982, it ruled on the so-called 'Quebec Veto'.[44] The Court's ruling came a full half year after the legal completion by the federal Government of the purely formal, symbolic 'patriation' of the Canadian constitution from the former 'parent', Imperial country, Great Britain, which had originally enacted the constitution in 1867 as the charter of a then purely subordinate, colonial territory within the British Empire overseas. The 'patriation' had been achieved by resolution of both Houses of the federal Parliament, followed by formal legislation by the British Parliament, and it was achieved without the concurrence of the Government of Quebec and, indeed, over its strong protests.[45] But the act was done, and it all seemed a little late for the Quebec Government now, after the event, to try to close the stable door after the horse had already bolted. Quebec asked the Courts to rule that such approach by joint resolution of the two federal Houses, without Quebec's consent, was unconstitutional. Surely the issue, by now, was moot? It was too late, legally, to reverse what had already been done, and there could be no further federal Government approach to the British Parliament since any residual British legislative power in relation to Canada, such as it might be, terminated with the act of 'patriation'. The Supreme Court of Canada did, indeed, answer NO! – that no consent of the Quebec Government was constitutionally necessary; but the better approach, and one much more in accord with the character of the judicial process, would surely have been to decline to rule at all on the basis that the issue, in strictly constitutional law terms, had become purely academic; and that if any *ex post facto* demand for satisfaction were now involved it might better be addressed through the ordinary, political processes and left to inter-governmental political-diplomatic negotiation and exchange.

110

NOTES

1. See, generally, the author's *Constitution-Making. Principles, Process, Practice* (1981).
2. *Ibid.*, p. 42 *et seq.*
3. Pound borrowed, here, from the great German legal philosopher, Kohler. See J. Kohler, *Lehrbuch der Rechtsphilosophie* (1908); Roscoe Pound, *Social Control through Law* (1942); Julius Stone, *The Province and Function of Law* (1946), pp. 355 *et seq.*, 487 *et seq.*
4. M. S. McDougal and H. D. Lasswell, 'The identification and appraisal of diverse systems of public order', 53 *American Journal of International Law* 1 (1959).
5. For the most comprehensive, in comparative law terms, analysis, see Chester James Anticau, *Constitutional Construction* (1982).
6. Reported in 26 *Australian Law Journal* 2, at p. 4 (1952).
7. *Judicial Review in the English-Speaking World* (4th ed., 1969), p. 76 *et seq.*
8. I.C.J. Reports 1966, p. 6.
9. *South West Africa, Preliminary Objections, Judgment,* I.C.J. Reports 1962, p. 319.
10. *Legal Consequences for States of the Continued Presence of South Africa in Namibia (South West Africa) notwithstanding Security Council Resolution 276 (1970), Advisory Opinion,* I.C.J. Reports 1971, p. 16.
11. Manley Hudson, *The Permanent Court of International Justice, 1920-1942,* at p. 511.
12. Cited by Fitzmaurice J., Dissenting Opinion, I.C.J. Reports 1971, p. 16, at p. 303.
13. I.C.J. Reports 1966, p. 6, at p. 441.
14. *Gopalan* v. *State of Madras,* 13 *Supreme Court Journal* (India) 174 (1950); A.I.R. *1950* S.C. 27.
15. *Ibid.*, pp. 214-215.
16. *Ibid.*, p. 217.
17. *Ibid.*, p. 186.
18. 14 *Supreme Court Journal* (India) 182 (1951); A.I.R. *1951* S.C. 128.
19. *Ibid.*, p. 185.
20. 4 Wheaton 316 (1819).
21. *Re Alberta Statutes* [1938] 2 D.L.R. 81.
22. [1938] 2 D.L.R. 81, at pp. 107-108 (per Duff, C.J.); at p. 119 (per Cannon J.).
23. *Judicial Review in the English-Speaking World* (4th ed., 1969), at p. 21 *et seq.*
24. See Leibholz' early, seminal study of the principle of Equality before the Law, written in the capacity of Professor in the between-the-two-World-Wars period: G. Leibholz, *Die Gleichheit vor dem Gesetz. Eine Studie auf rechtsvergleichender und rechtsphilosophischer Grundlage* (1925); G. Leibholz, *Das Wesen der Repräsentation unter besonderer Berücksichtigung des Repräsentativsystems.*
25. 297 U.S. 288, 345 (1936).
26. 297 U.S. 288, 346-348 (1936).
27. *Judicial Review in the English-Speaking World* (4th ed., 1969), p. 174 *et seq.*
28. *Thorson* v. *Attorney-General of Canada* [1975], 1 S.C.R. 138.
29. Supreme Court of Canada, decision of 1 December 1981.
30. A. V. Dicey, *Introduction to the Study of the Law of the Constitution* (9th ed., by E.C.S. Wade, 1939).
31. Supreme Court of Japan, Grand Bench, decision of 8 October 1952; John M. Maki, *Court and Constitution in Japan. Selected Supreme Court Decisions, 1948-60* (1964), at p. 362.
31a. *Massachusetts,* v. *Laird, Secretary of Defence.* 400 U.S. 886 (1970).
31b. *Ibid.*
32. Decision of 23 October 1952, 2 B Verf GE 1 (1953) (First Senate).

33. Decision of 17 August 1956, 5 B Verf GE 85 (1956) (First Senate).
34. Bonn Constitution, Art. 79 (2).
35. Bonn Constitution, Art. 93 (1).
36. Decision of 30 July 1952, 1 B Verf GE 396 (1952) (First Senate).
37. Decision of 9 December 1952, 2 B Verf GE 79 (1953) (*plenum*).
38. The federal President's request for Advisory Opinion had been made in terms of s. 97 (1) and (2) of the Court Statute, as originally enacted in 1951: in considerable measure as a result of the experience of its use in the EDC controversy, the Advisory Opinion jurisdiction was abolished in 1956, under s. 1 (19) of the Statute of that same year amending the Court Statute. The federal President's formal withdrawal of his request to the Court for Advisory Opinion is officially noted in the Court's records, 2 B Verf GE 143, at 147 (1953).
39. Decision of 7 March 1953, 2 B Verf GE 143 (1953) (Second Senate).
40. *Nuclear Tests (Australia v. France), Interim Protection, Order of 22 June 1973,* I.C.J. Reports 1973, p. 99; *Nuclear Tests (Australia v. France), Judgment of 20 December 1974,* I.C.J. Reports 1974, p. 253.
41. I.C.J. Reports 1974, p. 253, at pp. 264-268.
42. *Ibid.,* pp. 271-272.
43. I.C.J. Reports 1971, p. 16, at p. 303 (cited by Fitzmaurice J., Dissenting Opinion).
43a. *Military and Paramilitary Activities in and against Nicaragua (Nicaragua v. U.S.A.), Provisional Measures, Order of 10 May 1984,* I.C.J. Reports 1984, p. 169.
43b. United Nations, N.Y., Press Release, WS/11, 13 April 1984.
43c. *Nuclear Tests (Australia v. France), Interim Protection, Order of 22 June 1973,* I.C.J. Reports 1973, p. 99.
44. *Re Attorney-General of Quebec and Attorney-General of Canada,* 140 D.L.R. (3d) 385 (1982).
45. See, generally, the author's *Canada and the Constitution 1979-1982. Patriation and the Charter of Rights* (1982).

CHAPTER VI

THE COURTS AND THE CONSTITUTIONAL *GRUNDNORM*

We approach the very large problem of the general constitutional and governmental processes, and the *rôle* of the Courts in them. It is a problem with its own special contradictions and antinomies, and the responses of the Courts have not been uniform as between the different national legal systems surveyed, or even within the same legal system over different time periods. In the one sense because of the Courts are, themselves, an integral part of the general constitutional and governmental processes, they can claim a special knowledge of the internal organisation and workings of parallel, coordinate constitutional-governmental institutions, and a special competence, therefore, to arbitrate or regulate conflicts arising within them. On the other hand, simply because the judiciary, the executive, and the legislature are coordinate institutions, in no way subordinate the one to the other, separation of powers principles come into play involving constitutional obligations of mutual respect and deference, and self-restraint that apply *inter se*. The Court's obligations of self-restraint may become the stronger, in political and constitutional terms, if the judges are not elected, directly or indirectly, or submitted to legislature-based ratification of their appointments to the Courts; for their claims to constitutional legitimacy and to a mandate to control the popularly-elected institutions of government are then at their lowest. For this reason Courts in many different systems have developed special constitutional-legal categories for legally immunising themselves against the necessity to make pronouncements, on demand, as to the alleged constitutionality or unconstitutionality of particular exercises in constituent power or assertions of executive or legislative authority. Such categories, as developed and actively utilised by the Courts become instruments of judicial self-restraint: we see the doctrine of 'political question', in which, *ex hypothesi,* the Courts will not intervene, developed by the United States Supreme Court and applied also by other Common Law-based constitutional courts. It has its counterpart, in the French Civil Law, in the doctrine of 'acte de Gouvernement'. The contours and reach of the doctrine of 'political question' are not clear, though its consequences are: once they have decided a particular problem brought before them is a 'political question', the Courts will not intervene. The category has developed piecemeal, on a case by case basis, with little serious attempt at an overarching conceptualisation or synthesis. As we have seen, most great constitutional controversies are also political ones. The rule of judicial non-intervention seems to have emerged experientially, as a rule of judicial prudence, for fear of getting one's fingers burned. On the other hand, as we will see, the category itself and its list of non-justiciable, non-judicially reviewable constitutional-governmental actions has tended to contract in more recent years as judicial expertise and judicial confidence have increased, and also as the judges have come increasingly to accept that in relation to certain basic community problems, it is either a matter of the judges' intervening, or else of no one intervening, with the result that grave constitutional abuses will remain unsolved. In practical terms, the category of 'political question' has seemed, in the past, to involve the three main groups of problems: problems going to the *Grundnorm* or ultimate source of legal authority in the state; intra-Governmental, inter-institutional conflicts – what, in German terms, is classified as *Organstreitigkeiten;* and finally, electoral questions. Only the first of these three groups of problems would seem to be capable of argument as so intrinsically *political* as to be necessarily non-legal and non-justiciable: the argument, so far as it goes, would maintain that issues of the nature and survival of the state are absolute ones and properly beyond the competence of Courts. The second of the three, intra-Governmental, inter-institutional conflicts, raise separation-of-powers issues above all, and the Courts' non-intervention is predicated upon the obligation of deference and self-restraint *vis-à-vis* other, coordinate institutions of Government. The last of the three, electoral questions, were traditionally (and wrongly, it may be suggested) considered as involving technical problems beyond the ability of judges to comprehend or their expertise to resolve in useful ways.

The *Grundnorm,* as Kelsen defined it, is the authoritative starting point of any legal system.[1] It is, by definition, a pre-legal, meta-legal, *political* fact. Once the *Grundnorm* has been established, however, and that will also be a question of fact and usually self-evident, the legal system and its institutions, processes, and substantive principles flow logically from it. Many major legal systems begin with extra-legal, unconstitutional, potentially treasonable acts that are only validated in legal terms *ex post facto,* by the fact of the political success of the initially illegal acts. This is true, for example, of the ultimate historical origins of the present British constitutional settlement, the so-called 'Glorious Revolution' of 1688; of the very first American constitution after the political-military break with Imperial Britain in 1776, the Articles of Confederatin which were adopted in 1779 and endured until the present Constitution of the United States was adopted in 1787. It will be only rarely that the transition from one *Grundnorm* to another will occur peacefully and consensually and as an act of rational will in which one political *élite* hands over power to another and different *élite,* as with a few of the happier instances of Imperial decolonisation after World War II; or in which a politically mature and enlightened people attempts, without external pressures, to reform or restructure its own internal base of power and ground rules in order, variously, to widen popular participation in the system of government or to enable it better to handle and resolve pressing community problems. This latter situation applies, no doubt, in the passage from the Articles of Confederation to the new United States Constitution, a few years after Imperial Britain had legally accepted its military defeat in North America and abandoned its erstwhile pretensions to sovereignty over the former colonies; and in the movement from the Constitution of 1848 to the present Swiss Constitution of 1874; and perhaps in the so-called constitutional 'patriation' exercise in Canada in the period 1980-2,[2] in which the last purely ceremonial or symbolic links from a British colonial past were eliminated and attempts, (not completely successful, however), were made to provide a new constitutional starting point with new or remade constitutional institutions and processes and a new, constitutionally-entrenched Charter of Rights and Freedoms. Most often, however, the abandonment of an earlier *Grundnorm* and its replacement by another, will occur under conditions of national emergency, – military defeat, political or social revolution, or under the imminent threat of *force majeure,* and although it has proved possible to rally a surprising degree of national consensus and support for a new *régime* and for a new political-constitutional settlement under these circumstances, the resulting new constitutional charter will often be hurriedly conceived and drafted, ill-digested and contradictory in many places, and able to command support mainly on a *de minimis* basis because there is no consensus for anything more positive or more coherent and connected in philosophy.[3] The constitutional system of the Third French Republic, provisionally proclaimed with the French military defeat at Sedan in September 1870 and the downfall of Napoleon III, and consolidated, in successive steps, with organic laws of 1873 and of early and mid-1875, is an example of this, and it remains to note that like other *régimes* of transition, conceived and supported as such until further, broader consensus on its replacement should emerge, it performed adequately enough for most people and survived until the French military defeat of 1940. The post-World War II constitutional systems of Japan and West Germany have their origins in the disasters for the two countries of their participation, and loss, in the great military events that ended in 1945;

for this meant, in each case, prolonged military occupation, truncation (in the case of Japan) and truncation and political division (in the case of Germany) of the pre-War national territories, and also being charged with the enormous burden of moral guilt and economic reparation imposed by the victorious Allies, the United States, Great Britain, and the Soviet Union in their wholly Manichaean conception of historical causation and responsibility for the political origins of the then recent War. This explains some of the patent contradictions in the new *Grundnorm,* established in Japan in 1946, and in rump West Germany in 1949; for these contradictions reflect the political ambivalence of the Allied Occupation powers concerned at the time, (as well, perhaps, as the dangers of 'moralising' positions in foreign policy, that derive from essentially simplistic conceptions of history of the sort formed too easily in shooting Wars or even 'Cold Wars'). The new *Grundnorm,* as the authoritative starting point for Japan in the post-War era, reflects the political facts-of-life of the military defeat of 1945, the loss of the outer islands to the Soviet Union, the military occupation and government by the United States in displacement of the pre-existing system, and the enforced assumption by Japan of the total burden of 'War guilt' for the Pacific and South-East Asian theatres. The basic antithesis lies in the positive law entrenchment of Japanese War guilt in the new constitutional charter of 1946, in the 'No-War' sections that were deliberately designed to prevent Japan from ever rearming again or becoming a military power; and in the basic political fact-of-life that the United States and the other Western powers were eventually restoring legal sovereignty to Japan in the anticipation of integrating it into the Western political-military alliance system as a buffer against the Soviet Union (and eventually Communist China) in the then emerging East-West 'Cold War' conflict. It was inevitable, under these circumstances, that the Supreme Court of Japan would soon find itself at the centre of the battle between rival political forces inside Japan itself, and called upon to resolve the philosophical contradictions in the new post-War *Grundnorm* by producing a new political-legal synthesis.

The contradictions in the case of West Germany were essentially the same, though less acute perhaps in their representation in constitutional verbal formulation, since the three Western Military Occupation powers had, by that time, had just a little more time for reflection on *Realpolitik* dictates and for ridding themselves of some of the moral encumbrance of unilateral 'War guilt' assumptions. In restoring legal sovereignty to their own three zones of Germany, in 1949, as the rump state of West Germany, the Western Allies certainly intended and expected to be able to make West Germany an ally in the then already well-established, East-West 'Cold War' conflict; but deference to their own publicly proclaimed

War aims of the recent 1939-1945 military conflict period and to their own carefully nurtured public opinion in their own countries, required that the venture be rendered politically palatable by requiring the new West Germany to become 'democratic' as a condition of restoration of sovereignty. As in Japan, however, the Allied Military Occupation powers' own propaganda as to the War guilt burden had its own success with the local, occupied population concerned, and necessitated some skilful verbal compromises or contrived ambiguities in the ensuing new, local constitutional charter. A proclaimedly peaceful, permanently disarmed West Germany might still perhaps hope for eventual political reunification with Soviet-sponsored East Germany; while a West Germany, integrated into the Western political and economic system, and rearmed, might not. The new *Grundnorm* reflects, and the constitutional charter itself expresses, in terms, the contradictions: the necessary affirmations, in the Preamble and in the final Article of the new charter, of the goal, albeit a distant goal, of German reunification, and a deliberate silence, a consciously contrived constitutional gap, on the issue of military power. This gap was later filled, in measure, by express constitutional amendments effected in 1954 and 1968, [Bonn Constitution of 1949, Article 73 (1) as amended], when the contradictions had been substantially resolved at the political level, and a new national consensus formed on this point; but it was no doubt inevitable that the Courts, in West Germany, right from the outset and to some extent even now, should be asked by the contending political forces to resolve the antithesis, implicit in the *Grundnorm* of 1949, of a defeated and disarmed Germany and one effectively rallied to the Western political-military bloc.

While the new, post-decolonisation constitution of the post-War Republic of India was indeed the work of a wholly indigenous, national Constituent Assembly, the former Imperial power had done little or nothing to prepare the former colonial territory for a planned and staged, graceful devolution and transfer of power. There was, indeed, virtually no period of enlightened constitutional transition and preparation of representative democratic government. The national Constituent Assembly, hastily put together in 1946 when the Attlee Labour Government in Great Britain suddenly announced its decision to quit India, was of necessity a politically *élitist,* non-elected body, there being neither the time nor the constitutional machinery to endow it with a popular, elected base and mandate. Its dominant members were well-educated, often outside India, cultivated and well-to-do, and the narrowness of the political-social base was accentuated in ethnic-cultural terms with the withdrawal, shortly after the formation of the Constituent Assembly, of most of the Muslim delegates who moved away to form their own distinctive Constituent Assembly and, eventually, their own separate and autonomous, independent state of Pakistan, leaving the predominantly Hindu, rump state of India. The Constitution of the Republic of India, adopted in 1949 and coming into force in early 1950, simply because it was the product of a national Constituent Assembly freed from external, Imperial political pressures, comes as close as any organic law can ever achieve to being a reflex of the new political *Grundnorm* after independence. Without the substantial bloc of Muslim delegates, the constitutional charter in religious matters reflects the clear preference of the new post-independence political *élite* for a secular state; but in social and economic matters, the charter tends to reflect the narrowness of the social and economic base of that *élite* in their roots in *bourgeois* liberal values, and the conflicts presented with that same *élite's* openings, often through education in Imperial Britain, to politically enlightened social democratic ideas of the sort circulating in the British Universities in the between-the-two-World-Wars era. The basic antinomy between inherent, class-derived, liberal values, and educationally-acquired social democratic ideals, present in the Constituent Assembly, is reflected in the constitutional charter antinomy between the Fundamental Rights (Part III) and the Directive Principles of State Policy (Part IV), of the new charter, the one with a certain, express *laissez-faire* philosophy, and the other with a determinedly social and economic interventionist, outlook. It was inevitable again that this constitutional charter antinomy would end up before the Courts, as new, politically progressive, economic planning programmes were introduced by the fedeal Government, these programmes involving nationalisation or redistribution of wealth and property from the private to the public domain. In the 1960s and early 1970s, the courts and executive-legislative authority at the federal level became locked in political battle, as the federal Government attempted to counter hostile judicial decisions declaring such programmes to be unconstitutional by reference to the Fundamental Rights sections of the Constitution, by formally amending the Constitution to overcome the Court judgments by putting the constitutional text and intent beyond doubt and certainly beyond judicial tampering. The Courts, however, carried on the war with executive-legislative authority by venturing to examine the nature and quality of constitutional amendments, as such, and to set legally permissible limits thereto, beyond which, in the Courts' view, executive-legislative authority could not venture. Such issues go, of course, to the nature and quality of the *Grundnorm,* and to the constituent process itself – here the ability to change the *Grundnorm* by the constitutional amending machinery. We shall treat of this under the rubric of Constituent Power.

Finally, the Constitutions of the Fifth French Republic grew out of the evident breakdown of the Fourth Republic with its inability to resolve the Algerian War crisis. The Fourth Republic, itself, had been organised and established in 1946 after the failure of the original 'Liberation', Gaullist-led initiative for a complete renewal of French governmental institutions and processes, in the immediate, post-1944 Liberation era, in replacement of the politically discredited apparatus of the Third Republic on which, rightly or wrongly, so much of the political obloquy for the military disaster and political collapse of 1940 was heaped. General de Gaulle's constitutional programme in 1944-5 called for a strong presidential executive and a doing away with the Government-by-Assembly which had so weakened and frustrated governmental decision-making under the Third Republic. The failure of the Gaullist project, and General de Gaulle's consequent temporary withdrawal from public life meant that the remaining constitution-makers for the Fourth Republic built a constitutional charter very much in the image of the old Third Republic, and it was characterised, immediately it went into operation, by the same ministerial instability and games of musical chairs between rival political factions competing for the right to form Cabinets, that had so weakened the Third Republic. The Gaullist-made Constitution of the Fifth Republic, in reaction, deliberately established a strong presidential-executive *régime* and subordinated the legislature accordingly. The continuance, until the Presidential elections of 1981, of strong Gaullist, or Gaullist-supported, incumbents in the office of President and of parallel majority coalitions in the legislature meant that the original Gaullist design of the constitution, with a two-headed executive of strong President and subordinate Prime Minister designated by the President, was not seriously challenged, throughout the period, and neither were the basic social and economic values against which the charter had been adopted in 1958. We shall see various points at which constitutional issues going to the *Grundnorm* and to constituent power were thought to be involved – the innovation of direct popular election of the President, and the abortive regional reform of 1969 which was treated by President de Gaulle as the occasion for his own retirement – though none of these, it might be suggested, was fundamental in character.

1. CHANGE IN THE *GRUNDNORM:* LEGAL CONSEQUENCES

What should be the attitude of the Courts to a sharp, revolutionary break from the pre-existing *Grundnorm* and its replacement by a new one, in ways not conforming to the processes for fundamental constitutional change established under and required by the old *Grundnorm*. In the contemporary era of representative, participatory constitutional democracy, a sufficient constitutional legitimacy may be considered to be established for the new *Grundnorm* by its subsequent ratification in plebiscite or similar popular form. It is a rule of constitutional prudence not to make charters so difficult and time-consuming to change, by building in too many restrictions and limitations into the constitutional amending machinery, as to invite the by-passing of that constitutional amending machinery altogether in favour of a fresh appeal to direct democracy. Certainly, some of the constitutional charters of the French Revolutionary era, with their in-built constitutional guarantees against 'premature' or too rapid change, were ignored altogether as to those stipulations when the charters themselves became quickly dated or inconvenient; and no one was heard to impugn the constitutional legitimacy of the new constitutional charters that replaced them, by direct action without conforming to the pre-defined rules of the game as to constitutional change. Nevertheless, in the desire to make assurance doubly sure, to secure extra constitutional legitimacy, and perhaps simply to maintain the goodwill of a predecessor *régime,* many of the transitions, today, from an old (often Imperial) *Grundnorm* to a new (post-decolonisation) *Grundnorm* shew a scrupulous, surprisingly literal conformance to the old constitutional processes, and this sometimes when the actual transfer of power may have been preceded and finally induced only by a chain of bitter political events, passage of arms, or even a successful War of National Liberation. When Canadian Prime Minister Trudeau introduced his constitutional 'patriation' project in 1980, involving the ending of the last formal, purely symbolic and ceremonial links between Canada and the former parent, Imperial power, Great Britain, the process of constitutional adoption involved full respect for the pre-existing constitutional customs or conventions dating from the original Imperial days, of a resolution adopted by both Houses of the Canadian federal Parliament then submitted to the British Government and followed by legislation of the British Parliament formally enacting the Canadian Parliamentary Resolution. This original, Imperial-era process was enormously time-consuming and required, for its consummation, very difficult political compromises at the federal-provincial level within Canada itself; but the Canadian Prime Minister considered, no doubt correctly on the facts, that not to conform to the processual requirements as to change of the pre-existing *Grundnorm* would be a form of constitutional revolution that might weaken the subsequent political as well as constitutional legitimacy of the constitutional 'patriation' project, when adopted. To act otherwise was never seriously considered, even though the direct action route to 'patriation' of the Canadian Constitution, through federal Parliamentary action followed by popular plebiscite vote, would have offered enormous political attractions in terms of constitutional legitimation of the project.

The contemporary examples of active judicial testing of the legal consequences of transition from one *Grundnorm* to another tend to be relatively modest ones, explicable on other, non-constitutional legal grounds. Sometimes these will be Public International Law in character involving the principle of continuity of the state, and of the survival, as a matter of customary International Law, of legal rights and obligations, especially of a private law character, deriving from an earlier sovereign authority, and not manifestly incompatible with the successor sovereign authority or declared to be such. Such a Public International Law rule applies even to the quite extraordinary situation of foreign, belligerent occupation, and it would be rather surprising if ordinary, non-political legal relations – marriage, divorce, family law, tort law, contract law, private property law (at least where it does not conflict with the new sovereign's invocation of the power of eminent domain) would not benefit from a legal presumption of continuance after change in the *Grundnorm*. The Commonwealth case law, involving the political breakaway, (white) Government of the then British colony of Southern Rhodesia, which had made its Unilateral Declaration of Independence to forestall a very, very belated British Government acceptance of decolonisation and (black) majority rule, concerned, remarkably enough, the public law category of preventive detention, inherited from the British Imperial era when it was designed and used by the British Government against non-white political leaders agitating for independence. The Southern Rhodesian judges who heard the matter in the first instance managed to rule that while the 1965 (white) Constitution of Rhodesia adopted by the breakaway (white minority) Government was not the lawful constitution of Southern Rhodesia, nevertheless public law, legislative and administrative measures of that Government, including specifically preventive detention, should be given effect to by the Courts as being measures for the effective government of the country. [4] This decision was confirmed, on appeal, by the Appellate Division of the High Court of Southern Rhodesia, largely on the argument of effectiveness – that the breakaway Government had 'effective control of the territory and this control seems likely to continue'; but having ruled for the breakaway Government on the substantive legal issue involved, the Appellate Division then, in a graceful display of legal footwork, quashed the actual preventive detentions involved by ruling, on simple statutory construction grounds, that the actual regulations under which the parties had been detained were *ultra vires* the Emergency Powers Act under which they had been made, and that irrespective of whether the breakaway Government's Unilateral Declaration of Independence was valid. [5] The Southern Rhodesian Courts thus, in their final holding, managed to reconcile political realism – recognition of the political facts-of-life and the political limits to the judicial process – with the practical remedy of doing justice in the individual case. Assorted cases in Pakistan in the decade of the 1960s, when the Pakistan superior Courts faced, at the instance of various private litigants, the problem of trying to determine the precise legal consequences, in particular cases, of the successive changes in the *Grundnorm* as civilian government first gave way to direct military rule, and as one such military leader was then followed by another, as a result of a military *coup* or simple hand-over of power, hardly take the matter much further[6]: it is one involving recognition, in the ultimate, that judicial power is dependent power and that without a sufficiency of executive-legislative backing, the Courts run the risk of legislating in vain if they seek directly to counter those coordinate institutions of government. The general philosophical issues have been canvassed at length in the jurisprudential debate of the early post-World War II years, among West German scholars especially, as to the limits of positivism and the judicial duty of deference to the positive law created by an anti-democratic, totalitarian *régime* that itself denies constitutional rights. The debate on the general plane ended somewhat inconclusively, but with a general recognition of the limits of effective legal action, by the judges, in such cases. So much more do the arguments of the practical limits to Court powers *vis-à-vis* executive and legislative authority, apply when it is a matter going to the core of the *Grundnorm,* its content and character and the manner or process by which it has been changed.

2. SUSPENSION OF THE CONSTITUTION: CONSTITUTIONAL 'EMERGENCIES'

The much-discussed decision of the British courts in *Liversidge* v. *Anderson* in 1942[7] sets the stage for much of the subsequent debate over the constitutional *rôle* of the Courts when executive authority, in the name of constitutional 'Emergency', – which it will usually define itself and put beyond the scope of possible judicial scrutiny as to the existence of the claimed emergency – acts counter to the *Grundnorm* in its allocations and distribution of law-making authority or its stipulations as to the manner and method and the substantive contents of such law-making. If the constitutional charter itself includes, in terms, a constitutional Emergency Powers doctrine and spells out the incidents of its user, the only constitutional questions will be the objective factual basis, if any, for invocation of the doctrine, and possibly also some of the circumstances of its application if these are not enumerated *in extenso* in the constitutional charter itself. Sometimes, of course, the doctrine of constitutional Emergency Powers is not mentioned in the constitutional charter, and so its existence must be implied if it is to be invoked at all. Even where it is mentioned, in terms, in the charter, there will usually remain questions as to the constitutional basis of its invocation and concrete application.

In *Liversidge* v. *Anderson,* the matter arose under the unwritten British constitutional system, and concerned the application during World War II of the ultimately statute-based power of the executive, under the Defence (General) Regulations of 1939, to subject persons, by executive order alone, to preventive detention even though they had neither been convicted of nor charged with any crime or breach of law. The British Regulations in question were patterned on similar executive powers to order preventive detention developed in World War I, and with slight variations only were the models for similar preventive detention powers, applied by the British to their colonial Empire overseas, which we saw litigated and tested, constitutionally, in India immediately after decolonisation and independence, and in Southern Rhodesia after the Unilateral Declaration of Independence by the white minority *régime* in 1965. The power of the relevant British Cabinet Minister, the Home Secretary, to decree preventive detention for any person under the Defence (General) Regulations of 1939 was predicated upon his having – '*reasonable cause to believe*' any person to be of hostile origin or associations or concerned in acts prejudicial to public safety or the defence of the realm. The legal question was whether, objectively, the Minister must have such 'reasonable cause to believe', which would make the 'reasonableness' of the Minister's belief subject to judicial review and control; or whether it was enough, subjectively, for the Minister himself, in good faith, to think he had such 'reasonable cause to believe' which, the Minister's personal good faith being presumed, would effectively place the matter beyond Court enquiry and correction if needed. The Court majority, following a World War I precedent, *R.* v. *Halliday,*[8] concluded that they could not enquire into the reasonableness of the Minister's belief, this apparently on the policy consideration of not embarrassing the executive in time of war. The result involved a most beneficial judicial construction of the emergency powers conferred on the administration by statute law. The Court decision carried a very strong dissent by Lord Atkin who refused to concede that the phrase 'reasonable cause to believe' was ambiguous, as the Court majority had argued to justify their own preferred, pro-executive power, policy interpretation, and who argued, instead, as to the dangerous effects upon individual liberty if, in the many statutes in which a similar formula was employed, judicial enquiry should be barred.

The British Court majority position expressed in *Liversidge* v. *Anderson* in 1942 was echoed, in its narrower, preventive detention aspects, by the Indian Supreme Court in the *Gopalan* case in 1950,[9] as we have seen, and the Indian Court majority reach a conclusion very similar to that of the British judges. It is not too difficult to see in that the still pervasive influence, even after decolonisation and independence from Britain, of 'received' British legal thought-ways and legal attitudes and basic legal philosophy, in India not less than in other former Imperial colonies or Dominions. After Prime Minister Indira Gandhi's proclamation of a National Emergency in June, 1975, the Supreme Court of India, in a decision in the following year, by a 4 to 1 judicial majority, upheld the constitutionality of a Presidential (executive) proclamation, given under Part XVIII (Emergency Provisions) of the Constitution and, specifically, under Article 359, suspending the right of any person to move in the Courts for enforcement of the Part III (Fundamental Rights) section of the Constitution – especially Articles 14 (equal protection of the laws), 19 (constitutional freedoms), 21 (procedural due process), and 22 (right to a fair trial). The Court majority in *Jabalpur* v. *Shivkant Shukla* in 1976,[10] (Chief Justice Ray, and Justices Beg, Chandrachud, and Bhagwati, with Justice Khanna dissenting), simply refused to grant petitions of Habeas Corpus, holding that petitions of detainees were not maintainable during the Presidentially-invoked Emergency.

The Supreme Court of the United States, less beholden, certainly, than Indian or Canadian or other British-derived or British-influenced tribunals, to respect British precedents as to the judicial duty of deference to executive power, rejected, by a 6 to 3 majority, President Truman's invocation of the then current Korean War emergency as the constitutional authorisation for his Presidential executive order directing seizure of the nation's steel industry because of labour relations problems and a threatened cessaion of steel production.[11] The Opinion of the Court, written by Justice Hugo Black, was a relatively modest one addressed to the narrow issue of the constitutionality of Presidential action taken in the absence of a Congressional (legislative) grant of authority, in an area where Congress was competent to legislate to endow the President with the necessary authority. In a multi-opinion decision, the constitutional nuances of inherent Presidential power, in a claimed period of emergency, must be found in the specially concurring opinions filed in support of the Black Opinion of the Court. Only two of the majority judges, apart from Justice Black, would appear to have rejected the doctrine of inherent Presidential Emergency Powers. On the other hand, notwithstanding the ongoing Korean War at the time of decision, the case can hardly be viewed as concerning a major national crisis warranting testing, one way or another, in American constitutional terms, of the maxim *salus populi suprema lex.*

3. FUNDAMENTAL POLITICAL PREMISES OF THE STATE

While the *Grundnorm,* once established, will identify the source of legal power in the state and the institutions and processes by which authoritative legal decisions are effected, it is, as we have already noted, by defi-nition, a pre-legal, political fact. What if some part of that pre-legal, pol-itical, factual base is threatened or disturbed though without challenging the survival of the *Grundnorm* itself? Can and should, the Courts inter-vene at the behest of rival political forces in the state, to rule on (and, if need be, correct), the alleged danger to fundamental political premises of the state?

The legal issue has arisen in Japan and West Germany, understandably enough in view of the fact that their new, post-War constitutional sys-tems rested not merely on internal, domestic political adjustments or compromises but also on deference to certain fundamental political facts-of-life in the international arena. The Japanese Constitution of 1946 was adopted, after the defeat of Imperial Japan and its unconditional surren-der and during the period of Allied Military Occupation of Japan, with a strong Allied influence manifest in the project and outline for the new constitutional charter and even, as many have suggested, in the actual, detailed drafting of the charter. The Allied Military Occupation contin-ued after the adoption of the new constitution in 1946, right up to 28 April 1952 when the Treaty of Peace with Japan came into force, the Occupation was finally terminated, and full legal sovereignty was effec-tively restored in Japan. No Court jurisprudence involves the testing of the legality of the Allied Military Occupation, as such, from Japan's unconditional surrender in 1945 to the ending of the Occupation in 1952. What is involved, however, is the testing of some of the incidents of the Military Occupation by reference to the constitutional ideals and stan-dards established in the 1946 constitutional charter itself. There is also the policy issue of the latter-day constitutional force to be attributed to particular constitutional provisions, like the renunciation-of-War stipula-tions (Article 9), which had been deliberately inserted into the charter of 1946 under the influence, external as well as internal, of then current conceptions of a total Japanese War guilt and which were soon found to be legally very inconvenient for the Western powers' plans to integrate Japan into the Western military alliance against the Soviet Union and Communist China, in the emerging Cold War crisis.

In the so-called 'Red Flag' case, (*Sakagami* v. *State*) in 1953,[12] the Supreme Court of Japan had to rule on the banning of a Communist newspaper, *Akahata* and its successors. The case arose, ultimately, from a criminal prosecution instituted during the Occupation, for violation of a Cabinet Order of 1950 which provided for the 'Punishment of Acts pre-judicial to Occupation Objectives', the particular Occupation Objective involved in the present case being one set forth in Allied (SCAP) direc-tives prohibiting the editing, printing and distribution of the newspaper and other publications designated by SCAP as affiliates or successors.

The original trial court verdict convicting the defendant publisher was given while the Occupation was still in effect; a further judgment, on appeal, affirming the lower court decision was rendered in 1952 on the day the Peace Treaty was signed and the Occupation legally ended. A statute passed on that same day provided for the continuance of the original Cabinet Order of 1950, and several weeks later a further statute abolished the Cabinet Order, but with a saving clause as to – 'the application of the penal provisions to the acts done prior to the enforcement of this law'. The Supreme Court of Japan, by a 10 to 4 vote, reversed the lower court decisions and ordered the defendant publisher acquitted. With seven different Opinions, the exact *ratio* of the Court decision is not completely clear, but the Court did hold the continuation statutes, carrying on the SCAP Occupations Objectives in the post-Occupation era of full Japanese legal sovereignty, to be unconstitutional.

In the *Suzuki* case in 1952,[13] the Secretary-General of the Social Democratic Party had attacked the constitutionality of the 'National Police Reserve' which had been established by authority of the Allied Occupation authority, in July, 1950, shortly after the outbreak of the Korean War. Although the National Police Reserve was stated to be designed to maintain domestic security and armed only with light weapons, its potential application as an armed force was the subject of the petition to the Supreme Court, which asked for a ruling based on Article 9 (renunciation-of-War). The Supreme Court decided the petition on strictly procedural, adjectival law grounds, and thus ignored the substantive law (Article 9) issues raised in the petition. In a unanimous decision, the Court ruled that judgment might be sought in the courts – 'only when there exists a concrete legal dispute between specific parties', and that the courts had no – 'power to determine in the abstract the constitutionality of laws, orders, and the like, in the absence of a concrete case'. The Court's reasoning seems open to contest: since monies had already been voted and applied to creation of the new Police authority, by the time of the suit, it hardly seems possible to contend that the matter was an 'abstract' and not a 'concrete' one. A better constitutional ground, in the same large area of judicial self-restraint, might have been to deny a sufficient constitutional 'interest' to the petition, and thus to treat the acceptance of general, tax-payer's suits on a very restrictive basis – much in accord with *Massachusetts* v. *Mellon*[14] and United States Supreme Court jurisprudence in this area.

In the *Sunakawa* case in 1959,[15] the Supreme Court of Japan was again seized with the issue of the constitutional meaning and application of Article 9 (renunciation-of-War). The case arose from an incident of civil political violence, occurring on the edge of a major United States Air Force base, just outside Tokyo, in 1957, where the Japanese authorities had agreed to the U.S. Air Force's request for extension of the runways, with resultant substantial displacement of local farmers from their cultivated land. In the ensuing riot, there was some trespass on the U.S. base, though no damage to U.S. installations or attacks on American personnel; but seven of the Japanese rioters were arrested and charged with illegal entry on the U.S. base. In 1959, the trial division of the Tokyo District Court rendered a verdict of Not Guilty deriving directly from Article 9 of the Constitution: the Special Criminal Law under which the seven accused had been charged, the Court ruled, had been illegally enacted in implementation of the Japan-United States Security Treaty of 1951, which was itself unconstitutional (in Japanese legal terms) because it provided for the stationing of a U.S. force in Japan and this amounted to 'war potential', whose maintenance was specifically prohibited under Article 9. The Tokyo District Court decision was devastating in its domestic and foreign policy implications, and it was immediately appealed to the Supreme Court. The Supreme Court decision was unanimous, in quashing the Tokyo District Court decision; but there were no fewer than ten judicial expressions of qualification or disagreement with aspects of the judgment. The Opinion of the Court did expressly indicate that the renunciation-of-War stipulations in Article 9 of the Constitution, prohibiting the maintenance of 'war potential', were limited to – 'the war potential of our own country, and what is here termed war potential is not applicable to foreign military forces, even those which may be retained in our country'. While the Opinion of Court also suggested that the Security Treaty could be reconciled with the principle of self-defence, and with the inherent right of individual and collective self-defence recognised under the United Nations Charter, and thus reconciled with the Article 9 stipulations, the nub of the decision is to be found in the conclusion that the Security Treaty had – 'a highly political nature which... possesses an extremely important relation to the basis of the existence of our country as a sovereign nation... a character which, as a matter of principle, is not adaptable to review by a judicial court, which has as its mission a purely judicial function'. The decision, then, was that this was a 'political question', which should be left to the executive and legislature as the governmental institutions charged with the conclusion and ratification of Treaties (Constitution, Article 73), or to the people; but certainly not to the Courts. In a later case decided by the Sapporo Provincial Court of Appeals, the *Naganuma* case in 1976,[16] where part of a National Park had been resumed by the Agriculture Minister for the construction of a *Nike* missile base for the Air Defence Force, local farmers had opposed the resumption, arguing that no ground of public interest justifying the alienation of the forest land then dedicated as a National Park, existed. The lower court had upheld the farmers, basing its decision against the Government on Article 9 grounds; [17] but the Court of Appeals ruled the issue of constitutionality of the Defence Force to be a 'political question', beyond the competence of the Courts to decide. [18] The result in these cases is thus to establish the equivalent of the European *Acte de Gouvernement* which the other, elected arms of government would decide, and not the Courts. The consequence is that the Governmental acts concerned are upheld, without direct ruling on the substantive law-based constitutional objections raised against them.

We have already looked at the European Defence Community controversy, and its handling by the West German Federal Constitutional Court, separately and severally, in its two different Senates and in the *plenum* or Full Court. [19] Suffice it to repeat, now, that when the issue came before the Court in 1952, it was at a crucially important time in West German history, only three years after the three Western powers had restored legal sovereignty to their own particular Occupation Zones of defeated Germany and united them into the one, truncated state for that specific purpose. The Bonn Constitution of 1949 had acknowledged, in terms, the contradictory political goals and purposes of the new West German state by embracing, in its Preamble and in the final Article, the ideal of All-German reunification, East and West, in the one state, and by deliberately omitting a War or defence power from a new state founded, in part, on a German 'War guilt' legally imposed by all the Occupation powers; yet, by the opening of the 1950s, the Western powers were determined to integrate the new West German state into their own special system of military-political alliances, in opposition to the Soviet Union and Soviet bloc in the emerging Cold War crisis. The three divisions of the West German Court, – the Senates and the *plenum,* acting individually and, in public terms at least, without any concerted plan, achieved a common result whereby the Court disabled itself, on jurisdictional grounds, from ruling on the substantive legal issues of constitutionality, which, *faute de mieux,* were left to be resolved by the ordinary political-governmental processes, in the executive and legislative institutions of Government. In fact, the E.D.C. controversy was resolved by political events, without the need for potentially divisive Governmental action: opposition within the French legislature killed French participation, and without the French the whole E.D.C. project lapsed of its own accord.

In the Basic Treaty (*Grundlagenvertrag*) case of 1973, [20] the Second Senate of the Federal Constitutional Court had to rule on the constitutionality of the West German-East German Treaty, of 1972, the keystone of the Brandt Government's programme of *détente* with the Soviet Union and the Soviet bloc countries, through a 'politic of little steps' and the achievement of a series of bilateral, mini-treaties between West Germany and its Eastern European neighbours, guaranteeing the security and stability of existing, *de facto* territorial frontiers established at War's end in 1945. The attack on the West German-East German Basic Treaty had been initiated before the Court by the Government of the *Land* of Bavaria, whose original representatives, – years before, in the federal Parliamentary Council of 1948 that adopted what became the Bonn constitutional charter (*Grundgesetz*) of 1949 – had opposed adoption of the Bonn charter because of its being posited on a divided (West and East) Germany. The judgment of the Second Senate was rendered against a background of fierce partisan political controversy within West Germany. With the normal eight-man bench of the Second Senate, the Bavarian Government moved, desperately, to exclude one of those members, Judge Rottmann, a Free Democrat, from sitting on the case: the first motion by Bavaria, based on some public remarks by Judge Rottmann, was rejected by the Second Senate in May, 1972,[21] but a second motion by Bavaria, based on a letter written by the Judge in which he had praised the Brandt Government's *Ostpolitik* opening to the Soviet Union and Soviet bloc, was accepted by the Second Senate a year later.[22] With Judge Rottmann thus disqualified and the Second Senate reduced to a seven-member bench for the case, it still rejected the general Bavarian Government position by a unanimous vote.[23] The Bavarian Government had contended that the Basic Treaty of 1972 violated the constitutional command in the Preamble to the Bonn Constitution of 1949 to achieve the unity and freedom of Germany, and that, in fact, the 1972 Treaty resulted in the perpetuation of the partition of Germany into two sovereign states. In its decision, the Second Senate did take note of the principle of *judicial self-restraint,* itself using the English-language term:

'The principle of judicial self-restraint is aimed at holding open the area of free political operation that is guaranteed by the Constitution to the other constitutional institutions.'

But the Second Senate also felt it useful to address itself to the substantive legal merits and to dispose of the Bavarian Government's objections: so far from being at variance with the Bonn Constitution's dictum on reunification, the Basic Treaty of 1972 did not preclude the federal Government, either now or in the future, from doing all it could at all times on behalf of German reunification, and indeed the basic Treaty could be an initial step in a relatively long process aimed at the reorganisation of Germany on the basis of free self-determination by the German people. According to the Court, all constitutional organs in West Germany were obliged to work towards the achievement of reunification and, for this purpose, to keep alive, at home, the Basic Law's claim to reunification, and to represent it steadfastly in external relations.

One further decision of the Federal Constitutional Court, in 1975,[24] returned to the same general issue of the two Germanies and the Bonn charter's reunification imperative, but this time in regard to two other treaties in the Brandt Government's *Ostpolitik* mini-treaties series, the West German-Soviet Treaty of 1970 and the West German-Polish Treaty of 1970, and under the rubric of private rights – property, citizenship, family reunification – claimed to be abridged by the two treaties in violation of the Basic Rights sections of the Bonn Constitution (variously, Articles 14 (Property), 16 (Deprivation of Citizenship), 6 (Marriage, Family), and 2 (Rights of Liberty)). The Court dismissed all these arguments, which originated by way of individual constitutional complaint (*Verfassungsbeschwerde*), on the score that there was no immediate alteration of the complainants' position, to their disadvantage, as protected under the Bonn Constitution provisions referred to; and the Court supported this by looking to the terms of the two treaties and demonstrating that, in terms, they involved no such curtailment of the complainants' constitutional basic rights.

We have referred, in passing, to the Quebec 'Veto' case where the Supreme Court of Canada ruled, in December, 1982,[25] – after the federal Government of Canada's constitutional patriation project had been enacted into law, finally and irrevocably, – on the Quebec Government's claim that there was a binding constitutional custom (convention) in effect, under the Canadian constitution, requiring, as a matter of law, the Quebec Government's consent to any federal Government-sponsored constitutional amendment affecting either the legislative competence of the Quebec legislature or the status or *rôle* of the legislature or Government of Quebec within the Canadian federation. In the earlier discussion we examined the 'moot'-ness of the issue, the matter having already been disposed of politically at the time the Supreme Court of Canada rendered its decision.[26] Nevertheless, in rendering its decision, the Supreme Court did address itself to the substantive law issue of the existence or otherwise of such a convention involving a Quebec right of Veto on proposed constitutional change. Such a Right of Veto, as argued for by the Quebec Government, would amount to a fundamental political premise of the federal constitutional system, since not mentioned, in terms, in the Canadian constitutional charter – 'Canadian duality' as the Supreme Court of Canada referred to it, or 'Deux Nations' as the Quebec Government called it – and part of the *Grundnorm*. But the Supreme Court of Canada, in addressing itself to the substantive issue, concluded that the burden of proof of such a convention lay on the Quebec Government and that it had failed to establish its existence.[27]

NOTES

1. H. Kelsen, *Reine Rechtslehre* (1934).
2. See the present author's *Canada and the Constitution 1979-1982. Patriation and the Charter of Rights* (1982).
3. See, generally, *Constitution-Making, Principles, Process, Practice* (1981), ch. 2, p. 12 *et seq.*
4. *Madzimbamuto* v. *Lardner-Burke N.O. and others; Baron* v. *Ayre N.O. and others* (High Court of Southern Rhodesia, General Division, Lewis and Goldin J.J.A.) (Judgment No. GD/CIV/23/66, 9 September 1966) (Government Printer, Salisbury). And see, generally, R. S. Welsh, "The Constitutional Case in Southern Rhodesia', 83 *Law Quarterly Review* 64 (1967); Eekelaar, 'Splitting the *Grundnorm*', 30 *Modern Law Review* 156 (1967); C. Palley, 'The Judicial Process: U.D.I. and the Southern Rhodesia Judiciary', 30 *Modern Law Review* 263 (1967).
5. *Madzimbamuto* v. *Lardner-Burke N.O. and others: Baron* v. *Ayre N.O. and others* (High Court of Southern Rhodesia, Appellate Division, Beadle C.J., Quénet, Macdonald, Jarvis and Fieldsend J.J.A.) (Judgment No. AD 1/68, 29 January 1968) (Government Printer, Salisbury).
6. T. K. K. Iyer, 'Constitutional Law in Pakistan: Kelsen in the Courts', 21 *American Journal of Comparative Law* 759 (1973).
7. [1942] A.C. 206. And see the discussion, Sir W. S. Holdsworth, 58 *Law Quarterly Review* 1 (1942); A. L. Goodhart, 58 *Law Quarterly Review* 3 (1942); Sir C. K. Allen, 'Regulation 18 B and Reasonable Cause', 58 *Law Quarterly Review* 232 (1942); Julius Stone, *The Province and Function of Law* (1946), pp. 193-194.
8. [1917] A.C. 260.
9. 13 *Supreme Court Journal* (India) 174 (1950); A.I.R. *1950* S.C. 27.
10. A.I.R. *1976* S.C. 1207.
11. *Youngstown Sheet and Tube Co.* v. *Sawyer,* 343 U.S. 579 (1952).
12. Supreme Court of Japan, Grand Bench, Decision of 22 July 1953, 7 *Supreme Court Reports* (Japan) 1562 (1953). And see, generally, N. L. Nathanson', Constitutional Adjudication in Japan', 7 *American Journal of Comparative Law* 195, at 202-206 (1958); D. F. Henderson, *The Constitution of Japan. Its First Twenty Years, 1947-67* (1968), at pp. 127-133.
13. Supreme Court of Japan, Grand Bench, Decision of 8 October 1952; 6 *Supreme Court Reports* (Japan) 783 (1952); J.M. Maki, *Court and Constitution in Japan. Selected Supreme Court Decisions, 1948-60* (1964), p. 362 *et seq.;* and see, generally, Nathanson, *op. cit.,* 7 *American Journal of Comparative Law* 195, 196-199 (1958); D. F. Henderson, *op. cit.,* pp. 121-122; Hideo Wada and Hitoshi Itoh, 'A comparative overview of the Japanese Supreme Court', 28 *Jahrbuch des öffentlichen Rechts der Gegenwart 689, at 690 (1979).*
14. *262 U.S. 447 (1923).*
15. *Supreme Court of Japan, Grand Bench, Decision of 16 December 1959; J. M. Maki, op. cit.,* p. 298 *et seq.;* D. F. Henderson, *op. cit.,* pp. 124-125; Kosaku Tamura, 'Case on the conflict between the Constitution and a Treaty brought before the Judicial Court of Japan', *Problèmes Contemporains de Droit Comparé* (Japanese Institute of Comparative Law, Chuo University, Tokyo), vol. 1 (1962), p. 215 *et seq.*
16. Sapporo Provincial Court of Appeals, Decision of 5 August 1976. And see generally Teruya Abe and Masanori Shiyaka', Die Entwicklung des japanischen Verfassungsrechts von 1965-1976 unter besonderer Berücksichtigung der Rechtsprechung, 26 *Jahrbuch des öffentlichen Rechts der Gegenwart* 595, at 599-600 (1977).
17. Sapporo Provincial Court, Decision of 7 September 1973. Abe and Shiyaka, *op. cit., ibid.*

132

18. Sapporo Provincial Court of Appeals, Decision of 5 August 1976. Abe and Shiyaka, *op. cit., ibid.*

19. Decision of 30 July 1952, 1 B Verf GE 396 (1952) (First Senate); decision of 9 December 1952, 2 B Verf GE 79 (1953) (*plenum*); decision of 7 March 1953, 2 B Verf GE 143 (1953) (Second Senate). And see, generally, *Constitutionalism in Germany and the Federal Constitutional Court* (1962), p. 34 *et seq.*

20. Decision of 31 July 1973, 36 B Verf GE 1 (1974) (Second Senate). See Hans G. Rupp, 'Judicial Review of International Agreements: Federal Republic of Germany', 25 *American Journal of Comparative Law* 286, at 295-296 (1977); and see, generally, as to the *Ostpolitik* debate which led on to the negotiation and conclusion of the *Grundlagenvertrag,* the present author's *The International Law of Détente. Arms Control, European Security, and East-West Cooperation* (1978), ch. 5, p. 92 *et seq.*

21. Decision of 29 May 1973, 35 B Verf GE 171 (1974) (Second Senate). And see, generally, Donald P. Kommers, *Judicial Politics in West Germany. A Study of the Federal Constitutional Court* (1976), at pp. 198, 298.

22. Decision of 16 June 1973, 35 B Verf GE 246 (1974) (Second Senate). And see Kommers, *op. cit.,* at pp. 198, 298.

23. Decision of 31 July 1973, 36 B Verf GE 1 (1974) (Second Senate).

24. 40 B Verf GE 141 (1975). And see Rupp, *op. cit.,* 25 *American Journal of Comparative Law* 286, at 296-297 (1977).

25. *Re Attorney-General of Quebec and Attorney-General of Canada* (Quebec Court of Appeal), 134 D.L.R. (3d) 719 (1982); (Supreme Court of Canada), 140 D.L.R. (3d) 385 (1982).

26. 140 D.L.R. (3d), at 395-396 (1982) (Supreme Court of Canada).

27. *Ibid.,* p. 405.

CHAPTER VII

THE COURTS AND THE CONSTITUENT
AND GOVERNMENTAL PROCESSES

1. CONSTITUENT PROCESSES: CONSTITUTIONAL AMENDMENT

The Constituent Processes are part of the *Grundnorm* in so far as they establish the procedures by which it may be changed, and an orderly transition made from an old *Grundnorm* to a new or renewed one. They are ordinarily described as the constitutional amending machinery and may include a constituent assembly or Parliamentary committee endowed with the capacity to adopt or recommend constitutional novation or comprehensive change, and also provisions for partial or limited change in various elements, only, of the existing constitutional system. The area has become interesting, in comparative judicial terms since the Second World War, because of a trend to consider what was ventured only speculatively and in purely abstract terms during the vicissitudes of constitutional government in the dangeorus 1930s and also the wartime years, namely whether there are not – better still, in normative terms, should not be – certain substantive law limits to what can be attempted as a valid amendment to some existing constitutional system. The popularity of the new notion of 'unconstitutional' constitutional norms owes much, clearly, to the decline of Positivism and the revival of Natural Law thinking in the reaction, post-War, to the excesses of the authoritarian *régimes* of the pre-War and wartime period who justified so much of their actions, with a spurious constitutional legality, by pointing to a conformity to the letter, if not the spirit, of the existing ground rules of constitutional change.[1] There are obviously practical limits of the effectiveness of legal action attaching to the whole notion of substantive law bounds to the operation of the constituent processes; for it can only have reality as constitution law-in-action in a society that still respects the basic concept of a Government of Laws and not of Men, and that is either prepared to accept such imposed limits to its power to change the constitutional system, or at least prepared to fight against them or seek to counter them only by further action that is itself within the existing constitutional ground rules.

Such a society, certainly, is to be found in post-independence India, where the period of the late 1960s, and the early 1970s, saw a continuing struggle between the Congress Party Government at the federal level, which, deriving inspiration from the Directive Principles of State Policy (Part IV) of the Constitution, was determined to enact social planning and economic equalisation measures, and a Supreme Court majority which insisted on using the rather more conservative, *laissez-faire*-oriented, Fundamental Rights (Part III) of the Constitution,[2] to contest the federal Government at every step. The struggle between the federal Government and the Court represented more of a war than a single battle, each legislative initiative of the Government receiving a counter-attack from the judges, provoking further legislative initiatives by the Government and still further ripostes by the judges. It was all facilitated by the machinery for constitutional change under the Constitution (Part XX, Amendment of the Constitution, Article 368), which allows constitutional amendments (with a few exceptions only), to be effected by a Bill introduced in either House of Parliament and then adopted by each House by a two-thirds majority of the members present and voting. Since, from inauguration of the Constitution in 1950, until the formation of the short-lived Janata Government in 1977, the dominant Congress Party always enjoyed two-thirds majorities in each House of Parliament, there were no practical constitutional-legal obstacles to effecting constitutional amendments, and they became a vehicle for 'correcting' or overriding unpopular or unwanted Supreme Court decisions, – as had, in fact, been envisaged, in theory at least, for the United States, in the late 19th century, but had never been capable of practical realisation because of the much more complex and difficult U.S. constitutional amending machinery (U.S. Constitution, Article V), with its requirement of two-thirds majorities in each House of Congress, plus majorities in three-fourths of the states, for the effecting of constitutional changes. The relative ease of operation of constituent power, under the post-independence Indian Constitution's Article 368, and the fact that the federal Government was prepared to make use of it and did so successfully and frequently, created, it might be argued, a certain encouragement for the Supreme Court majorities to use their powers of judicial review to frustrate current federal legislative majorities by invocation of 'higher law' constitutional grounds, for the judges knew full well that their decision in any case would not be irrevocable but would always be subject to possible 'correction' by a constitutional amendment, if the federal Government felt strongly enough about it. Constituent Power that is readily rendered operational and that is functional as law-in-action, creates its own species of political and constitutional legitimacy for judicial activism applied against popular majorities in the other, coordinate arms of government.

There were, in fact, no less than forty-four constitutional amendments enacted, through the constituent power under Article 368, by the three Congress Party *régimes* – the Nehru, Shastri, and Gandhi Governments – in power from 1950 to 1977, and, according to the records, half of these touched on the Supreme Court, and more than half of these again involved major policy conflicts.[3]

In *Golak Nath* in 1967,[4] the Supreme Court of India, by a six-to-five majority, overruling a very early case »*Shankari Prasad,* in 1951),[5] held that the federal Parliament did not have the power to amend the Constitution under Article 368, so as to take away or abridge the Fundamental Rights (Part III) of the Constitution. The issue had emerged, tangentially, two years before (in *Sajjan Singh* in 1965),[6] when a strong Chief Justice, Gajendragadkar, speaking for the three majority judges in a three-to-two decision given on other grounds, had reaffirmed the *Shankari Prasad* ruling of 1951 that the federal Parliament could, under Article 368, amend the Constitution so as to take away or abridge the Fundamental Rights.[7] What was involved in *Sajjan Singh* in 1965, and again in *Golak Nath* in 1967, was the Seventeenth Amendment to the Constitution, adopted in 1964, directed to the politically difficult area of agrarian reform which had, however, been a crucial element in the Congress Party Governments' social and economic planning and land redistribution programmes from 1950 onwards.[8] The Indian Constitution, as originally enacted, contained the guarantee that – 'No person shall be deprived of his property save by authority of law' (Article 31 (1)), and this was accompanied by a requirement of 'compensation' in the case of property 'acquired for public purposes' (Article 31 (2)). Successive Supreme Court decisions throughout the 1950s and into the 1960s had hedged in the Government's power of eminent domain and acquisition of property for public purposes by close judicial scrutiny of the procedures and the actual amounts of compensation, insisting, variously, on reviewing the financial adequacy of the compensation offered for taking of land. The Seventeenth Amendment, upheld, in *Sajjan Singh* in 1965,[9] was designed to amend Article 31 (Right to Property) by establishing, as the legal criterion for determining adequacy of compensation, 'payment of compensation at a rate which shall not be less than the market value thereof'.

The Indian Government's attack on the *Golak Nath* decision and the attempt to 'correct' it for the future, had the two objectives, – the narrower one of removing the judicially-imposed standards of financial compensation in respect to Government exercises in eminent domain and acquisition of land and other property for public purposes, and the broader and much more long-range one of removing the judicially-created barriers to the operation of constituent power in amendment to the Constitution. The two constitutional vehicles to realise the Government's twin objectives were the Twenty-Fourth and Twenty-Fifth Amendments to the Constitution, both adopted in 1971.[10] The Twenty-Fourth Amendment was addressed directly to Constituent Power, and to Article 368 of the Constitution. Article 368 now saw its title changed to – 'Power of Parliament to amend the Constitution and procedure thereof', while a new, opening paragraph was inserted (Article 368 (1)): –

'Notwithstanding anything in this Convention, Parliament may in exercise of its constituent power amend by way of addition, variation or repeal any provision of this Constitution in accordance with the procedure laid down in this Article.'

The Twenty-Fifth Amendment was addressed to Article 31 of the Constitution. It substituted for the existing Article 31 (2) as to compensation for compulsory acquisition or requisition of property for public purposes, a new clause which included the stipulation, designed to exclude judicial review as to the 'adequacy' of such compensation: –

'and no such law shall be called in question in any court on the ground that the amount so fixed or determined is not adequate or that the whole or any part of such amount is to be given otherwise than in cash.'

In addition, the Tenty-Fifth Amendment added a new section, clause C, to Article 31, specifying that no law enacted in pursuance of the 'property' principles (Article 39 (b) and (c)) of the Directive Principles of State Policy, – which, in contradistinction to the 'property' provisions (Article 31 itself) of the Fundamental Rights part of the Constitution, were broadly social democratic in character and qualified property rights by reference to distribution to 'subserve the common good' (Article 39 (b)) and to avoiding 'concentration of wealth and means of production to the common detriment' (Article 39 (c)), – should be deemed void on account of inconsistency or conflict with Article 14 (Right to Equality), Article 19 (Right to Freedom), or Article 31. The new Article 31 C then went on to make assurance doubly sure by stipulating that –

'No law containing a declaration that it is for giving effect to [Article 39 (b) and (c) of the Directive Principles of State Policy] shall be called in question in any court on the ground that it does not give effect to such policy.'

It might be thought that, with the adoption of the Twenty-Fourth and Twenty-Fifth Amendments in 1971, the Gandhi Government had effectively bolted the door against any further Court-based attempt to frustrate its land reform and property and wealth redistribution programmes. This was not to be, however. In *Kesavananda Bharati*, in 1973,[11] the Supreme Court, in a decision rendered by its Full Bench, with thirteen judges, gave a curiously mixed ruling that held, variously, that the part of the Twenty-Fifth Amendment in effect giving Parliament final say on the amount of compensation was unconstitutional; but that Parliament did have authority to amend the Constitution, including Fundamental Rights. The decision included, however, a Parthian shot as to this particular part of its ruling: constitutional amendments that purported to alter the 'basic structure' of the Contitution would be unconstitutional. Former Indian Supreme Court justice, J. L. Kapur, has identified the *ratio decidendi* of *Kesavananda Bharati,* – difficult enough with any multi-member tribunal that practices separate opinion-writing, but especially complex with the present case because of the multiple issues involved – as follows:[12] –

(i) By a majority of seven-to-six, that Article 368 does not enable Parliament to destroy or alter the basic structure or framework of the Constitution. (Chief Justice Sikri defined that 'basic structure' of the Constitution, which cannot be altered, as consisting of the Supremacy of the Constitution, the Republican and Democratic form of Government, the secular character of the Constitution; the Separation of Powers between Legislature, Executive and Judiciary; and the Federal character of the Constitution. With the other judges, the 'basic structure' is largely left undefined or vague).

(ii) By a majority of twelve-to-one, that the power to amend the Constitution is to be found in Article 368 (as it stood even before the Twenty-Fourth Amendment) and not elsewhere; that Article 368 contains both the power and procedure for amending the Constitution; and that Parliament can enhance its own power of amendment.

(iii) By a majority of seven-to-six, that there are no implied limitations on the power of amendment under Article 368.

The constitutional sequel to the *Kesavananda Bharati* ruling of 1973 soon became caught up in the turbulent political events leading to Prime Minister Indira Gandhi's proclamation of Emergency, the defeat of her Government, and the Janata Government *interregnum* from 1977 to 1980. Madame Gandhi necessarily rejected the 'basic structure' limitation to the constitutional amending power, and brought forward, in 1976, on the eve of her departure from office, a further constitutional amendment, the Forty-Second, very long and detailed but with the objective of removing from the Supreme Court altogether the power of review over the politically most sensitive issues like land reform and property rights, and to put constitutional amendments wholly beyond the scope of judicial review. The successor Janata Government introduced, in 1977, its own constitutional amendment, the Forty-Third, restoring to the Courts some of the powers stripped away by the Forty-Second Amendment; while a further Janata Government measure, the Forty-Fourth Amendment to the Constitution, adopted in 1979, repealed still more of Madame Gandhi's Forty-Second Amendment, but at the same time deleted property from the Fundamental Rights (Part III) of the Constitution transferring it to a less conspicuous part near the end. Prime Minister Gandhi was returned to power again in February, 1980, and was greeted, almost immediately, by the decision in the *Minerva Mills* case where the Supreme Court examined the Gandhi Government's Forty-Second Amendment to the Constitution by the 'basic structure' test developed by Chief Justice Sikri in the earlier, seven-to-six, holding in *Kesavananda* in 1973, and struck down several portions of the Forty-Second Amendment by reference to that test. The Court, in *Minerva Mills,* in 1980,[13] by a four-to-one majority, (with Justice Bhagwati dissenting), maintained the 'basic structure' limitation to the constitutional amending power, declaring that the harmony and balance in the Constitution between Part IV, Directive Principles of State Policy, and Part III, Fundamental Rights, must not be disturbed, since an essential feature of the Constitution. The Court majority, through its Chief Justice Chandrachud, rejected by implication Prime Minister Gandhi's assertion of the primacy of the social democratic-leaning Directive Principles over the more traditional Fundamental Rights. With Prime Minister Gandhi looking at the possibility of review of the *Minerva Mills* judgment by a Full Bench of the Court, and considering further experiments with Court structuring for constitutional jurisdiction, it seemed likely that the new emphasis in the struggle between the Government and the judges might shift, as in the United States and in other countries in past years, to questions of Court organisation and Court personnel, supplementing the initiatives as to the executive appointing power that Prime Minister Gandhi had already taken, twice before, in 1973 and in 1976, in by-passing traditional practice as to a more or less automatic, mechanical promotion of the next most senior judge on the Court when a vacancy occurred in the Chief Justiceship, and superseding these particular judges by candidates more in keeping with the Government's general policy objectives.

Challenges under other legal systems going to the nature and limits of the constituent processes and the constitutional amending power generally, and the ability of the Courts to control them, have hardly been so sustained, in point of time; nor have the Courts been so persistently aggressive in defence of their own claims to review. The Constitution of the Fifth French Republic provides that constitutional amendments may be made either by an initiative of the President of the Republic approved by a three-fifths majority of the two Houses of Parliament, the Senate and National Assembly, meeting together; or else by a project of revision approved by each of the two Houses, and then approved by a popular referendum vote (Article 89). However, another Article of the Constitution allows the President of the Republic to submit to direct, popular referendum vote any project of law 'bearing on the organisation of the public powers' (Article 11).[14] This particular section of the Constitution, Article 11, was utilised by President de Gaulle in 1962 to modify those sections of the Constitution dealing with the election of the President of the Republic. President de Gaulle wanted to change the mode of Presidential elections from a cumbersome, indirect system involving an electoral college composed of Members of Parliament, members of the Departmental (regional district) Councils, members of the Assemblies of Overseas Territories, in addition to the elected representatives of the Municipal Councils (the Mayors and Deputy-Mayors of the smaller municipalities, ranging on to all the municipal Councillors for *communes* of more than 9,000 inhabitants, plus extra, nominated delegates for all *communes* of more than 30,000 inhabitants). (Constitution of 1958, as originally adopted, Article 6). [15] It was all very complicated, likely to prove very cautious and conservative in operation, and undoubtedly frustrating to someone, like de Gaulle, more sympathetic to ideas of representative, plebiscitarian democracy and the popular mandate conferred by direct, popular election. President de Gaulle proposed to change the Presidential elections system to one of direct popular election by universal suffrage, sweeping away the old; and he utilised Article 11 of the Constitution to go directly to the people by way of referendum to approve the proposed constitutional change, by-passing altogether Article 89 and the normal procedures of constitutional change. An attempt to block the special procedure of Article 11 of the Constitution, launched by the President of the Senate, Gaston Monnerville, a political opponent of President de Gaulle, was rejected by the *Conseil constitutionnel,* on jurisdictional grounds. [16] The *Conseil constitutionnel* grounded its refusal on a very strict reading of the establishment of its own jurisdiction under Article 61 of the Constitution, such jurisdiction being limited to consideration of the conformity to the Constitution of organic laws and ordinary laws. As the *Conseil* said in its judgment:

> 'It results from the spirit of the Constitution which has made of the *Conseil constitutionnel* a regulatory organ of the activity of public powers that the laws which the Constitution has intended to allude to are solely laws voted by the Parliament and not those which, adopted by the people following on a referendum, constitute the direct expression of national sovereignty,' [17]

It followed from this, in the *Conseil's* opinion, that it had no competence to pronounce on the matter. It is difficult to fault this ruling, either in constitutional-legal or in high-political terms. In the end, the argument that the President of the Republic had violated the constitutional ground rules as to exercise of constituent power by by-passing those rules and going directly to the people by way of referendum vote, would be determined by the ultimate source of constituent power in the state, the people, by their referendum vote, one way or another, on the proposal to replace indirect, electoral college-based election of the President of the

Republic by direct, popular election. With the way thus cleared by the *Conseil's* refusal to intervene, the referendum vote approved of the change to direct, popular election of the President.

In Canada, the constitutional 'patriation' project, sponsored by the federal Government, and involving the termination of the last purely formal and symbolic links between Canada and the former Imperial power, Great Britain, and the adoption of a constitutionally entrenched Charter of Rights and Freedoms of the citizen,[18] was attacked before the Supreme Court by a number of Provincial (regional) governments within Canada, on the argument that the constituent process used for the legal adoption of the 'patriation' project violated existing constitutional norms – in this case, according to the argument, purely unwritten, customary (conventional) law and practice. The Canadian Constitution, as originally adopted in 1867 when Canada's legal status was that of a dependent colony within the then British Empire, contained no internal machinery for its own amendment. The Constitution had been granted, in effect, as an expression of the sovereign, British Imperial power, in the form of a statute of the British Parliament; and in the absence of any internal amending machinery, any future amendments to the Constitution had to be achieved as still further statutes of the British Parliament. Such an essentially 'colonial' procedure became increasingly inelegant and politically unacceptable, with the decline of British Imperial power in modern times; and this was one of the reasons for the federal Government of Canada's project, in the period 1980-2, to effect a very belated 'patriation' of the Constitution by removing all the Imperial, British vestigial links, including the 'made-in-Britain' amending machinery.[19] Very much earlier, however, in order to render the 'made-in-Britain' amending machinery politically palatable in a Canada that had, since the Imperial Conferences of 1926 and 1930, and the last great Imperial Act, the Statute of Westminster of 1931, had its full independence and sovereignty *vis-à-vis* Great Britain recognised in International Law terms,[20] a bilateral Canadian-British, inter-Commonwealth, International Law-based practice had developed whereby, in effecting amendments to the Canadian Constitution by way of statutes of the British Parliament, the British Government would treat its *rôle* as a purely mechanical, non-discretionary one, in which it would act at the request of the federal Government of Canada, and only at the request of the federal Government of Canada, and in accord with the strict letter of the advice given to it by the federal Government of Canada. Political opponents of the federal Government 'patriation' project, within Canada and based in certain of the Provincial (regional) Governments, attempted to block the 'patriation' project within Great Britain itself by 'lobbying' the British Government and rank-and-file British Parliamentarians to vote against it. These were politely, but very firmly, rebuffed in Great Britain in their demands: as Governments of purely internal sub-divisions of the sovereign state of Canada, those regional administrations were, in International Law terms, legal non-persons and legally non-receivable in Great Britain or any other outside state. Having failed in Great Britain itself, these recalcitrant regional administrations then tried to block the federal Government of Canada from presenting its 'patriation' project to the British Government, through blocking action in the Courts of Canada. Since the Canadian Courts would be legally incompetent, according to established jurisprudence, to pass on the Canadian Government's foreign policy actions abroad (here, with Great Britain), their examination of the 'patriation' project was perforce limited to the priority of the constituent process up to (but not beyond) the presentation of a request from the Canadian Government to the British Government for formal enactment of the 'patriation' project as the last 'made-in-Britain' amendment to the Canadian Constitution. The main focus, then, was on the issue whether, in presenting such a request to the British Government, the Canadian Government was required, as a matter either of Canadian law or Canadian custom, to have the prior consent of the different Provincial (regional) administrations within Canada – all of them, a majority of them, or even some of them, for it was not too clear what exactly was being contended for, here. Two further questions were, of course, implicit here. Assuming there was such a custom of asking the Provincial administrations for their prior consent, would such a custom – not being law – be binding, legally, upon the Canadian Government; and would it, in any case, be proper for the Courts, as a matter either of constitutional jurisdiction or of ordinary judicial self-restraint in regard to 'political questions', to try even to rule on the existence of such a custom?

The answer given by the Supreme Court of Canada, in late 1981,[21] to these questions is not, it must be admitted from the outset, particularly satisfying, either in Court organisational or in doctrinal-legal terms. It all indicates, once again, the dangers that may befall Courts when they rush, too easily, into great political conflicts where Angels (and other, politically more experienced Supreme Courts in other jurisdictions) might prudently fear to tread. With no compelling precedents from its past jurisprudence to argue for its intervention, the Supreme Court resolved to grasp the nettle and to answer the main substantive questions, as to the alleged law and the alleged custom, on the merits. The only problem was that the Court could not produce any large, overriding consensus within its own ranks as to just what, and how, it was deciding. In the analytical jurisprudence terms developed by Dr. Goodhart,[22] there is no discernible *ratio decidendi,* or lowest common denominator statement of the majority grounds of decision. It is a multiple opinion, no-clear-majority decision, without the unifying element of an agreed majority Opinion of Court tying together its disparate elements, and characterised as much by evidence of ideological or personal cross-currents within the Court as by common intellectual meeting points. In sum, however, by a 7-to-2 vote,[23] the Supreme Court held that there was no requirement, in *law*, that the federal Government consult with, or *a fortiori* obtain the consent of, all or any of the Provincial administrations before making a request to the British Government for a formal amendment to the Constitution. Correlatively, by a 6-to-3 vote,[24] the Supreme Court held that there was a constitutional *custom* that the federal Government consult with the Provincial administrations and obtain the consent of some of them – exactly how many was not specified, presumably because it was impossible to obtain any consensus among the six judges, holding for the existence of such a *custom,* on this point. When the 7-to-2 vote *against* existence of any *legal* requirement, and the 6-to-3 vote *for* existence of a *customary* requirement are put together, we find that there are three judges voting solidly against the existence of any requirement, *legal or customary;* and two judges voting solidly for the existence of a requirement, *legal and customary.* The majorities for these two distinct and disparate positions taken by the Supreme Court are provided by four silent judges, who vote *against* the existence of a *legal* requirement, but *for* the existence of a *customary* requirement, but without in any way trying to reconcile the two positions, – for the law reviews and the general public, – by way of filing a separate opinion or opinions rationalising their own highly nuanced judicial positions. In the result, the Canadian 'patriation' decision, rendered by the Supreme Court of Canada, is now completely academic; for the project, once adopted, terminated the last British connection in favour of wholly autonomous, self-operating, all-Canadian, constitutional amending machinery for the future, operating through majorities in both Houses of the federal Parliament and majorities also in the Provincial legislatures, the number of Provincial legislatures in which majorities would be required varying according to the subject matter. As a matter of history, the federal Government, in spite of the Court's 7-to-2 majority ruling that it had no *legal* obligation to consult with the Provincial administrations, did indeed acknowledge the Court's 6-to-3 view that there was a *custom* to that effect, by actively consulting those Provinces and eventually obtaining the consent of nine out of the ten Provinces before making the request for formal amendment to the British Government. But the political price paid for this deference to 'custom', as distinct from 'law', seemed high, for it involved a compromising and attenuation of the principles of the new Charter of Rights and Freedoms of the citizen, in order to achieve the accord of a majority of the Provincial administrations. For the Supreme

Court, the exercise tended to confirm the doubts arising from the empirical experience of other jurisdictions, of judges' venturing into the heady political stuff of the nature and quality of the constitutional *Grundnorm* or the scope and limits of Constituent Power itself. A further issue, arising from the constitutional 'patriation' decision, which we have looked at already under the rubric of judicial self-restraint and 'political questions', and which we will have occasion to examine further, in other contexts, concerns the political and legal merits of the Court's volunteering to pass on governmental practice as distinct from law, and on the existence or otherwise of a claimed constitutional custom or convention and on just what its incidents might happen to be.

2. GOVERNMENTAL PROCESSES

(a) *Institutional equilibrium*

Here we are concerned with the relationships between the main organs of government – executive, legislative, and judicial; the institutional balance between them and the constitutional controls, if any, over their interactions; and, finally, the supervision of their working operations and guaranteeing of procedural and substantive due process therein. In a large sense, these are the matters covered by the German constitutional concept of *Organstreitigkeiten,* – the original object of constitutional review as classical German constitutional theory understood it. It is hardly surprising, therefore, that the West German Federal Constitutional Court, of all the final national tribunals, seems to shew most confidence in handling this type of question, and resolving it on its substantive law merits and not simply treating it on the preliminary, jurisdictional issue (usually by by-passing it altogether on procedural, adjectival law grounds) as other tribunals, particularly the Common law or Common Law-influenced ones, have tended to do. For such Common Law or Common Law-influenced courts, indeed, the issue of the internal workings or procedures of a coordinate institution of government like the executive or the legislature, has normally been treated as one proper for the application of judicial self-restraint – this, it would seem, on the basis of separation-of-powers concepts and the mutual respect and deference owed by the main organs of constitutional government, the courts included, to each other. When the courts have intervened, usually only under conditions of great public interest and pressure, as in the 'Watergate' era in the United States, it has, as we will note, been with a certain lack of constitutional sureness, or any certainty as to the past precedents or general constitutional-philosophical grounds for rationalising such judicial interventions in the executive or legislative processes.

In West Germany, in February, 1983, the Second Senate of the Federal Constitutional Court ruled upon the constitutionality of the dissolution, by the federal President, of the lower House of the federal legislature (*Bundestag*).[25] The issue had arisen as a result of a wholly contrived, artificial crisis within the *Bundestag*. The long-time Social Democrat-Free Democrat (liberal) coalition, headed by Chancellor Helmut Schmidt, had broken up at the beginning of October, 1982, because of disagreements over economic policy between its two elements; and the small Free Democratic party, which held the numerical balance of power in the *Bundestag* between the two large, opposing parties, the Social Democrats and the Christian Democrats and its (Bavarian) Christian Social Union faction, had then immediately joined with the Christian Democrats to form a new coalition government with the Christian Democratic leader, Helmut Kohl, being elected as Chancellor under what is known as a 'constructive no-confidence' motion which simultaneously designated Mr. Kohl and displaced Mr. Schmidt in the one vote which, as required by the Bonn Constitution (Article 67), was carried by an absolute majority of the members of the *Bundestag,* though barely so. The new Chancellor then devoted his skills to setting up a further no-confidence vote which, though having with his new coalition partner an absolute majority in the *Bundestag,* he would arrange to lose. The reason for this artifice was that the Bonn Constitution, in an endeavour to reduce the political chances of unstable or frequently changing Governments which were thought to have weakened the preceding Weimar Republic, had prescribed that the *Bundestag,* whose constitutionally-prescribed term (Article 39 (1)) was four years, could only be dissolved before expiry of that term if a motion of the Chancellor for a vote of confidence should not be carried by a majority of the members of the Bundestag (Article 68 (1)). The intent of the drafters of the Bonn Constitution of 1949 was to shore up the stability of the federal legislature by guaranteeing it a fixed term-of-years unless, demonstrably, government backed by majority vote did not exist. This was why, for example, in the 'constructive no confidence' vote on 1 October 1982, the then Chancellor Schmidt, no longer having a majority, ceded to the new Chancellor Kohl, without having the further constitutional option, (as under the British-derived Parliamentary system), of himself dissolving the legislature for fresh elections. In mid-December, 1982, the confidence motion, introduced by Chancellor Kohl, under Article 68 (1) of the Bonn Constitution, failed to carry, Chancellor Kohl's Christian Democrats and his coalition Free Democrats abstaining from voting and allowing the Opposition Social Democrats to defeat the motion. Chancellor Kohl then, armed with his defeat, went very happily to the federal President and asked him to dissolve the *Bundestag* for fresh elections (Article 68 (1)). The federal

President, after three weeks delay, agreed to the request, and general elections were then called for March, 1983.

The issue was whether a polite constitutional charade of this sort, which clearly violated both the historical intent and also the spirit of the Bonn charter, should be upheld as constitutional on the score of its literal compliance with the text of Article 68 (1). The issue arose squarely before the Federal Constitutional Court because four Parliamentary deputies petitioned it to declare the federal President's dissolution of the *Bundestag* as unconstitutional. [26] The matter had not been without a certain political embarrassment for the federal President, Dr. Carstens, himself a member of Chancellor Kohl's Christian Democratic party and a former Member of the *Bundestag* and Minister. Dr. Carstens was reported, in the Press, at the time he granted dissolution of the *Bundestag,* to harbour doubts about the no-confidence motion device employed by Chancellor Kohl, but to have comforted himself, in the exercise of his discretion as federal President, by the thought that it was not his job to act as spiritual confessor of the Members of the *Bundestag* and to enquire as to their actual motives in withholding confidence from the Kohl Government by doing, as the Christian Democratic-Free Democratic coalition members did, in abstaining *en masse* in the actual vote and so ensuring its passage through the Social Democratic minority's votes. Under the Bonn charter, Members of the *Bundestag* were to be 'subject only to their conscience' (Article 38 (1)); and the ordinary political processes, through the forthcoming general elections, could supply any political corrective that might be needed.

The complaint before the Federal Constitutional Court, brought by the four deputies (one Christian Democrat, two Free Democrats, and one independent and former Social Democrat), arose under the *Organstreitigkeiten* aspect of the Court's jurisdiction, involving conflicts between different, coordinate Constitutional institutions – here the federal President and the *Bundestag,* through its individual Members, the four deputies contending that their rights as Members of the *Bundestag* (Article 38 (2)) had been directly threatened by the federal President's action in dissolving the *Bundestag.*

In its decision, the Second Senate of the Federal Constitutional Court cleared one preliminary, jurisdictional hurdle quite easily, granting standing-to-sue to the four deputies under the Court Statute (sections 63 and 64 (1)), and being unanimous on this point. On other, substantive issues, however, the Court divided. By majority vote, the Second Senate held that the Presidential order dissolving the *Bundestag* was in conformity with Article 68 (1) of the Constitution, the judges concluding that the grant or decline of dissolution was a high political decision that belonged to the constitutional discretion of the President. On the specific objection that the Presidential dissolution power under Article 68 (1) was predicated upon a *bona fide* demand by the federal Chancellor to the *Bundestag* for a confidence vote (and not, as here, an artificial or contrived request in which the Chancellor was submitting the motion in the expectation, and hope, of being defeated) the Court, again by majority, concluded that it could not go behind the formal record and examine the factual basis of the federal Chancellor's request to the *Bundestag* for a confidence vote. These parts of the Second Senate's decision were rendered by a 6-to-2 majority, Judges Rinck and Rottmann each filing dissenting opinions in which they recorded their own views that, at the time Chancellor Kohl submitted his demand for a confidence vote, a situation of political instability such as might justify such a demand did not exist within the *Bundestag*. For this reason, the two dissenting judges felt that both the confidence motion and the dissolution order by the President were unconstitutional in terms of Article 68 (1). The Rinck dissenting opinion, in particular, is a most impressive examination of the legislative history of the adoption of the dissolution clauses of the Bonn Constitution, and the intentions of the 'Founding Fathers' as to their operation. However, the Second Senate majority judgment, arrived at with unusual speed so as not to interrupt or delay the federal electoral processes, then under way, and announced in mid-February, 1983, received a clear form of popular electoral ratification in the March elections, Chancellor Kohl's Christian Democratic-Free Democratic coalition being returned to office for a full term. The final electoral resolution of the problem seemed to confirm the practical political wisdom of the federal President's original decision to grant dissolution, in spite of constitutional doubts, and to allow the matter to be determined, one way or another, by the ordinary political and electoral processes which could come into operation immediately the dissolution had been granted. The majority judgment of the Second Senate raises, then, the principle of judicial self-restraint, in relation, first of all, to 'political questions' which are deemed to be properly non-justiciable because of their high political content, and, secondly, to the duty of deference and respect for the discretionary judgment of another, coordinate institution of government acting within the ambit of its constitutionally-defined powers. On the substantive law side, however, a new constitutional 'gloss', tolerating an enlarged area of executive discretion as to the granting of a dissolution of the *Bundestag,* beyond the rather narrow conditions stipulated in the Constitution, had clearly been created by the Federal Constitutional Court's judicial self-restraint.

In Japan, an almost identical question involving the executive power of dissolution of the legislature had come to the Supreme Court of Japan in its early post-War era. In August, 1952, Prime Minister Yoshida had secured the dissolution of the lower House of the Diet by means of an

Imperial decree under Article 7 of the Constitution which stipulates the powers of the Emperor, to be exercised 'with the advice and approval of the Cabinet', as including 'dissolution of the House of Representatives'. The House's term is stipulated, elsewhere (Article 45), as being four years, subject to earlier dissolution. Article 69 of the Constitution reads: –

> 'If the House of Representatives passes a non-confidence resolution, or rejects a confidence resolution, the Cabinet shall resign *en masse,* unless the House of Representatives is dissolved within ten (10) days.'

This clearly had not happened with Prime Minister Yoshida's dissolution. The Prime Minister had by-passed Article 69 altogether, in making no attempt to meet its requirements. A member of the Parliamentary Opposition asked the Supreme Court to declare the dissolution null and void, but the Court, in a unanimous holding, in 1953, refused, invoking the doctrine of 'political question'.[27] The case has an extra interest because its very succinct and laconic judgment is accompanied by a long concurring opinion by Justice Mano which looks, nevertheless, to the constitutional merits of the question and concludes that the power of dissolution of Parliament is contained in Article 69 and that its conditions must be met before dissolution can be granted.[28] Judge Mano related the power of dissolution to the general system of constitutional checks and balances established under the 1946 Constitution, the separation of powers, and the desire to contain and limit by Article 69 the executive's control over the Diet. Judge Mano reaches out for pre-War German law – here Hitler's dissolution of the *Reichstag* – as an example of what the post-War Japanese constitution-makers tried to avoid in their new charter. Justice Mano's opinion is, of course, an extended *obiter dictum,* not affecting the unanimous Opinion of Court, to which he adhered, declining to rule on the complaint for preliminary, procedural reasons not going to its substantive constitutional law merits. The Supreme Court, in a later decision of 7 March 1962, again refused to exercise judicial review over the legislature's internal operations – in this case, the question whether the Diet's 19th session had been legally extended at the time it voted amendments to the Police Law, the Court indicating that it must defer to the autonomy of the Diet.

In France, the *Conseil constitutionnel,* had no hesitation – perhaps because of its own legislative roots in the old Fourth Republic's *Comité constitutionnel,* perhaps also because of the direct legislative experience of some of its nine members – in moving in where other tribunals have chosen to apply a prudent self-restraint. On 20 December 1979 – the exact date becomes relevant because of the time sequence – the Socialist Opposition party in the National Assembly took advantage of the highly permissive 1974 Amendment to the *Conseil* statute whereby any 60 deputies of the National Assembly (or any 60 Senators) may seize the *Conseil* with a constitutional question, [29] to launch, (in company with the President of the National Assembly, M. Chaban-Delmas, a prominent Gaullist), a challenge to the constitutionality of the Barre Government's finance and budget law. [30] The actual issue was a complicated procedural one, not going to the substance of the Barre budgetary proposals. A General Ordinance, in existence since 1959, required budget laws to be in two parts, the first part establishing the general conditions of financial equilibrium, and the second part comprising the actual voting of credits. The Barre Government had been defeated in the National Assembly on the first part of its budget law; but it had then moved on to parliamentary adoption of the second part of the budget law, by making use of Article 49 (3) of the Constitution which allows a Prime Minister, by treating the matter as one of 'confidence', to have it considered as being legally adopted by the National Assembly unless a motion of motion of censure, filed within the next twenty-four hours, be passed by the National Assembly. The *Conseil constitutionnel,* within four days of receiving the constitutional complaint, ruled on 24 December 1979 that the budget law did not conform to the Constitution. [31] The constitutional vice was not one of substance, but of procedure and specifically of the chronology of the vote on the budget. The Barre Government's reaction to this ruling by the *Conseil constitutionnel* was immediately to convoke the National Assembly and to have adopted by the National Assembly, on 27 December 1979, a further law authorising the Government to collect, in 1980, already-existing taxes. The *Conseil constitutionnel* was immediately seized of the issue by the necessary number (sixty) of Communist and Socialist deputies, and it now ruled, on 30 December 1979, that this latest statute authorizing the Government to collect, in 1980, the already existing taxes, conformed to the Constitution. [32] This latest *Conseil* ruling allowed the Government to carry on until such time as the National Assembly could be convoked again, in regular session early in 1980, to consider the Barre Government's budget project. What was involved was no *crise de régime,* for in fact, aided by the *Conseil's* second ruling, the Barre Government was able to extricate itself easily and quickly from the constitutional impasse created by the first *Conseil* ruling, by taking limited 'corrective' action immediately and then planning more substantial budgetary project modifications at its leisure. [33] If the *Conseil,* in its first ruling, ventured, on the demand of Opposition members of the National Assembly, to examine the working of the internal, law-making procedures of the legislature on a matter as notionally fundamental as adoption of the budget, thus invoking its constitutional arbitration *rôle* against the executive, it balanced this constitutional activism by a studied restraint and pragmatism in upholding the Government's 'corrective' action. The *Conseil* also gave its ruling with unusual speed, so as to cause the least possible practical disruption to the executive-legislative processes.

We have already, in the general discussion of the Courts and the constitutional *Grundnorm* and its specific application to suspension of the constitution or constitutional safeguards under the 'emergency' doctrine, looked at the Indian Supreme Court's ruling on the constitutional 'emergency' proclaimed by Prime Minister Indira Gandhi's Government in the period 1975-6. In *Jabalpur v. Shukla,* in 1976,[34] the Court, by a four-to-one majority, upheld executive (Presidential) proclamation suspending the right of any person to move the Courts for the enforcement of Article 19 of the Constitution (Right to Freedom) rights, and refused to hear Habeas Corpus petitions by political detainees on the basis that these were not maintainable during the emergency. The Court also, in a unanimous decision of a five-member bench in 1975, in *Indira Nehru Gandhi v. Raj Narain,*[35] upheld Prime Minister Gandhi's appeal from a lower Court (Allahabad High Court) ruling which had purported to nullify her election to the lower House of the Indian Parliament in 1971, and thereby impugn her right to continue as Prime Minister. The Indian Parliament had already, in adopting the Thirty-Ninth Amendment to the Constitution, nullified the lower Court ruling on the validity of the Prime Minister's election as Member of Parliament, and though the Supreme Court now made some criticisms, in passing, of the Thirty-Ninth Amendment, the result of the Supreme Court's holding was clear. If, in *Jabalpur v. Shukla,* the Supreme Court applied self-restraint in relation to a 'political question' involving executive high political, discretionary powers, in the *Indira Nehru Gandhi* case it recognised the ultimate reality that it could not sit, in effect, as a court of disputed electoral returns, looking into the actual application of particular individual constituencies' election processes. This is quite a different proposition, of course, from a judicial setting or reviewing of constitutional norms as to electoral fairness, or ensuring equality before the law in the electoral laws themselves, on a basis generally applicable to all constitutuencies, as we shall see in the discussion, *infra,* on the Courts and the electoral processes. But, on the particular facts of the *Indira Nehru Gandhi* case, the original challenge to her election as a Member of Parliament seemed inspired, at the political level, by purely mischievous motives, and it would have been an act of judicial irresponsibility for the Supreme Court itself to appear to condone such actions, – in a period of admitted political instability and conflict in the country at large, – by countenancing any Court review of the merits of the Prime Minister's original election as a Member. The corrective, if any be needed, should be left to Parliament itself or to the ordinary political processes at the next general elections.

In the United States, the Supreme Court has always recognised the full authority of the federal legislature (Congress) to determine its own rules and procedures, as matters not subject to judicial review. The leading cases go back to the late 19th century – *U.S.* v. *Ballin*,[36] and *Field* v. *Clark*,[37] in 1892, and encompass, also, the so-called 'enrolled bill' rule, whereby the signatures of the presiding officers of the two Houses are conclusive as to the contents and authority of measures adopted by Congress, and cannot be impeached in the Courts. Some interesting questions as to the limits of the Court powers *vis-à-vis* Congress and the Presidency arose during the 'Watergate' crisis of 1973-4, and not all of them were resolved at the time in so far as the resignation of the President forestalled any final action on a number of them. The United States Constitution contains a specific clause (Article II (4)) on Impeachment of the President, Vice-President and civil officers of the United States, the actual constitutional phrasing prescribing removal from office on – 'Impeachment for, and Conviction of, Treason, Bribery, or other high Crimes and Misdemeanours'. On ordinary principles of constitutional construction it would appear that the indictment, (and *a fortiori* the conviction), for Impeachment is constitutionally predicated upon the commission of *criminal* acts; but some of the counts formulated by various Congressmen and pressed for adoption in the proposed proceedings against President Nixon shewed a tendency to pass over and confuse, (perhaps deliberately), the frontiers between actual criminal misconduct and asserted errors of political judgment – the same essential blurring of the distinction between the stricter, criminal impeachments and the much looser political impeachments, present in the original English constitutional law of impeachment from mediaeval times onwards.[38] Such questions might, arguably, have been meet for judicial review and control, but the issue became otiose when the President resigned, leaving unclear whether any Impeachment bill could also have included alleged political errors not in themselves involving criminal acts. One question that was, however, resolved by the Courts in very decisive terms, flowing from the 'Watergate' crisis, was the scope of the so-called Executive Privilege. The Supreme Court of the United States, in 1974, in a unanimous decision, *U.S.* v. *Nixon*,[39] refused to quash a *subpoena* to the President, issued on the motion of the 'Watergate' Special Prosecutor, directing production of certain tape recordings and documents relating to Presidential conversations with staff and advisers which, the Prosecutor contended, were necessary as evidence in criminal proceedings. The public interest in the affair was very great, and the resultant political pressures on the Court may have contributed to a ruling which, in retrospect, seems to go very far in limiting the political discretion and judgment of another, coordinate institution of constitutional government to the Court. Could not, or should not, the matter have been left to determination, ultimately, by the political-legal processes established under the Impeachment sections of the Constitution for constitutional pursuit of an incumbent President? The Court itself seems to have had some doubts: it recognised, in its Opinion of Court delivered by Chief Justice Burger, that there is a presumption of privilege for Presidential communications, but insisted that this privilege could only be a qualified one and must yield to other, countervailing legal interests, such as use in pending criminal proceedings. The Chief Justice also, in an *obiter dictum,* indicated that – 'a claim of need to protect military, diplomatic, or sensitive national security secrets' might be upheld as a valid exercise of Presidential Executive Privilege, in the future, against Court review.

(b) *The executive in Foreign Affairs*

We have seen how, in *Massachusetts* v. *Laird* in 1970,[39a] the United States Supreme Court, by a 6-to-3 vote, refused to accept jurisdiction over a suit by the Massachusetts legislature to determine the constitutionality of the American participation in the Vietnam armed conflict. The dividing line between a Court ruling directed to the preliminary, procedural, adjectival law, standing-to-sue issue and one that overcomes that first hurdle but then goes on to apply judicial self-restraint as to the substantive law issue, under the 'political questions' legal rubric, is not always clearly established. Justices Harlan and Stewart, in differing from the Court majority's refusal of jurisdiction in *Massachusetts* v. *Laird,* favoured hearing legal argument on both standing-to-sue and also the 'political questions'-justiciability issue; while Justice Douglas, in his formal dissenting opinion filed to the Court's refusal of jurisdiction, addressed himself at length to both points.[39b] In *Holtzman* v. *Schlesinger,* in 1973,[39c] the same substantive issue of the constitutionality of American involvement in the Vietnam War was presented again to the Supreme Court, and this time the Court addressed itself directly to the 'political questions' issue. Notwithstanding what one of its members, Justice Marshall, described as a 'respectable and growing body of lower court opinions' to the effect that cases challenging the U.S. Presidential (executive) war-making in Vietnam did, indeed, offer justiciable controversies,[39d] the Supreme Court majority refused to support a lower Court determination that the Presidential-directed bombing of Cambodia was unconstitutional.[39e] The Supreme Court majority concluded that the Presidential-authorised use of the armed forces abroad, in the absence of a formal declaration of War, constituted a non-justiciable 'political question' that could not be reviewed by the Courts.[39f] Justice Marshall, for his part, would have preferred to add a nuanced and qualified statement establishing substantive legal limits, nevertheless, to such Presidential power: 'it seems likely that the President may not wage war without some form of congressional approval – except, perhaps, in the case of a pressing emergency or when the President is in the process of extricating himself from a war which Congress once authorised'.[39g] The Supreme Court decision, in *Holtzman* v. *Schlesinger* in 1973, to apply the 'political questions' doctrine as an absolute bar to Court examination of the constitutional merits of executive action in armed conflicts, was given at the height of the American civil disobedience campaign against American involvement in Vietnam and at a time, also, when Congressional attacks on alleged abuses of Presidential power in the Watergate affair were also at their strongest. The Supreme Court itself, in *U.S.* v. *Nixon,* in the following year, 1974,[39h] did, indeed, establish clear positive law limits to Presidential claims of inherent, prerogative powers; and so the Court's refusal to intervene in *Holtzman* v. *Schlesinger,*[39i] in spite of all the cognate, enormous public pressures upon it, must be regarded as constituting the high-water mark of the 'political questions' exception to Court jurisdiction, in its modern form.

We have already examined, in the case of Japan, the Supreme Court's disposition, in *Suzuki (1952),*[40] *and Sunakawa* (1959),[41] of various political challenges to the Japanese Government's attempts, notwithstanding Article 9 of the Constitution and the 'renunciation-of-war' imperative therein imposed upon Japan, to integrate Japan into the Western political and military alliance system in the Cold War period. The decisions in both cases, in situations where the legality of the para-military National Police Reserve and of Japanese adherence to the Japan-U.S. Security Treaty was sought to be impugned, avoided the substantive law issues and turned instead on procedural issues – the necessity for a concrete case/controversy and not a purely abstract question, the doctrine of 'political questions'. There is no doubt of their main thrust – judicial self-restraint and the duty of Court deference to executive-legislative authority in highly delicate issues of foreign policy, which, in Japan's case, since involving U.S. Military Occupation policies at the time of the effective reestablishment of the Japanese state, post-war, went to its very legal foundations or *Grundnorm.*

In practical terms, and with somewhat similar post-War political events of foreign military occupation preceding the return of political sovereignty and the establishment of the truncated West German state, the West German Federal Constitutional Court, as we have seen, effectively disabled itself, on procedural grounds, from passing on the substantive law questions involved in any West German adherence to the projected

European Defence Community, which the three former Western military occupation powers were pressing upon the Adenauer Government at the opening of the 1950s. In applying a conscious policy of judicial self-restraint, the Court, in the result, immunised such highly controversial political issues from judicial review and left them to be determined by the ordinary political processes, as they, in fact, were when the E.D.C. project was abandoned in 1954 when it failed of adoption in the French legislature. In somewhat parallel political circumstances, involving once again the issue of West German rearmament and West German commitment to the Western military alliance system, but this time the possibility of equipping the armed forces with Atomic weapons, on which the *Bundestag* had voted favourably, the Federal Constitutional Court positively intervened against *Länder* (regional) governments to prevent their embarrassing the federal Government in the conduct of its foreign policy, as against the argument that the federal Government's rearmament policies ran counter to the general mandate, under the Bonn Constitution, for reunification of Germany, West and East. Two of the *Länder,* the city-states of Bremen and Hamburg, which had Social Democratic *régimes* politically opposed to the Christian Democratic government at the federal level, had proceeded to pass statutes authorising popular advisory referenda, within their regions, on the question of arming the West German military forces with atomic weapons. The Federal Constitutional Court, in the decision of its Second Senate in 1958,[42] granted injunctions against the holding of the proposed referenda – this on the application of the federal Government. The Court reasoned that the holding of the referenda, even though their results would not be binding on the *Länder* concerned, or *a fortiori* on the federal Government, nevertheless would subject the *Bundestag* and the federal Government to undesirable political pressures in discharging their political responsibilities in an area of concededly exclusive federal responsibility under the Bonn Constitution. The Court's decision, here, turns not so much on the issue of judicial self-restraint *vis-à-vis* the federal executive in its conduct of foreign policy, as on another, *federal* principle – the *Bundestreue* (federal comity), – which we will have occasion to look at again, which enjoined the *Länder* (state) governments in the present case to exercise constitutional self-restraint and to respect the constitutional allocation of powers, federal-*Länder,* and the exclusive control over foreign policy established thereunder in the federal Government.

We have already discussed, earlier, the decision of the Federal Constitutional Court in the *Grundlagenvertrag* (Basic Treaty) decision of 1973,[43] where the Court's Second Senate applied judicial self-restraint in regard to that innovatory exercise in executive foreign policy, the Brandt Government's *Ostpolitik,* and refused to intervene against the keystone

Treaty in that *politik,* the West German-East German Treaty normalising political-legal relations between the two parts of divided Germany. In December, 1983, the Second Senate of the Federal Constitutional Court, in a unanimous decision as to its end results, though with one negative vote as to its legal grounds, declined to strike down on constitutional grounds the stationing of U.S. middle-range nuclear weapons ('Pershing II Missiles') on West German territory.[43a] The matter had originated in an application for an interlocutory injunction to forbid the introduction of the Pershing Missiles into West Germany, on the part of the West German 'Green Party' and other pacifist groups. The narrow ground of the decision is to be found, above all, in constitutional separation-of-powers considerations, going to the deference that the Courts owe to the other, coordinate, (executive and legislative), organs of government in the exercise of their constitutional powers. As the Court expressly noted, the Foreign policy and the Defence policy of the Federal Republic belong to those other, constitutionally competent organs, with any possible risks involved in such policies to be weighed by those organs and any resultant political responsibility to be accepted by them. So far, it is a classical application of the principle of judicial self-restraint *vis-à-vis* the other, coordinate, non-judicial branches of government; and a judicial recognition that Foreign and Defence policy raises difficult political issues going beyond the Courts' special competence. The Second Senate of the Federal Constitutional Court did, however, go on to add to its essentially technical, procedural ruling the laconic comment – reminiscent, perhaps, of a Common Law judicial *obiter dictum* – that the postulated grave threat, (the subject of the application for interlocutory injunction) stemmed not so much directly from the nuclear weapons stationed in the Federal Republic of Germany as from the nuclear weapon potential outside the Federal Republic; though the Second Senate acknowledged that that postulated threat could nevertheless be an indirect consequence of the conduct of the Federal Republic.[43b] One further decision of the Federal Constitutional Court in the foreign affairs field, though it is rooted more in federal constitutional principles than in either executive-in-foreign-affairs constitutional power considerations or even judicial self-restraint, has a special interest for us, for it was rendered by the German judges in full awareness of Canadian and United States leading decisions in parallel cases, and with an evident conscious preference for the rationale of the one, rather than the other, as to the application of federal principles to foreign affairs – here to treaty-making and treaty-implementation. In the *Reichskonkordat* decision of 1957,[44] the Federal Constitutional Court had to pass on the constitutionality of *Land* (Niedersachsen) legislation providing for common, non-denominational education for all school children within the *Land,* notwithstanding its incompatibility with the provisions of the German-Vatican treaty or *Concordat* of 1933 guarante-eing separate education for all Roman Catholic students in Germany. In balancing the federal Government's constitutional power over foreign affairs (and also a very specific provision, Article 123, continuing in force (pre-Bonn Constitution) 'state treaties concluded by the German Reich concerning matters for which, according to this Basic Law, *Land* legisla-tion is competent') against the undoubted *Länder* constitutional power over education within the *Land,* the Federal Consitutional Court, man-aged to reconcile the two apparently conflicting policies, federal and *Land,* by holding that while the *Land* legislation was fully constitutional, the Treaty of 1933 was, nevertheless, still valid and binding at law upon West Germany. The Court reasoned that the mere fact that the federal Government might be obligated at International Law under a still-con-tinuing treaty with a foreign country, could not give it power, in the implementation of the treaty, over subjects otherwise (in terms of the Bonn federal system) belonging to the *Länder,* this argument not being affected by the fact that at the actual time of conclusion of the treaty in 1933, the subject matter might then have been within the federal Gov-ernment's power (under the old Weimar Constitution of 1919). The Court recognised, in its opinion, that difficult problems might be pre-sented for the West German Government because of the potential gap between International Law obligations assumed by the federal Govern-ment under the treaty-making power, and the federal Government's pow-ers, under the Bonn Constitution, effectively to implement those obliga-tions within West Germany in internal, municipal law. In such cases, the Court said, the remedy, if one be needed, must be found in the inner harmony of the Bonn Constitution, the principle of the *Bundestreue* (fed-eral comity)[45] and cooperation by the *Länder* in the fulfilment, at the treaty-implementation, municipal law level, of any such International Law obligations.

In the parallel Canadian and American leading cases, in the same field, (which the West German judges were aware of at the time they rendered their *Reichskonkordat* decision though they do not refer to them, in terms, in their judgment), what is manifest is a clear difference of opinion as to the importance of the federal question in the national polity, and perhaps, also, different approaches to functional federalism and the ren-dering operational of a complex, territorially divided system of govern-ment and government decision-making power, within the one state. In the great decision of the United States Supreme Court in *Missouri* v. *Holland* in 1920,[46] Mr. Justice Holmes, writing the Opinion of the Court in one of his most brilliant judicial essays, had ruled that the foreign affairs power of the national government must be broadly construed and that it covered, in particular, the concluding and implementation of treaties in areas of subject matter which, in the absence of the treaty, might not otherwise be within national authority since not coming within the express grant of national powers under the United States Constitution. In terms of the comparative constitutional law of federalism, *Missouri* v. *Holland* undoubtedly represents the high-water mark of national power as to treaty-making and treaty-implementation in a federal state. In the *Labour Conventions* ruling, rendered by the Imperial Privy Council in 1937,[47] sitting then in its erstwhile historical *rôle* as final appellate tribunal for Canada as part of the then British Empire and Commonwealth, the other side of the coin is presented. The Privy Council viewed the division of legislative powers under the Canadian constitutional charter in rigid and static terms, and insisted on treating them as being, so to speak, in 'watertight compartments', without any carry-over between federal Government legislative powers and those of the regions (Provinces). The subject matter, with the multilateral treaties involved in *Labour Conventions,* being conditions of labour, and this being a regional (Provincial) power under the Canadian constitutional charter, the only legislative power to implement the Treaty obligations which, the Privy Council conceded, had been validly entered in to by the federal Government, lay with the regional (Provincial) administrations. As to a possible gap, then, between Treaty-making (federal power), and Treaty-implementation (regional (Provincial) in the present case), the Privy Council had little practical advice to offer in its 1937 decision. It is widely interpreted that the non-Canadian (British) judges, sitting on the Privy Council for its *Labour Conventions* ruling, had wanted to render a 'Provincial Rights' opinion, weighted towards the regional units of Canada in the spirit of constitutional pluralism established by earlier Boards of the Privy Council in relation to Canada, under the great Scottish liberal pluralist philosophers and judges, Lord Watson and his intellectual disciple, Lord Haldane, who had dominated Privy Council rulings on Canada at the end of the 19th century and the beginning of the 20th century. The matter is not free from doubt, however, as Watson and Haldane were long since gone from the Privy Council by 1937; the single Opinion of the tribunal is not especially well written or reasoned; and we now know that, (for an anonymous tribunal that never divulged its actual vote, at that time) the decision was only rendered by a four-to-three vote.[48] In *Reichskonkordat,* however, in 1957,[49] there is little doubt that the West German judges made a conscious decision, responding to pragmatic considerations, at the time, of the need for strengthening the *rôle* of the *Länder* in West German government as a bulwark in the Bonn constitutional charter's attempts to prevent any return to the marked centripetal tendencies and concentration of decision-making power in the national administration that were considered, historically, as one of the principal contributing factors to the political downfall of the preceding, Weimar Republic. The opting for a decentralised, pluralistic federalism is the more striking because there were other avenues to decision-making available which would have enabled the West German Court to have reached the same result, – but avoiding the substantive constitutional law issues that it in fact decided, – by following the United States constitutional maxim of always avoiding the constitutional law issue wherever possible. It could, for example, have ruled that the *Concordat,* being made with the Vatican, was not really a Treaty but some lesser form of international law accord not having the full substantive legal character or consequences of a treaty; or that the German adherence to the *Concordat* in 1933, being made under the general machinery of the Nazi *régime's* Enabling Act of 1933, (itself a form of constitutional *voie de fait*), was not really an effective adherence; or that the claimed binding character of the *Concordat* today must be interpreted as subject to reexamination and revision under the International Law doctrine of *clausula rebus sic stantibus.* The decision rendered by the Second Senate of the Court, in *Reichskonkordat,* reflects the thinking of its most prominent personality and constitutional philosopher, Judge Gerhard Leibholz, and the policy of judicial activism in behalf of strengthening the regions (*Länder*) and thus West German federalism as functional democracy.[50] It is a high-water mark in West German federalism, somewhat artificial and 'constructed' as the *Länder* were in the politically *truncated* West Germany of 1949; and, as a judicial policy, begins to decline from the 1960s onwards as the sociological facts of an increasingly mobile West German society begin, in turn, to operate on and correct the federal ideal-constructs imposed by the constitutional charter.

In France, the *Conseil constitutionnel* is faced with some quite specific provisions in the Constitution itself which define, and also limit, its own *rôle* in reveiw of treaties, international engagements, and foreign affairs generally. Under Article 52, the President of the Republic negotiates and ratifies treaties; under Article 53, treaties take effect after having been ratified and approved; and under Article 55, treaties and other agreements, once ratified and approved – 'have, from the time of publication, an authority superior to that of laws'. Under Article 54, if the *Conseil constitutionnel,* being consulted by the President of the Republic, the Prime Minister, or the President of either the Senate or National Assembly, has –

> 'declared that an international obligation includes a clause contrary to the Constitution, authorisation to ratify or approve it may be accorded only after revision of the Constitution'.

It follows from this that it is only, really, *projects* for treaties that the

Conseil constitutionnel can consider in terms of their conformity to the Constitution; for a treaty or similar international engagement, once ratified and approved, has an authority superior to that of laws. Further, if the *Conseil* should judge a projected treaty text as incompatible with the Constitution, it is suggested by two of its leading interpreters, Favoreu and Philip, that it is the Constitution itself that should be amended to bring it into line with France's projected international obligation, not the project of treaty.[51] The constitutional Fathers of the Constitution of 1958, on this view, wanted to reconcile the principle of the supremacy of International Law with the desire to establish a constitutional safety net against the adoption of international agreements putting in issue the Constitution itself and notably national sovereignty. Luchaire speaks, in this regard, of a 'Gaullist spirit' in those who drafted these particular Articles of the Constitution, especially one of the main architects of the Constitution, Michel Debré, who was very attached to the idea of national independence and wanted to lock the door to the supra-nationalist partisans of a European constitutional federation, who were in a majority in the Parliament of 1958.[52] It was thus not a question, as with the rest of the *Conseil constitutionnel* jurisdiction, of controlling the constitutionality of laws or of preventing Parliament from breaking out of its competences, and certainly not of safeguarding the rights and freedoms of the individual. According to Luchaire, the possibility of this control in relation to international engagements is quite simply the manifestation of a nationalist reflex directed principally against the European Community.[53] This control does not, however, have the effect of introducing into each treaty signed by France a general reservation as to its compatibility with French Constitution. It simply results in the complication of the procedure for ratification of an international engagement contrary to the Constitution by subordinating such ratification to a preliminary amendment of the Constitution, under the normal provisions for Amendment of the Constitution (Article 89) that we have already looked at. It will be noted that Article 54 of the Constitution limits the power to seize the *Conseil* with the question whether a projected international obligation is counter to the Constitution, to the President, the Prime Minister or the presiding officers of each of the two legislative Houses. The 60 deputies or 60 Senators now authorised by the reform in the *Conseil* statute of 1974,[54] to seize the *Conseil* with various questions cannot, apparently, raise this type of matter; although in its decision of 29-30 December 1976 on the issue of direct election to the European Parliament, the *Conseil* indicated that the said 60 deputies or 60 Senators could indeed seize it with a complaint going to a law authorising the ratification or approval of such an international agreement.[55] There have been two main decisions bearing on section 54. In its decision of 19 June 1970,[56] the *Conseil,* on the request of the Prime Minister, ruled on whether the treaty signed in April, 1970, modifying certain budgetary provisions of the Treaties instituting the European Communities and the Treaty instituting a single Council and a single Commission of the European Communities, as well as the decision of the Council of the Communities in April, 1970, concerning replacement of financial contributions of member-states by resources appropriate to the Communities, were compatible with the Constitution. The *Conseil* ruled in favour of constitutionality.

In its decision of 29-30 December 1976,[57] the *Conseil,* on the request of the President of the Republic, ruled on the question of the compatibility of the agreement of September, 1976, which envisaged the election of Members of the European Parliament by universal suffrage, with the French Constitution, and again the *Conseil* ruled in favour of constitutionality. In both cases, though it was the executive – the Prime Minister, and the President of the Republic – who had seized the Court with the matters, the executive action had been largely provoked by political contestation within the French Parliament on the issue of constitutionality of the international engagements *vis-à-vis* the French Constitution; and the executive action in approaching the *Conseil* for an expectedly favourable ruling was designed to dispel the doubts and prevent their gaining ground among other members of the Government's Parliamentary majority. Both cases concerned the European Communities, and it was the arch-Gaullist and former Gaullist Prime Minister, M. Debré, who in fact had raised the Parliamentary storm over direct elections to the European Parliament and its compatibility with Gaullist notions of national sovereignty thought to be embodied in the Constitution of 1958.[58] In its 1976 decision, the *Conseil* rendered some comfort to the opponents of European integration by stating, in its decision, that nothing in the Constitution authorised the transfer of national sovereignty to any international organisation of whatever sort. But in the substance of its decision, it essentially adopted the argument advanced in public by President Giscard d'Estaing and Prime Minister Barre that what was involved in the direct election project neither modified the competences and powers already attributed, on a strictly defined basis, to the European Communities, nor modified the character of the European Assembly (Parliament).[59] To the objections of those who contended that direct election by universal suffrage would create a 'dynamic of sovereignty' and risk to transform the European Parliament into a sort of European constituent assembly, the *Conseil* suggested that such direct election by universal suffrage could have neither result since any evolution of this sort could only result from a new modification of the existing Treaties and the putting under way of the constitutional procedures envisaged in this eventuality.[60] The 1976 decision, as with the preceding 1970 decision, fully defers to the executive *rôle* in determination and application of foreign policy, in a way analogous to the judicial self-restraint that we have seen with other tribunals, outside France, having to rule in the same domain. It was evidently bitterly contested within the *Conseil,* for *Le Monde* of 1 January 1977 reported it as having been rendered only by a five-to-four vote, even with the qualifications as to safeguarding of national sovereignty for the future already introduced into the judgment.[61] Maurice Duverger, in fact, qualified it as a Pyrrhic victory for the French 'Europeanists', and as representing a break with the 'slow movement to supra-nationalism' that had been interrupted by President de Gaulle in 1958 and that had taken on again after his departure in 1969.[62]

NOTES

1. The idea was much discussed in the early post-War years – significantly, among those constitutionalists actively interested in re-establishing a 'robust' democratic constitutionalism in Western Europe who had themselves the twin, German Civil Law and Anglo-Saxon Common Law, constitutional experience. See, in general, Carl J. Friedrich, *Constitutional Government and Democracy* (rev. ed., 1950), p. 132 *et seq.;* Friedrich, *The Impact of American Constitutionalism Abroad* (1967); Friedrich, *Limited Government. A comparison* (1974); Karl Loewenstein, *Political Power and the Governmental Process* (1957); Gerhard Leibholz, *Die Gleichheit vor dem Gesetz* (2nd ed., 1959), p. 88 *et seq.*

2. P. K. Tripathi, in *Constitutionalism in Asia. Asian Views of the American Influence* (L. W. Beer, ed., 1979), p. 68 *et seq.;* S. N. Ray, *Judicial Review and Fundamental Rights* (1974), p. 117 *et seq.*

3. See, generally, George H. Gadbois Jr., 'The Supreme Court of India: a preliminary report of an empirical study', 4 *Journal of Constitutional and Parliamentary Studies* 33 (1970).

4. *Golak Nath* v. *State of Punjab,* A.I.R. *1967* S.C. 1643. And see, gneerally, S.P. Sathe, *Fundamental Rights and the Amendment of the Indian Constitution* (1968), especially at p. 11 *et seq.;* J. L. Kapur, 'The Constitution of India and some recent Amendments made therein', 23 *Jahrbuch des öffentlichen Rechts der Gegenwart* 505, at pp. 520-534 (1974); P. K. Tripathi, *op. cit.,* at p. 61; S. N. Ray, *op. cit.,* at pp. 115, 126.

5. *Shankari Prasad* v. *Union of India,* A.I.R. *1951* S.C. 458; Sathe, *op. cit.,* pp. 8-9.

6. *Sajjan Singh* v. *State of Rajasthan,* A.I.R., *1965* S.C. 845; Sathe, *op. cit.,* pp. 8-9; and see also P. K. Tripathi, 'Mr. Justice Gajendragadkar and Constitutional Interpretation', 8 *Journal of the Indian Law Institute* 479, at 578-583 (1966).

7. A.I.R. *1965* S.C. 845, at 856 *et seq.* (*per* Gajendragadkar C.J.).

8. S. P. Sathe, *Fundamental Rights and Amendment of the Indian Constitution* (1968), p. 8; S. N. Ray, *Judicial Review and Fundamental Rights* (1974), p. 232 *et seq.;* J. L. Kapur, 23 *Jahrbuch des öffentlichen Rechts der Gegenwart* 505, at 520-534 (1974); H. C. L. Merillat, *Land and the Constitution in India* (1970).

9. A.I.R. *1965* S.C. 845.

10. J. L. Kapur, *op. cit.,* pp. 524-534; S. N. Ray, *op. cit.,* pp. 248-252.

11. *Kesavananda Bharati* v. *State of Kerala,* A.I.R. *1973* S.C. 1461.

12. J. L. Kapur, *op. cit.,* at p. 532.

13. *Minerva Mills Ltd. and others* v. *Union of India and others*, AIR *1980* S.C. 591.
14. François Luchaire, *La constitution de la république française* (1980), p. 252 *et seq.*
15. Luchaire, *op. cit.*, p. 180 *et seq.*
16. L. Favoreu and L. Philip, *Les Grandes Décisions du Conseil constitutionnel* (1975), p. 181.
17. *Ibid.*
18. *Canada and the Constitution 1979-1982: Patriation and the Charter of Rights* (1982), p. 52 *et seq.*
19. Ch. 7 ('Cutting the imperial Gordian Knot'), *ibid.*, p. 65 *et seq.*
20. See, generally, R.T.E. Latham, 'The Law and the Commonwealth', in *Survey of British Commonwealth Affairs* (W.K. Hancock, ed.) (1937), vol. 1, p. 533; Sir Ivor Jennings, The Statute of Westminster and Appeals to the Privy Council, 52 *Law Quarterly Review* 173 (1936); N. Mansergh, *The Commonwealth Experience* (rev. ed.), vols: 1 and 2 (1983).
21. *Reference re Amendment of the Constitution of Canada (Nos. 1, 2 and 3)*, 125 D.L.R. (3d) 1 (1982).
22. A.L. Goodhart, *Essays in Jurisprudence and the Common Law* (1931).
23. 125 D.L.R. (3d) 1, at 12 *et seq.* (1982).
24. 125 D.L.R. (3d) 1, at 79 *et seq.* (1982).
25. Decision of 23 February 1983, – B Verf GE – (1983) (Second Senate). (Advance text, *Aus Politik und Zeitgeschichte,* Bonn, B 8-9/83, 23 February 1983).
26. 'Entsprach die Auflösung des Bundestages dem Grundgesetz? Verhandlung vor dem Bundesverfassungsgericht: Vier Abgeordnete Klagen', *Frankfurter Allgemeine Zeitung,* 26 January 1983.
27. Supreme Court of Japan, Grand Bench, Decision of 15 April 1953. J.M. Maki, *Court and Constitution in Japan. Selected Supreme Court Decisions, 1948-60,* p. 366 *et seq.* And see, generally, Kisaburo Yokota (sometime Chief Justice of the Supreme Court), 'Political Questions and Judicial Review: a comparison', in *The Constitution of Japan. Its First Twenty Years, 1947-67* (Dan Fenno Henderson, ed.) (1968), p. 141 *et seq.*
28. Maki, *op. cit.*, p. 368 *et seq.*
29. Constitution of the Fifth Republic, Art 61 (as amended 29 October 1974).
30. Jacques Robert, 'La sauvegarde du droit', *Le Monde,* Paris, 27 December 1979.
31. Michel Debré, La République consolidée, *Le Monde,* Paris, 27 December 1979.
32. *Le Monde,* Paris, 5 January 1980.
33. 'Le bilan de la Session parlementaire d'Automne', *Le Monde,* Paris, 8 January 1980.
34. A.I.R. *1976* S.C. 1207. And see, also, Alice Jacob and Rajeev Dhavan, 'The Dissolution Case: Politics at the Bar of the Supreme Court'. *Journal of the Indian Law Institute 355,* at 357-358 (1977).
35. A.I.R. *1975* S.C. 2299; Jacob and Dhavan, *op. cit., ibid.*
36. 144 U.S. 1 (1982).
37. 143 U.S. 649 (1892).
38. Discussed by the present author in 'Congress and the Presidency and the Impeachment Power', 7 *Indiana Law Review* 833 (1974); 'The English and American Impeachment Powers and the constitutional Separation of Powers', 24 *Jahrbuch des öffentlichen Rechts der Gegenwart* 577 (1975).
39. 418 U.S. 683 (1974).
39a. 400 U.S. 886 (1970).
39b. *Ibid.*
39c. 414 U.S. 1304 (1973).
39d. 414 U.S. 1304, 1311 (1973).
39e. *Holtzman* v. *Schlesinger,* 361 F. Supp. 553 (E.D.N.Y. 1973).

162

39f. 414 U.S. 1304 (1973).

39g. 414 U.S. 1304, 1311-1312 (1973).

39h. 418 U.S. 683 (1974).

39i. 414 U.S. 1304 (1973).

40. Supreme Court of Japan, Grand Bench, Decision of 8 October 1952; Maki, *op. cit.,* p. 362 *et seq. (supra,* ch. 6).

41. Supreme Court of Japan, Grand Bench, Decision of 16 December 1959; Maki, *op. cit.,* p. 298 *et seq. (supra,* ch. 6).

42. Decision of 30 July 1958, 8 B Verf GE 104 (1959) (Second Senate). And see Wolff, 9 *Jahrbuch des öffentlichen Rechts der Gegenwart* 69, 71 (1960).

43. Decision of 31 July 1973, 36 B Verf GE 1 (1974) (Second Senate) *(supra,* ch. 6).

43a. Decision of 16 December 1983, – B Verf GE – (1983) (Second Senate).

43b. *Ibid.*

44. Decision of 26 March 1957, 6 B Verf GE 309 (1957) (Second Senate); *Constitutionalism in Germany and the Federal Constitutional Court* (1962), p. 46 *et seq.* And see, generally, W. Wengler, *Völkerrecht und Reichskonkordat von 1933* (1956).

45. H.-W. Bayer, *Die Bundestreue* (1961); *Constitutionalism in Germany and the Federal Constitutional Court* (1962), p. 51 *et seq.;* Heinz Laufer, *Das föderative System der Bundesrepublik Deutschland* (3rd ed., 1977), p. 63 *et seq.;* K. Doehring, *Staatsrecht der Bundesrepublik Deutschland* (2nd ed., 1980), p. 116 *et seq.;* K. Hesse, *Grundzüge des Verfassungsrechts der Bundesrepublik Deutschland* (2nd ed., 1968), p. 101 *et seq.;* P. M. Blair, *Federalism and Judicial Review in West Germany* (1981), p. 162 *et seq.*

46. 252 U.S. 416 (1920).

47. *Attorney-General for Canada* v. *Attorney-General for Ontario* [1937], A.C. 326 (P.C.).

48. See the discussion by Lord Wright (one of the British judges sitting on the Board of the Privy Council that decided the case), in 33 *Canadian Bar Review* 1123 (1955); and the resulting discussion in 34 *Canadian Bar Review* 114, 115, 243 (1956). And see, generally, *Comparative Federalism. States' Rights and National Power* (2nd ed., 1965), at p. 43 *et seq.*

49. Decision of 26 March 1957, 6 B Verf GE 309 (1957) (Second Senate).

50. *Constitutionalism in Germany and the Federal Constitutional Court* (1962), p. 46 *et seq.*

51. L. Favoreu and L. Philip, *Le Conseil constitutionnel* (1978), p. 90 *et seq.;* and see also F. Luchaire, *La constitution de la république française* (1980), p. 671 *et seq.*

52. Luchaire, *op. cit.,* at p. 686 *et seq.*

53. Luchaire, *op. cit.,* p. 710. And see, also, Luchaire, *Le Conseil constitutionnel* (1980), p. 225 *et seq.*

54. Constitution of the Fifth Republic, Art. 61 (as amended, 29 October 1974).

55. Favoreu and Philip, *op. cit.,* p. 90 *et seq.*

56. Decision of 19 June 1970 *(Traités des Communautés européennes), Les Grandes Décisions du Conseil constitutionnel* (L. Favoreu and L. Philip, eds.) (1975), p. 257 *et seq.*

57. Decision of 30 December 1976 *(Journal Officiel,* 31 December 1976); *Le Monde* (Paris), 1 January 1977.

58. See F. Luchaire, 'Faut-il réviser la Constitution?', *Le Monde,* 6 November 1976; F. Luchaire, «L'Europe et le droit: Faut-il modifier la Constitution?' *Le Monde,* 11 December 1976; L. Philip, 'L'Election du Parlement des "Neuf": Le Conseil constitutionnel est-il compétent?', *Le Monde,* 13 November 1976.

59. See the varying appraisals of the *Conseil's* decision: Jean Verges, 'Une Assemblée aux pouvoirs limités', *Le Monde* (Paris), 1 January 1977; Maurice Duverger, 'Une victoire à la Pyrrhus', *Le Monde,* 4 January 1977.

60. Decision of 30 December 1976; *Le Monde,* Paris, 1 January 1977 (André Laurens, 'Le Conseil constitutionnel met des limites à la supranationalité tout en acceptant l'élection du Parlement européen au suffrage universel').
61. *Le Monde* (Paris), 1 January 1977 (André Laurens, 'Le Conseil constitutionnel met des limites à la supranationalité...').
62. Duverger, *op. cit., Le Monde,* 4 January 1977.

CHAPTER VIII

THE COURTS AND THE POLITICAL-GOVERNMENTAL PROCESSES: FEDERALISM AND REGIONALISM

1. THE 'OPEN SOCIETY' AND ITS CONSTITUTIONAL VALUES

In his Opinion of the Court, in *U.S.* v. *Carolene Products Co.* in 1938,[1] a case which need not concern us, in its substantive law elements, for it relates to the regulation of inter-state commerce within the U.S. federal system, Mr. Justice (later Chief Justice) Harlan Stone offered an interesting *obiter dictum* on the judicial process and postulated judicial obligations of affirmative policy-making in certain areas of public activity. Mr. Justice Stone's suggestions, dropped as Mr. Justice Frankfurter later criticised it, with all the 'casualness of a foot-note' (foot-note 4) to his Opinion, acquired a seminal influence, nevertheless, on subsequent American constitutional development. Stone had been one of the frequent judicial dissenters to the 'Old Court', conservative majority which, up to the Roosevelt-inspired 'Court Revolution' of 1937, had insisted on invalidating social and economic planning or interventionist measures, federal or state, in the name of a 'liberty of contract', in the abstract, and similar economic *laissez-faire* principles supposedly embodied in the Due Process clauses of the Fifth and Fourteenth Amendments to the United States Constitution.[2] In his *Carolene Products* case Opinion, Mr. Justice Stone referred to that general Presumption of Constitutionality in favour of governmental action which the liberal dissenters to the 'Old Court' majority before 1937, who were now the post-1937 liberal majority on the Court, had sought to draw from the thinking of the late, great, Justice Oliver Wendell Holmes, jr., as a judicial rationale for upholding so much of the Roosevelt New Deal legislation. A beneficial Presumption of Constitutionality is, of course, itself an application of the principle of judicial self-restraint; and it was the absence of self-restraint, and indeed the charge of a wilful and arrogant desire to substitute their own (conservative) social and economic values for the more liberal values of the popularly-elected and popularly-mandated President and Congress, – and this despite the actual words of the Constitution and the historical intentions of its drafters – that was the principal political indictment of the 'Old Court' majority up to 1937. On this view, not merely did their (conservative) judicial activism involve a conscious distortion of the Constitution's text, but it was basically un-democratic in so far as it set a non-elected judiciary over an elected, and then overwhelmingly re-elected, President. The twin objections to the 'Old Court', then, were rooted both in substantive values (conservatism *versus* liberalism), and institutional considerations (the legitimacy of judicial review in relation to the other, popularly-mandated institutions of Government).

Mr. Justice Stone's reference to the normal Presumption of Constitutionality in favour of executive-legislative action was his point of departure for his foot-note musings on constitutionalism: –

'... The existence of facts supporting the legislative judgment is to be presumed, for regulatory legislation affecting ordinary commercial transactions is not to be pronounced unconstitutional unless in the light of the facts made known or generally assumed it is of such a character as to preclude the assumption that it rests upon some rational basis within the knowledge and experience of the legislators.'[3]

But, after that, the foot-note qualification, raising the issue of whether there should not be some limits, nevertheless, to judicial self-restraint *vis-à-vis* executive-legislative action, and, if so, what limits: –

'There may be narrower scope for operation of the presumption of constitutionality when legislation appears on its face to be within a specific prohibition of the Constitution, such as those of the first ten amendments, [U.S. Constitution, Bill of Rights], which are deemed equally specific when held to be embraced within the Fourteenth. [citations omitted].

'It is unnecessary to consider now whether legislation which restricts those political processes which can ordinarily be expected to bring about repeal of undesirable legislation, is to be subjected to more exacting judicial scrutiny under the general prohibitions of the Fourteenth Amendment than are most other types of legislation. On restrictions upon the right to vote; on restraints upon the dissemination of information; on interferences with political organisations; as to prohibition of peaceable assembly. [citations omitted].

'Nor need we enquire whether similar considerations enter into the review of statutes directed at particular religions; or racial minorities; whether prejudice against discrete and insular minorities may be a special condition, which tends seriously to curtail the operation of those political processes ordinarily to be relied upon to protect minorities, and which may call for a correspondingly more searching judicial enquiry.' [citations omitted].[4]

This is the genesis of the 'political process' concept of judicial review, basing a judicial right and duty positively to intervene to keep the ordinary political processes open, and free and unobstructed by removing clogs to their effective operation. Although Mr. Justice Stone was not a speculative man and so did not cast his notion in terms of contitutional theory, it may be suggested that the duty of judicial self-restraint *vis-à-vis* executive-legislative authority is predicated upon such authority's having a *bona fide* claim to popular mandate and, therefore, to being democratically constituted in the first place. The implications for an affirmative judicial review of the fairness and representativeness of the electoral system were clear enough, though it would take some more years for Justice Stone's judicial initiative to overcome, in his own country, the 'political questions' barrier which earlier Supreme Court majorities had erected against judicial review of the constitutional electoral process. The links, also, to 'Open Society' values – freedom of speech and of the press and of information generally – on which informed and honest elections must also be predicated, is clear enough; and, there, the link to the judicial concept of the 'preferred position' of the First Amendment, Free Speech guarantees in competition with all other constitutional values and constitutional guarantees, – associated, especially, with Justices Black and Douglas,[5] is proximate and direct. In West Germany, the greatest of the constitutionalists of the post-War era, and one of the most courageous and innovatory jurists of the Western World, Gerhard Leibholz, had already worked out in his pre-War, University career and his academic writings,[6] ideas, stemming ultimately from the constitutional princple of equality before the law, that involved the consideration, as part of the constitutional system and therefore as deserving of that more exacting, 'higher law' scrutiny to which constitutional law as distinct from ordinary statute law is subjected, of the whole electoral processes, including the electoral laws proper but also organisation and operation of political parties and even their financing. To the conception of the electoral processes as deserving of special constitutional protection, Leibholz added a special concern for federalism and the federal order as a means of decentralising and thus limiting state authority; plus establishment of the equality principle as constitutionally paramount, and acceptance of the judicial watchdog *rôle* as the most effective constitutional-institutional guarantee of the Rule-of-Law state (*Rechtsstaat*).[7] Since Leibholz was elected to the first bench of the Federal Constitutional Court on the Court's establishment in 1951, and remained on its Second Senate for twenty years until his retirement in 1971, he was in a unique position to translate his constitutional ideas from the level of philosophical abstractions to operational principles of the evolving West German constitutionalism – from law-in-books to law-in-action. In fact, in the area of the electoral processes, and judicial control over their basic fairness and conformity to ultimate constitutional-democratic principles, the West German Court, in its decisions, actually anticipated, by some years, developments in the United States, and seemed more comprehensive and philosophically coherent in purpose and concrete application.

Mention of Leibholz, in intellectual juxtaposition to Stone of the U.S.

Supreme Court, directs attention to the still-important *rôle* of the judicial 'man-of-ideas' who tries to unify disparate case-law decisions in search of ultimate, ordering constitutional principles – what, in International Law terms, is referred to as *Jus Cogens,* or 'imperative principles' of law, superior to and, if necessary, overriding other, ordinary legal rules. It becomes a sort of empirically-based Natural Law and, when exercised on a comparative, inter-systemic basis, as the post-War years with their easier communications and exchanges and borrowings between different legal systems have certainly encouraged, it begins to take on a *Jus Gentium* quality, much like that highly pragmatic, experiental law administered by the *Praetor Peregrinus* at Rome which, because of its self-evident common-sense and its basic eclecticism (and hence appeal to people of many different cultures, who found it to be reasonable in their own legal terms), rivalled and quickly displaced much of the old and rigid, inherited *Jus Civile.* The trans-national comparisons add, however, one further, important point, for they necessarily mean emancipation from too literal adherence to constitutional texts, created as those were, so very often, by casual accidents of personal taste and preference among the individual members of the constituent assembly or committee drafting those constitutional texts in the first place. The differences between a short, lapidarian text and a long, professorial or didactic one, and between a poetic, literary formulation and a technical, legalistic one, become secondary to the reaching out and embracing of constitutional first principles – the 'spirit of the Constitution', rather than a narrow, textual exegesis. It is this judicial quest for constitutional first principles that gives a certain coherence and order and rationality to otherwise rambling and interminable constitutional documents – the Canadian and the Indian charters, as simply the more notable among these – and facilitates, and also clarifies for later public study and criticism, the judicial decisions upon them. Judicial activism is encouraged, but also, because it is more open and usually also frankly acknowledged, it can be more easily subjected to the democratic correctives existing within the constitutional system. The constitutional broad strokes, rather than the *petit-point* needlework, become the vehicles of judicial policy-making today, transcending the often too low-level and specific, and hence too quickly dated, directives from original constitution-makers, or from those operating the subsequent constituent processes through the constitutional amending power.

2. FEDERALISM AND REGIONALISM

Leibholz had made, of federalism, one of the post-War constitutional imperative principles, ranking with Equality before the Law as he had earlier developed it, in his pre-War thinking, as the ultimate ordering principle of democratic constitutionalism. Leibholz' concern with federalism, post-War, corresponded to similar concerns of the Founding Fathers of the Bonn Constitution at their original Herrenchiemsee conference, and with a clear motivation of the main political leaders of the new West German state, from Chancellor Adenauer downward. [8] They were all responding to the conceived lessons of the earlier, Weimar Republic and its collapse in 1933 to anti-democratic forces; for the concentration of power in the popularly elected federal President and other federal institutions, and the resultant centralisation of all community decision-making power was thought to have facilitated the political tactics of the authoritarian parties, of both the Right and the Left, to discredit Weimar democracy by attenuating potential countervailing power groups at the regional or local level. The most striking constitutional expression, within the Weimar Republic, of the frustration of regional democracy and the federal principle, and an example present in the minds of the Bonn constitution-makers, had been the '*Preussenschlag*' of July, 1932, [9] in the twilight of the Weimar Republic. The federal President had then invoked Article 48 of the Weimar Constitution and the doctrine of constitutional Emergency, to suspend the government of the state of Prussia and to occupy its government premises by the Army, and to install federal Government administrators in their place, and to exercise the functions of the deposed state (Prussian) Government. This action was taken by President Hindenburg, at the instance of the federal Chancellor, von Papen; and while it was immediately contested before the courts, the *Staatsgerichtshof,* exercising a form of limited, embryonic judicial review, in a decision handed down in October, 1932, upheld the federal President's action against legal challenge. [10] The Court decision itself was mixed, reflecting both the arbitrary and colourable character of Chancellor von Papen's political manoeuvring that had led to the Presidential decree, and also ultimate power realities of the time: the Court confirmed the removal of the Prussian Ministers from the exercise of their office, but declared that a formal dismissal of them could not constitutionally be made by the federal President under Article 48 (2) of the Weimar Constitution. In the immediate result, of course, the Court decision changed nothing in the practical political situation: it reflected the agony and dilemma of constitutional judges facing a present political situation they were powerless to control, but might at best hope to influence or limit in respect to any future, similar action. But, as a leading case on the death-knell of Weimar federalism, it seemed to have lessons to offer for the new, post-War Bonn constitutionalism.

It must be admitted that there was a large element of contrivedness in the federalism established under the Bonn Constitution for the politically truncated West Germany that had been created by combining the three Western powers' Military Occupation zones in Germany. As one of the most perceptive American authorities, Taylor Cole,[11] referring to some current German criticisms, described it:

> 'The weakness of the German states as constituent units provides, it is alleged, a flimsy base for the federal system and encourages the centripetal pressures. Most of the states are artificial entities created by the fiat of occupying powers largely through the post-war dismemberment of Prussia. They are today 'simply places of residence for a geographically mobile population''. Only Bavaria and the Hansa cities of Bremen and Hamburg have tradition, historic continuity and community consciousness. Early opinion polls in the 1950s found little popular support for the retention of the states.'

The emphasis given by the Adenauer administration, and by the Federal Constitutional Court in its decisions in the first decade at least of its jurisprudence, to the federal idea, reflects the influence of constitutional thinkers like Leibholz, and the great German-American constitutionalist and Harvard professor, Carl Friedrich, who was very active in the U.S. Military Occupation period and much respected by Bonn political leaders and the early judges of the Court.[12] For Leibholz and Friedrich, federalism was a constitutional idea whose time had come, in view of the post-War drives, in Western Europe, for supra-national integration and association, while retaining the ethnic-cultural identity and autonomy of the constituent states. It is not surprising that both Leibholz and Friedrich were confirmed 'Europeans', and intellectual leaders in the political movements that gave rise to the European 'federal' idea, and that culminated in formation of the European Coal and Steel Community at the opening of the 1950s.[13] For the political leaders in Bonn, however, the approach to federalism was rather more instrumental: how to ensure, in advance, against an excessive concentration of decision-making power in Bonn that might pave the way to a return to authoritarian government that could not be completely excluded, as a political hypothesis, because of all the problems, political and economic, and all the pressures from outside, facing the new, politically divided German state. Constitutional safeguards could be built in, on a *de jure* basis, and *a priori*, by, for example, limiting the mandate of the President, under the Bonn charter, through a system of indirect election to that office, where the earlier, Weimar Constitution had endowed the President with all the extra political prestige and authority and effective power flowing from direct, popular election, in nation-wide vote. On a *de facto*, operational basis, federalism, if accepted in the Bonn constitutional charter and properly encouraged and developed at the political-administrative level in the early years, could provide an effective counter-weight at the regional and local level to the national government. We have already looked at the

Reichskonkordat decision of 1957,[14] where the Federal Constitutional Court opted for the Canadian 'divided competences'-federalism, rather than the U.S. strong national federalism approach, and, at the price of some practical inconvenience in the federal Government's treaty-implementation power, enunciated the principle of Federal Comity (*Bundestreue*)[15] and insisted that where the subject matter of a pending international engagement concerns matters otherwise belonging to the regional (*Länder*) administrations – here, education – the federal Government must treat with the regional governments as to the practical adoption of the international treaty or other legal obligations involved. In the *Referendum on Atomic Weapons* decision,[16] rendered one year later, the Federal Constitutional Court presented the other side of the coin as to Federal Comity, and insisted on the reciprocal duty of the regions (*Länder*) to respect and defer to the federal Government's constitutional competences under the Bonn charter. Federal Comity, on this approach, with its reciprocal, two-way, right-duty relationships becomes a highly refined and civilised legal concept for regulating inter-governmental relations within a federal system – cooperative, inter-governmental federalism in the best sense.

In the Television (*Fernesh*) case, in 1961,[17] the Federal Constitutional Court, on some contemporary views, really came of age politically, for, for the first time, its decision put the Court into direct conflict with the federal Government on a matter of policy which the federal Government considered vital, and yet the Court was able to emerge from the battle bloodied but unconquered. The Adenauer Government had, in 1953, resolved on the creation of a second television channel within West Germany, to supplement the existing channel already created over the preceding few years by the regions (*Länder*) in collaboration with various private associations. The Bonn decision to intervene in television and television control was evidently prompted by consideration of the necessity for some sort of comprehensive, central governmental coordination of the granting of television licences in the restricted land area of post-War West Germany. The right of the federal Government to regulate such television matters was contested by the regional (*Länder*) administrations on the argument that they fell within recognised *Länder* competence over cultural matters. The *Länder* proposed an inter-governmental compact or agreement, dividing the jurisdictional competence over television between the federal Government and the *Länder,* but, in the Summer of 1960, Chancellor Adenauer acted to put the matter beyond further negotiation by creating, by federal law, a federal Governmental authority to have charge of television, the German Television Company. The compatibility of the new federal, television company with the Bonn constitutional charter was immediately challenged by four of the *Länder,* all of them having Social Democratic administrations that were politically opposed to the Adenauer Government, in proceedings before the Second Senate of the Federal Constitutional Court. Since the Bonn charter did not, in terms, allocate authority over television, the federal Government's case for its own competence had to rest on generic interpretation of other, more traditional heads of federal authority under the Bonn Constitution, – for example, Article 73 (7) (Posts and Telegraphs). The Court, however, ruled that while this Article might extend to the regulation of the arrangements as to the technical modes of transmitting television, it could not cover the so-called studio technique and certainly not the organisation and fashioning of programmes of the sender. This was enough, on legal grounds, to dispose of the case and thereby to reject the federal Government's claisms to constitutional control over television. The Court went on, however, beyond this, and in an extended *obiter dictum* ventured on certain constitutional first principles to govern the judicial determination and allocation of federal-*Länder* legislative competence under the otherwise somewhat cryptic formulae provided in Articles 70 to 75 of the Bonn charter. The Court found that the Adenauer Government had infringed the Basic Rights sections of the Bonn charter, – specifically, Article 5 guaranteeing freedom of expression, opinion and information, which, as the Court saw it, prohibited the federal Government directly or indirectly from having control of a company to arrange the transmission of television. The Court declared that television must be recognised, as with newspapers and the press generally, as the indispensable modern mass communication medium, and, more than that, as a major factor in public opinion formation. Article 5, in the Court's view, with its freedom of expression imperative, must prohibit the conferring of a monopoly control over television to the one government. There are elements, in the Court's reasoning, here, that seem derived from the American Anti-Trust legislation, whose motor principles, preaching the avoidance of concentration of too much power, economic or political-economic, in any one set of hands, had been preached by American Military Government officials, in Germany, with almost evangelical fervour in the immediate post-War years. There are links, too, to the Open Society ideal and the necessity for affirmative action to remove clogs on the free flow of information and ideas represented by present-day trends to large-scale monopoly control in the communications industry generally. The Court also, in passing, took the opportunity to invoke the Federal Comity principle and to castigate the Adenauer Government for the manner in which it conducted its negotiations with the *Länder* over the control of television: it tried to deal only with those *Länder* controlled by its own, Christian Democratic party and allies, and to exclude from the negoatiations, altogether, those controlled by the Opposition Social Democrats. This was a 'divide and conquer' approach, and the gravamen of the offence was increased when the federal Government peremptorily broke off negotiations altogether, and resolved to reject all *Länder* counter-proposals to its own proposals and to proceed unilaterally to form its own monopoly company controlling television. Such a style and procedure was not, in the Court's view, reconcilable with the command to inter-governmental moderation in a federal system, which the *Bundestreue* principle enjoined.

The decision by the Federal Constitutional Court was a crucial one, in several respects. In retrospect, it stands out as the high-water mark in judicially-based and judicially-created federalism in West Germany:[18] the giving of the benefit of the doubt, in judicial construction of the constitutional charter, to the *Länder* and not to the federal Government, in a situation where the constitutional charter itself was not merely not controlling but open-ended; the pragmatic, functional approach to federalism, involving accepting the possibility of division of governmental competence over television by allocating the medium (regulation of the modes of transmission) to the federal Government, and the message itself (programme content) to the *Länder;* the disapproval of governmental monopoly power, in general, in the communications field; and, finally, the insistence on a code of inter-governmental good manners – Federal Comity (*Bundestreue*) – in federal-*Länder* negotiations within the federal system. As a second main point, however, Chancellor Adenauer, although clearly very annoyed by the Court decision, accepted it, and accepted it with good grace, in spite of the public political rebuff involved in it; and that was a signal and happy event in executive-judicial relations within the federal Government itself, and an important event also in the political consolidation and legitimation of the power of judicial review under the Bonn constitutional system. Thereafter, no major judicial testing of the federal idea emerges; and the governmental trends, in fact, are all the other way, being centripetal in character and designed to consolidate and extend the federal Government's authority and competences. These trends were facilitated by two factors – the federal tax power and the complicated system of allocating tax revenues which left the *Länder* with restricted avenues for financing their activities; and the relative ease with which the constituent processes could be made to operate and the constitutional amending power used to increase federal Government involvement and responsibility.[19] This occurred in important areas of community policy-making where either the actual legislative competence was not clear between federal Government and *Länder,* as with health; or where the matter had been traditionally viewed as the preserve of the *Länder,* as with education, environmental protection, police and internal security, and uniform legislation concerning civil service pensions and compensation. The financial setting for these and other developments was provided by the financial-taxation reforms of 1969-71, which also involved a series of constitutional amendments and a substantial alteration, in the process, of the fiscal relationships within the federal system and the balance of revenues between federal, *Länder*, and local (municipal) administrations. By most counts, these financial reforms involved a practical redistribution of powers in favour of the federal Government and a reduction of *Länder* discretion in the exercise of their former taxing powers, adding momentum to the pattern of centralisation. [20] If we add to this the absence, in the historical-sociological patterns of the West German state, (and apart from the several exceptions already noted, – Bavaria, Bremen, Hamburg), of any 'natural' federal element, and the departure from the political scene at Bonn and also from the Court itself of the consciously pro-federalist, Founding Fathers of the earlier Bonn years, the decline of federalism in the Court jurisprudence becomes readily understandable. The particular West German political needs that were felt to make judicial activism in behalf of federalism a constitutional preferred policy of the decade of the 1950s had all been satisfied by the end of that time, with the obvious success of the Bonn system as an exercise in democratic constitutionalism; and there was no particular need or reason for continuing to press the federal idea, as a judicial construct, at least where it did not arise normally in the cases coming to the Court in the ordinary way. No doubt this situation would continue, unless and until a new federal problem should arise with any All-German state of the future that might reunite West and East Geramny peaceably, on a necessarily federal base.

The artificial, politically or judicially contrived, character of West German federalism under the Bonn constitutional charter, where the sociological forces are, and will continue to be, centripetal in character and when the federal idea is really invoked in aid of other, non-federal policies – such as, in the early Bonn years, guarding against any possible, Weimar Republic-style, descent into authoritarian government, by making assurance doubly sure that the *de jure* constitutional checks and balances will be supplemented by geographical dispersal of authority in (somewhat artificial) territorial units, – has some parallels, perhaps, in North American experience in federalism in both the United States and Canada. The original Southern States of the United States and fortress Quebec in Canada to one side, as special historical cases with still-subsisting major political-legal influences, both major North American federal states have been characterised, in sociological terms, by 'moving frontiers' where newly-arrived immigrants tend to be dispersed in a number of different centres and regions throughout the country, with distinct ethnic-cultural and linguistic communities from overseas becoming absorbed into a genuine 'melting-pot' national community; and where even 'original', long-standing settler communities display frequent and widespread mobility in search of more favourable employment or professional opportunities and the pursuit of wealth and well-being generally. Federalism becomes, under these circumstances, as in West Geramny, less a matter of the constitutional recognition of ethnic-cultural, linguistic, religious or similar sociological particularity established on a more-or-less fixed or stable geographical-regional base, than a means of satisfying other, distinct and different constitutional values which are not any the less legitimate because of that fact but which may, nevertheless, need to be brought into the open for the democratic corrective of public debate and criticism of any judicial decisions seeking to incorporate or realise them in constitutional terms. One such, 'other' constitutional value would be the felt desire, as in West Germany at the end of the 1940s and in the decade of the 1950s, to impede any possible future concentration of governmental decision-making power, even if it meant fostering or keeping alive politically-contrived or artificial, notional special local communities. Another such postulated constitutional value would be to create legal obstacles, throught Court litigation based on the protection of the claimed federal character of the constitution, against governmental social and economic planning legislation or socially interventionist measures, whether emanating from a federal Government or from regional (state, Provincial) administrations as the case may be. Federalism becomes, in such cases, another last-ditch means of defence of economic *laissez-faire* and the special economic interests favouring it, against popular majorities in the legislature; and the Courts and their judges are sought to be invoked in aid of such special interests groups.[21] We shall have occasion to examine, in a later chapter, that politically most controversial and charged aspect of judicial review as a defence of economic and property claims of private interest groups against democratically-elected legislatures; and it is amply evidenced in the constitutional jurisprudence of the United States, Canada, India and other countries. For present purposes, constitutional federalism, as a legal argument, is simply one aspect of that larger legal battle between the state on the one hand and private economic and property interests. It is surprising how often the claim of 'States Rights' or 'Provincial Rights', and 'maintenance of the federal balance' of the constitution and an existing constitutional charter-based division of legislative competences between various geographical levels of government, has been sought to be raised, and allowed by the Courts to be raised, without any serious question, by special interest groups that, by no colour of legal right, can claim to wear the mantle of regional (state/Provincial) governmental authority. Why have not the Courts and their judges been more vigilant in lifting the claimed veil of state authority, or, at least, directly inviting the governmental authority whose name has been invoked to appear and intervene in the suit and, if it wishes, to repudiate the claim of 'State Rights' advanced in its name?

The history of the case law on the U.S. Commerce power, where the federal Governmental constitutional competence to 'regulate Commerce... among the several states', is invoked to strike down local, state regulatory action, is a sustained record, over half a century until the 'Court Revolution' of 1937, of a successful Court-based guerilla war of litigation against legislative action at the State level, complementing equally successful litigation, on other constitutional arguments, against legislative action at the federal level, in the endeavour to create a legislative 'No Man's Land' against governmental regulation of whatever nature, federal or state, in the community interest.[22]

In Canada, in the absence, until the adoption of the constitutionally-entrenched Canadian Charter of Rights and Freedoms, of any constitutional Bill of Rights guarantees which could be invoked in defence of economic and property special interests, the constitutional battles over such claims and in their defence have been based squarely upon the federal nature of the constitution and the division of legislative competences, under sections 91 and 92 of the Constitution, between federal and Provincial (state) authority. The so-called Bennett 'New Deal' legislative programme, enacted during the Depression era by the federal Government and patterned on President Franklin Roosevelt's economic recovery programme in the United States of the time, was rejected by the Imperial Privy Council, sitting in its then capacity as final appellate tribunal for Canada, largely on these special 'federal' constitutional grounds, by invoking 'Provincial Rights' to strike down the programme.[23] As late as 1978, two private corporations, Canadian Industrial Gas and Oil Ltd.,[24] and Central Canada Potash Co. Ltd.,[25] successfully invoked before the Supreme Court of Canada the argument of invasion of federal Governmental powers, and persuaded the Court to strike down regulatory legislation of the Province of Saskatchewan. In the first case, – the oil case, – the social democratic (New Democratic Party) Government of Saskatchewan had tried to tax the unexpected windfall profits accruing to the oil company, not through any special efforts or investment or intelligence on the oil company's part, but because of the general World energy crisis that followed on the OPEC group's massive increases in World oil prices in 1973. When Canadian oil companies began to increase their own prices in response to the World price increases, the Province of Saskatchewan legislated in 1974 to provide that any increase in the price of Saskatchewan oil above the 1973 level should go to the Saskatchewan Government and not to the oil company. The Supreme

Court of Canada, by a seven-to-two majority, struck down the Provincial legislation as an invasion of federal Governmental power. [26] In the second case, – the potash case – the Supreme Court of Canada, by a unanimous, seven-to-nil vote, ruled unconstitutional, again as an invasion by the Province of federal Governmental power, a Saskatchewan law establishing a pro-rationing scheme designed to stabilise and regulate the potash industry of the Province. [27] In both cases, the federal Government of Canada did choose to enter the litigation, as intervenor in the oil case and as co-plaintiff in the potash case. The Saskatchewan Premier of the day, Premier Blakeney, complained publicly, in late 1976, at the time of the federal Government's legal interventions in both cases, that the federal Government's position in these resource cases demonstrated a – 'systematic and deliberate attempt to destroy, through court action, the provincial rights of resource ownership'. [28]

Equally unhappy, in terms of the angry political reactions to its decisions, have been the Supreme Court of Canada's essays in judicial policy-making involving the Province of Quebec and its claims, variously, to a special constitutional status within Canadian federalism; to special historical, vested rights as to the constitutional protection of the French language and distinctive French culture within Quebec; and to a Quebec Governmental 'Right of Veto' over projected constitutional change in the federal system, either (in its more modest form) projected constitutional change touching Quebec and the French language and culture within Quebec, or (in its broadest form) projected constitutional change of whatever nature, and whether or not involving Quebec beyond the involvement of the other Provinces. [29] The broadest Quebec claim involved a generalised Quebec 'Right of Veto' over constitutional change and bears comparisons, obviously, (though there is apparently no direct historical link) to Calhoun's insistence on the need for the double, 'concurrent majorities' in the pre-Civil War, United States, in respect to projected U.S. federal Government action touching the Southern States' special interests, and in particular the institution of slavery. [30] In the case of Quebec, the special historical-sociological fact of the French-speaking, overwhelmingly French-Canadian, 'homeland' of Quebec, within Canadian federalism, has been tested at the two levels, political and judicial, on the argument, essentially, that the 'French fact' constitutes an integral element or part of the Canadian constitutional *Grundnorm*. At neither level has it had too much public recognition: at the judicial level, hardly at all, though at the federal political level it seems to have been accorded some tacit deference as one of those fundamental political facts-of-life of Canadian federalism that one acts against only with due deliberation and with knowledge of potentially unpleasant political consequences. In the Quebec Cablevision case, in 1977, [31] the Supreme Court of Canada ruled on a challenge, by a private citizen, to the constitutionality of a Quebec Provincial Government board created to license the operation of cable television within the Province of Quebec. The Supreme Court of Canada, by a six-to-three majority, (with all three judges from Quebec dissenting), ruled that the Government of Quebec had exceeded its constitutional powers in its statute creating the board. The Quebec Government, with constitutional reasoning very similar to that of the *Länder* in the West German *Fernseh* case in 1961, which we have already discussed (although there seems to have been absolutely no direct link between the two), had argued that cable television was intended primarily for public education, stressing the 'message' (the subject matter communicated), rather than the 'medium' (the technical modes of communicating the message), as a basis for characterising the Quebec law as concerning education and thus as falling within Provincial power. The Supreme Court majority, however, refused to accept this argument, ruling, instead, that broadcasting, including cable distribution, consisted of a unified system that was necessarily federal and hence beyond Provincial power. [32] The Court's decision was complicated by the existence of a precedent, dating back half a century to the old Imperial Privy Council, involving radio broadcasting. [33] Yet the Canadian constitution contains nothing, in terms, on television or even on radio broadcasting in its allocation of governmental law-making competences between the federal and the Provincial Governments; and the Privy Council judgments of an earlier, more primitive era in the history of communications hardly seem so persuasive or compelling, intellectually, as to stand in the way of a rational reallocation and distribution of law-making competences in accordance with more contemporary thinking on communications. This might point to a recognition, as in West Germany, that the subject of cable television is a complex one in contemporary governmental decision-making terms, calling for cooperation between the different levels of government in a joint, shared or concurrent competence, rather than for abstract, *a priori* allocations of monopoly competence to one or other order of government alone. In respecting so fully the early Privy Council precedent, the Supreme Court of Canada passed up an opportunity for recognising Quebec's claims, such as they were presented, for constitutional recognition of the special need to protect the French language and culture within Quebec.

In relation to language and the Quebec Government's constitutional claims to special protection of the French language within Quebec, the political imperatives of Quebec's own 'Quiet Revolution', or intellectual reawakening, from the opening of the 1960s onwards, were concretised, in statutory form, with the passing by the Bourassa Liberal Government of Quebec, in 1974, of the so-called Bill 22, establishing French as the

Official Language, Language of Work, and Language of Education within Quebec, – a measure which was reinforced, as to its main principles, and also somewhat extended, by the Lévesque *Parti québécois* Government's Bill 101 of 1977.[34] All this occurred shortly after the adoption, by the federal Government in 1969, of the federal Official Languages Act which establishes official bilingualism (French and English) at the federal level, in respect to federal institutions and services throughout Canada. There is, of course, absolutely no reason for constitutional collision or conflict between these two language policies, Quebec and federal, since the Quebec law-making competence as to language can only operate validly in relation to Quebec Government institutions and services within Quebec, and the federal law-making competence operates validly only in relation to the larger federal policy. In constitutional theory terms, a Quebec Provincial constitutional *Grundnorm* that incorporates the primacy of the 'French fact', can operate within, and politically coexist with, a larger federal constitutional *Grundnorm* that establishes French and English bilingualism as one of its elements. When the two Quebec French Language laws were adopted in 1974 and 1977, Quebec spokesmen pointed out, correctly, that they were only doing, in express, positive law terms (establishing the primacy of one language, French, within the Province), what the other, English-speaking Provinces had always managed, historically, to achieve, *de facto,* as a political-sociological fact – absolute primacy of the one language, (English), within their Provinces, to the exclusion of French. The key factor in all this, of course, with the emphasis on political coexistence of different language policies, federal and Provincial, within the one, large, plural federal society, is cooperation and commonsense and the conscious avoidance of a guerrilla war of litigation between the two levels of government. It cries out for the exercise of that spirit of mutual tolerance bound up in the German concept of Federal Comity (*Bundestreue*), as adumbrated by the West German Federal Constitutional Court. It lies beyond the scope of the present study to canvass the matter in too much further detail. Suffice it to say that while some private interest and political pressure groups have tried to challenge both the federal and the Provincial language laws before the Courts, sometimes with evident motivations of making political mischief between French and English, the key political players, and especially perhaps the federal Government, have shewn a sufficient political modesty and awareness of the risks involved in terms of future French-English relations within Canada, to confine their own interventions in the private interests-based litigation to a politically tolerable level of juridical activism.[35] The federal-Provincial conflicts, here, have tended to be confined to political campaign rhetoric, which may have been fortunate since respecting the reality of the two language policies, federal and Quebec, operaging side-by-side within Quebec and each at its own separate and distinct level of governmental authority. The Canadian political *Grundnorm* certainly seems to include such a practical coexistence of linguistic policies today. Even in its constitutional 'patriation' project and accompanying Canadian Charter of Rights and Freedoms, adopted as part of the Canadian Constitution in 1982, the federal Government seems to have been at pains to avoid a constitutional collision course with Quebec language policies. The only point at which the new Charter in its bilingual (French and English) stipulations conflicts with, and therefore constitutionally overrides, Quebec's language policies, concerns the rights of Canadian citizens as to the language of education of their children, when they move to Quebec from another Province within Canada. (Canadian Charter of Rights and Freedoms, sections 23 (2)). This point had already been conceded by Premier Lévesque of Quebec, several years before, as not being fundamental and therefore negotiable on a *quid pro quo,* political bargaining basis. [36] The other main stipulations in the new Canadian Charter as to language of education, which could impinge adversely on Quebec's language policies, (section 23 (1) (a)), were, as a political gesture by the federal Government to Quebec, expressly made subject, as to their future legal operation and application within Quebec, to their prior authorisation by the legislature or Government of Quebec (Canadian Charter of Rights and Freedoms, section 59). As for the Courts, taking their cue, perhaps, from the conscious pragmatism and federal 'good manners' applied by the federal Government in regard to trying to reconcile federal and Quebec language policies, they have shewn little tendency to judicial aggrandisement in this area. The judges could, perhaps, have shewn more self-restraint as to conceding standing-to-sue and constitutional 'interest' sufficient to raise the language issue before it, to some of the more patently politically unrepresentative or unreasonable private persons or groups seeking to invoke the Courts' jurisdiction in their own political causes. On the main issue, constitutionality of Quebec's first language law, – Bill 22 of 1974 – the very great Chief Justice of the *Cour supérieure* in Montreal, Jules Deschênes, in an impressively researched and reasoned judgment rendered in 1976, in the *Protestant School Board* case, [37] disposed of the various constitutional objections so completely and decisively as to leave the issue beyond any real doubt for the future; and to establish the Court's ruling as a land-mark decision even though rendered by an intermediate court and not the Supreme Court of Canada. The later judgment of the Supreme Court of Canada, in late 1979, in the *Blaikie* case, [38] was directed only to a constitutionally somewhat marginal (if politically important) aspect of Quebec's Bill 101 of 1977 and did not address itself to, or threaten, its main principle, as with Bill 22 of 1974, of primacy of the French language within Quebec. Though the Supreme

Court did invalidate, in its unanimous ruling, two sections of Bill 101, the Court ruling was easily 'corrected' – as the Supreme Court itself had no doubt envisaged and would have accepted, itself – by further Quebec Provincial legislation of an omnibus character retroactively passing in English, as well as French, all laws adopted, since the passage of Bill 101 in 1977, in French only.[39] Unless and until the federal Government is prepared, for political considerations, to change its own apparent policy of tolerated coexistence of federal and Quebec language policies, and to launch its own frontal War, in the Courts, on the Quebec language laws, or to intervene aggressively, in the Courts, in behalf of private interest groups seeking the same end, there is little reason to expect that the present relative absence of judicial activism in this area will not continue for the future. The main actors, here, however, in respect to acceptance or rejection of Quebec's special federal constitutional claims as to the French language and culture within Quebec, are political ones – the federal Government – and not judicial.

We have already examined the Supreme Court of Canada's ruling, in late 1982, on the Quebec 'Right to Veto' claim,[40] where Supreme Court rejected, categorically, the Quebec Government claim as being historically and constitutionally unfounded. Our suggestion, then, was that since the issue, in fact, if it ever existed in constitutional law terms, had become legally 'moot' with the final legal adoption of the constitutional 'patriation' project, in April, 1982, notwithstanding Quebec's refusal of support, the Supreme Court of Canada need not, and on ordinary principles of judicial self-restraint should not, have ruled on the issue at all. Unless they raise concrete and immediate issues of the constitutionality of application in specific cases of specific statutes or governmental orders and decrees, – such as we may have seen in relation to the 'language' cases, – purely abstract, and high level and general, philosophical questions going to the nature of the *Grundnorm,* seem better left by the Courts to the popularly-elected institutions of government for political debate and, if need be, political resolution, or else to the people.

In India, the sweeping powers of the central Government in relation to the regional, state administrations have always raised questions of just how genuinely federal the Indian constitution really is, both as a matter of the abstract, constitutional law-in-books, and also the constitutional law-in-action of governmental practice. The larger federal option for the Indian sub-continent, in process of decolonisation and independence after 1946, of maintaining the imposed political unity of the former British Raj in one necessarily, constitutionally plural, federal state, for the future, had been, of course, foreclosed, very early, when the Muslim delegates broke away from the All-India Constituent Assembly to form what became, very shortly, their own separate, independent state of Pakistan, leaving rump India to form the present Republic of India. In the federal Dissolution case, *State of Rajasthan* v. *Union of India*,[41] decided by the Supreme Court of India in 1977, the Court, in a unanimous decision, necessarily resolved some of these fundamental issues as to the constitutional nature of Indian federalism. After Prime Minister Indira Gandhi's defeat in the general elections of March, 1977, the newly elected Janata Government, with an eye, it is said, on the then forthcoming Indian Presidential election for which the various State Assemblies formed the electoral college, 'invited' the Chief Ministers of various States, having Congress Party majorities in their Assemblies that were politically opposed to the Janata Government, to dissolve their State Assemblies and submit them to fresh State elections, – with the expectation that this would lead to defeat of those Congress Party State administrations by pro-Janata forces.[42] The suggestion was that this 'invitation' by the federal Government to the various Chief Ministers of the States was simply a political ploy to build the political ground for a subsequent constitutional request by the federal Government to the federal President to dissolve the State Assemblies in question by Presidential Proclamation under the Emergency Provisions of the Constitution (Part XVIII, Emergency Provisions: Article 356 (Breakdown in States)). Such a Presidential Proclamation would have enabled the legal imposition of direct, federal (Presidential) rule on the States concerned and also dissolution of their legislatures. Nine of the States, however, promptly filed suits under Article 131 (a) of the Constitution, on the basis of existence of a federal-State dispute, and were joined by individual members of a State legislature who claimed that their property rights under the Constitution – here their right to continue to draw their parliamentary salaries, – were impaired. Moving with speed, however, the Supreme Court of India dismissed all the suites.[43] There were a number of interesting constitutional criticisms advanced against the Court's unanimous decision. Two very perceptive Indian students of the Constitution, Professors Jacob and Dhavan,[44] note the unusual haste with which the Court ruling was announced and point out that the Presidential Proclamation, at the time the suits were brought, was only threatened or foreshadowed and not an actual and concrete invasion of the petitioners' rights; and that the ruling, therefore, was 'premature' or on an as yet 'hypothetical' question. In fact the Presidential Proclamation was issued only after the Court had disposed of the case, though it is in fact commented on in Mr. Justice Chandrachud's opinion. The decision in *State of Rajasthan* v. *Union of India*[45] is a multi-opinion one, and there is the inevitable difficulty in ascertaining the *ratio decidendi,* or common grounds of decision. By and large, however, the decision is an application of the doctrine of 'political questions' and of judicial self-restraint and non-involvement in the scrutiny of the actual exercise of executive discretionary powers under the constitution. If the criticism that the Court acted 'prematurely' in ruling *before* the Presidential Proclamation had actually been made, seems not too weighty an objection in contemporary constitutional terms, as Jacob and Dhavan themselves note,[46] the Court's non-examination of the factual issue of the existence or otherwise of an emergency, on which a Presidential Proclamation is predicated, raises the same questions of constitutional construction that we have seen in the British case of *Liversidge* v. *Anderson.*[47] Article 356 (1) of the Indian Constitution speaks, in this regard, of the following conditions:

'If the President, on receipt of a report from the Governor... of a State or otherwise, is satisfied that a situation has arisen in which the government of the State cannot be carried on in accordance with the provisions of this Constitution, the President may by Proclamation...'

On objective tests, involving judicial scrutiny of any Presidential conclusion that the governments of the States concerned could not 'be carried on', there might have been difficulty in the Court's confirming that the legal conditions prerequisite to user of Presidential power under Article 356 had been constitutionally met. On the *Liversidge* v. *Anderson* approach, where it is a matter for the subjective determination by the President himself, there is no basis for judicial review of the actual exercise by the President of his discretionary power, including the pre-conditions to its exercise. The result, in any case, through judicial self-restraint and application of the 'political questions' doctrine, is judicially to sanction a sweeping exercise in executive federalism whereby any federal character of the constitution is subordinated to the central Government's felt political needs, through utilisation of the constitutional Emergency Provisions.

In France, the *Conseil constitutionnel* ruled in February, 1982, on the constitutionality of two reform projects of the new Mitterand Presidency, the first project concerning the conferment of a 'special status', involving limited self-government or 'Home Rule', for Corsica;[48] and the second project concerning a general process of Regionalisation or devolution of the highly centralised French administrative structure, inherited from the Napoleonic era, involving conferment of much greater legal autonomy upon elected, local, municipal, administrations.[49] In both cases, Parliamentary deputies of the two Opposition parties, amounting to more than the minimum number of sixty deputies required under Article 61 (2) of the Constitution, as amended in 1974, to seize the *Conseil* with a matter, had sought to impugn the new Socialist administration's projects.

The objections raised to the 'special status' for Corsica project, included its alleged uniqueness in constitutional terms (Article 72 of the

Constitution); and its effects upon the constitutional principles of 'indivisibility' of the French Republic (Article 2), of 'equality before the law' in so far as it envisaged special amnesty provisions in Corsica (also Article 2). In rejecting these objections, the *Conseil* indicated, however, that the constitutional equality principle required that the special electoral *régime* – proportional representation on a regional list – proposed for Corsica, either be applied to all regional councils or else the Corsican scheme be modified to accord with the general system. Nothing permitted the special *régime* proposed for Corsica to derogate, on this point, from the electoral Common Law applicable to all regions.[50]

On the Regionalisation project, the *Conseil constitutionnel* picked up Article 72 (3) of the Constitution, which makes the Government delegate in the administrative *départements* and territories responsible for the national interests and for the administrative control and observance of the laws. Before the adoption of the Mitterand Regionalisation project, the Government delegate or prefect could personally annul illegal acts of a municipal council, whereas thereafter he could only seize the administrative tribunals with jurisdiction to examine those acts and pronounce on their legality. The *Conseil* accepted the general principle of this reform, and qualified it only in certain respects going to refusal of executory character to such acts of municipal councils pending their legal review under the new system.[51]

The two *Conseil* decisions concern French Governmental projects which, contrary to more general trends in comparative constitutionalism in modern times, involve a conscious policy of decentralisation and devolution of power on a territorial, geographical basis, by creating new, and unique, constitutional entities, in the case of Corsica; and by confering more autonomy of decision and independence from the central Government to the popularly-elected municipal councils, in the case of the Regionalisation project. Save for some rather technical and easily severable dispositions, the *Conseil* upheld both projects. But in attaching such conditions to the projects, in its decisions, the *Conseil,* in Professor Luchaire's view,[52] served notice that the legislator did not have *carte blanche,* and that the *ensemble* of the Constitution of the Republic and its general principles created limits to constitutional decentralisation for the future – 'No federalism', in Professor Luchaire's words.[53]

NOTES

1. *United States* v. *Carolene Products Co.,* 304 U.S. 144 (1938).
2. See, generally, Walton Hamilton, 'The Path of Due Process of Law', *The Constitution Reconsidered* (1938), p. 167 *et seq.*

3. 304 U.S. 144, 152, n. 4 (1938).

4. *Ibid.*

5. See, especially, Black, J. (dissenting), *Dennis* v. *United States,* 341 U.S. 494, 580-581 (1951); and see also per Reed, J., *Kovacs* v. *Cooper,* 336 U.S. 77, 88 (1949). And see, generally, Edmond Cahn, 'The doubter and the Bill of Rights', 33 *New York University Law Review* 903, 915 (1958).

6. See, for example, Gerhard Leibholz, *Die Gleichheit vor dem Gesetz* (1st ed., 1925; 2nd rev. ed., 1959).

7. See, generally, *Die moderne Demokratie und ihr Recht. Festschrift für Gerhard Leibholz zum 65. Geburtstag* (K.D. Bracher *et al.,* eds.) (2 vols.) (1966); H.-J. Rinck, 'Introduction', G. Leibholz and H.-J. Rinck, *Grundgesetz für die Bundesrepublik Deutschland* (6th ed., 1981); Norbert Kamp, *Gerhard Leibholz* (Georg-August-Universität Göttingen, 1982).

8. H. Laufer, *Verfassungsgerichtsbarkeit und politischer Prozess* (1968), p. 35 *et seq.;* H. Laufer, *Das föderative System der Bundesrepublik Deutschland* (3rd ed., 1977), p. 32 *et seq.;* K. Doehring, *Sozialstaat, Rechtsstaat und freiheitlich-demokratische Grundordnung* (1978).

9. Henning Grund, *'Preussenschlag' und Staatsgerichtshof im Jahre 1932* (1976).

10. *Ibid.,* p. 79 *et seq.*

11. R. Taylor Cole, 'West German Federalism revisited', 23 *American Journal of Comparative Law* 325, 325 (1975); R. Taylor Cole, 'New dimensions of West German Federalism', in *Comparative Politics and Political Theory* (Pinney, ed., 1966), p. 117.

12. See, generally, C.J. Friedrich, *The impact of American Constitutionalism abroad* (1966), p. 41 *et seq.;* C.J. Friedrich, *Limited Government. A comparison* (1974), p. 50 *et seq.*

13. See *Studies in Federalism* (R.R. Bowie and C.J. Friedrich, eds., 1954).

14. Decision of 26 March 1957, 6 B Verf GE 309 (1957) (Second Senate).

15. H.-W. Bayer, *Die Bundestreue* (1961); and see generally *Constitutionalism in Germany and the Federal Constitutional Court* (1962), p. 51 *et seq.*

16. Decision of 30 July 1958, 8 B Verf GE 104 (1959) (Second Senate).

17. Decision of 28 February 1961, 12 B Verf GE 205 (1961) (Second Senate).

18. *Constitutionalism in Germany and the Federal Constitutional Court* (1962), p. 60 *et seq.;* R. Taylor Cole, 'West German Federalism revisited', 23 *American Journal of Comparative Law* 325, at 333 (1975); P.M. Blair, *Federalism and Judicial Review in West Germany* (1981), at 176.

19. R. Taylor Cole, 23 *American Journal of Comparative Law* 325, at 329 (1975).

20. *Ibid.*

21. See the comments by Robert H. (later Mr. Justice) Jackson, *The Struggle for Judicial Supremacy* (1941), at p. 21.

22. Carl Brent Swisher, *American Constitutional Development* (2nd ed., 1954), p. 207; Edward S. Corwin, *The Constitution and what it means today* (1948), p. 44 *et seq.*

23. *Judicial Review* (4th ed., 1969), p. 71; W.P.M. Kennedy, 'The Interpretation of the British North America Act', 8 *Cambridge Law Journal* 154 (1943); Vincent C. MacDonald, 'The Canadian Constitution Seventy Years After', 15 *Canadian Bar Review* 401 (1937).

24. *Canadian Industrial Gas and Oil Ltd.* v. *Government of Saskatchewan* [1978] 2 S.C.R. 545.

25. *Central Canada Potash Co. Ltd. and Attorney-General of Canada* v. *Government of Saskatchewan* [1979] 1 S.C.R. 42.

26. [1978] 2 S.C.R. 545.

27. [1979] 1 S.C.R. 42.

28. *Quebec and the Constitution. 1960-1978* (1979), pp. 88-89, 104.

29. *Ibid.,* p. 21 *et seq.*

186

30. Carl Brent Swisher, *op. cit.,* p. 234 *et seq.*
31. *Public Service Board* v. *Dionne* [1978] 2 S.C.R. 191; *Quebec and the Constitution* (1979), pp. 99-102.
32. [1978] 2 S.C.R. 191.
33. *In re Regulation and Control of Radio Communication in Canada* [1932] A.C. 304 (P.C.).
34. *Quebec and the Constitution* (1979), p. 56 *et seq.*
35. *Canada and the Constitution. 1979-1982* (1982), p. 118.
36. *Quebec and the Constitution* (1979), p. 72.
37. *Protestant School Board of Greater Montreal* v. *Minister of Education of the Province of Quebc,* 83 D.L.R. (3d) 645 (1978): *Quebec and the Constitution* (1979), p. 65 *et seq.*
38. *Attorney-General of Quebec* v. *Blaikie* [1979] 2 S.C.R. 1016.
39. *Canada and the Constitution* (1982), p. 24.
40. *Re A.-G. Quebec and A.-G. Canada* (1982) 140 D.L.R. (3d) 385.
41. A.I.R. *1977* S.C. 1361. And see Alice Jacob and Rajeev Dhavan, 'The Dissolution case: Politics at the Bar of the Supreme Court', 19 *Journal of the Indian Law Institute* 355 (1977); and compare J.L. Kapur, 'The federal structure of the Indian Republic. Its nature and extent', 21 *Journal of the Indian Law Institute* 227 (1979); J. L. Kapur, 'Jurisdiction of the Supreme Court over Election Matters relating to or connected with Presidential elections', 24 *Jahrbuch des öffentlichen Rechts der Gegenwart* 663 (1975).
42. Jacob and Dhavan, *op. cit.,* 19 *Journal of the Indian Law Institute* 355, 357-359 (1977).
43. A.I.R. *1977* S.C. 1361.
44. 19 *Journal of the Indian Law Institute* 355, at 359-362 (1977).
45. A.I.R. *1977* S.C. 1361.
46. Jacob and Dhavan, *op. cit.,* at p. 361.
47. [1942] A.C. 206.
48. *Loi no. 82-214 du 2 mars 1982 portant statut particulier de la région de Corse: organisation administrative, Journal Officiel de la République Française,* 3 March 1982, p. 748.
49. *Loi no. 82-213 du 2 mars 1982 relative aux droits et libertés des communes, des départements et des régions, Journal Officiel de la République Française,* 3 March 1982, p. 730; *Le Monde* (Paris), 30 January 1982.
50. *Conseil constitutionnel,* decision of 25 February 1982 (decision no. 82-138 DC), *Journal Officiel,* 27 February 1982, p. 696; and see 'Corse: statut "non contraire" à la Constitution', *Le Monde,* 27/28 February 1982.
51. *Conseil constitutionnel,* decision of 25 February 1982 (decision no. 82-137 DC), *Journal Officiel,* 3 March 1982, p. 759. And see F. Grosrichard, 'La décision du Conseil permet l'application rapide de la décentralisation', *Le Monde,* 28 February/1 March 1982.
52. François Luchaire, 'La politique et le droit: pas de fédéralisme, *Le Monde,* 28 February/1 March 1982; and see also Michel Debré, 'Contre l'arbitraire', *Le Monde,* 20-21 February 1982.
53. Luchaire, *op. cit., Le Monde,* 28 February/1 March 1982.

CHAPTER IX

THE COURTS AND THE ELECTORAL PROCESSES

1. THE CONSTITUTIONALISATION OF POLITICAL REPRESENTATION

Constitutional charters do not normally include detailed rules as to political representation.[1] The reasons for this gap are partly aesthetic or stylistic ones, going to the length of the charter and the understandable desire of constitution-makers to confine it, essentially, to general principles uncluttered by too much low-level detail of the sort normally necessary for the spelling out, for example, of electoral systems. Other reasons have to do with the desire for a certain degree of stability and long-range continuity in the constitutional charter: in no area of constitutional law do tastes seem to change so easily or frequently as with electoral systems, and in entrenching those rules in the constitution itself one would either be condemning oneself to constitutional permanence or else forced into the time-consuming and arduous task of trying to make often very antiquated and rigid constitutional amending systems work frequently. A third explanation has to do with traditional, 'classical' conceptions of what a constitutional charter should do and also contain: right up until the present day many constitution-makers still seem to envisage such charters as being limited to the institutions and processes of *government* only – the main community decision-making organs (executive, legislative, and judicial), how they are to make and publish their decisions, and their institutional equilibrium *inter se*. The emphasis on inclusion in such charters of constitutional Bills of Rights, on the American and French late 18th century models, is a latter-day trend in general constitutinalism, dating really only from the era between the two World Wars. The emphasis on 'constitutionalising' political representation, through stipulating in the constitution itself minimum or limiting principles as to elections and their conduct and also the organisation and control of political parties, is even more recent, as is the attempt by the Courts to create their own constitutional 'ground rules' on political representation either as an alternative to constitutional charter-defined norms where these do not exist, or as a supplement to such norms where they do exist but need fleshing-out or up-dating to be rendered operational and constitutional law-in-action.

The Constitution of the United States, as originally adopted in 1787, did include certain rules as to political representation – among these the principle of minimum representation of each state of the federal system in the lower house of the federal legislature (Article I (2) 3), and also the age and citizenship qualifications of candidates for election (Article I (2) 2); the principle of equal representation of each state in the federal Senate, and of delegation of the Senators from each state by the relevant state legislature, and the length of term of office of such Senators (Article I (3) 1); the principle of election of the federal President by an electoral college composed of members selected from each state (Article II (1)). These provisions, as originally adopted, have been modified, with the passage of time, in accordance with long-range trends in democratic constitutionalism – sometimes by constitutional custom and convention developing as a gloss on the constitutional text as written, as with the change in the nature and character of the members of the electoral college for the federal Presidency, from genuine electors having their own full discretion (as envisaged in Article II (1), and also the Twelfth Amendment to the Constitution adopted in 1804) to persons exercising a purely mechanical, automatic *rôle* in strict accord with the popular majority vote cast within their states at the Presidential elections. At other times, the original constittutional rules have been changed by formal constitutional amendment, as with the substitution for the original system of indirect election or delegation of Senators by state legislatures, of direct, popular election of the Senators within their respective states, this being effected by the Seventeenth Amendment, adopted in 1913, and reflecting the more general, long-range trend in comparative constitutionalism away from 'aristocratic', hereditary or nominated or indirectly selected, upper houses, to popularly elected legislatures at the upper house as well as the lower house level.

The major changes in the positive law of the constitution as to electoral representation in the United States occur by way of constitutional amendments. The Fifteenth Amendment, adopted in 1870, as the third of the post-Civil War, 'Reconstruction Amendments', declares that:

'The right of citizens of the United States to vote shall not be denied or abridged by the United States or by any State on account of race, colour, or previous condition of servitude.'

The historical intent of the Fifteenth Amendment, and its general egalitarian impulse and motivation, were clear from the outset. It cannot be divorced from its companion Amendments – the Thirteenth, adopted in 1865, declaring that 'neither slavery nor involuntary servitude' should exist within the United States; and the Fourteenth, adopted in 1868, which both extended the Due Process of Law guarantees of the Fifth Amendment (adopted in 1791 and applying to the federal Government) to the individual states, and also established the general constitutional principle of 'the equal protection of the laws'. But the constitutional history of the Thirteenth, Fourteenth, and Fifteenth Amendments is that their egalitarian principles, at the level of constitutional law-in-action, became nominal and not normative. They were caught up in the political reaction, after the brief 'Reconstruction' period, to the hardships of the Civil War and to the harshness and excesses of the initial federal Government dealings with the defeated Southern States. The spirit of reconciliation and political realism dictated that deference to another, *federal* constitutional principle – here the ability of the legislatures of the Southern States and their governments to determine their own future, within the United States, – should prevail over the constitutionally egalitarian norms inscribed in the three 'Reconstruction' Amendments. And while the largest impact of this new 'federal' priority was in those areas of civil rights having to do with race relations in education and housing and community life generally, there were direct consequences, also, in the area of political representation involving State action, executive or legislative, differentiating on the basis of race in terms of access to and participation in the electoral processes, that was effectively tolerated by the Court's invoking legal principles of judicial non-intervention in such matters in spite of the clear constitutional norms. In general, the change in judicial attitudes, – back to the spirit and letter of the United States Constitution and its Thirteenth, Fourteenth, and Fifteenth Amendments, – would have to wait on a new judicial activism, itself the product of the 'Court Revolution' of 1937 and of the general civil libertarian activist drives in the community from the Second World War onwards.

2. JUDICIAL SELF-RESTRAINT IN ELECTION CASES: 'POLITICAL QUESTIONS'

Race relations in the practice and operation of the electoral laws shade off into the larger issue of constitutional scrutiny and control, according to constitutional charter-stipulated norms or to the general spirit of the constitution, of political representation, including here the electoral processes as a whole and political parties as the main public organs for political representation. The United States Supreme Court, as late as 1946, had refused to intervene against the distorted, 'gerrymandered' federal electoral districts within the State of Illinois, as apportioned under Illinois State law. The Court, in its official opinion in *Colegrove* v. *Green*,[2] written by Mr. Justice Frankfurter, ruled the matter to be 'of a peculiarly political nature and therefore not meet for judicial determination'. As Mr. Justice Frankfurter commented:

'Of course no court can affirmatively re-map the Illinois districts so as to bring them more in conformity with the standards of fairness for a representative system. At best we could only declare the existing electoral system invalid. The result would be to leave Illinois undistricted and to bring into operation, if the Illinois legislature chose not to act, the choice of members for the [federal] House of Representatives on a state-wide ticket. The last may be worse than the first.'[3]

In suggesting that – 'the remedy ultimately lies with the people', Mr. Justice Frankfurter noted that the Court had – 'traditionally held aloof' from scrutinising 'party contests'; that it was 'hostile to a democratic system to involve the judiciary in the politics of the people'. But the decision in *Colegrove* v. *Green* contained a strong dissent, by Justices Black, Douglas, and Murphy,[4] who considered the issue to be judicially cognisable; and also a concurring opinion by Justice Rutledge[5] who, though with the Court majority on other grounds, nevertheless considered the substantive issue of the constitutionality of the Illinois apportionment according to Article I (2) and the Fourteenth Amendment, to be judicially cognisable. It was obvious that judicial self-restraint in regard to intervening to correct abuses in the electoral processes would soon be challenged. The Court had already, in *Smith* v. *Allwright* in 1944,[6] rejected the distinction, from its earlier jurisprudence, between 'State' action which would be violative of the Fourteenth and Fifteenth Amendments, and 'private' action, in ruling that a political Party's primary election to choose its candidates for the federal Senate and House of Representatives was an integral part of the general electoral system, and that as primaries were conducted under State authority, the Pary became, in effect, an agent of the State. The exclusion of voters, therefore, from the Texas Democratic Party primary, on account of race and colour, amounted to a violation of Article I (2) and of the Fourteenth and Fifteenth Amendments of the Constitution.

3. JUDICIAL ACTIVISM: 'EQUAL PROTECTION OF THE LAWS' IN ELECTIONS

In *Gomillion* v. *Lightfoot,* in 1960,[7] the Supreme Court invoked the Fifteenth Amendment to the Constitution to invalidate a State reapportionment plan that would have denied almost all the Negro voters within the City of Tuskegee, Alabama, their pre-existing municipal vote by removing them from within the city's limits. It was, however, in *Baker* v. *Carr,* in 1962,[8] that the Court really came to grips, frontally, with its earlier, *Colegrove* v. *Green,* 1946,[9] holding where it had applied self-restraint and refused to intervene in electoral cases. An action had been brought by voters within the State of Tennessee challenging, on the score of their denial of federal constitutional rights and specifically the Fourteenth Amendment's Equal Protection clause, the State's apportionment statute for elections to the State legislature. In sixty years since the enactment of that State statute, the population distribution within the State had altered markedly, creating severe disproportions – in the ratio, in the extreme cases, of more than nineteen to one as between different State electoral districts; but no new apportionment had been made. The U.S. Supreme Court, re-examining *Colegrove* v. *Green,* now held such electoral questions to be justicially cognisable, and therefore reversed lower court judgments denying jurisdiction and remanded the case for application of Fourteenth Amendment Equal Protection principles. This landmark decision, holding electoral issues to be justiciable and conceding legal standing-to-sue to individual voters, opened the flood-gates to constitutional litigation designed to effect more equitable and more 'representative' legislative apportionment systems for both federal and state elections. This was achieved, as to equality of federal Congressional electoral districts, in *Wesberry* v. *Sanders* in 1964;[10] and as to State legislatures (and, in the actual instance involved, a State upper house) in *Reynolds* v. *Sims,* also decided in 1964,[11] from which the 'One Man, One Vote' principle evolved. Where *Wesberry* v. *Sanders,* as to federal electoral districts, was based squarely upon Article I of the Constitution, *Reynolds* v. *Sims,* with the contested Alabama upper house's thirty-five senatorial districts, each electing one State senator, ranging in population from 15,000 to more than 600,000 persons, was related by the Court directly to the Fourteenth Amendment Equal Protection principle.

The implications of the new jurisprudence were clear and substantial, not merely in terms of ensuring honest and fair political representation systems at both federal and State levels, and thus in Justice Harlan Stone's spirit, as enunicated in the *Carolene Products* case in 1938,[12] for keeping the general political processes free and unobstructed; but also for the Court's own work-load and its claims to specialist, as distinct from general professional expertise. Courts could, manifestly, annul unjust electoral laws and practices on constitutional grounds, but unless they were prepared themselves to sit as a sort of continuing electoral boundaries commission they might, as Justice Frankfurter had noted as a rationale for his 'self-restraint' approach in *Colegrove* v. *Green* in 1946, have to accept the temporary substitute of elections-at-large, on a State-wide basis, for federal or State elections as the case may be, while depending on the goodwill and desire to cooperate in good faith of the relevant State legislature for affirmative, follow-up action to any Court decisions striking down existing State laws as unconstitutional. A further constitutional amendment, the Twenty-Fourth, adopted in 1964,[13] at the time the land-mark, judicial activist, interventionist decisions on voting laws were being rendered by the Supreme Court, indicated just such an affirmative will to cooperate on the part of both the federal legislative majorities that formally initiated it as a constitutional amendment, and the State legislative majorities that then ratified it as a constitutional amendment. The Twenty-Fourth Amendment struck down the 'poll tax' – a device adopted in many of the defeated Southern States, after the Civil War, to restrict access by Negroes to the electoral laws – and gave the federal legislature power to enforce that ban, by appropriate legislation. Since the members of both federal Houses are elected in each State, according to State electoral laws, the establishment of such federal constitutional norms – in the Fifteenth and Twenty-Fourth Amendments – controlling and overriding State laws, and authorising further federal enforcement laws if needed – becomes crucial, as does continuance of the supervisory, monitoring *rôle* as to fairness of electoral laws assumed by the Supreme Court since the early 1960s in particular. In 1965, pursuant to the Fifteenth and Twenty-Fourth Amendments, Congress, with strong Presidential pressure applied to it, enacted the Voting Rights Act establishing substantial federal authority to break down State discriminatory barriers of a racial character in the State electoral laws.[14] The 1965 federal statute abolished literacy tests, waived accumulated poll taxes, and gave the federal Attorney-General vast discretionary powers to deal with areas suspected of discrimination against Negro voters, including power to send in federal examiners to any county in which 50 percent or more of the voting age population was not registered, and power in such federal examiners then to list all qualified voters and to declare them eligible to participate in elections. Portions of the 1965 federal statute were challenged, in *South Carolina* v. *Katzenbach* in 1966,[15] and the challenges were rejected by the Supreme Court, with Chief Justice Warren taking the opportunity to deliver a sweeping constitutional endorsement of the federal law's basic philosophy, in terms of the Fifteenth Amendment above all, of massive federal Governmental intervention and activism in support of voting rights. In a further statute, the federal Voting Rights Act of 1970,[16] Congress went even further, prohibiting the use of literacy tests in all elections, where such tests were not already proscribed by the 1965 Act, and this prohibition was upheld by the Court; for, faced with evidence that literacy tests had reduced voter participation in a racially discriminatory manner, a nation-wide ban on literacy tests had become appropriate (*Oregon* v. *Mitchell*).[17]

With the main issue of the justiciability of election questions, on constitutional grounds, now disposed of in favour of affirmative exercise of Court jurisdiction, and with Governmental activism at the executive-legislative level in favour of affirmative protection and extension of voters' rights now increasingly popular, the Courts became seized with some extremely interesting and complex cases involving, often, different constitutional libertarian principles in direct competition. The task for the Court, in such cases, involves resolving the consequent constitutional antinomies. In *United Jewish Organisation, Inc.* v. *Carey,* in 1977[18] – which we will have occasion to look at again, later, when we examine the *rôle* of the Courts in relation to Minority Rights – what was involved was a New York State law reapportioning the State electoral districts in New York City, with the evidence indicating that the electoral boundaries had been drawn with the deliberate intent of creating non-white (Puerto Rican and Negro) racial majorities as a means of increasing such non-white representation in the State legislature. The effect of the State of New York's 'affirmative action' on behalf of the Puerto Rican and Negro voters, however, was to diminish markedly the value of the votes of another minority group, the Hasidic Jewish community of Brooklyn, whose voting strength, originally concentrated in the one State Assembly (lower house) and the one State Senate (upper house) electoral constituency, was now dissipated by being split between several constituencies, effectively depriving the Hasidic Jewish community of the power to elect their own community representatives to the State legislature. The Supreme Court of the United States had no difficulty in proceeding to decide the case on the merits, and, in a seven-to-one majority judgment based directly on the Fifteenth Amendment to the U.S. Constitution and the federal Voting Rights Act of 1965 designed to implement it, upheld the New York reapportionment in its focus upon racial minorities and ways of securing their more effective exercise of the electoral franchise. Mr. Justice White, for the Court, found that – 'neither the Fourteenth nor the Fifteenth Amendment mandates any *per se* rule against using racial factors in districting and apportionment';[19] and Mr. Justice Brennan, in his specially concurring opinion, endorsed that form of 'benign discrimination' which, in his view, was –

'permissible because it is cast in a remedial context with respect to a disadvantaged class rather than in a setting that aims to demean or insult any racial group.'[20]

We have come a very long way, by now, from the judicial self-restraint and conscious judicial disengagement from the electoral processes, manifested in *Colegrove* v. *Green* in 1946.[21] The new judicial attitudes not merely reflect the conclusion, flowing from Justice Stone's inspired *dicta* in *Carolene Products* in 1938,[22] that judicial deference to the legislature and legislative majorities bound up in the judicial presumption of constitutionality in favour of legislative action, is predicated upon the legislatures concerned being representative, and honestly and fairly elected in the first place; but they also reflect the increasing judicial sophistication in the examination of the theory and also the actual practice of political representation and different voting plans, that is a necessary concomitant of the new judicial activism in regard to the electoral processes generally. [23]

4. POLITICAL PARTIES AND THE ELECTORAL LAWS: CONSTITUTIONAL EQUALITY

The Bonn Constitution of 1949 has several major Articles devoted to political representation. In Part III of the Constitution (the *Bundestag*), Article 38 (Elections) lays down the basic principle that members of the *Bundestag* are to be –

> 'elected in general, direct, free, equal, and secret elections. They shall be representatives of the whole people, not bound by orders and instructions, and shall be subject only to their conscience.' (Article 38 (1))

There are several other constitutional provisions, such as the establishment of the legal age for voting as eighteen (Article 38 (2)), and the prescribing of a fixed, four-year term for the *Bundestag* (Article 39 (1)), that need not now concern us. The other, major constitutional provision, contained in Part II of the Constitution (The Federation and the *Länder*), Article 21 (Political Parties), lays down constitutional ground rules for the character, organisation and conduct of political parties:

> Article 21:
> '(1) The political parties shall participate in the forming of the political will of the people. They may be freely established. Their internal organisation must conform to democratic principles. They must publicly account for the sources of their funds.
> (2) Parties which, by reason of their aims or the behaviour of their adherents, seek to impair or abolish the free democratic basic order or to endanger the existence of the Federal Republic of Germany, shall be unconstitutional. The Federal Constitutional Court shall decide on the question of unconstitutionality.'

Schweitzer, himself a former deputy in the *Bundestag,* comments upon the relation of tension between Article 21 (Political Parties) and Article 38 (Elections), in actual legislative practice within the *Bundestag.* Is the *Bundestag* member to have his own freedom-of-decision, or should he conform to the policy of his political party? [24] Both Articles reflect main objectives of the original Herrenchiemsee Conference preceding adoption of the Bonn Constitution in 1949, where the constitutional Founding Fathers endeavoured to profit from the lessons of the failure of the Weimar Republic and to constitutionalise, within the new charter, adequate institutional and procedural safeguards to prevent any recurrence of the Weimar weaknesses in the future. The express constitutional stipulation as to 'unconstitutional' political parties (Article 21 (2)) reflected the informed view, among West German political leaders in 1948-9, that the politically extremist parties of both the Right and the Left had deliberately undermined the stability and coherence of the Weimar constitutional system and had shown a contempt for its democratic principles.[25] In two decisions in the early 1950s, the First Senate of the Federal Constitutional Court applied Article 21 (2) to outlaw, first, in 1952, the neo-Nazi Socialist Reich Party and to order its immediate dissolution and the vacation of all parliamentary seats held by its members;[26] and then, in 1956, after a process arising at the same time as the Socialist Reich Party case but in respect to which, for reasons we have already canvassed, decision was delayed, for political reasons, for a number of years, the West German Communist Party.[27] These two decisions, as noted, were rendered by the First Senate of the Court, but most of the Court jurisprudence on political representation and the electoral processes flows, for special jurisdictional reasons, from the Second Senate, and the main judicial *rapporteur* in those cases is known to have been Judge Leibholz who, in his pre-War as well as his post-War career as a University Professor and writer, had been responsible for the development of very much of the critical, scientific-legal theory as to political representation in the modern democratic state and its concrete expression in constitutional ground rules as to political parties and election processes.[28] Judge Leibholz, after the experience of the Weimar Republic years of the relative passivity or supineness of the democratic political parties in face of the totalitarian, anti-democratic parties of the Right and the Left, and also the political fractiousness and indiscipline of the myriad of moderate, centrist, liberal democratic and social democratic parties, when confronted with the deliberately disruptive tactics of the extremist parties, posited the formation of a vibrant, operational constitutional democracy under the new Bonn system, upon the achievement of several main principles. First, a vigilant, combative democracy that would not be afraid to fight to defend its constitutional principles. Second, the establishment of a genuine, plural-Party state in which the system of political representation would be grounded in effectively-functioning, cohesive political parties, applying democratic principles, under law, as to their internal organisation and practice, and also unity and self-discipline as to the maintenance of intra-parliamentary consensus in support of Party policies. And third, the guarantee that the Party state, while necessarily plural and not monolithic to ensure a genuinely dialectical, inter-Party, give-and-take in the making of parliamentary decisions, would not distintegrate in a mass of small, splinter-parties or fractions that would be mutually destructive in the way that had effectively prevented the formation of stable, coalition majorities of the centre under the Weimar Republic. [29] The last point in the Leibholz philosophy of political representation was the necessary application of the key-stone constitutional principle of Equality before the Law (Article 3 of the Bonn Constitution) to the electoral processes both to ensure honest and constitutionally fair electoral representation, and also to ensure public respect for the integrity of the election system as a whole. All these principles were represented, in measure, in the Bonn constitutional charter in 1949, but giving them teeth was the work, essentially, of an activist judicial majority within the Second Senate of the Federal Constitutional Court, with Leibholz's own *rôle* as intellectual animator within the Second Senate, veiled as it necessarily was for most of the time because of the Court's traditions and practice of collegiality and anonymity, a very vital one. The key decision, and the most controversial in its immediate political background since involving, first, the Second Senate's disqualification, by four-to-three majority vote, with Judge Leibholz himself abstaining from that vote, of Judge Leibholz, [30] and then a four-to-three majority decision, on the substantive constitutional issue, by the rump Second Senate, again without Judge Leibholz, [31] was the decision in the Party Financing case in 1966. [32] A key element in the conception of an effectively functioning plural-Party system as the foundation of modern constitutional democracy was the notion that such political parties should have proper economic resources for financing their general operations and election campaigns. The Second Senate of the Federal Constitutional Court, in 1958, had invalidated a federal law permitting individual and corporate deductions from their taxation of a percentage of their financial contributions to political parties, [33] and this decision was understandable enough since it would, demonstrably, have favoured those political parties supported by the more affluent sections of the community and by the large corporations and thus violated the constitutional Equality principle. A new federal law met the problem of state support for political parties head-on, by providing for direct public financing, across the board, to all main political parties represented in the *Bundestag,* and it was this law that the Second Senate ultimately rejected, in 1966, in its four-to-three vote on the substantive issue of constitutionality. [34] For purposes of contesting the federal law before the Court, an un-Holy Alliance soon formed between extreme Right wing political splinter-groups who objected to the new federal law because, in recognition of the post-Weimar lesson of encouraging a plurality of stable, competing political parties but not a multiplicity of minor splinter-parties or fractions, that federal law designedly excluded from the federal government financial subsidies to political parties those parties that failed to

obtain a certain minimum percentage of the popular vote in the general
election and thus a certain minimum number of seats in the federal
legislature; and the then main federal Opposition party, the Social Democrats, moving through their local regional Government of the *Land* of
Hessen, the Social Democrats having, because of their own large independent sources of funds from trade unions and similar labour syndical-
ist groups, little need for extra financial subsidies, in comparison to the
federal Government (Christian Democratic) parties.[35] The majority
opinion of the Second Senate, perhaps because of the very close nature of
the internal division within the Court, is not always too clear or too
concrete in its formulation of its constitutional grounds.[36] It refers, rather, to general constitutional principles of the 'free democratic basic
order', and to a 'free-from-the-state, and open, popular, opinion and
will-formation', which it relates to Article 20 (2) (Basic principles of the
Constitution), and which it considers as 'guarding against any form of
state-institutional consolidation of the activity of the political parties,
and as forbidding their insertion in the sphere of organised state authority'. If the majority opinion of the Second Senate did declare unconstitutional the present *general* financing statute, which provided *general*
subsidies, by the state, to political parties, it did not, in terms, purport to
invalidate all possible schemes of public financing of political parties.
Insofar as political parties were constitutional organs of the state for purposes of securing popular input into government, the state might reim-
burse them for 'necessary expenses' incurred during the course of an
election campaign. To finance parties between campaigns, or to provide
for their general support, however, would involve an unconstitutional
interference with the freedom of the political processes. Political parties,
being in substance social organisations, were entitled to no greater claim
to state support than other politically-oriented voluntary associations.

What followed upon the Second Senate's decision of 1966 is a good
illustration of the thesis that the courts and the other, (executive and
legislative), institutions of government don't have to be mutually anta-
gonistic, and that a great deal can be achieved by their trying to work in
tandem, as mutually complementary, community problem-solving institutions. The federal Government responded to the 1966 decision invalidating the *general* financing of political parties statute by enacting, in
1967, a new Statute on Political Parties which is really a comprehensive
code of rules defining political parties, as such, and their constitutional
rôle; laying down legal principles as to parties' internal governance and
administration; establishing the legal rights and duties of party members
and rules as to the conduct of party assemblies; establishing the principle
of the reimbursement of political parties' election expenses and also
detailed rules for its implementation; requiring the publication of the

names and contributions of individual and corporate donors to political parties, above a certain limit (20,000 Marks in the case of individuals; 200,000 Marks in the case of corporations). The 1967 statute's new scheme of public financing of political parties' election expenses was itself challenged before the Federal Constitutional Court's Second Senate; and the Court, in 1968, (with Judge Leibholz participating this time) did in fact strike down certain elements of the 1967 statute. One of the vices of the earlier *general* financing scheme, struck down by the Second Senate in its 1966 decision, had been that it was limited to the parliamentary parties already represented in the federal legislature, thereby excluding minor parties or new parties. The 1967 statute, in an endeavour to meet the 'Open Society' test of allowing free and unobstructed access to the political processes, had predicated the state reimbursement of parties for their campaign expenses on their receiving a minimum of 2-1/2 percent of the national popular vote. This 2-1/2 per cent floor the Second Senate now ruled to be unconstitutional as violating the constitutional Equality principle. [37] The suit had been brought by a minor party excluded, by virtue of the 2-1/2 per cent floor, from the 1967 statute's financial benefits; and the Second Senate, noting that the 1967 statute thereby imposed a special hardship on such minor parties, went on to suggest in its judgment that a 0.5 per cent statutory floor, as a condition to reimbursement of electoral expenses, might meet the test of constitutional Equality. The federal Government immediately picked up the Court's implied invitation, and the 1967 Statute on Political Parties was promptly amended, in 1969, to lower the statutory floor, accordingly, to 0.5 per cent. The statutory provision, as now amended, has been free from subsequent challenge, and the statute as a whole stands as a legal code defining and governing the operation of political parties as constitutional organs of government in West Germany.

In it main outlines, the Bonn constitutional charter's design of constitutionalising political representation has been confirmed and extended by the Court. Thus, the basic federal electoral plan of a 'mixed' system whereby one-half of the members of the *Bundestag* are elected in single-member, geographically-based electoral constituencies, and the other half on a party list system using proportional representation based on the actual party vote cast, was upheld by the Court in 1952. [38] The system of proportional representation, as such, was upheld in 1957. [39] The five percent rule, which requires a political party to attain that threshold, in the popular vote, before being eligible for representation in the *Bundestag,* and which was the key legislative instrument in the Bonn attempt to profit from the Weimar Republic lesson of the dangers of allowing too many splinter-parties or fractions in the legislature, was also upheld in 1957. [40] The 'one man-one vote' rule was recognised by the Court in

1963.[41] Other Second Senate decisions, in 1957[42] and 1961,[43] establishing modalities of application of these principles, including the limitation of the political parties' discretion in the designation of order of priority on the party candidates' list before and after the actual popular vote,[43a] help to reinforce the effective constitutionalisation of the electoral process and the *rôle* of the political parties in them.

There are no exact parallels, in the other systems we have surveyed, to the Bonn Constitution's 'entrenchment' of political parties as constitutional organs of the state. The Bonn Constitution of 1949, as a latter-day charter, had benefit from all the latter-day constitutional wisdom and learning as to the extent to which abstract charters, if they are ever to become constitutional law-in-action, are dependent upon vibrant, democratically functioning, extra-governmental institutions like political parties and similar cultural, social and economic interest groups. The study of constitutional institutions can no longer be limited today to the old, triadic, executive-legislative-judicial scheme of division; and the constitutional ground rules must take account of these new institutions like the political parties and provide for their democratic conduct and governance. This had been Judge Leibholz' teaching, as professor, and it was echoed by so many of the Founding Fathers of Bonn constitutional democracy in 1949, who had lived through the earlier, Weimar Republic when the constitutionally unregulated and undisciplined parties had contributed so greatly to its eventual downfall. West Germany in 1949 thus led the way in terms of constitutional entrenchment and regulation of political parties, pioneering in the idea of public reimbursement of such parties for their direct campaign expenses and also serving as a model for other constitutional systems which had no express mention of political parties, as such, in their own constitutional charters. In the United States, as we have seen, the Supreme Court had moved, through its case-law jurisprudence, to accord a degree of constitutional recognition and control of political parties as early as 1944, with its decision in *Smith* v. *Allwright*.[43b] It had there been held that the political party 'primary' elections, even though purportedly the activity of private (non-public) organisations, were an integral part of the electoral processes, virtually guaranteeing, in the case of effective one-party states, the final election; and so the political party 'primary' elections should be subject to constitutional regulation and control under the Fourteenth and Fifteenth Amendments to the Constitution. In *Buckley* v. *Valeo*, in 1976,[43c] the U.S. Supreme Court struck down, on First Amendment, free speech grounds, provisions of the Federal Election Campaign Act of 1971 limiting independent political expenditures by individuals and groups, and fixing ceilings on overall campaign expenditures by election candidates. These statutory limitations, the Court held, were constitutionally imper-

missible burdens on the right of free expression under the First Amendment, and could not be sustained on the argument of countervailing governmental interests in preventing the actuality or appearance of corruption, or in equalising the resources of candidates. The Supreme Court
did, however, at the same time, uphold the imposition by the Federal
Election Campaign Act of ceilings on political contributions, against the
objection of violation of First Amendment speech and association rights
or invidious discrimination against non-incumbent candidates and minority party candidates, the Court deferring, here, to what it felt to be
substantial governmental interests in limiting corruption and the appearance of corruption. In *Democratic Party of U.S., and Edward Mezvinsky
v. National Conservative Political Action Committee,* in 1983,[43d] a U.S.
District Court extended the protection of the First Amendment Free
Speech guarantee to the activities of the so-called Political Action Committees, operating independently of the main political parties and seeking
to spend their own monies, during election campaigns, to influence the
outcome of those campaigns. The U.S. District Court reasoned that the
attempt, under the Presidential Election Campaign Fund Act of 1974, to
limit financing of election campaigns to the major political parties was,
(in the words of Judge Becker), to – 'give the institutionalised political
parties an almost impervious monopoly over the agenda and terms of
debate in presidential electoral campaigns'. The U.S. District Court, in
its judgment, directly invoked *Buckley* v. *Valeo,* as authority for the proposition that expenditures by Political Action Committees constitute
speech that is constitutionally protected by the First Amendment. The
U.S. District Court decision, and the Supreme Court decision in *Buckley*
v. *Valeo* on which it relied, were both expressions of the Open Society
ideal and its proclaimed imperative of keeping the political processes as
free and unobstructed as possible. For these purposes, the two Court
decisions treated political parties and other political interest groups (here
the Political Action Committees) on the same plane of constitutional
equality and as being entitled, equally, to First Amendment Free Speech
protections. This goes beyond the jurisprudence under the West German
Constitution. However, the West German constitutional charter of 1949
formally 'entrenches' political parties and thereby gives them a species of
constitutionally preferred status in relation to other political interest
groups; and the Statute on Political Parties of 1967, enacted pursuant to
the constitutional charter 'entrenchment' provisions, establishes an ela-
borate code of legal rules protecting rights of party members and regulating due process of law in internal party proceedings, thereby ensuring
that the political parties themselves, as constitutional organs, conform to
the Open Society ideal. In contrast, the U.S. Constitution says nothing, in
terms, as to political parties, or for that matter other political interest

groups. The dual system of legal regulation of political parties in the United States – federal as to some overriding constitutional norms (mainly going to constitutional Free Speech and Equality interests) and state (local) as to all other matters – is neither comprehensive in range and philosophy nor fully coordinated; and the practical effect of leaving so much to state (local) regulation has been to confirm a duopoly of the two old-line national parties and to erect legal barriers against third parties and the emergence of new political ideas, thereby frequently stultifying the Open Society ideal. The U.S. District Court decision in *Democratic Party of U.S., and Edward Mezvinsky* v. *National Conservative Political Action Committee* in 1983 reflects this thinking. It was under appeal to the U.S. Supreme Court at the time of writing.

In a Canadian test case, *National Citizens Coalition and Colin Brown* v. *Attorney-General of Canada,* in 1984,[43e] a Provincial Supreme Court was asked to rule on the constitutionality of the federal Government's attempt, under the Canada Elections Act, as amended, to restrict federal electoral campaign expenditures to 'registered' political parties, such 'registered' parties being effectively limited, in terms of the Act, to those fielding at least 50 candidates in the federal elections concerned. The legal attack on the Canada Elections Act was launched by a private interest group, and the constitutional arguments advanced were Open Society ones, based on freedom of speech and freedom of association (sections 2 (b) and 2 (d)), and the right to vote (section 3) of the then recently enacted, and constitutionally entrenched, federal bill of rights – the Canadian Charter of Rights and Freedoms of 1982. In Canada, as in the United States and in contrast to West Germany, there is no formal constitutional entrenchment of political parties; and one of the constitutional arguments advanced against the Canada Elections Act (as amended) restriction of electoral campaign activities and expenses to 'registered' political parties was that it attempted to do, by indirection, and as an afterthought to legislation adopted for other purposes, what the Canadian constitution-makers had not chosen to do directly, either at the time of original adoption of the Constitution in 1867 or even at the time of the Constitution's renewal in 1982 when, *inter alia,* the Charter of Rights and Freedoms had been adopted – namely, 'establish' the already existing political parties as the only constitutionally approved organs for purposes of the federal electoral processes. Evidence led to the Provincial Supreme Court at the hearing demonstrated that, under the system of public reimbursement of political parties for election expenses, provided by the Canada Elections Act, 98 per cent of the public reimbursements made for election expenses incurred in the then last two federal general elections held in 1979 and 1980, had gone to the three political parties already represented in the federal Parliament. The practical effect of the Canada

Elections Act, as amended, on this view, was to consolidate existing political orthodoxies, rather than, as the great Mr. Justice Oliver Wendell Holmes of the U.S. Supreme Court had suggested, many years earlier,[43f] to promote a genuine competition and interaction of ideas in the general marketplace of ideas represented by a free democratic society. It is clear that, in Canada as well as in the United States, the constitutional-dialectical process is not yet complete of giving new meaning and content to constitutional freedom of speech and freedom of association and right to vote guarantees in the light of latter-day perception of the new *rôle,* in the political and general constitutional processes, of the mass political parties. So far as the parties should be constitutionally 'entrenched', *de jure* or *de facto,* there would seem to be a correlative constitutional obligation to subject those parties, as constitutional organs of the state, to constitutional requirements of due process in their internal operations as well as to all the tests of constitutional free speech and constitutional equality. The political and general constitutional processes would also seem to need to be kept constitutionally open to new political interest groups and new political ideas not yet able to secure effective representation or expression in already established, orthodox political parties. The West German constitutional experience of recent years, though much more advanced and detailed than in other countries, still rests on special 'German' societal factors – the historical experience with the breakdown of party democracy under the earlier Weimar Republic, and the express inclusion in the constitutional charter of 1949 of the status of political parties as constitutional organs of the state – that need to be comprehended before direct transfer of the West German experience to other constitutional-legal systems is undertaken or contemplated. The comparative law exercise involved is properly rooted in sociological jurisprudence, with congruence as to both Law and Society necessary for purposes of a successful and useful legal 'reception'.

In the Canadian case just referred to, Mr. Justice Medhurst of the Supreme Court of the Province of Alberta, in a judgment handed down in June, 1984,[43g] rightly recognised in his Opinion that recourse to comparative law, to be helpful in a Canadian context, must proceed from and be based upon comparative sociology of law, involving not merely comparison of the abstract, positive law texts as written but also comparison of the different societal conditions to which those positive law exercises had been designed to respond. In a judgment based squarely upon the new Canadian Charter of Rights adopted in 1982, and specifically its s. 2 (b) constitutional guarantee of freedom of expression (rather than its s. 3 constitutional guarantee of the right to vote), the Alberta Supreme Court invoked dicta by Chief Justice Duff in an earlier Canadian Supreme Court *cause célèbre* ruling of 1938, the *Alberta Press* case,[43h] to invalidate the Canada Elections Act, as amended, in its prohibitions upon electoral campaign activities conducted by private citizens or interest groups outside the *aegis* of the established political parties officially registered, as such, under that Act. What is surprising in the whole matter is less the actual ruling by the Alberta Supreme Court; for the Canada Elections Act, as amended, seemed cavalier and widesweeping in its range and also overly restrictive in its impact upon historically recognised constitutional liberties. The real surprise was the almost immediate public announcement by the federal Attorney-General and Minister of Justice that he would not appeal the adverse ruling by the Alberta Court,[43i] thus allowing its judgment to invalidate the federal statute, as amended, to stand. Though there were undoubtedly considerations of immediate political expediency behind the federal Government's decision not to appeal, with the desire to avoid further public debate on the general issue (with a federal general election then imminent), there was apparently also an overriding recognition that the federal law, as amended, had been unnecessarily broadly drafted in the first place, and that the federal Government should go back to the legislative drafting board and try to devise a better integrated law on political parties that would be more consonant with 'Open Society' ideals.

5. JUDICIAL SELF-RESTRAINT AND THE CONSTITUTIONAL EQUALITY PRINCIPLE

The evident success of this aspect of Bonn constitutionalism, the lack of timidity of the judges in approaching the constitutional surveillance of the electoral pre-conditions to any democratic decision-making by legislatures and legislative majorities, and the degree of skill the judges have displayed in acquiring the specialist knowledge involved in scrutinising the internal operations of political parties and the practical workings of the electoral laws, suggest that Courts in other jurisdictions may have deferred too much, in the past, to doctrines of judicial self-restraint in regard to 'political questions' predicated upon the alleged difficulty or impossibility of the Courts' comprehending the electoral processes or prescribing effective, operational remedies for alleged abuses in them. The post-War Japanese Constitution of 1946, like the Bonn Constitution of 1949, contains specific stipulations as to the electoral processes, and also key general constitutional principles, such as the principle of 'equality under the law' (Article 14) that the Supreme Court has had no difficulty in holding as fully applicable to guarantee fairness in the electoral system and its practical operation. Article 43 of the Constitution states that both Houses of the legislature are to consist of 'elected members, representative of all the people'. Article 44 requires that, in fixing the qualifications of members of both Houses and also their electors, there shall be – 'no discrimination because of race, creed, sex, social status, family origin, education, property or income'. Article 47 states that electoral districts, method of voting, and other matters pertaining to the method of election of members of both Houses, are to be fixed by statute law. These Articles all fall within Chapter IV of the Constitution, dealing with the Diet (legislature). In Chapter III (Rights and Duties of the People), we have already referred to Article 14:

> 'All of the people are equal under the law and there shall be no discrimination in political, economic or social relations because of race, creed, sex, social status or family origin.'

Article 15 adds to this, in regard to elections, that – 'the people have the inalienable right to choose their public officials and to dismiss them'; and it also guarantees 'universal adult suffrage... with regard to the election of public officials', plus – 'in all elections, secrecy of the ballot'.

All these provisions of the Constitution came together in the *Koshiyama* case, decided by the Grand Bench of the Supreme Court of Japan on 5 February 1964.[44] A Tokyo voter had challenged the 1962 election of Tokyo representatives to the upper House of the legislature on the grounds that the apportionment of seats was based on a 1946 census, and that the electoral law violated the constitutional guarantee of Equality under the Law in Article 14. The argument was that the Constitution required the number of representatives to be proportionate to population, and that in the absence of affirmative grounds justifying an imbalance between the number of representatives and the number of voters in terms of the 'value of a vote', a law that exceeded the maximum limit of tolerable imbalance violated the constitutional Equality principle. The Supreme Court rejected this complaint, stating that while the apportionment of Diet seats to each election district in proportion to the population of the electorate was definitely desirable in terms of the constitutional Equality principle, there was no impediment to the consideration of many additional factors, for example, historical background, and a balance between the number of members and the number of separate administrative divisions. The key consideration was that the Diet possessed a discretionary authority, as the legislature, to determine the number of members in each House, the election districts, and the apportionment of members to each election district. Therefore, the Court reasoned, except in a case in which the number of Diet members in an election district created an extreme inequality in the voter's enjoyment of the right to elect, the percentage of seats apportioned to each election district was a matter of legislative policy subject to the Diet's authority as the legislative branch. The mere fact that the apportionment of Diet seats was not proportionate to the population of electorates did not make it contrary to the Article 14 constitutional Equality principle. The problem was still one of propriety of legislative policy, and the Court could not recognise the emergence of a problem of unconstitutionality. The Supreme Court judgment reduces, thus, to much the same considerations of judicial self-restraint and judicial deference to the legislature's judgment in electoral apportionment matters, that we saw in the United States Supreme Court judgment in *Colegrove* v. *Green* in 1946,[45] now put aside in *Baker* v. *Carr* in 1962.[46] The Japanese Supreme Court's exception of a possible situation where it might intervene – a situation, as it mentioned, of '*extreme inequality* in the voter's enjoyment of the right to elect', which it did not find to exist on the facts of the instant case – drew a supplementary (specially concurring) opinion from Justice Kitaro Saito,[47] who invoked Justice Frankfurter's dissenting opinion to *Baker* v. *Carr*[48] to resist even this mild limitation to a policy of judicial self-restraint, and judicial abstention on the ground of 'political questions' from review of constitutional fairness or equality of the election processes. In fact, the practical result of the electoral apportionment complained of in the *Koshiyama*[49] case was that the 'value' of a vote in the Tokyo prefecture, for upper House elections, was only one-quarter of its value in some other prefectures. On 25 April 1974, the First Petty Bench of the Supreme Court of Japan followed the jurisprudence of the Grand Bench (full Court) in *Koshiyama* in 1964, and rejected a similar petition involving a value difference between electoral districts of five-to-one, again involving upper House elections.[50] On the other hand, in the case of lower House elections, the Grand Bench of the Supreme Court of Japan, in the *Kurokawa* decision of 14 April 1976, rules that apportionment of representatives in the House should be prorated to the number of voters in each electoral district.[51] An action had been initiated to annul the lower House elections of December 1972, on the ground that votes in the Hyogo Prefecture's fifth district had five times the weight of votes in the Chiba Prefecture's first district. The Supreme Court held that this imbalance violated the Article 14-based constitutional Equality principle, and that the apportionment of lower House seats should be proportionate to the population of the electoral districts. But the majority opinion was not in favour of nullification of the whole elections, the Court reasoning that even an unconstitutional apportionment should not be invalidated if a review of all the circumstances indicates that invalidation is not wise.[52] The 1976 decision thus evidences the general reluctance of the Japanese Supreme Court to intervene in election cases. It is suggested that the opening to judicial activism made in the *Kurokawa* case in 1976 in regard to electoral apportionments to the *lower* House, as opposed to the jurisprudence following *Koshiyama* in 1964[53] as to electoral apportionments for the *upper* House, may stem from the fact that the lower House electoral districts are multi-member ones, each district having between three and five members. On the other hand, Professor Osanai, who opts for the judicial self-restraint explanation of the Supreme Court of Japan's general reluctance to intervene and seek to control the legislature's judgment (rather than any American-style, 'political questions' doctrine),[53a] bases the Supreme Court's apparent partial shift from *Koshiyama* (1964), in *Kurokawa* (1976), on the conceptual breakthrough for the judges involved in their now separating the general principle from the remedy. The general principle vindicated by the Supreme Court in *Kurokawa* in 1976 was the unconstitutionality of the lower House legislative apportionment, because of the 'impermissible inequality' it had created in the individual votes from one electoral district to another; the logical remedy – invalidation of the actual election result because of such unconstitutional inequality – the Supreme Court refused to apply in *Kurokawa* as being, for practical reasons, unacceptable. The frequent step-by-step character, manifested in judicial legislation in a number of countries, in complex questions involving the legislature's discretion as to legislative apportionment, should not be overlooked, here. If the Supreme Court of Japan did not go as far, in *Kurokawa* in 1976, as the U.S. Supreme Court has chosen to move in its more contemporary review of election cases, Osanai still suggests that it was a gain, in constitutional terms, to have the Supreme Court, in its official opinion, castigate the national legislature for its indolence in approaching legislative reapportionment on equitable grounds. There is an affirmative jurisprudential value in such judicial opinions which are themselves a contribution to political thinking and a potential influence on the evolution of the legislature's own policy-making.[53b]

Some remaining Japanese Supreme Court decisions on election questions involve the Grand Bench refusal, in a decision of 9 February 1955 (stemming from elections within the Nagano Prefecture to the lower House),[54] to overrule on constitutional grounds the suspension of rights of suffrage and eligibility for election, of certain persons convicted of a number of violations of the Public Offices Election Law; and a refusal by a Petty Bench of the Court, in a decision of 21 November 1967, in the *Taniguchi* case,[55] to strike down on constitutional grounds [mainly Article 15 ('inalienable right of people to choose their public officials')] the ban in the Public Offices Election Law on door-to-door election canvassing. The ban on door-to-door canvassing apparently stemmed from the legislature's belief that it encouraged unfair electoral practices, bribery, and inducement to vote for vested interests, and that it disturbed the voters' peace; and the ban was applied in the *Taniguchi* case against canvassers for two Communist Party candidates for the upper House. In the *Iwasaki* decision of 14 March 1962,[56] the Grand Bench of the Supreme Court approved of the invalidation, by lower Court, of the election of a member of the Hiroshima Prefecture local Assembly, because of election laws violations by his campaign manager and the campaign manager's conviction for that, the Grand Bench rejecting constitutional arguments by the member concerned based, variously, on Article 15 ('inalienable right of people to choose their public officials'), Article 13 ('right to life, liberty, and the pursuit of happiness'), and Article 31 ('no person shall be deprived of life or liberty, nor shall any other criminal penalty be imposed, except according to procedure established by law'). All this jurisprudence evidences the general conservatism of the Supreme Court in relation to interventions in electoral cases, the Court's rejection of constitutional complaints being posited, essentially, on self-restraint considerations rather than the substantive constitutional arguments themselves.

The French *Conseil constitutionnel's* jurisdiction, as established under the Constitution of the Fifth Republic, includes the supervision of – 'the election of the President of the Republic with a view to ensuring its regularity' (Article 58); and deciding – 'in disputed cases, on the regularity of the election of Deputies and Senators' (Article 59), as well as supervising the 'conduct of referenda' (Article 60). Luchaire notes that the constitutional control of elections is quite old in France, going back to the verification by the pre-Revolutionary Estates-General of the powers of its members. Up until 1958, the control was exercised by the two Houses of the legislature, which validated the election of each one of their members and thus systematically controlled *all* elections. The Constitution of the Fifth Republic entrusted legislative elections disputes to the *Conseil constitutionnel,* and thereby suppressed the systematic control of *all* elections, for the *Conseil* will only intervene if it is seized with a request contesting a particular election. The change, according to Luchaire,[57] was made because the two Houses of the legislature, in their pre-1958 verification of elections, often committed abuses, too often deciding for political reasons without taking account of the most elementary juridical considerations: thus, after the national elections of 1951, the same juridical problem (the method of calculation of the seats going to a particular party in application of proportional representation) received absolutely contradictory solutions in two different electoral departments by reason of the personality of one of the elected, General Koenig; while in 1956, numerous elected candidates of the Poujade (populist) movement had their elections invalidated without any solid juridical reason. Favoreu and Philip record[58] that in its first two decades of work, the *Conseil constitutionnel* heard some four hundred disputed elections cases. During the same period there were twenty-seven applications to the *Conseil* relating to various aspects of the Presidential elections (covering the Presidential elections of 1958, 1965, 1969, and 1974); and a mere handful (eight) of applications to the *Conseil* relating to the various referenda of 1961, April 1962, October 1962, 1969, and 1972. None of these matters involved major rulings of constitutional principle. It will be remembered that in the matter of the Referendum Law of 6 November 1962, concerning the election of the President of the Republic by direct, universal suffrage, which had been adopted by the people by referendum vote on 28 October 1962, the *Conseil constitutionnel,* though seized with the issue of constitutionality by the President of the Senate under Article 61 (2) of the Constitution, had declined to exercise jurisdiction, ruling that the matter lay outside its own competence as defined in the Constitution.[59] Favoreu and Philip suggest, however, that the *Conseil* was sharply divided within itself as to the merits of exercising self-restraint and declining jurisdiction, and that the *Conseil* decision was only reached by a six-to-four vote.[60] (The highly unusual tenth vote, added to the votes of the nine elected members, was that of the 'as-of-right' (former President of the Republic) life-member, Vincent Auriol, who felt sufficiently strongly on the matter to break his firm habit, since May 1960, of not sitting in the *Conseil*).[61]

NOTES

1. *Constitution-Making. Principles, Process, Practice* (1981), p. 96 *et seq.*
2. 328 U.S. 549 (1946).
3. *Ibid.,* at 556.
4. *Ibid.*
5. *Ibid.*
6. 321 U.S. 649 (1944).
7. 364 U.S. 399 (1960).
8. 369 U.S. 186 (1962).
9. 328 U.S. 549 (1946).
10. 376 U.S. 1 (1964).
11. 377 U.S. 533 (1964).
12. 304 U.S. 144, 152, n. 4 (1938).
13. Bernard Schwartz, *Constitutional Law* (2nd ed., 1979), pp. 394-395. And compare, as to the historical intentions as to voting rights, Chester J. Antieau, *The original understanding of the Fourteenth Amendment* (1981), pp. 49-56.
14. Louis Lusky and Michael Botein, 'The Law of Equality in the United States', in *Constitutional Protection of Equality* (T. Koopmans, ed.) (1975), p. 46; Schartz, *op. cit.,* p. 396.
15. 383 U.S. 301 (1966).
16. Lusky and Botein, *op. cit.,* p. 47; Schwartz, *op. cit.,* p. 397.

17. 400 U.S. 112 (1970).
18. 430 U.S. 144 (1977).
19. *Ibid.*
20. *Ibid.*
21. 328 U.S. 549 (1946).
22. 304 U.S. 144, 152, n. 4 (1938).
23. As reflected in *United Jewish Organisations, Inc.* v. *Carey,* 430 U.S. 144 (1977).
24. Carl Christoph Schweitzer, *Der Abgeordnete im parlamentarischen Regierungssystem der Bundesrepublik* (1981).
25. G. Leibholz and H.J. Rinck, *Grundgesetz für die Bundesrepublik Deutschland* (4th rev. ed., 1971), p. 456 *et seq.;* H. Laufer, *Verfassungsgerichtsbarkeit und politischer Prozess* (1968), p. 534 *et seq.*
26. Decision of 23 October 1952, 2 B Verf GE 1 (1953) (First Senate).
27. Decision of 17 August 1956, 5 B Verf GE 85 (1956) (First Senate).
28. G. Leibholz, *Das Wesen der Repräsentation unter besonderer Berücksichtigung der Repräsentativsystems* (1929); G. Leibholz, *Die Gleichheit vor dem Gesetz* (1925); (2nd rev. ed., 1959).
29. Karl Dietrich Bracher, *Die Auflösung der Weimarer Republik. Eine Studie zum Problem des Machtverfalls in der Demokratie* (1960), especially at pp. 37, 64, 96.
30. Decision of 3 March 1966, 20 B Verf GE 9 (1966) (Second Senate).
31. Decision of 19 July 1966, 20 B Verf GE 56 (1966) (Second Senate).
32. G. Leibholz and H.J. Rinck, *Grundgesetz für die Bundesrepublik Deutschland* (4th rev. ed., 1971), p. 446 *et seq.;* H. Laufer, *Verfassungsgerichtsbarkeit und politischer Prozess* (1968), p. 505 *et seq.;* H. Laufer, 'Zur staatlichen Finanzierung der politischen Parteien, *Aus Politik und Zeitgeschichte* (no. 44, 1966).
33. Decision of 24 June 1958, 8 B Verf GE 51 (1959) (Second Senate); H. Laufer, *Verfassungsgerichtsbarkeit und politischer Prozess* (1968), at p. 507; G. Leibholz and H.J. Rinck, *Grundgesetz für die Bundesrepublik Deutschland* (4th rev. ed., 1971), p. 446; D. P. Kommers, *Judicial Politics in West Germany* (1976), p. 239.
34. Decision of 19 July 1966, 20 B Verf GE 56 (1966) (Second Senate).
35. Leibholz and Rinck, *op. cit.,* p. 447; Laufer, *op. cit.,* pp. 509, 512.
36. Decision of 19 July 1966, 20 B Verf GE 56 (1966) (Second Senate); Laufer, *op. cit.,* p. 520 *et seq.*
37. 24 B Verf GE 300 (1968) (Second Senate); and see K. Hesse, *Grundzüge des Verfassungsrechts der Bundesrepublik Deutschland* (11th ed., 1978), p. 75; Leibholz and Rinck, *op. cit.,* p. 455; Kommers, *op. cit.,* p. 242.
38. Decision of 5 April 1952, 1 B Verf GE 208 (1952) (Second Senate). And see, generally, Laufer, *op. cit.,* p. 553 *et seq.;* Leibholz and Rinck, *op. cit.,* p. 520 *et seq.;* Hesse, *op. cit.,* p. 239 *et seq.;* Kommers, *op. cit.,* p. 236. And see, generally, G. Leibholz, *Der Strukturwandel der modernen Demokratie* (3rd ed., 1967), p. 112 *et seq.*
39. Decision of 3 July 1957, 7 B Verf GE 63 (1958) (Second Senate).
40. Decision of 23 January 1957, 6 B Verf GE 84 (1957) (Second Senate).
41. Decision of 22 May 1963, 16 B Verf GE 130 (1964) (Second Senate).
42. Decision of 9 July 1957, 7 B Verf GE 77 (1958) (Second Senate).
43. Decision of 26 August 1961, 13 B Verf GE 127 (1962) (Second Senate).
43a. 13 B Verf GE 127 (1962) (Second Senate).
43b. 321 U.S. 649 (1944).
43c. 424 U.S. 1 (1976).
43d. U.S. District Court for the Eastern District of Pennsylvania, decision of Becker, J. (Circuit Judge sitting by designation), 12 December 1983.
43e. Court of Queen's Bench of Alberta, Judicial District of Calgary (Medhurst J.) decision of 25 June 1984.

210

43f. Per Holmes, J. (dissenting), *Abrams* v. *U.S.*, 250 U.S. 616, 624 (1919).

43g. Court of Queen's Bench of Alberta, (Medhurst J.), decision of 25 June 1984.

43h. *Re Alberta Statutes*, [1938] 2 D.L.R. 81, at 107-108 (*per* Duff, C.J.).

43i. *Globe and Mail* (Toronto), 12 July 1984.

44. Supreme Court of Japan, Grand Bench, Decision of 5 February 1964; *The Constitutional Case Law of Japan. Selected Supreme Court Decisions, 1961-70* (Hiroshi Itoh and L.W. Beer, eds. 1978), p. 53; and see generally Teruya Abe and Masanori Shiyake, 'Die Entwicklung des japanischen Verfassungsrechts von 1965-1976 unter besonderer Berücksichtigung der Rechtsprechung', 26 *Jahrbuch des öffentlichen Rechts der Gegenwart* 595, 604 (1977). And see also Satoru Osanai, 'An explanatory study of Judicial approach to legislative malapportionment in Japan', *Comparative Law in Perspective. Collected Essays in Commemoration of the Thirtieth Anniversary of the Institute of Comparative Law in Japan, (Chuo University, Tokyo)*, 75, at 92 *et seq.* (1982).

45. 328 U.S. 549 (1946).

46. 369 U.S. 186 (1962).

47. Supreme Court of Japan, Grand Bench, Decision of 5 February 1964; Itoh and Beer (eds.), *op. cit.*, p. 55.

48. 369 U.S. 186 (1962).

49. Supreme Court of Japan, Grand Bench, Decision of 5 February 1964. As to Justice Saito's supplementary opinion and his disagreement with the Court majority's *rationale*, see Osanai, *op. cit.*, 75, at 97-99.

50. Cited by Professor Shuzo Hayashi, *Japan Echo* (Tokyo) (vol. 5, no. 3) (1978) 17, 19-20. And see also Osanai, *op. cit.*, 75, at 103-104.

51. Supreme Court of Japan, Grand Bench, Decision of 14 April 1976; Teruya Abe and Masanori Shiyake, *op. cit., 26 Jahrbuch des öffentlichen Rechts* 595, at 604-605 (1977); Osanai, *op. cit.*, 75, at 104 *et seq;* Nobushige Ukai, 'The significance of the reception of American Constitutional Institutions and Ideas in Japan', in *Constitutionalism in Asia* (L.W. Beer, ed.) (1979), p. 114 *et seq.;* Hideo Wada and Hiroshi Itoh, 28 *Jahrbuch des öffentlichen Rechts* 689, at 692 (1979).

52. Supreme Court of Japan, Grand Bench, Decision of 14 April 1976; and see Teruya Abe and Masanori Shiyake, *op. cit., 26 Jahrbuch des öffentlichen Rechts* 595, at 604-605 (1977).

53. Supreme Court of Japan, Grand Bench, Decision of 5 February 1964.

53a. Osanai, *op. cit.*, 75, at 85.

53b. Osanai, *op. cit.*, 75, at 107-108.

54. Supreme Court of Japan, Grand Bench, Decision of 9 February 1955; *Court and Constitution in Japan. Selected Supreme Court Decisions, 1948-60* (John M. Maki, ed.) (1964), p. 182.

55. Supreme Court of Japan, Petty Bench, Decision of 21 November 1967; Hiroshi Itoh and L.W. Beer (eds.), *op. cit.*, p. 149.

56. Supreme Court of Japan, Grand Bench, Decision of 14 March 1962; Hiroshi Itoh and L.W. Beer (eds.), *op. cit.*, p. 151.

57. François Luchaire, *La constitution de la république française* (1980), p. 744; Luchaire, *Le Conseil constitutionnel* (1980), p. 292.

58. L. Favoreu and L. Philip, *Le Conseil constitutionnel* (1978), pp. 39-40.

59. *Conseil constitutionnel,* decision of 6 November 1962, *Journal Officiel,* 7 November 1962, p. 10778; *Les Grandes Décisions du Conseil constitutionnel* (L. Favoureu and L. Philip, eds.) (1975), p. 181; G. Berlia, 'Le mode d'élection du Président de la République et la procédure de l'article 11', *Revue du Droit Public* (1962), p. 931.

60. L. Favoreu and L. Philip, *Le Conseil constitutionnel* (1978), pp. 27-28.

61. L. Favoreu and L. Philip, *op. cit.*, p. 14; and see also (as to M. Auriol), *Le Monde* (Paris), 3 July 1960.

CHAPTER X

THE COURTS AND ECONOMIC AND PROPERTY INTERESTS

1. HISTORICAL RELATIVISM: THE SPACE-TIME DIMENSION OF ECONOMIC AND PROPERTY INTERESTS

This has been, in terms of comparative legal science, the philosophically most troubling, and politically most controversial, area of judicial inter-pretation and judicial application of the constitution, for it has raised charges, in a number of countries, putting in question traditional judicial claims to independence and to neutrality on issues of community social and economic policy-making coming before the Courts, and thus has put in question the integrity of the judicial process as a whole. Stated shortly, constitutional texts that were politically-ideological neutral in them-selves, and that were, in any case, as a matter of the original intentions of the constitutional Founding Fathers who actually drafted them, histori-cally intended to mean something else, were consciously and deliberately manipulated by judicial majorities in the Courts, in a last-ditch, judicial-ly-based defence of private economic and property interest groups and pressure groups, to uphold *laissez-faire* economic principles against de-mocratically-elected majorities in the executive and legislative arms of government. According to the thesis, those who could no longer hope to control the legislatures looked to the Courts as guardians of their special economic privileges. [1]

At the political level, the charge has been embarrassing for the Courts for it has based most of the contemporary trends in democratic consti-tuionalism around the World towards producing judicial accountability or answerability to the popularly-elected arms of government, or to the people at large: in the most extreme form, provision for popular recall, by popular petition, of judges whose decisions or opinions are deemed unacceptable in current political terms, but more normally provision for public, legislature-based examination, prior to appointment, of candi-dates for judicial office, as to their professional credentials and also their general philosophical or value-position on law and also specific, current or pending, legal controversies – as with the U.S. Senate Committee examination of the first woman nominee to the United States Supreme Court, as to her past actions as a State legislator, and also her current intellectual attitudes, on the right to choice/right to life, legalised abortion controversy. The best political counter to charges of 'Court over Constitution', or 'Government by the [non-elected] judiciary', – to recall some of the political catch-words of the period, around 1937, of President Franklin Roosevelt's battle against the conservative, 'Old Court' majority that had been holding up his 'New Deal' legislative programme throughout his first Presidential term – is, of course, some more open processes of screening of candidates for high judicial office, and some form of public participation in the judicial appointment processes themselves, either by way of legislature-based election of the judges or else through legislative ratification and confirmation of executive nominations to those offices. Insofar as that would then confer on the judges some form of political mandate in their own right, it would meet, in measure, the criticism that judicial review is 'undemocratic' by providing it with its own special form of constitutional legitimation.

The philosophical objections to judicial review, based on the empirical record of judicial behaviour in the economic and property cases in a number of countries, are rather more difficult to dispose of. Various types of 'conspiracy' theories have been advanced. First, as to the actual words of the constitutional charters concerned, that they always had a covert, in-built, *laissez-faire* philosophy, corresponding to the economic special interests of those who drafted them, and that, for example, the Fourteenth Amendment to the U.S. Constitution, adopted in 1868, while nominally in the interests of the newly-freed slaves, was actually intended, from the beginning, to serve the interests of the Republican Party corporation lawyers who so largely determined its language.[2] That thesis might be capable of being supported by historical research into the intentions of the dominant political and legal *élites* active in the adoption of the Fourteenth Amendment in the immediate post-Civil War years; but one has difficulty in transferring it to other national legal systems – India, for example – where parallel constitutional provisions were treated by the Courts in essentially the same way that the U.S. Supreme Court used the Fourteenth Amendment to protect economic vested interests, but where it is clear, as a matter of history, that the constitutional Founding Fathers, being aware of the unhappy U.S. experience, consciously tried, in advance, to prevent its being followed by deliberately wording their own constitutional charter clauses differently from the American Charter's Fourteenth Amendment.

Another aspect of the 'conspiracy theory' is directed to special lawyer-client relationships as conditioning judicial reflexes in constitutional cases, when the professional legal advocate is later translated to the Court

– as in all the Common Law, and 'received' Common Law, constitutional systems – and then has to pass on his former clients' interests, or ones
analogous to them in economic and property terms. In the Common Law
or 'received' Common Law constitutional systems – in the United States,
Canada, India, for example – the best way to the Supreme Court historically tended to be through successful corporate practice. There seems
little basis for alleging positive judicial bias, in such cases, and it would,
in any case, be a basis for a request for judicial disqualification if a judge
were to be called to sit on a case involving former professional clients.
Only one case, involving a Privy Council ruling, more than half a century
ago, on the Labrador boundary issue between the then British Crown
Colony of Newfoundland, and the Province of Quebec within Canada,
and with important mineral and natural resource questions turning on
the outcome of the Court ruling, appears to have raised any question of
direct personal conflict-of-interest (because of personal association with
the corporations benefiting from the decision in the case) on the part of
judges taking part in the case.[3] The criticism here is, rather, the more
subtle one that too frequent association with one particular category of
propertied clients, on the upward ladder of professional success and
eventual Court appointment, brings an inevitable identification with
those clients' particularist claims as being self-evident and beyond the
need for constitutional demonstration, that is the more pervasive because
it is a largely unconscious identification on the part of the judges. This is
a criticism, as we will see, that may, on the historical evidence, be capable of being validated in the empirical record of the United States
Supreme Court in the so-called 'Gilded Age' of American capitalism in
the period from after the Civil War until the 'Court Revolution' of 1937,
and in the empirical record of the Indian Supreme Court jurisprudence
throughout the first two decades of the Court's post-independence history. It may also find support in the performance of the Imperial Privy
Council sitting in judicial review of the Canadian Constitution (in effect,
as final appellate tribunal for Canada, up to the abolition of its jurisdiction *vis-à-vis* Canada in 1949); although, as we will note, there are also
other – 'federalist', or, if you wish 'liberal pluralist' – explanations for
the Privy Council's behaviour in relation to Canada, which seem even
more persuasive, though also involving a conscious and wilful judicial
manipulation of the text of the constitutional charter to achieve a judi-
cially-desired, particular 'policy' result, that can only with difficulty be
reconciled with the 'ordinary rules' of constitutional construction professedly applied by the Privy Council – though it may be fully justifiable
on other, extra-legal, political, 'policy' grounds.

A still further explanation of the special record of the judges in the
Common Law, and 'received' Common Law, constitutional systems, in

defence of private economic and property interests against popular majorities in the legislative assemblies, and in defiance both of the text of the constitutional charter itself and also historical intentions of original constitutional Founding Fathers, raises fundamental questions of the nature and character of constitutionalism. This has importance, long-range, both for the survival of democratic constitutionalism in the very Western societies in which it originated, as those societies move, or have already moved, from *laissez-faire* to more consciously interventionist, social democratic principles and practice of government; and also for the potential usefulness of democratic constitutionalism, export-variety, for 'reception' and engrafting in other, non-Western societies that may only recently have decolonised and become independent, and that are looking for constitutional-governmental models capable of helping them move quickly through the different stages of economic growth and development and achieve orderly and equitable institutions and processes of community decision-making. Is it in the essence of democratic constitutionalism – part of its inherent value system and structure – that it should specially protect special private economic interests against larger community interests, even or especially where those countervailing community interests are expressed through democratic majorities in popularly-elected executive-legislative institutions? In other words, is there a necessary, symbiotic relation between democratic constitutionalism and *laissez-faire* political and economic philosophy, and *a fortiori* Western-style, *laissez-faire* thinking? If the answer were to be affirmative, it would not say too much for the future of democratic constitutionalism in the present era of transition in our own internal societies and in the World Community generally. For it would identify it as being purely relativist in temporal terms and hence historically dated in the present post-*laissez-faire* era; and it would also condemn it, in ethnic-cultural terms, as a purely Western ethno-centric, '*Eurocentrist*' conception of not too much operational range and significance in the larger, plural, predominantly non-Western World Community of today. As it happens, the experience of other Civil Law, or 'received' Civil Law, constitutional systems – West Germany, Japan, France – suggests that the connections, in space-time terms, are neither necessary nor inevitable, and that with new or renewed constitutional charters and a certain constitutional wit and imagination, judges can indeed liberate themselves from their own special socio-economic predilections or preferences, and render decisions that represent both fidelity to the text of the constitutional charter, in accord with the historical intentions of its constitutional Founding Fathers, and also respect for the popular mandate of the representative, democratically-elected, coordinate executive-legislative institutions of government.

2. SUBSTANTIVE DUE PROCESS: THE 'GILDED AGE' IN AMERICAN CONSTITUTIONALISM

The starting point is the Fourteenth Amendment, adopted in 1868 as the second of the three, post-Civil War, 'Reconstruction Amendments' to the Constitution, and, *inter alia,* applying to the States of the United States what the Fifth Amendment (adopted in 1791 as part of the original Bill of Rights, the first ten Amendments) had already long since applied to the federal Government:

'... nor shall any State deprive any person of life, liberty, or property, without due process of law.'

On the Thirteenth, Fourteenth, and Fifteenth Amendments generally it can be said that an overriding constitutional purpose, stemming from the Radical Republic majorities in the post-*bellum* federal legislative houses operating without the representatives from the defeated rebel Southern States, is clear, and manifest in the language of the Amendments themselves: the *Thirteenth Amendment* directing that 'neither slavery nor involuntary servitude' should exist within the United States; the *Fourteenth Amendment* granting citizenship of the United States and of the State of residence to 'all persons born or naturalised in the United States, and subject to the jurisdiction thereof', and forbidding any State to 'abridge the privileges or immunities of citizens of the United States', or to 'deprive any person of life, liberty, or property, without due process of law', or to 'deny to any person within its jurisdiction the equal protection of the laws'; and the *Fifteenth Amendment* stipulating that 'the right of citizens of the United States to vote shall not be denied or abridged by the United States or by any State on account of race, colour, or previous condition of servitude'. In the case of each of the three Amendments, the federal legislature was given power to enforce 'by appropriate legislation'.

As for the Due Process clause itself, it had, as noted, been in the original Bill of Rights of 1791 and applicable to the federal Government and all its activities for three quarters of a century up to its reenactment and application to the States with the Fourteenth Amendment. Its historical roots were, through Blackstone, in the early and mid-17th century, constitutional struggles in Great Britain between the supporters of Royal, prerogative power and the Parliament-based political forces allied against them. In 17th century English constitutional-legal history the phrase had seemed to mean procedural fairness and to denote a legally guaranteed absence of arbitrariness or irregularity in Court trials and similar proceedings. If the constitutional history, in its origins in 17th century Great

216

Britain seems clear, it is also true that as a matter of textual interpretation of the U.S. constitutional charter's Fifth and Fourteenth Amendment according to the 'ordinary rules' of constitutional construction, the due process guarantee should not have presented any particular problems. The benefits of the constitutional guarantee are limited, in terms, to a 'person', and the thrust of the guarantee is *procedural;* there is, in terms, no substantive guarantee of 'life, liberty, or property', *tout court,* but merely a legal limitation as to the manner and mode of their taking – to be valid, it must be effected with 'due process of law'. The translation of the due process guarantee from a *procedural* one to a *substantive* one, required considerable judicial ingenuity and verbal dexterity, that could hardly be attempted or achieved in one decision but required a species of conscious and continuing judicial legislation, over a period of years and on a step-by-step, case to case basis. In the *Slaughter-House Cases* in 1873,[4] the constitutionality of a Louisiana statute of 1869 granting to one corporation the exclusive right for twenty-five years to maintain slaughter-houses in New Orleans, had been put in issue by several other private concerns adversely affected by the monopoly grant; and various arguments involving the Thirteenth Amendment to the Constitution (creation of an involuntary servitude) and the Fourteenth Amendment (abridgment of the privileges and immunities of citizens of the United States, denial of equal protection of the laws, and denial of property without due process of law) were invoked by the plaintiffs in support of their attack on the monopoly. Mr. Justice Miller, in delivering the Opinion of the Court in the United States Supreme Court, had little difficulty in disposing of these arguments in which, as he noted, the Supreme Court was called upon for the first time to give construction to the Thirteenth and Fourteenth Amendments' articles. In Mr. Justice Miller's words:

'The most cursory glance at these articles discloses a unity of purpose, when taken in conjunction with the history of the times, which cannot fail to have an important bearing on any question of doubt concerning their true meaning... Fortunately that history is fresh within the memory of us all, and its leading features, as they bear upon the matter before us, free from doubt... In the light of this recapitulation of events, almost too recent to be called history, but which are familiar to us all; and on the most casual examination of the language of these amendments, no one can fail to be impressed with the one pervading purpose found in them all, lying at the foundation of each, and without which none of them would have been even suggested; we mean the freedom of the slave race, the security and firm establishment of that freedom, and the protection of the newly-made freeman and citizen from the oppressions of those who had formerly exercised unlimited dominion over him.'[5]

On the argument that the State grant of monopoly violated the *due process* clause of the Fourteenth Amendment, Mr. Justice Miller, for the Supreme Court, was quite categorical. Noting that the *due process* clause had been in the U.S. Constitution since the adoption of the First Amendment, as a restraint on federal Government power, in 1791, and that it was also to be found in the constitutions of nearly all of the States as a restraint upon the power of the States, he concluded:

'We are not without judicial interpretation, therefore, both State and National, of the meaning of this clause. And it is sufficient to say that under no construction of that provision that we have ever seen, or any that we deem admissible, can the restraint imposed by the State of Louisiana upon the exercise of their trade by the butchers of New Orleans be held to be a deprivation of property within the meaning of that provision.'[6]

Two strong dissenting opinions – by Justice Field (who had been appointed to the Court in 1863 and would sit on it until 1897), and by Justice Bradley (appointed in 1870, and continuing on the Court until 1892), were harbingers of the future majority Supreme Court philosophy, which would be brought about by retirements and changes in Court membership. While Mr. Justice Field's dissent was directed, especially, to the privileges and immunities section of the Fourteenth Amendment, Mr. Justice Bradley, in dissent, addressed himself to the due process clause:

'In my view, a law which prohibits a large class of citizens from adopting a lawful employment, or from following a lawful employment previously adopted, does deprive them of liberty as well as property, without due process of law. Their right of choice is a portion of their liberty; their occupation is their property.'[7]

The procession from the *procedural* to the *substantive* conception of due process, under the Fourteenth Amendment requires several more judicial stages, to be achieved; and the dialectical interaction, within the Court, of minority, dissenting opinions upon the majority, can be observed in the flow of decisions after the *Slaughter-House Cases*. In *Munn* v. *Illinois* in 1877,[8] the Supreme Court was concerned with one of a group of cases inspired by the Grange agrarian reform movement, the question here being the power of the legislature of the State of Illinois to fix the maximum charges that might be imposed by warehousemen for the storage of grain in warehouses in Chicago and other large centres. In upholding the State legislation, Chief Justice Waite, for the Court majority, invoked the old English Common Law concept, from the 17th century and Lord Chief Justice Hale, of businesses being 'affected with the public interest' and hence ceasing to be *juris privati* in character. This concept was used by Chief Justice Waite to reject constitutional objections based on the Fourteenth Amendment due process clause, among others. But in directing attention to nature and quality of the subject matter being regulated, rather than to the *method* of regulation employed, Chief Justice Waite had made the fatal opening of the way for substantive, rather than procedural, due process as a test of the constitutionality of economic and property regulation by State legislatures. The Court majority Opinion was accompanied by forceful dissents by Justices Field and Strong. Mr. Justice Field, in particular, excoriated the majority Opinion of Court:

'The principle upon which the opinion of the majority proceeds is, in my judgment, subversive of the rights of private property, heretofore believed to be protected by constitutional guarantees against legislative interference. ... If this be sound law, if there be no protection, either in the principles upon which our republican government is founded, or in the prohibitions of the Constitution against such invasion of private rights, all property and all business in the State are held at the mercy of a majority of its legislature... There is, indeed, no protection of any value under the constitutional provision, which does not extend to the use and income of the property, as well as to its title and possession.'[9]

While it was not until 1897, in *Allgeyer* v. *Louisiana*,[10] that a State law was struck down, for the first time, on Fourteenth Amendment due process grounds, the case is notable because it could have been decided on lesser, non-constitutional grounds – the non-application of a Louisiana State statute, regulating insurance companies within the State, to transactions wholly concluded within another State. The Supreme Court, through Mr. Justice Peckham, was clearly anxious to rule on the substantive constitutional issue. The high-water mark of the Fourteenth Amendment due process clause, in its new, Court-majority sanctioned, substantive aspect, is, however, in *Lochner* v. *New York,* in 1905,[11] where the Supreme Court, by a five-to-four majority, ruled unconstitutional a New York State statute prescribing the maximum hours of labour within bakery shops in New York as ten in any one day, or sixty in any one week. The Court majority had to do some fine footwork to 'distinguish' an earlier decision, rendered only seven years before in *Holden* v. *Hardy* in 1898,[12] whereby the Court majority (with Justices Brewer and Peckham dissenting) had upheld a State of Utah statute limiting employment in smelters and underground mines to eight hours per day, the distinction now seized upon being that the Utah State statute was not to apply in emergencies. The Opinion of the Court, in the *Lochner* case in 1905, was rendered by Mr. Justice Peckham. As Mr. Justice Peckham saw it, the question before the Court reduced to the following:

'Is this a fair, reasonable and appropriate exercise of the police power of the State, or is it an unreasonable, unnecessary and arbitrary interference with the right of the individual to his personal liberty or to enter into those contracts in relation to labour which may seem to him appropriate or necessary for the support of himself and his family? Of course the liberty of contract relating to labour includes both parties to it. The one has as much right to purchase as the other to sell labour.'[13]

Mr. Justice Peckham went on to conclude, within this statement of the basis for decision, that there was –

'no reasonable foundation for holding this to be necessary or appropriate as a health law to safeguard the public health or the health of the individuals who are following the trade of a baker. If this statute be valid, ... there would seem to be no length to which legislation of this nature might not go.'[14]

Mr. Justice Peckham concluded with assorted remarks on the social condition of the baking industry:

'To the common understanding the trade of a baker has never been regarded as an unhealthy one. Very likely physicians would not recommend the exercise of that or of any other trade as a remedy for ill health... It is unfortunately true that labour, even in any department, may possibly carry with it the seeds of unhealthiness. But are we all, on that account, at the mercy of legislative majorities? A printer, a tinsmith, a locksmith, a carpenter, a cabinetmaker, a dry goods clerk, a bank's, a lawyer's or a physician's clerk, or a clerk in almost any kind of business, would all come under the power of the legislature, on this assumption. No trades, no occupation, no mode of earning one's living, could escape this all-pervading power, and the acts of the legislature in limiting the hours of labour in all employments would be valid, although such limitations might seriously cripple the ability of the labourer to support himself and his family.'[15]

After this parade of possible horrors of State legislative regulation of conditions of employment if the New York State statute should be upheld, Mr. Justice Peckham, for the Court majority, ruled that it was an unconstitutional violation of the 'liberty of contract', under the Fourteenth Amendment due process clause, not merely of the employer but also of the employee to whose benefit, of course, the State statute had been directed. It was left to Mr. Justice Holmes, in dissent — in perhaps his most famous opinion – to put the Court majority holding in social perspective:

'This case is decided upon an economic theory which a large part of the country does not entertain... The Fourteenth Amendment does not enact Mr. Herbert Spencer's Social Statics... Some of these laws embody convictions or prejudices which judges are likely to share. Some may not. But a constitution is not intended to embody a particular economic theory, whether of parternalism and the organic relation of the citizen to the State or of *laissez-faire*...

General propositions do not decide concrete cases. The decision will depend on a judgment or intuition more subtle than any articulate major premise... I think that the word liberty in the Fourteenth Amendment is perverted when it is held to prevent the natural outcome of a dominant opinion unless it can be said that a rational and fair man necessarily would admit that the statute proposed would infringe fundamental principles as they have been understood by traditions of our people and our law.'[16]

The Holmes' dissent represents the classical statement of the principle of judicial self-restraint, and, in particular, of judges not substituting their own social and economic preferences or prejudices – those 'inarticulate major premises' to Court decisions – for the social and economic standards of the community at large as reflected in the statutes enacted by popularly-elected majorities in the executive and legislative institutions of government. Aided by further egregious, Court-made distinctions to take care of exceptional cases which might otherwise have been politically highly embarrassing for the Court majority, 'liberty of contract', as held to be constitutionally guaranteed by the Fourteenth Amendment in its new *substantive* due process manifestation, against any form of State regulation, survived as a constitutional dogma, with very concrete, *laissez-faire* legal consequences, until 1937. In *Muller* v. *Oregon,* in 1908,[17] on the basis of the distinction between women and men, of which the Court took judicial notice – aided by the Brandeis Brief, the submission of (later Mr. Justice) Louis Brandeis, as counsel appearing before the Court, of impressively-researched sociological data, from many countries, of Government restrictions on the hours of labour of women in industry – the Court 'distinguished' the *Lochner* holding of three years earlier and upheld an Oregon State statute establishing a maximum ten-hour day for female employees in industry, here a laundry. In *Adkins* v. *Children's Hospital,* in 1923,[18] the Supreme Court, in a majority decision with Mr. Justice Holmes again dissenting, distinguished, this time, *Muller* v. *Oregon*[19] as having dealt only with the 'incidents' (hours of labour) of the contract of employment of women in industry, and as not having affected the 'heart of the contract'. On the basis of this postulated distinction between 'incidents' of a contract and the 'heart of the contract', the Court majority applied the *Lochner* holding of 1905[20] to strike down a federal statute, applying to the federal District of Columbia and fixing minimum *wages* for women and children in industry within the District, as violative of substantive due process-based 'liberty of contract' (as guaranteed, in this case, in relation to the federal Government, by the Fifth Amendment). Are not, however, *hours* of labour (whose State regulation is constitutionally permissible after *Muller* v. *Oregon*)[21] and *wages* of labour (now, by the present holding, constitutionally impermissible in terms of State regulation), merely different elements of the same women's employment contract? Mr. Justice Holmes, in his dissent, suggested that the Court majority was employing a distinction without a difference, and raised again the basic question of whether 'freedom of contract is a misnomer as applied to a contract between an employer and an ordinary individual employee'.

The substantive due process 'liberty of contract' constitutional principle was applied, for the last time, in *Morehead* v. *New York, ex rel. Tipaldo,* in 1936,[22] another five-to-four decision, this time striking down a New York State law prescribing minimum wages for women in industry, as applied to women employees in a laundry. In 1937, with President Franklin Roosevelt triumphantly re-elected to his second term in the November, 1936, Presidential elections, and with the Presidential 'Court-packing' plan for increasing the Court membership from nine to fifteen judges, to allow balancing of 'conservative' incumbents, now pending, one of the judges in the conservative five-man majority in the *Morehead* five-to-four ruling the previous year fortuitously switched his vote; and so a new Court majority, by a five-to-four vote, now, in a judiciously balanced opinion by Chief Justice Hughes, upheld a Washington State law establishing minimum wages for women in industry, in this case a chambermaid working in a hotel.[23] The *Adkins* ruling of 1923[24] was itself overruled, and substantive due process disappeared into history, President Roosevelt, for his part, eventually dropping his 'Court-packing' plan which had now become politically unnecessary and irrelevant, the Court having changed its mind, and not merely for the present case. Consolidated by the quick departure of the ideological conservatives on the Court, the so-called 'Four Horsemen' – Van Devanter in 1937, Sutherland in 1938, Butler in 1939, and McReynolds in 1941 – President Roosevelt was able to remake the Supreme Court very much in his own preferred, liberal activist image, with eight new judges appointed between 1937 and his death in 1945 and a ninth, Harlan Stone, promoted from within the Court's ranks to the Chief Justiceship, after Hughes, in 1941. The Court-imposed barriers against popular will, as expressed through the Presidency and Congress in the wave of 'New Deal' legislation, were now removed and, in its place, applying Holmes' principle of judicial self-restraint and deference to legislative majorities, a new judicial presumption of constitutionality emerged in favour of legislation, federal and State. It was balanced, also, by a new liberal activism, at the judicial level, whose intellectual paternity the judicial liberals sought to accredit to Holmes too, and which involved a conscious judicial diligence in relation to the administration of State laws and State police power and its conformity to the *procedural* due process aspects of the Fourteenth Amendment and also to First Amendment free speech guarantees as now held by the judges to be 'incorporated' within the more general Fourteenth Amendment protections[25] and to be given a constitutionally 'preferred portion' therein.[26]

3. PROPERTY RIGHTS AND 'PUBLIC WELFARE': POST-WAR JAPANESE CONSTITUTIONALISM

Our concern has been, however, with *substantive* due process, and with the steps by which, under judicial interpretation, the original Fifth and

222

Fourteenth Amendment formulations were transformed – one might almost say 'transmogrified' – in spite both of the words of the constitutional text and also the original historical intentions of its two successive waves of constitutional Founding Fathers in 1791 and in 1868, into a constitutional dogma specially protecting private corporate economic interests from governmental regulation. This special American constitutional experience became a text-book example to be avoided by constitution-makers in other countries. In the post-World War II era of constitution-making, it became accepted as an axiom for constitutional drafting that one should positively avoid having, in terms, a 'due process' clause in one's constitution. Thereafter, while seeking to embrace explicit constitutional charter guarantees of procedural fairness and against arbitrary Court or administrative processes, everyone has been at pains to avoid copying the U.S. Constitution's language on this point. With the post-War Japanese Constitution, for example, both in the SCAP Original Draft prepared by the U.S. Military Occupation officials and also in the Constitution as actually adopted in 1946, there was a conscious and deliberate attempt to separate 'property' from the 'life, liberty, or property' aphorism contained in the U.S. Constitution's Fifth and Fourteenth Amendment due process clauses. The formulation in the Constitution, Chapter III, Rights and Duties of the People, Article 29, which corresponds substantially to the provisions spread over the three Articles (27 to 29) of the SCAP Draft, is devoted solely to property, and expressly subjects the definition of property to the 'public welfare' and also allows its taking 'for public use upon just compensation':

Article 29'
'The right to own or to hold property is inviolable.
Property rights shall be defined by law, in conformity with the public welfare.
Private property may be taken for public use upon just compensation.'

To make assurance doubly sure that the property right under the Constitution, subject as it is, in terms, to the public welfare, should not be confounded with substantive due process, American-style, 'life and liberty' and their correlative of fair procedure are consigned to their own autonomous Article which also spells out prosaically, and in a way that, presumably, will exclude any equivocation in the future, just what that limitation is to mean:

Article 31:
'No person shall be deprived of life or liberty, nor shall any other criminal penalty be imposed, except according to procedure established by law.'

As the expert *rapporteur,* Hideo Tanaka, noted in his report to the Japanese Cabinet Commission on the Constitution (Takayanagi Commission) at the opening of the 1960s,[27] the question most debated in relation to this Article concerned the question of the post-War land reform projects. The key to the land reform was requiring landowners to sell a large portion of their agricultural land, defined in detail by statute and resulting orders, to their leasehold tenants for a price calculated by formulae established by statute. The fundamental principle underlying the price formulae was stated to be the capitalisation of profit to be raised under the then existing Rent Control Act. The price that was fixed at the outset was originally very high, but the post-War inflation markedly reduced its real value. In brief, the land reform project, which was one of the most important economic changes sponsored by the American Military Occupation authorities, more than doubled the number of owner-cultivators of agricultural land in Japan, and virtually eliminated landlords because of the limitation of landholding to a maximum of eight acres. Some five million acres of land was stated to have been transferred under the reform. In a suit brought by former landlords, Article 29 of the Constitution was directly invoked, particularly its third paragraph with the two limitations to taking of private property of 'public use' and 'just compensation'. The Grand Bench of the Supreme Court of Japan, however, in a major decision of 23 December 1953, rejected the complaints, with four judges dissenting from the majority holdings.[28] The majority Opinion of Court held that land could still be 'taken for public use' even though the title to the land would rest in the former tenants; and that the phrase 'taken for public use' should be construed as including 'taking for public interest' and as not necessarily meaning that the property taken should be used by the public in general. On the issue of 'just compensation', to which, apparently, the former landlords' constitutional complaint had been principally directed, the Court majority upheld the arrangements provided under the statutory formulae, reasoning that since the exercise of property rights might, compatibly with the second paragraph of Article 29, be restricted by law 'in conformity with the public welfare', compensation could legally be based upon the value of the property as calculated under the state of things existing at the time of the taking. Mr. Justice Kuriyama Shigeru, in a specially concurring opinion, perhaps best expressed the philosophical *rationale* of the post-War Supreme Court's approach to economic and property rights under the Constitution:

'It is a commonly held idea in the free countries of the world at the present time, particularly after the first and second world wars, when capitalism has reached a high stage of development, that since the right of private property is regarded as capital and that those who possess it can control and direct the many who do not, the right of property carries with it the social responsibility to conform with the public welfare. That our own Constitution has emerged naturally from the same concept is clear when the provisions of Article 29 are matched with those of Articles 25 and 28.'[29]

Article 25 of the Constitution guarantees to all people the 'right to maintain the minimum standards of wholesome and cultured living', and obligates the State, in all spheres of life, to 'use its endeavours for the promotion and extension of social welfare and security, and of public health'. Article 28 guarantees – 'the right of workers to organise and to bargain and act collectively'. The social character of property rights under the post-War Japanese Constitution thus becomes clear. In the Takayanagi Commission discussions on reform of the Constitution, the special *rapporteur* Hideo Tanaka noted some objections that, even as it stood, Article 29, especially in its first paragraph, was redolent of 19th century constitutions and that it should be positively rephrased so as to stress the social character of property rights, taking into consideration the 20th century constitutions of other nations, the Constitution of the Weimar Republic here being cited. [30] There were also some proposals within the Takayanagi Commission to reverse the order of the first and second paragraphs of Article 29. [31]

Article 25 of the Constitution (right to minimum standards of wholesome and cultured living) had been subject to some fanciful constitutional testing in the early post-War years when it was invoked by persons convicted and sentenced to prison for violation of the laws controlling the acquisition of staple foods: the Grand Bench of the Supreme Court, in a decision of 29 September 1948, [32] dismissed the appeals on the basis that the food rationing system was designed to guarantee staple foods supplies for the people and to avoid maldistribution or disappearance of such foodstuffs through buying up, hoarding, or the holding back of goods in the expectation of a better price. Article 29 itself was also considered by the Grand Bench of the Supreme Court in a further decision of 26 June 1963, [33] involving families that had been cultivating the bank of a reservoir for generations, and that were charged with, and convicted for, violating a regional Prefectural Ordinance prohibiting farming on the banks of a reservoir. The Court decision was based on the conclusion that an administrative (Prefectural) order amounted to a defining of property rights 'by law' in accordance with the second paragraph of Article 29, and that compensation was not required in terms of the third paragraph of Article 29 since the present restriction of property rights was a reasonable one inherent in the right to own a reservoir. An American 'liberty of contract'-style constitutional argument, based on Article 22 of the Constitution (freedom to choose one's occupation' to the extent that it does not interfere with the public welfare') raised by an unlicensed taxi-cab operator against the statutory system of licensing and regulation, among a defined number of taxi-cab operators only, of the road transportation business, was also rejected by the Grand Bench of the Supreme Court, in a decision of 4 December 1963, [34] by reference to the 'public welfare' limitation to the constitutional freedom to choose one's occupation. The Grand Bench of the Supreme Court had ruled, in an early decision of 15 November 1950,[35] that neither Article 29, nor Article 28 (the right of workers to organise and to bargain and act collectively), gave workers the right to take over production in a factory as a means of continuing a dispute with management – the so-called 'production control' strike. The Supreme Court jurisprudence indicates, on the whole, a substantial deference to State, public activity limiting private property rights claims under Article 29 by reference to the 'public welfare' norms expressed in Article 29 itself and elsewhere in the Constitution, and also a judicial indisposition to be too adventurous in conceding novel property claims when advanced by private, as distinct from State interests. The social character of property rights under the Constitution, and the limitation of private claims by deference to larger, community considerations, is evident.

4. DUE PROCESS REINCARNATED: PROPERTY RIGHTS UNDER THE INDIAN CONSTITUTION

We have already seen that the constitutional Founding Fathers of the Indian Republican Constitution had considered the possibility of having a Due Process clause. As Tripathi has pointed out, clause 16 of Sir Benegal Rau's draft of a Constitution had included it, *sans* property admittedly: 'No person shall be deprived of his life or personal liberty without due process of law'.[36] But when Rau visited Washington,[37] Mr. Justice Felix Frankfurter of the U.S. Supreme Court, whom he had come to consult in private, advised him that it would not only be undemocratic (because of the veto power over legislation that it would give the judges), but that it also would throw an unfair burden on the judiciary; while Judge Learned Hand had even gone so far as to suggest treating all fundamental rights as moral precepts only and not as formal fetters in the Constitution.[38] Governor Munshi's draft of a Constitution[39] had, indeed, included a Due Process clause, *cum* property, in its Article V (4): 'No person shall be deprived of his life, liberty or property without due process of law'. In the drafting sub-committee of the Constituent Assembly it had then been subjected to the criticism that it would defeat the land tenancy reforms contemplated in several of the States within the Indian federal system. It was only after Rau's return from the United States and his report of his conversations with American judges and other senior jurists, however, that the drafting committee could be persuaded to remove the expression 'due process' altogether, and to replace it by a new, supposedly un-colourable legal phrasing borrowed directly from the post-War Japanese Constitution's Article 31 formula – 'except according to procedure established by law'. It was thought that the Japanese constitutional formulation, which had been specially designed in Japan to avoid any judicial tendency to borrow from or copy the American Substantive Due Process 'liberty of contract' jurisprudence, would have a similar saving quality and effect in the new Indian Constitution.[40] Rephrased slightly, it became the first paragraph of Article 31 (Right to Property), in the Indian Constitution, Part III (Fundamental Rights):

Article 31 (1):
'No person shall be deprived of his property save by authority of law'.

The affirmative aspect of the property right is expressed in Article 19 (Right to Freedom):

Article 19 (1):
'All citizens shall have the right –
...
(f) to acquire, hold and dispose of property.'

If Article 19 (1) (f) is balanced, in measure, by Article 31 (1), it also finds a certain philosophical antithesis in Part IV of the Constitution, Directive Principles of State Policy, with their concededly social democratic inspiration. Among the Directive Principles, the ones most relevant for present purposes are the following:

Article 38:
'The State shall strive to promote the welfare of the people by securing and protecting as effectively as it may a social order in which justice, social, economic and political, shall inform all the institutions of the national life.'

Article 39:
'The State shall, in particular, direct its policy toward securing –
'(a) that the citizens, men and women equally, have the right to an adequate means of livelihood;
'(b) that the ownership and control of the material resources of the community are so distributed as best to subserve the common good;
'(c) that the operation of the economic system does not result in the concentration of wealth and means of production to the common detriment.
'...'

Article 41:
'The State shall, within the limits of its economic capacity and development, make effective provision for securing the right to work, to education and to public assistance in case of unemployment, old age, sickness and disablement, and in other cases of undeserved want.'

We have already in other contexts, examined the constitutional antinomy presented by Part III (Fundamental Rights) with their more conventional, eclectically traditional, enunciation of 'classical'-style constitutional rights, and Part IV (Directive Principles of State Policy) with their determined openings to the newer, social democratic rights, a constitutional antinomy that is not completely resolved by the repeated affirmation that the Directive Principles are 'non-justiciable' for they represent, in a very real sense, the challenge of the 'new' constitutionalism to the 'old'. We have also looked at property rights under the Constitution interstitially to our discussion of the Constituent Processes, the constitutional amending power, and whether in fact there are areas of the Constitution which the amending power cannot validly touch – '*unconstitutional* constitutional amendments', in the Continental European terminology. This particular dilemma of constitutional theory arose, directly, in connection with the Supreme Court's adjudication of constitutional property rights claims advanced by private economic groups as an attempted legal counter to government regulation and control; and then the subsequent attempts by the federal Government, through use of the constitutional amending power, legally to 'correct' or overcome Supreme Court decisions upholding those private interest groups against the community regulation and control. The constitutional battle begins as an economic struggle between the private economic interest groups which had already lost their political ability to influence or control the legislatures, and which then turned to the Supreme Court as last-ditch guardian of their special interests, and the popularly-elected executive-legislative majorities moving against them in the name of larger community interests; but it becomes transformed, then, into a protracted institutional-governmental struggle that pits the judges directly against those same popularly-elected executive-legislative majorities, and at a certain point the original economic interests become merged or submerged in the conflict over constituent and governmental processes in the continuing, step-by-step political-legal development of Court move, governmental counter-move, further Court response and further governmental counter-response. Having already examined, in some detail, the constituent and governmental processes aspects of the struggle over economic and property rights, we will look, now, rather at the substantive, political and economic values involved in the attempts at community regulation, and the Court response thereto in terms, strictly, of the Fundamental Rights, Directive Principles, 'values' Parts of the Constitution. Three great cases, following in quick succession at the end of the 1960s and the beginning of the 1970s, illustrate very well the political and legal dilemmas of judicial interpretation and judicial policy-making involved; the *Golak Nath* case in 1967,[41] the *Bank Nationalisation* case in 1970,[42] and the *Privy Purses* case in 1971.[43]

Chris Merillat, one of the more perceptive and sensitive foreign observers of the Indian constitutional scene in its earlier years, has amply recorded the importance of the land and agrarian reform issue to the post-independence Indian political leaders,[44] and the personal commitment made by Pandit Nehru and other key Congress Party figures to legislative intervention by the government, on achievement of the constitution, in behalf of an activist programme of land redistribution. Did the new Constitution, as drafted, give a positive mandate for such a programme? We have referred already to the antinomy between the more 'classical' statement of the right to property under the Fundamental Rights Part of the Constitution, and the more avowedly community interventionist, 'social purpose' formulation under the Directive Principles Part. Any too easy conclusion, however, that the constitutional Founding Fathers were divided on the issue of policy choice, and simply recorded their constitutional ambivalence in the constitutional charter itself, is tempered by the consideration that Article 31 within the Fundamental Rights Part, even as originally drafted and adopted, envisaged, in terms, a community taking of property but simply conditioned its being done upon the application of legal processes – 'by authority of law', according to Article 31 (1); and upon the providing of 'compensation', for which either the 'amount' was to be fixed in the law concerned or else the principles and manner of determination and award to be specified in the law (Article 31 (2)). The subjects of agriculture and land were both local, State matters under the Indian federal system – Part XI, Relations between Union and States (Chapter I, Legislative Relations, Distribution of Legislative Powers), Article 246. As set out in the Seventh Schedule appended to Article 246, the legislatures of the States had exclusive power to make laws over:

> List II, State List:
> '14. Agriculture, including agricultural education and research, protection against pests and prevention of plant diseases.'
> '18. Land, that is to say, rights in or over land, land tenures including the relation of landlord and tenant, and the collection of rents; transfer and alienation of agricultural land; land improvement and agricultural loans; colonisation.'

Moving very energetically, State legislatures, many of them having governments that were the local, regional affiliates of the dominant federal Congress Party, enacted by the early 1950s a good deal of agrarian reform legislation. It was then that the matter came to the Courts on legal challenge, most of it being directed to the issue of the compensation provided for the taking of land. The Courts insisted, from the outset, not merely on the principle of compensation – which would hardly be denied in view of its specification, in terms, in Article 31 (2), but also on their own right, *qua* Court, to scrutinise the amount of such compensation and to rule on that compensation's adequacy in financial terms and, if it deemed it wanting, to invalidate the State taking of the land on constitutional grounds. This second position taken by the Courts is much more contestable on strictly legal grounds. As a matter of the 'ordinary rules of construction', such a *quantitative* review of the compensation provided under the State law in question – to be exercised by the judges – would seem to have no warrant under the terms of Article 31 (2). To read in such a right of judicial review as to the particular merits of the compensation provided – going beyond determining whether (as specified in Article 31 (2)) the State law has fixed the amount of compensation or specified the principles and manner of determining and awarding such compensation – one would have to make a very considerable judicial leap into the policy field, involving a judicial policy interpretation of otherwise clear and unambiguous constitutional charter language. The explanation and justification for such a judicial policy leap has to be found – because the ordinary rules of construction, ordinarily applied, do not support it – in some form of judicial 'inarticulate major premise' of a political-economic character. A politically frustrating series of Court decisions throughout the 1950s which had the effect of defeating agrarian reform laws adopted in a number of States, brought federal Government intervention in support of the States by way of recourse to the constitutional amending power to put the issue of the State legislative power to resume land and to determine the actual amount of compensation, without any judicial second-guessing, beyond constitutional doubt or question. The federal Government then had, however, the even more frustrating experience of seeing such constitutional amendments, when adopted, themselves effectively negated by further harsh judicial construction which defeated their purpose. This was the fate, for example, of the First Amendment to the Constitution, adopted in June 1951, which added a new Article 31A to the existing Article 31 (Right to Property), stipulating that –

'no law providing for the acquisition by the State of any estate or of any rights therein or for the extinguishment or modification of any such rights shall be deemed to be void on the ground that it is inconsistent with, or takes away or abridges any of the rights conferred by, any provisions of this Part.'

The same constitutional amendment also sought to protect specific, named State laws or regulations from judicial overruling by enacting a new Article 31B which listed thirteen such State laws in a new, Ninth Schedule to the Constitution, and which declared that none of those laws was 'deemed to be void, or ever to have become void', on the ground of

230

inconsistency with any of the rights conferred by that Part of the Constitution; and that –

> 'notwithstanding any judgment, decree or order of any court or tribunal to the contrary, each of the said Acts and Regulations shall, subject to the power of any competent legislation to repeal or amend it, continue in force.'

In the sustained and protracted battle between the Congress Party Government at the centre, moving in aid of the reformist State legislatures, and the Courts, one saw further specific constitutional amendments directed to 'correcting' hostile Court decisions, like the Fourth Amendment, adopted in 1955, which sought to remove the adequacy of compensation from the scope of judicial review by specifying that no law compulsorily acquiring or requisitioning property for a public purpose should be –

> 'called in question in any court on the ground that the compensation provided by that law is not adequate.'

It also amended Article 31A to strengthen its defences against the judiciary still further by specifying that no State law acquiring estates, or taking over the management of any property, or amalgamating corporations, or extinguishing or modifying mining leases or licences, should be deemed to be void on the ground of inconsistency, specifically, with Article 14 (right to equality), Article 19 (right to freedom), or Article 31 (right to property).

The guerilla warfare before the Courts against State agrarian reform laws continued, notwithstanding the powerful legal support provided to the embattled States by the federal Government's intervention in their support with 'corrective' constitutional amendments. Faced with tenacious judges, the Congress Party majority at the federal level made political concessions at one level, by conceding the principle of compensation – 'at a rate which shall not be less than the market value' – in the case of estates acquired by the State where the land comprised therein was held by a person – 'under his personal cultivation'. This provision, in the Seventeenth Amendment to the Constitution adopted in 1964, was accompanied by a further listing of forty-four State laws which were to be added to the Ninth Schedule to the Constitution and thereby exempted from the scope of judicial review. This made a total of sixty-four such State agrarian reform laws in effect shut off from the judicial power to control or defeat. It was the Seventeenth Amendment to the Constitution which was at the core of the decision, in 1967, in *Golak Nath* v. *State of Punjab*[45] when the Supreme Court, by a narrow, six-to-five vote, ruled directly on the constitutional amending power and declared that the federal legislature did not have the power to amend the Constitution so as to take away or abridge the Fundamental Rights in the Constitution. The Supreme Court had, only two years before, in *Sajjan Singh* v. *State of Rajasthan* in 1965,[46] in a three-to-two decision, held exactly the opposite. The changes in judicial personnel, as between *Sajjan Singh* and *Golak Nath* from 1965 to 1967, and also the differences between a five-man panel and a Full Court bench of eleven judges, explain the political difference in the two results. It was Chief Justice Gajendragadkar, who had something of Marshallian sweep in his approach to constitutionalism, who rendered the majority opinion in the *Sajjan Singh* panel decision;[47] whereas a new Chief Justice, Subba Rao, delivered the majority opinion, the other way, of the Full Court in *Golak Nath*.[48] The philosophical difference in the two decisions can only be explained, as Professor Sathe rightly points out, on an 'inarticulate major premise' of the *Golak Nath* majority that fundamental rights guaranteed by the Constitution were – 'transcendental and therefore must not be allowed to be whittled down by any majority in Parliament'.[49] In positive law terms, the new majority in *Golak Nath* justified its holding, variously, on the basis that Article 368 (Amendment of the Constitution) did not contain the plenary statement of the power to amend the Constitution but only dealt with the procedure of such amendment; that Article 368 did not contain the authority for amending the Constitution so as to take away or abridge Fundamental Rights; that even if Article 368 did contain the power to take away or abridge Fundamental Rights, it was subject to Article 13 (2) of the Constitution (which denied the (legislative) power of the State to take away or abridge the Fundamental Rights and made any law in contravention of Article 13 (2) itself void); that the constitutional amending power at best envisaged only minor alterations or modifications of the existing provisions and not any major change; and that if it were indeed desired to amend the Fundamental Rights guarantees, this could only be done by a new Constituent Assembly specially established, by law, by the federal legislature.[50]

In the *Bank Nationalisation* case – *R.C. Cooper* v. *Union of India* – in 1970,[51] the Supreme Court ruled on the constitutionality of the Banking Companies Acquisition and Transfer of Undertakings Act of 1969, under authority of which fourteen major commercial banks had been nationalised, with some provisions included for payment of compensation to the companies concerned and their shareholders. It was these compensation provisions which were challenged under Article 31 (2) of the Constitution, on the score that the principles and method of compensation involved did not amount to compensation as defined in that Article. The Supreme Court majority holding, written by Mr. Justice Shah, struck down the Act as violative of the Fundamental Rights and not protected by Article 31 (2). The decision in the *Bank Nationalisation* case was perhaps the more surprising in that, only the previous year, in *State of Gujarat* v. *Shantilal Mangaldas,* in 1969,[52] the Supreme Court had seemed to develop a new, beneficial approach to the State power to resume or acquire land and to allowing the State to determine the quantum of compensation therefor, for purposes of Article 31 (2) as amended. A distinguished jurist, J.L. Kapur, himself a retired Judge of the Supreme Court of India, suggests that the general conception, in political circles, that the *Bank Nationalisation* judgment had directly overruled *Shantilal,* was incorrect, and that some of the resulting political sound and fury against the Court and the prompt federal Governmental attempt to 'correct' *Bank Nationalisation* by a further constitutional amendment were constitutional over-reactions and constitutionally unnecessary.[53] However that may be, *Bank Nationalisation*[54] was followed, in 1971, by the Supreme Court ruling in the *Privy Purses* case (*Madhav Rao Scindia* v. *Union of India*),[55] where what was involved was the 'derecognition' of the old princely Rulers of various Indian States who had accepted the sovereignty of the British Crown under the old British Imperial *Raj,* and whose privileges and also financial pensions (which were to be exempt from income tax) were continued, as a charge on the Consolidated Fund of India, after Indian independence, by special Articles of the new Constitution (Article 291 (Rulers' Privy Purses), Articles 362, 363 (Rights, etc., of Rulers)). The Congress Party, in 1967, had passed a resolution for abolition of these vestigial Privy Purses (pensions), and the federal Government had then attempted to negotiate with the Princes for fresh financial settlements, but without any results. The federal Government then proceeded by the constitutional amendment route of Article 368, securing the necessary two-thirds majority in the lower House but failing only by the narrowest margin to secure the necessary two-thirds vote in the upper House for a project to repeal Articles 291 and 362 of the Constitution. The indirect, 'de-recognition' route was adopted by the federal Government in consequence of the failure of the direct, constitutional amendment process, and it involved, very simply, a Presidential order formally withdrawing the recognition of all the Princely rulers.[56] The Presidential order was challenged by the Princely rulers under Article 32 of the Constitution (right to constitutional remedies), the Princes invoking both Article 19 (1) (f) and Article 31 on the score that their privileges and also the financial benefits payable under the Privy Purses amounted to property rights guaranteed as Fundamental Rights under the Constitution. Chief Justice Hidayatullah, for the Supreme Court, rejected the argument, on behalf of the federal Government, that de-recognition was a 'political act' or Act of State, and, as such, beyond the jurisdiction of the Court.[57] The Chief Justice held that the Act of State doctrine could not operate against a citizen of the country, which the Princely rulers, in the Court's view, had become, after integration of their former territories in to India, and that the Privy Purses were, indeed, property and as such governed by Articles 19 and 31 of the Constitution.

The Congress Party Government then moved rapidly and proceeded to enact in 1971 and 1972 the Twenty-Fourth, Twenty-Fifth, and Twenty-Sixth Amendments to the Constitution, respectively 'correcting' the *Golak Nath, Bank Nationalisation,* and *Privy Purses* decisions. In 1972, the Government moved, further, to enact the Twenty-Eight Amendment, designed in part to forestall litigation over the Privy Purses' abolition; and the Twenty-Ninth Amendment, again directed to shoring up the agrarian reform State legislation against further Court harassment. The Twenty-Fourth Amendment, in particular, inserted an express provision in Article 368 to indicate that the source of the constitutional amending power would be found in that Article itself, now given a new title, expressive of that fact – 'Power of Parliament to amend the Constitution and procedure thereof'. With its original clause now being renumbered as paragraph (2), a new paragraph (1) stipulated that when the federal Parliament made a constitutional amendment, it acted – 'in exercise of its constituent power'. Finally, it was stipulated in both the new, revised Article 368 and also in Article 13, that Article 13 was not to apply to any amendment of the Constitution made under Article 368.

Constitutionality of the Twenty-Fourth Amendment was challenged, almost immediately, in *Kesavananda Bharati* v. *State of Kerala.*[58] The Supreme Court, with a full Bench of thirteen judges, decided, after a record, 68-day hearing by a seven-to-six majority, to overrule the *Golak Nath* decision of 1967,[59] the Court's decision, however, carrying the sting in its tail of the 'basic structure' limitation to future constitutional amendments. On the main point, however, the Court majority conceded that Article 368 contained both the *power* and the *procedure* to amend, including the power to amend the Fundamental Rights Part III of the Constitution. The 'basic structure', as enunciated by Chief Justice Sikri, and which would still apply to limit the substantive content of constitutional amendments, concerned inter-governmental, inter-institutional aspects of the Constitution, and not Fundamental Rights. Apart from the 'basic structure' concept there were no inherent or implied limitations on the constitutional amending power.[60]

We have, already, looked at the determined follow-up campaign launched by Prime Minister Indira Gandhi, to build on the successes of her earlier counter-attacks on Court decisions adverse to agrarian and land legislation and to property reforms generally, culminating in the Forty-Second Amendment of 1976 seeking to 'de-judicialise' most of these matters, and also to put constitutional amendments beyond the scope of judicial review. [61] The defeat of the Gandhi Government in the 1977 General Elections saw the new Janata Government's attempt to reverse the Forty-Second Amendment, with its own Forty-Third and Forty-Fourth Amendments, but at the same time, in fulfilment of a Janata Party election pledge, removing property rights from the Fundamental Rights, Part III of the Constitution and consigning them, instead, to a much less conspicuous place as a new Article 300A. With the return of the Gandhi Government to power, once more, the long struggle between executive-legislative authority and the judges, over the issue of relating property interests, like all other constitutional interests, to the broader, community interest, seemed on the way to being resolved – as it could always have been resolved, in the past – by a conscious and forward-looking executive policy as to the choosing of judges for the Supreme Court, in the future, as judicial vacancies should occur from time to time through death or retirement at age sixty-five. Even before her electoral defeat in early 1977, Prime Minister Gandhi had begun to recognise this basic political fact-of-life with her departure from the normal 'seniority rule' of promotion to Chief Justice of the next most senior, currently serving Justice, and her advancing Chief Justice Ray ahead of three other, more senior, serving judges, in 1973, after Chief Justice Sikri's retirement. [62] This constitutionally novel exercise of the Prime Ministerial discretion as to judicial appointments, occurred immediately after the decision in the *Kesavananda Bharati* case. Prime Minister Gandhi applied a similar 'supersession' principle in 1977, just before her giving way to the Janata Government, in advancing Justice Beg to the Chief Justiceship, ahead of his more senior colleague, Justice Khanna. Court jurisprudence, even as to property rights, can be changed by other, subtler and more patient methods – at least where the executive judicial appointment power is relatively free and unencumbered – as well as by the direct, frontal assaults involved in the constitutional amending power.

5. FEDERALISM, AND ECONOMIC AND PROPERTY INTERESTS: THE
CANADIAN EXPERIENCE

The Canadian Constitution amounts to a special, *sui generis* study in the application of the ordinary rules of construction, by judges, to a constitutional text in cases involving economic and property interests, insofar as the constitution, as originally drafted and adopted in 1867, as a statute of the British Parliament designed as the charter of one of the self-governing colonies in its then Overseas Empire, contained no constitutional Bill of Rights or similar listing of fundamental rights of the person, including property rights. It was not until 1982, and then as part of the Trudeau federal Liberal Government's constitutional 'patriation package', that a constitutionally entrenched Bill of Rights was added; and when it was added, it was without any mention of property rights, early suggestions for including, variously, 'property', or 'God and property' having been dropped for reasons that included awareness of their history, as Natural Law-style absolutes operating under the U.S. Constitution's Due Process clause in its 'substantive' era of interpretation, to block social and planning reforms that a clear majority of the community, through its legislative majorities, had found necessary and desirable.[63] Chalk up yet another example of the negative influence of the U.S. Constitution's jurisprudence on Due Process!

And yet economic and property interests have received special judicial protection under the Canadian Constitution, as under the U.S. and Indian and other Common Law or 'received' Common Law constitutional systems, long after legislative majorities have concluded that their regulation in the wider, community interest should be undertaken. In the absence of a constitutional Bill of Rights as in the United States and India, it all had to be done within the interstices of the constitutional provisions allocating law-making competences, in federal terms, between the two different levels of government, federal and local (Provincial). You do not, it seems, need a constitutional Bill of Rights or similar formalised guarantees, for Natural Law-style considerations of the desirable limitation of governmental power (federal or Provincial, as the case may be), to operate in judicial review of the constitution. Except that they operate, this time, covertly, and more as 'inarticulate major premises' to the judicial decision-making; and will rarely be rendered explicit in the judicial opinions filed in support of the Court decisions and in rationalisation of their legal grounds. The jurisprudence was mainly the work of the Privy Council, sitting as final appellate tribunal for Canada in its capacity as the highest Court of the old British Colonial Empire Overseas, including Canada – which it remained until 1949 when the Canadian Parliament finally legislated, of its own accord, to cut the Imperial Gordian Knot, in legal appeals at least, by abolishing all appeals from Canadian Courts, henceforth, to London, and leaving the Canadian Supreme Court as final tribunal for Canada.[64] During this same time period, up to 1949, the Canadian Supreme Court essentially accorded with the Privy Council's jurisprudence on Canada, though there is some doubt as to whether it did this simply because of the deference it owed, as a then intermediate court only, to the ultimate appeal court within its own hierarchy, or because it genuinely approved of the Privy Council decisions – as to their end results when applied to Canada and also their intrinsic legal reasoning.[65] There is no doubt, however, of the Privy

Council's own satisfaction with its work in relation to Canada, and its freedom from self-doubt and backward glances. The Scottish legal philosopher, Lord Watson and his intellectual disciple and philosopher in his own right and sometime activist, reformist politician, Lord Haldane, who dominated Privy Council interpretation of the Canadian Constitution for three decades from the end of the 1890s on well into the 1920s, were liberal pluralists in their political philosophy and decentralisers in their applied federal constitutional thinking. Perhaps moved by a latter-day desire to make constitutional retribution to French-Canada for the past injustices of British colonial wars and casual colonial military victories, decided by mere hundreds of men but effectively cutting off a grand French historical venture in colonial development in North America with the Battle of Quebec in 1759, Watson and Haldane became convinced 'Provincial Righters' and effectively and decisively tilted the balance of Canadian federalism away from a strong, centralised authority, as apparently intended by the original constitutional drafters of 1867, in reaction to the then recent American Civil War and the 'weak' central government that was thought to have contributed to it.[66] In producing, by conscious judicial effort and much persistence over the years, a strongly decentralised system of government in Canada, Lord Watson and Lord Haldane after him reached, in the words of Professor H.A. Smith, writing in 1927, a 'result which the historian knows to be untrue'.[67] Professor (later Mr. Justice) Vincent MacDonald put it even more caustically that a Constitution which –

'(rightly or wrongly) embodied a Centralised Federalism in which Dominion legislative power was of paramount importance... has yielded a Decentralised Federalism in terms of legislative power; and one, moreover, that is ill-adapted to present needs.'[68]

In brief, the *general* grant of law making power of the federal Government of Canada, under section 91 of the Constitution, was cut down by the Privy Council by deference to the specific heads of local (Provincial) power enumerated in section 92; and it was held that the federal Government could not legislative under the general power in section 91 if the effect would be to 'trench' upon the local (Provincial) categories of subjects. Lord Haldane, indeed, went even further than Lord Watson and enunciated the so-called 'emergency' doctrine under which the federal Government's general legislative power under section 91 should be confined to use in periods of national 'emergency', such as war, famine, or pestilence.[69] While Lord Haldane, in 1923, in paying eloquent tribute to his predecessor and mentor Lord Watson, hailed him for having –

'put clothing upon the bones of the Constitution, and so covered them over with living flesh that the Constitution of Canada took a new form. The Provinces were recognised as of equal authority coordinate with the Dominion, and a long series of decisions were given by him which solved many problems, and produced a new contentment in Canada with the Constitution they had got in 1867. It is difficult to say what the extent of the debt was that Canada owes to Lord Watson.'[70]

On the other hand the later Chief Justice of the Canadian Supreme Court, Bora Laskin, writing, in 1947, of the Privy Council's record in relation to the Canadian constitution, asserted that –

'if anything, [the course of decisions] indicates conscious and deliberate choice of a policy which required, for its advancement, manipulations which can only with difficulty be represented as ordinary judicial techniques.'[71]

The passage of time, the rise of French-Canadian nationalism after the 'Quiet Revolution' of 1960, and the emergence of new, Quebec-based claims for a 'special constitutional status' for Quebec within Canadian federalism,[72] have softened some of the originally very harsh, Anglo-Canadian criticisms of the Privy Council's intrusions into Canadian federalism which, in striking down affirmative social and economic planning legislation, enacted by the federal Government, in the name of an abstract 'Provincial Rights', reached that result by a mode of judicial interpretation that both ignored the ordinary meaning of the text of the constitutional charter, and also the known historical intentions of its drafters of 1867. The resultant judicial favouring of the private economic special interest groups that so largely invoked the constitutional claim of Provincial Rights in the law courts, is clear enough. Its possible political justification, in terms of its end results, on other and different, federalist grounds, raises other issues of constitutional policy beyond the scope of our immediate enquiry.

6. NEW CONSTITUTIONAL PROPERTY CONCEPTS: THE SOCIAL MARKET ECONOMY, SOCIAL DEMOCRACY, IN WEST GERMAN AND FRENCH CONSTITUTIONALISM

The Bonn Constitution of 1949, because both of its timing and also the balance of Christian Democratic and Social Democratic thinking represented in the political discussions and debate preceding its adoption, reflects the newer, interests-balacing approach to property interests and to the degree of protection to be accorded to them in community policy-making. Thus,

Article 14 (Property, right of inheritance, expropriation):
'(1) Property and the right of inheritance are guaranteed. Their content and limits shall be determined by the laws.

'(2) Property imposes duties. Its use should also serve the public weal.

'(3) Expropriation shall be permitted only in the public weal. It may be effected only by or pursuant to a law which shall provide for the nature and extent of the compensation. Such compensation shall be determined by establishing an equitable balance between the public interest and the interests of those affected. In case of dispute regarding the amount of compensation, recourse may be had to the ordinary courts.'

This is followed by *Article 15 (Socialisation)*:

'Land, natural resources and means of production may for the purpose of socialisation be transferred to public ownership or other forms of publicly controlled economy by a law which shall provide for the nature and extent of compensation. In respect of such compensation the third and fourth sentences of paragraph (3) of Article 14 shall apply *mutatis mutandis.*'

Article 14, as well as Article 9 (Freedom of association), were invoked before the Federal Constitutional Court by twenty-nine Employers' Associations, as well as nine Companies, who were contesting the constitutionality of Co-Determination Act enacted by the *Bundestag* in 1976,[73] after two years of debate, by an overwhelming, All-Party vote of 391 to 22. The Act, applying to all Companies employing more than 2,000 persons – some 450 Companies, in fact – required the Companies to have a supervisory board with an equal number of worker and Company shareholder-designated directors, and with the Chairman (who was elected by the Company shareholders) having the casting vote. The principle of worker/employer co-determination and co-management in industry had been extensively debated in the pre-constitution political debates of 1948, when the issue was establishment of factory committees; and legislation of the early 1950s had partly realised the principle, particularly in regard to the coal and steel industry under 1951 legislation. The 1976 statute, however, was comprehensive and universal in its application to Companies with more than 2,000 employees, and represented the legal concretisation of the 'co-determination' approach to user of economic power in the modern state, and no doubt that is why the Employers' Associations decided to make a political and legal stand against it. In addition to the Article 14, property rights, objection, the argument was made by the Employers' Associations, based on Article 9, that the 1976 statute would mean a curtailment of free collective bargaining insofar as it would create a conflict of interest for trade unionists serving at once as directors on the Company board and as representatives of the workers in labour negotiations. This would violate, it was contended in picturesque language, the 'liberty of the opponent' which was indispensable in collective bargaining, and could thereby lead to changes in Company structures. All these constitutional objections were rejected by the First Senate of the Federal

Constitutional Court in its decision of 1 March 1979.[74] The Court noted that, with the shareholders-elected chairman of the new supervisory boards having the casting, tie-breaking vote in the event of a deadlock between the shareholders-elected and the workers-elected directors, the board membership was neither *de jure* nor *de facto* equal representation, the employers thus enjoying a slight superiority under all conditions. The Court said it was uncertain how this slightly less than equal co-determination would affect future development, but assuming a willingness on both sides to cooperate loyally, workers' participation would have a different effect than it would if the atmosphere in a company were to be marked by mutual distrust or indeed enmity. Emphasis was given to the favourable predictions by the lawmakers, but if these should fail to materialise and a Company become paralysed in its operations by co-determination, then corrective measures would become mandatory. The Federal Constitutional Court agreed that the 1976 Co-Determination Law would bring about major changes in the economic order. But it noted that the Bonn Constitution did not prescribe a specific economic order, and the lawmakers in the *Bundestag* therefore enjoyed a far-reaching liberty as to economic policy which could not be restricted by constitutional construction. The Court verdict was widely hailed, as had been the adoption of the 1976 Law itself, as sanctioning the extension of political and social democracy to the economic sphere; and as creating a new and better balance in the relationship of capital and labour, and between the right of disposition over property on the one hand and the right of individual self-fulfilment on the other. In a statement on behalf of the federal Government, issued by the Ministers of Labour, Justice, and the Interior on 9 March 1979, the Bonn Government expressed pleasure that the Court had –

'expressly recognised that the Constitution is neutral as regards economic policy. Thus the verdict spells an end to attempts to confer constitutional status on a market-economy system that in fact is based upon considerations of expediency.[75]

On the constitutional guarantee of property under Article 14, the Bonn Government suggested that the Court's decision took heed of the –

'special aspects of property in the form of shares. The Court makes clear – in a sequel to its former judicial interpretations – that such property-ownership is modified by an extensive social obligation, in that possession of shares confers no benefits without the employment of manpower in our large business entreprises.'[76]

The French Presidential elections of the Spring of 1981 brought a change from the right-of-centre political forces that had governed, since the inception of the Fifth Republican constitutional system in 1958, under, successively, de Gaulle, Pompidou, and Giscard d'Estaing. The new Socialist administration of President Mitterand, having won at the Presidential level and, almost immediately after, gained a clear majority in the elections for the National Assembly, moved swiftly to enact a socialist economic programme, the most important element in which was the Nationalisation Law of 1981 which affected five industrial groups or trusts (reported by *Le Monde* to control 194 billion francs and to employ 650,000 persons), and also thirty-six banks (or ninety-eight banks, counting those banks that they controlled, and representing 75 percent of all credits distributed and 74 percent of all bank deposits).[77] The Nationalisation Law had been passed by the National Assembly in October, 1981, by a vote of 332 to 154.[78] A group of right-of-centre deputies, amounting to more than the sixty necessary to seize it with a matter under Article 61 (2) of the Constitution as amended in 1974, promptly requested the *Conseil constitutionnel* to rule on the constitutionality of the project, the political expectation being that with its membership dominated by appointees from the de Gaulle, Pompidou, and Giscard eras, the *Conseil* would find the Nationalisation project in conflict with the Constitution. The constitutional issues raised were ones of high policy. The Preamble to the Constitution of the Fifth Republic of 1958 refers to, and in effect adopts, the Declaration of the Rights of Man and the Citizen of 1789, as 'confirmed and completed by the Preamble to the Constitution of 1946' [of the preceding, Fourth French Republic]. Article 17 of the Declaration of 1789 stipulated the right of property in the following terms:

'Property being an inviolable and sacred right, no one can be deprived of it, save when the public need, legally established, clearly requires it, and on condition then of a just compensation paid in advance.'

In the Preamble of the Constitution of 1946 (paragraph 9), however, property interests were defined somewhat differently, and in much more qualified terms that recognised the community interest:

Preamble of Constitution of 1946, paragraph 9:
'All property and all entreprises that now have, or subsequently shall have the character of a national public service or of a monopoly in fact, must become the property of the community.'

In fact, the *Conseil constitutionnel* had two looks at the Nationalisation project, the first in its decision of 16 January 1982 when it ruled that certain clauses, only, of the Nationalisation Law were not in conformity with the Constitution; and that several of these clauses, going to determination of the value of shares for purposes of compensation, could not be severed from the whole Law, thereby compelling, in effect, the Government to amend that Law.[79] The second decision, rendered by the *Conseil constitutionnel* on 11 February 1982, on a further demand by sixty or more Opposition deputies, seizing the *Conseil* with jurisdiction under Article 61 (2) of the Constitution as amended in 1974, in respect to the Nationalisation Law as now adopted by the National Assembly in revised form in the light of the earlier *Conseil* ruling, declared the Nationalisation Law to be in conformity with the Constitution.[80] The key elements of the *Conseil's* thinking are to be found in its decision of 16 January 1982 and the recitals made therein in justification of the decision.[81] In these recitals, while taking due note of the continued constitutional operation of Article 17 of the Declaration of the Rights of Man and the Citizen of 1789, the *Conseil* also referred to the evolution after 1789 and right up to the present day of the content and conditions of exercise of the right of property,[82] referring here both to paragraph 9 of the Preamble of the Constitution of 1946, and also to Article 34 of the present Constitution of 1958:

Constitution of 1958, Article 34: ...
'Laws determine also the rules concerning:
'... nationalisations and the transfer of property from the public to the private sectors.'

As the *Conseil* went on:

'It results from the *travaux préparatoires* of the law submitted to the *Conseil constitutionnel's* examination that the legislator intended to base the nationalisations effected by the said law on the fact that the nationalisations would be necessary to give to the public power the means to counter the economic crisis, to promote economic growth and to combat unemployment, and would thus proceed from public necessity in the sense of Article 17 of the Declaration of 1789. 'The appreciation brought by the legislator on the necessity of the nationalisations decided by the law submitted to the examination of the *Conseil constitutionnel*, could not, in the absence of manifest error, be challenged by the *Conseil* at least until such time as it should be established that the transfers of goods and of entreprises presently operated would restrain the field of private property and the liberty of entreprise to the point of misunderstanding the dispositions already cited of the Declaration of 1789.'[83]

The revisions made by the Mitterand Administration to the original Nationalisation Law as a result of the *Conseil's* specific criticisms involved, principally, the substitution of a new formula of compensation for the nationalised properties, based this time on the Stock Market listings augmented by the rate of inflation in 1981, in place of the preceding, multi-criteria formulae (average of Stock Market listings 1978-1980, plus certain augmentations).[84] The Mitterand Government was reported as being anxious to take a new step in favour of shareholders in the nationalised trusts and banks and at the same time to keep it simple.[85] In any case the *Conseil,* having made its point with its first decision and compelled Government delay and Government amendments to the Nationalisation Law as originally presented and adopted by the National Assembly,[86] was not disposed to press the matter further. The *Conseil* decisions, in sum, represent a pragmatic approach by a purely appointive tribunal to a Governmental economic measure which the President of the *Conseil,* the old Gaullist, Roger Frey, and his eight colleagues, would no doubt have disapproved of, personally, on political-ideological grounds.[87] The balance between activism – in compelling changes in the precise manner and mode of exercise of the nationalisations, – and self-restraint on the part of the *Conseil* members in deferring to the Government on the general principle and also, finally, on the fact, of its nationalisations,[88] is there, the self-restraint also reflecting, in measure, the balance between private interests and the wider, community, social or public interest already achieved in the text of the Constitution of 1958 with its express incorporations from the Declaration of 1789 and the Preamble of the 1946 Constitution.

NOTES

1. Compare per Waite J. (Opinion of the Court), *Munn* v. *Illinois,* 94 U.S. 113, 134 (1876): 'For protection against abuses by legislatures the people must resort to the polls, not to the courts'.
2. See, for example, Walton Hamilton, 'The Path of Due Process of Law', *The Constitution Reconsidered* (1938), p. 167 *et seq.;* Graham, 'The "Conspiracy Theory" of the Fourteenth Amendment', 47 *Yale Law Journal* 371 (1938).
3. See, generally, Jacques Brossard, 'La souveraineté politique: le territoire', *L'accession à la souveraineté et le cas du Québec* (1976), pp. 484, 488-490; H. Dorion, *La Frontière Québec – Terre-Neuve* (1963).
4. 16 Wall. 36 (1873).
5. *Ibid.*
6. *Ibid.*
7. *Ibid.*
8. *Munn* v. *People of Illinois,* 94 U.S. 113 (1877).
9. *Ibid.*
10. 165 U.S. 578 (1897).
11. 198 U.S. 45 (1905).
12. 169 U.S. 366 (1898).
13. 198 U.S. 45 (1905).
14. *Ibid.*
15. *Ibid.*
16. *Ibid.*
17. 208 U.S. 412 (1908).
18. 261 U.S. 525 (1923).
19. 208 U.S. 412 (1908).

20. 198 U.S. 45 (1905).
21. 208 U.S. 412 (1908).
22. 298 U.S. 587 (1936).
23. *West Coast Hotel Co.* v. *Parrish,* 300 U.S. 379 (1937).
24. 261 U.S. 525 (1923).
25. *Adamson* v. *California,* 332 U.S. 46 (1947), par Black and Murphy JJ. (dissenting); per Reed J. (Opinion of the Court), *ibid.,* (adopting Cardozo J. (Opinion of the Court) in *Palko* v. *Connecticut,* 302 U.S. 319 (1937)).
26. See, for example, *Kovacs* v. *Cooper,* 336 U.S. 77, 88 (1949), (per Reed J.); criticised by Frankfurter J., (concurring opinion), *ibid.,* at 90. And see, generally, Alpheus T. Mason, 'The Core of Free Government 1938-40: Mr. Justice Stone and "Preferred freedoms",' 65 *Yale Law Journal* 597 (1956); E.V. Rostow, 'The Democratic Character of Judicial Review', 66 *Harvard Law Review* 193 (1952); Edmond Cahn, 'The Doubter and the Bill of Rights', 33 *New York University Law Review* 903, 915 (1958).
27. Hideo Tanaka, 'Chapter III, Rights and Duties of the People', (Position Paper), *Cabinet Commission on the Constitution (Japan)* (1962).
28. Supreme Court of Japan, Grand Bench, Decision of 23 December 1953; *Court and Constitution in Japan. Selected Supreme Court Decisions, 1948-60* (John M. Maki, ed., 1964), p. 228.
29. *Ibid.,* (John M. Maki, ed., 1964), et p. 238.
30. Hideo Tanaka, *op. cit.*
31. *Japan's Commission on the Constitution: The Final Report* (transl. and ed., John M. Maki) (1980), pp. 287-289.
32. Supreme Court of Japan, Grand Bench, Decision of 29 September 1948; *Court and Constitution in Japan. Selected Supreme Court Decisions, 1948-60* (John M. Maki, ed., 1964), p. 253.
33. Supreme Court of Japan, Grand Bench, Decision of 26 June 1963; *The Constitutional Case Law of Japan. Selected Supreme Court Decisions, 1961-70* (Hiroshi Itoh and L.W. Beer, eds., 1978), p. 73.
34. Supreme Court of Japan, Grand Bench, Decision of 4 December 1963; *ibid.,* p. 80.
35. Supreme Court of Japan, Grand Bench, Decision of 15 November 1950; *Court and Constitution in Japan. Selected Supreme Court Decisions, 1948-60,* p. 273.
36. P.K. Tripathi, *Constitutionalism in Asia* (L.W. Beer, ed., 1979), 59, at 82 *et seq.*
37. *Ibid.,* at 67-69 and 85.
38. *Ibid.,* at 69.
39. *Ibid.,* at 82-83.
40. *Ibid.,* at 85.
41. *I.C. Golak Nath* v. *State of Punjab,* A.I.R. *1967* SC 1643.
42. *R.C. Cooper* v. *Union of India,* A.I.R. *1970* SC 564.
43. *Madhav Rao Scindia* v. *Union of India,* A.I.R. *1971* SC 530.
44. H.C.L. Merillat, *Land and the Constitution in India* (1970).
45. A.I.R. *1967* SC 1643.
46. A.I.R. *1965* SC 845.
47. *Ibid.;* and see P.K. Tripathi, 'Mr. Justice Gajendragadkar and Constitutional Interpretation', 8 *Journal of the Indian Law Insitute* 479 (1966).
48. A.I.R. *1967* SC 1643.
49. S.P. Sathe, *Fundamental Rights and Amendment of the Indian Constitution* (1968), p. 8.
50. *Ibid.,* at pp. 12-13.
51. A.I.R. *1970* SC 564.
52. A.I.R. *1969* SC 634.
53. J.L. Kapur, 'The Constitution of India and some recent amendments made therein', 23

244

Jahrbuch des öffentlichen Rechts der Gegenwart 505, at 522, 524 (1974).

54. A.I.R. *1970* SC 564.
55. A.I.R. *1971* SC 530.
56. Kapur, *op. cit.,* at 524 *et seq.*
57. A.I.R. *1971* SC 530; Kapur, *op. cit.,* at 526-527.
58. A.I.R. *1973* SC 1461.
59. A.I.R. *1967* SC 1643.
60. A.I.R. *1973* SC 1461.
61. As to the Forty-Second Amendment, see the comments by Rajeev Dhavan, 'Amending the Amendment: the Constitution (Forty-Fifth Amendment) Bill, 1978', 20 *Journal of the Indian Law Institute* 249, at 249-251 (1978).
62. See the comments by Alice Jacob and Rajeev Dhavan, in 19 *Journal of the Indian Law Institute* 355, 355 (1977).
63. *Canada and the Constitution 1979-1982. Patriation and the Charter of Rights* (1982), at pp. 57-58, 112.
64. See, generally, the author's *Judicial Review* (4th ed., 1969), at p. 61 *et seq.*
65. *Ibid.,* at p. 73.
66. *Ibid.,* at pp. 64-70.
67. H.A. Smith, 9 *Journal of Comparative Legislation and International Law* 160 (1927).
68. Vincent C. MacDonald, 'The Constitution in a Changing World', 26 *Canadian Bar Review* 21, 44 (1948).
69. *In re Board of Commerce Act,* [1922] 1 A.C. 191 (P.C.); *Toronto Electric Commissioners v. Snider,* [1925] A.C. 396 (P.C.).
70. Lord Haldane, 'The Judicial Committee of the Privy Council', 1 *Cambridge Law Journal* 143, 150 (1923).
71. Bora Laskin, '"Peace, Order and Good Government" Re-examined', 25 *Canadian Bar Review* 1054, 1086 (1947).
72. *Quebec and the Constitution,* 1960-1978 (1979).
73. See, generally, H. Wiedemann, 'Codetermination by Workers in German Enterprises', 28 *American Journal of Comparative Law* 79 (1980).
74. Decision of 1 March 1979, – B Verf GE – (1979) (First Senate); *The Bulletin* (Bonn) (Government of West Germany), 28 March 1979.
75. *The Bulletin* (Bonn), 28 March 1979.
76. *Ibid.*
77. 'Le débat sur les Nationalisations', *Le Monde* (Paris), 23 October 1981.
78. *Le Monde,* 28 October 1981.
79. *Conseil constitutionnel,* Decision of 16 January 1982; *Journal Officiel de la République Française,* 17 January 1982, p. 299. And see Jean-Michel Quatrepoint, 'La mauvaise surprise', *Le Monde,* 19 January 1982.
80. *Conseil constitutionnel,* Decison of 11 February 1982; *Journal Officiel,* 12 February 1982, p. 560.
81. *Journal Officiel,* 17 January 1982, p. 299.
82. *Ibid.,* 300-301.
83. *Ibid.,* 300.
84. Loi de nationalisation (no. 82-155 du 11 février 1982), *Journal Officiel,* 13 February 1982, p. 566.
85. 'Le rejet par le Conseil constitutionnel de plusieurs articles de la loi de nationalisation: le gouvernement entend présenter rapidement une nouvelle formule d'indemnisation', *Le Monde,* 19 January 1982.
86. André Laurens, 'Les Nationalisations: l'épreuve de force ou la patience', *Le Monde,* 23 January 1982.
87. Philippe Boucher, 'Le pouvoir et ses juges', *Le Monde,* 19 January 1982.

88. Generally, see Ulrich Wölker, 'Die Nationalisierung in Frankreich 1981/82. Darstellung und juristische Untersuchung der dritten Verstaatlichungswelle', 43 *Zeitschrift für ausländisches öffentliches Recht und Völkerrecht* 213 (1983).

CHAPTER XI

THE COURTS AND SOCIAL POLICY:
ETHNIC-CULTURAL AND OTHER MINORITIES

1. PUBLIC MORALS: 'RIGHT-TO-LIFE' AND 'RIGHT-TO-CHOICE'

We have seen how, in the area of economic and property rights, the judges have, without too much intellectual difficulty – and whether or not it was so intended by the constitutional Founding Fathers or the constitutional charter text required it that way – come out in defence of private special interest groups against governmental regulation. It has required, indeed, a fairly sharp and distinct and verbally categorical break from the constitutional past, in a new constitutional charter, and also a particularly resolute group of judges practising self-restraint as to their own political-economic predilections or preferences, for the newer, interest-balancing approach to be realised that sees economic and property claims placed on the same plane of constitutional equality as other societal claims and to be weighed against them, pragmatically, upon a concrete factual record in the instant case, and not elevated *a priori* to the rank of abstract constitutional absolutes. In the area of social policy, we see the same high degree of subjectivity present in judicial reactions to the complex cases coming before them, and a tendency to liberate oneself from the conceived tethering confines of constitutional text itself and historical intent of constitutional drafters, in favour of free, 'policy' decisions; except that, granted the degree and variety of judicial training and experience both individually, and also collectively and collegially insofar as judges may reflect the dominant social values of the particular era in which the working majority of their Court was put together, the clash and dissonance as to policy choice is far greater. The Law and Society symbiotic relationship is, understandably, far more evident in the area of social policy as conceived and applied by the courts than it is in other Court business.

All this is amply indicated in the jurisprudence on issues of social policy commonly conceived of as involving public morality or moral choice by individual citizens or groups. Two major constitutoinal tribunals, the Supreme Court of the United States and the Federal Constitu-

248

tional Court of West Germany, passed on the issue of constitutionality of abortion laws, and this within two years of each other in the early 1970s. In early 1975, the First Senate of the Federal Constitutional Court divided, six-to-two, on the issue of constitutionality.[1] By the accidents of the regular Parliamentary elections of the judges of the Court, five of the eight judges in the First Senate deciding the case were acknowledged members of the Opposition Christian Democrats, and the other three had Social Democratic affiliations. The two dissenting judges[2] were both Social Democrats, and included the only female judge in the First Senate; and, incidentally, as was noted at the time, both dissenting judges were of the Protestant religion. The First Senate, in its majority decision, ruled as unconstitutional a criminal law reform, sponsored by the Social Democrat-Free Democrat coalition Government at the federal level, which had amended the old German Criminal Code which, in its section 218, established criminal penalties for performing abortions. The Abortion Law Reform Bill had been adopted by the *Bundestag* in 1974, by 247 votes to 233, the vote following Party lines almost exactly, with the Opposition, Christian Democrat and Christian Social Union parties united against the new law. Immediately on its signature by the federal President, the law was challenged before the Federal Constitutional Court by 193 deputies of the Christian Democratic-Christian Social Union Opposition parties in the *Bundestag,* joined by five Provincial (*Länder*) Governments controlled by the same parties. The case arose before the Court as an Abstract-Norm-Control process initiated, in terms of Article 13 (6) of the Court Statute, by 'one third of the Members of the *Bundestag*'. Party feelings ran deeply, reflecting, in measure, a certain religious-sectarian weighting in their composition. The 1974 law had amended the German Criminal Code in a number of important respects: first, the non-penalising of abortions within the first twelve weeks of pregnancy; second, the non-penalising of abortions after the first twelve weeks, if medical or eugenic grounds were present. The majority decision of the First Senate of the Court was based on two Articles from the Part I, Basic Rights, of the Bonn Constitution, both of them formulated at a very high level of generality and abstraction – Article 2 (Rights of Liberty) and Article 1 (Protection of human dignity):

Article 2 (2):
'Everyone shall have the right to life and to inviolability of his person.'

Article 1 (1):
'The dignity of man shall be inviolable. To respect and protect it shall be the duty of all state authority.'

Reading these two Articles together, the Court majority found a positive obligation on the part of the state to protect life, developing life, even against the mother, and this was the basis for holding the 1974 reform uncontitutional. The two dissenting judges, in their common opinion, hardly debate the majority on substantive law grounds, their dissent being directed, much more, to the structures of government and to judicial deference to, and respect for, the community judgment, on controversial issues of social policy, effectively exercised by the legislative majority in its decision to amend the Criminal Code with the 1974 Law. The Court decision declared as unconstitutional those parts of the 1974 Law concerning the termination of pregnancy within the first three months – the proposed new section 218a of the Criminal Code which had read:

'A termination of pregnancy conducted by a doctor with the permission of the pregnant woman is not punishable under Paragraph 218 if no more than twelve weeks have elapsed since conception.'

The Court decreed interim rules to operate until a new law could be passed by the *Bundestag,* and in terms of which abortion should not carry a penalty if performed after consultation with a doctor and if any one of the following grounds existed: danger to the health or life of the mother, not avoidable by other means; the existence of an irremediable defect in the unborn child that would make continuation of the pregnancy unreasonable (this within the first twenty-two weeks); origins of the pregnancy in rape or sexual abuse of a child or another serious offence (this within the first twelve weeks). Following on the Court's decision, the Social Democrat-Free Democrat federal Government introduced a new law permitting abortions when performed by a doctor, if the mother had approved and after she had had social and medical consultation, and if the doctor had determined that any one of a number of grounds (medical, ethical, eugenic, or emergency situation) existed. The new project was passed by the *Bundestag* in 1976, in a close vote according with strict Party lines, with the Christian Democratic forces voting against the measure, and became law in the same year.

The West German decision contrasts sharply with the United States Supreme Court decision in *Roe* v. *Wade* in 1973,[3] which followed closely on the decision in *Griswold* v. *Connecticut* in 1965[4] in which the Court had struck down, as violative of what Mr. Justice Douglas, writing the Opinion of the Court, had called –

'a right of privacy older than the Bill of Rights – older than our political parties, older than our school system' –

an 1879 Connecticut State statute forbidding the use of contraceptives, a statute which even a dissenting judge, Potter Stewart, did not hesitate to describe as 'an uncommonly silly law'.[5] In *Roe* v. *Wade,* in 1973,[6] what was involved was a Texas State law prohibiting abortion unless procured by medical advice for the purpose of saving the life of the mother. Mr. Justice Blackmun, giving the Opinion of the Court, invoked the 'right of privacy', which, as he conceded, is not explicitly mentioned in the U.S. Constitution but might be related to the 'Fourteenth Amendment's concept of personal liberty and restrictions upon state action', or even, as the federal District Court had determined, in the 'Ninth Amendment's reservation of rights to the people'.[7] Whatever its origins, in Mr. Justice Blackmun's view, the right of privacy was – 'broad enough to encompass a woman's decision whether or not to terminate her pregnancy'. While rejecting the argument that the woman's right was absolute and that she was – 'entitled to terminate her pregnancy at whatever time, in whatever way, and for whatever reason she alone chooses', and while noting that a State might –

> 'properly assert important interests in safeguarding health, in maintaining medical standards, and in protecting potential life,'[8]

Mr. Justice Blackmun concluded that the – 'right of personal privacy includes the abortion decision'. The Justice rejected, in passing, the argument that the unborn fetus was a 'person' within the meaning of the Fourteenth Amendment, this on a basis of language of the charter, 19th century historical practice, and comparative religion and comparative theological teaching. As Mr. Justice Blackmun held:

> 'We do not agree that, by adopting one theory of life, Texas may override the rights of the pregnant woman that are at stake...
> 'With respect to the State's important and legitimate interest in the health of the mother, the "compelling" point, in the light of present medical knowledge, is approximately at the end of the first trimester... It follows that, from and after this point, a State may regulate the abortion procedure to the extent that the regulation reasonably relates to the preservation and protection of maternal health...
> 'This means, on the other hand, that, for the period of pregnancy prior to this "compelling" point, the attending physician, in consultation with his patient, is free to determine, without regulation by the State, that, in his medical judgment, the patient's pregnancy should be terminated. If that decision is reached, the judgment may be effectuated by an abortion free of interference by the State.'[9]

Applying these criteria to the Texas State statute involved in the present case, which restricted legal abortions to those 'procured or attempted by medical advice for the purpose of saving the life of the mother', Mr. Justice Blackmun found that the statutory sweep was too broad, that there was no distinction between abortions performed early in pregnancy and those performed later, that the legal justification for abortion procedures was limited to the single reason of saving the mother's life; and that

the State statute was, therefore, unconstitutional.[10] The U.S. Supreme
Court decision carried strong dissents by Justices White and Rehnquist,
Justice White charging the Court majority with abandoning judicial self-
restraint in order to substitute its own values for those of the State of
Texas in an area of social policy which he considered should be – 'left
with the people and to the political processes the people have devised to
govern their affairs'.[11] Justice Rehnquist, while taking issue with the
Court majority in their holding that the unborn fetus was not to be
regarded as a 'person' for purposes of the Fourteenth Amendment, also
questioned whether the Court should have exercised jurisdiction in the
first place in conceding legal standing-to-sue to plaintiffs whose 'interest'
no longer existed insofar as the pregnancy had already terminated.[12] In
the result of the U.S. Supreme Court and the West German Court rulings,
we have two majority, 'policy' decisions directed to the substantive legal
issues involved but reaching different 'policy' results and reflecting different majority judicial values, in situations where the constitutional
charter texts concerned offer little in the way of concrete guidance. The
constitutional Articles invoked by the judicial majorities in each case
were high-level and general and abstract, and hardly compelling, one way
or another, any more than the historical intentions of the constitutional
Founding Fathers, assuming that these latter might have existed on the
point. Is the road of the judicial dissenters, in each case, perhaps more
persuasive, with the suggestion, in the one case, of insisting on observance of strict procedural rules as to standing-to-sue before the Courts
should intervene and rush to judgment on a highly controversial issue of
community policy-making; and the strong recommendation, in both
cases, for application of judicial self-restraint and judicial deference to
the political judgment, in such issues of social policy, of the popularly-
elected organs of Government?

The decision of the *Conseil constitutionnel* of 15 January 1975[13] on the
law then recently adopted by the French National Assembly on the
Voluntary Interruption of Pregnancy has an interest not merely because
of the *Conseil's* ruling on substantive law provisions of the Constitution
of the Fifth Republic and elements like the Declaration of the Rights of
Man and the Citizen of 1789 that are incorporated into that Constitution
through its Preamble, but also because of the express affirmation by the
Conseil in its decision of the limits of its own competence *qua* constitutional tribunal. The *Conseil* had been seized with the matter by 81 deputies of the National Assembly belonging to the Government majority
forces, under Article 61 (2) of the Constitution of the Fifth Republic as
amended only several months earlier, in October, 1974, to facilitate
access to the *Conseil* by just such a group of deputies or Senators (in
addition to the official dignitaries – the President of the Republic, the

Prime Minister, or the President of either House of the legislature –
allowed to invoke the *Conseil* jurisdiction under the Constitution as originally adopted in 1958). The petition to the *Conseil* was thus a political
testing of the new and expanded jursidiction by a 'majority within the
majority' in the National Assembly when it adopted the law, and who
wished to have a second chance to attack a legal reform project on a
highly sensitive and politically controversial issue of social policy by
transferring the battle from the legislative arenas to the judicial arenas
and thereby making the *Conseil* a sort of court of appeal from Parliamentary decisions. The analogues, potential and actual, to the political trans-
formation of the United States Supreme Court, in the late 19th century,
to a judicial battleground for special economic interests that had already
lost out in the legislatures, seemed to be there. But the *Conseil* replied
firmly on this point:

> '*Article 61 of the Constitution does not confer on the Conseil constitutionnel a general
> power of evaluation (appréciation) and of decision identical to that of Parliament*, but
> gives it competence only to pronounce on the conformity to the Constitution of laws
> submitted to its examination.'[14]

In truth, the enlargement of the procedures of seizing the *Conseil* with
constitutional matters and, in particular, the enlargement of those entitled to seize the *Conseil* to include general political, as well as strictly
Governmental, petitioners, was not without certain political dangers for
the *Conseil,* as in the present case, with a problem of a high philosophical
or religious content. And it seems clear that it was for these reasons that
the *Conseil,* in its decision, shut the door to any temptation to becoming
a 'government by the judiciary'. On the substantive legal issues themselves, the *Conseil's* approach is technical, and modest in policy terms.
As to the Declaration of the Rights of Man and the Citizen of 1789,
incorporated into the Constitution of the Fifth Republic through the
Preamble to the Constitution, the references in Article 2 of the Declaration of 1789 to the – 'goal of every political association... the preservation of the natural and imprescriptible rights of man...' and the inclusion
therein of the 'right to liberty', were not offended by the new law. As the
Conseil affirmed:

> 'The law on the voluntary interruption of pregnancy *respects the liberty of the persons
> called on to have recourse to, or to assist in, an interruption of pregnancy,* and it is a
> question of a situation of distress or of therapeutic reason. On this account, the law
> does not offend the principle of the liberty contained in Article 2 of the Declaration of
> the Rights of Man and the Citizen.'[15]

The law did not offend against anyone's liberty, insofar as it did not
compel anyone either themselves to undergo an abortion or to participate

(as medical doctor, for example) in such an operation. As for other general constitutional principles which had been invoked before the *Conseil* as being incorporated in the Constitution of the Fifth Republic through its Preamble – for example, the provisions contained in the Preamble of the Constitution of the preceding, Constitution of the Fourth Republic of 1946, proclaiming –

- 'every human being, without distinction of race, religion, or belief possesses inalienable and sacred rights;
- 'The law guarantees to all, notably to the child, to the mother and to elderly workers, the protection of health...'

these provisions (with their references to 'every human being' and to the guarantee to the 'child' of the 'protection of health'), were not offended by the present Law on the Voluntary Interruption of Pregnancy, which was, 'in fact, in no way contrary' to them. As the *Conseil* noted, laconically, in its judgment:

'The law referred to the *Conseil constitutionnel* only permits touching on the principle of respect for every human being from the commencement of life, recalled in its Article 1, *in case of necessity and according to the conditions and limitations that it defines.*'[16]

In firmly passing up any temptations to base itself on the 'fundamental principles recognised by the laws of the Republic', mentioned in the Preamble of the Constitution of the Fourth Republic, and incorporated, through its own Preamble, in the Constitution of the present, Fifth Republic, the *Conseil* thus eschewed recourse to Natural Law and high policy considerations. In basing itself upon the particular law that had been referred to it and its particular text, the *Conseil* opted for judicial self-restraint and deference to executive-legislative authority and its judgment on a burning issue of community social policy on which the constitutional charter offered no firm guidelines.

2. LAW AND SOCIETY IN RACE RELATIONS

The decision handed down by the United States Supreme Court in the school-segregation cases, *Brown* v. *Board of Education of Topeka,* in 1954,[17] marked the completion of a cycle in policy attitudes that began with the adoption of the Reconstruction Amendments – the Thirteenth, Fourteenth, and Fifteenth Amendments – in the aftermath of the Civil War, that was highlighted by the Supreme Court decision in *Plessy* v. *Ferguson* in 1896,[18] and that made full turn with the 1954 land-mark decision. The ultimate legal source of the 1954 decision is to be found in the period immediately after the Civil War when Radical Republican majorities in both Houses of the federal legislature pushed through a series of proposals designed to translate into constitutional law-in-action President Lincoln's Proclamation of 1 January 1863 declaring all persons held as slaves in the rebel Southern States to be free. These proposals were all, within the space of a few years, successfully ratified as the Reconstruction Amendments to the Constitution. The three Amendments reflected the special political temper of the times when they were adopted: they were imposed on the defeated Southern States by the dominant Republican majorites in Congress immediately after the Civil War, and ratification of them was made a condition prerequisite to the readmission of the defeated Southern States to their full constitutional status within the federal Union. When the U.S. Supreme Court had to rule, in 1873, in *Railroad Company* v. *Brown,*[19] on the device of segregating white and non-white passengers into separate but identical railroad cars on the same train, it had little difficulty, against the background of the dominant public policies of the time, in finding that the statute amounted to a denial of equality in violation of the Fourteenth Amendment. This 1873 Supreme Court decision clearly represented the high-water mark of Radical Republican sentiment immediately after the Civil War.

The resiling that then occurred seems partly to have been a response to the hitherto unsuspected difficulties in integrating the newly-freed slaves into full community life in the United States. Partly, also, it seems to have been a reaction by politically enlightened Northern opinion against the indignities inflicted upon the defeated rebel Southern States in the first flush of military victory, in that Manichean conception of historical causation that all military victors seem to have to the defeated. There was a new disposition among Northern, political leaders to let the Southern States solve their own problems without further intervention. Mr. Justice Miller of the Supreme Court, a great Northern liberal himself, had seemed to foreshadow this change of heart in his opinion in the *Slaughter-House Cases,*[20] rendered in the same year, 1873, as *Railroad Company* v. *Bonn.* Though the *Slaughter-House Cases* had nothing to do with race relations, being concerned with the grant of an economic monopoly by the 'carpet-bag' (federally-imposed) legislature of the State of Louisiana, Mr. Justice Miller, in ruling on whether the grant of a monopoly to one company at the expense of others violated the 'privileges or immunities of citizens of the United States' guaranteed by the Fourteenth Amendment, had little difficulty in concluding that it did not do so. But he then went on to postulate a new 'States-Rights' approach to the Constitution:

'We do not see in those [Reconstruction] Amendments any pressure to destroy the main features of the general system. Under the pressure of all the excited feeling grow-ing out of the war, our statesmen have still believed that the existence of the states with powers for domestic and local government, including the regulation of civil rights, the rights of persons and of property, was essential to the perfect working of our complex form of government, though they have thought proper to impose additional limitations on the states, and to confer additional power on that of the nation.'[21]

In 1883, in the *Civil Rights Cases,*[22] the Supreme Court had to pass on the constitutionality of prosecutions launched under the federal Civil Rights Act of 1875 (enacted in implementation of the Reconstruction Amendments) for denial of certain facilities to negroes on account of race and colour – variously, accommodation in inns or hotels, admission to the dress circle of a theatre in San Francisco, admission to the Grand Opera House in New York, use of the ladies car in a train. Mr. Justice Bradley, for the Court, held that though Congress could, by affirmative legislation like the federal Civil Rights Act of 1875, enforce the Four-teenth Amendment against State laws or acts done under State authority – that is, Congress could 'correct' *State* action – there was no 'general' federal legislative power over civil rights sufficient to reach purely *private* (as distinct from *State*) action. In setting up the distinction between 'cor-rective' action (permitted to the federal Government under the Four-teenth Amendment) and 'general' action (denied to the federal Govern-ment), and making its application turn on whether what was involved in the denial of civil rights was *State* or *private* action, Mr. Justice Bradley set up a new constitutional dichotomy – *public,* as opposed to *private* – with the correlative proposition that only public, and not private, action denying rights on account of race or colour, could be reached by federal legislation. The U.S. Supreme Court, by this decision, thus erected a major legal barrier, persisting to the present day, against any very com-prehensive fedeal civil rights programme.

When, eventually, the Supreme Court was asked to rule, in 1896, in *Plessy* v. *Ferguson,*[23] on a Louisiana State statute, enacted in 1890, which provided for separate railway carriages for the white and coloured races, the temper of the American people had evidently changed considerably from the egalitarian attitudes reflected in the 1873 decision in *Railroad Company* v. *Brown.* As Mr. Justice Brown declared in his Opinion of the Court, in *Plessy* v. *Ferguson* in 1896:

'The object of the [Fourteenth] amendment was undoubtedly to enforce the absolute equality of the two races before the law, but in the nature of things it could not have been intended to abolish distinctions based upon colour, or to enforce social, as dis-tinguished from political, equality, or a commingling of the two races upon terms unsatisfactory to either. Laws permitting, and even requiring their separation in places where they are liable to be brought into contact do not necessarily imply the inferiority

256

of either race to the other, and have been generally, if not universally, recognised as within the competence of the state legislatures in the exercise of their police power. The most common instance of this is connected with the establishment of separate schools for white and coloured children, which have been held to be a valid exercise of the legislative power even by courts of states where the political rights of the coloured races have been longest and most earnestly enforced.'[24]

Mr. Justice Brown concluded the Opinion of the Court by referring to the difficulties confronting any official attempt to counteract social prejudices:

'The argument [of the plaintiff] assumes that social prejudices may be overcome by legislation, and that equal rights cannot be secured to the negro except by an enforced commingling of the two races. We cannot accept this proposition. If the two races are to meet on terms of social equality, it must be the result of natural affinities, a mutual appreciation of each other's merits and a voluntary consent of individuals...'[25]

The *Plessy* v. *Ferguson* decision, in upholding the Louisiana State railway segregation statute against constitutional attack under the Fourteenth Amendment, introduced the principle of 'separate but equal' into American constitutional law; and as a general constitutional formula for applying the mandate of the Fourteenth Amendment and for reconciling, under law, the relations between white and negro in the United States, 'separate but equal', erected into constitutional dogma, prevailed until *Brown* v. *Board of Education of Topeka* in 1954.[26] In strictly constitutional-legal terms, the switch from *Railroad Company* v. *Brown* in 1873 to *Plessy* v. *Ferguson* in 1896, reflects, in part, the competition between two different judicial policies, both having claims to being liberal in character: the liberal activist, determinedly egalitarian judicial policy that insists on full social justice for negroes, and the liberal pluralist judicial policy that stresses *local* determination of policy and a new Court favouring of 'States-Rights' in the name of a belated post-Civil War reconciliation between victors and vanquished. Other, cross-currents to the changes in the Court majority's policy attitudes are represented in the judicial comments on the relations between Law and Society, and the societal limits to the effectiveness of legal action. These reflect, in measure, both judicial pessimism as to the possibilities of judicial activism in behalf of social policies, and also a certain lack of judicial sophistication – understandable enough for the times – of the affirmative possibilities of the positive law in itself shaping, and not simply being the prisoner of, societal attitudes. It is unnecessary, for our present purposes, to speculate on whether the changes in Court majority policy attitudes do not also reflect – and the 'public'/'private' dichotomy, established as a judicial gloss on the Fourteenth Amendment, is perhaps the most controversial, here – 'inarticulate major premises' containing particularist judicial preferences and prejudices as to race relations in general. The race relations cases illustrate, once more, the complexity of the judicial process and the presence of a number of different, competing policies bearing on judicial decision-making, in addition to the 'ordinary rules' of construction, textual interpretation and history, which seem much more readily put aside, here, than in other areas of constitutional law, presumably because of the very strong community pressures and the pendulum-like swings in such community attitudes, over the years.

Once enunciated in *Plessy* v. *Ferguson* in 1896, the 'separate but equal' formula, as the legal antithesis to the Radical Republican-sponsored, racially egalitarian sentiment of the Reconstruction Amendments, begins to be challenged, and we can observe the unfolding of the dialectic in the Court decisions after 1896 and right down to *Brown* v. *Board of Education of Topeka* in 1954. It is unnecessary to canvass the case law in detail, but in general it may be said that the Court, accepting the 'separate but equal' formula as a constitutional *donnée* – (and it could hardly do otherwise, because of its categorical formulation) – becomes increasingly activist in assuring that, in its factual application in concrete cases, that formula will be used honestly and in its full spirit. If there is to be constitutionally-sanctioned separation of white and negro, then, that equality that is also enjoined must be a real one. This was especially true, by the late 1930s and the 1940s, in the education cases – in law school and graduate education, for example; while as early as 1917, in *Buchanan* v. *Warley*,[27] and again in 1948, in *Shelley* v. *Kraemer* (with Chief Justice Vinson writing the Opinion of the Court),[28] the Court, notwithstanding the 'public'/'private' constitutional dichotomy, had little difficulty in concluding that what Chief Justice Vinson, in the 1948 decision, called the 'full coercive power' of the State lay behind, for example, city zoning ordinances denying negroes the right to occupy houses in blocks where the greater number of houses were occupied by whites, and also restrictive covenants as to race entered into by private landowners among themselves. By insisting that the 'public', in the 'public'/'private', original, Court-made constitutional dichotomy, be interpreted in the concrete, and not in the abstract, the Supreme Court was able to conclude – without having to challenge the old constitutional doctrine head-on – that, as applied in the concrete cases before the Court, it meant a denial of that equal protection of the laws guaranteed by the Fourteenth Amendment. The way had thus been prepared, by the beginning of the 1950s, through the judicial chipping away at the old constitutional dogmas, through rigoriously fact-oriented judicial scrutiny of their concrete application by State or even professedly private actors, for their final judicial overthrow. In this sense, the judgment of the Supreme Court in *Brown* v. *Board of Education of Topeka*, in 1954 – in the unanimous opinion written by

Chief Justice Earl Warren, who had replaced Chief Justice Vinson after his sudden death a year before and while the case was, so to speak, in full argument before the Court – represented the culmination of a whole series of smaller, more fact-oriented decisions and, thus, the ultimate synthesis in a judicial dialetical process on race relations begun with *Railroad Company* v. *Brown* in 1873, and joined in issue with *Plessy* v. *Ferguson* in 1896. In ruling, for the unanimous Court, that:

'We conclude that in the field of public education the doctrine of "separate but equal" has no place. Separate educational facilities are inherently unequal,'[29]

Chief Justice Warren, in his Opinion of the Court, refused to become the prisoner of a purely static conception of history – what might have been intended as to segregation in education at the time of the adoption of the Fourteenth Amendment in the late 1860s when, of course, as the Chief Justice noted:

'In the South, the movement toward free common schools, supported by general taxation, had not yet taken hold. Education of white children was largely in the hands of private groups. Education of Negroes was almost nonexistent, and practically all of the race were illiterate. In fact, any education of Negroes was forbidden by law in some states.'

In opting for a developmental approach to legal history, and not a static, contemplative one, Chief Justice Warren noted that the Court could not –

'turn the clock back to 1868 when the Amendment was adopted, or even to 1896 when *Plessy* v. *Ferguson* was written.'[30]

Once enunciated, the overruling of the 'separate but equal' formula and the acceptance of the principle of racially integrated education, at the lowest, grade school level as well as for college, graduate and professional schools, raised some very immense practical, as well as philosophical, dilemmas for the Court. Education being a State matter under the U.S. Constitution, State implementing action would obviously be required if the Court decision, on the general principle of desegregation, rendered in *Brown* v. *Board of Education of Topeka* in 1954, were ever to become constitutional law-in-action. Too much Court pressure on the States would raise issues of federalism. Too much attempt at centralisation of the decision-making, and decision-applying, processes would run the risk of ignoring special, regional or local, societal factors and thus complicate the business of rendering the principle of desegregation genuinely operational, on a nation-wide basis, as quickly as possible. We enter, now, on to questions of sociological jurisprudence, the societal limits to effective legal action, and the dilemmas of judicial policy-making on social issues where a high and continuing degree of attention to societal factors is required – of the sort touched upon, albeit somewhat primitively, by Mr. Justice Brown more than half a century before in *Plessy* v. *Ferguson.* The Supreme Court which had rendered the 'general principle' decision, in 1954, was fully aware of the practical problems and so, one year later, in a follow-up decision, *Brown* v. *Board of Education* in 1955,[31] it tried to embrace the tools and techniques of sociological jurisprudence by, in effect, accepting the possibility of delay in enforcement of the 'general principle' decision of 1954, and this on a regional or geographical basis related to the particular political and social facts of the individual region concerned. The Court, in its 1955 'application' decision, essentially decided to remit the question of concrete enforcement and implementation of the 1954 'general principle' decision to the lower federal, District courts, so that these might fashion remedies according to distinctive local conditions, such as they might be, and not necessarily requiring immediate, complete desegregation. The watchword, invoked by the Court, in its 'application' decision of 1955, was to be the phrase (suggested by Mr. Justice Frankfurter, and borrowed from English Equity), of moving – 'with all deliberate speed'.[32] However realistic this may have been in Law and Society terms – and there is no reason other than to conclude that the alternative Court approach of immediate and full desegregation, ordered by the Court without qualification, would have been a politically largely futile, King Canute gesture, without active State cooperation – there is no doubt of the result. It condemned the federal courts to many years of patient and continuing supervision and monitoring of local school board activity, requiring special technical skills that not all judges have or seem willing to acquire, since outside their normal legal domain. In a very real sense, when Courts enter into the mechanics of practical application, as a means of implementing the 'general principle' decision of 1954, of school busing systems involving the transportation of white or negro students, as the case may be, from one suburb of the city where they reside, to another which may be many miles away, in order to achieve a notional, and, in the end, necessarily somewhat arbitrary, 'percentage' racial balance in the grade schools concerned, then they are very far away from traditional conceptions of the judicial process and from traditional legal training. It is not surprising, therefore, if judicial patience should become frayed at political criticisms that the Courts are sacrificing individual children's best interests and welfare in the pursuit of an abstract legal principle, or individual interests to postulated group interests. The practical problems and dilemmas for the Court are best illustrated in *Swann* v. *Charlotte-Mecklenburg Board of Education,* in 1971,[33] where the Court sanctioned a lower court-ordered, busing plan for Charlotte, North Carolina, that involved conversion to a racially-integrated system of education through remedial altering of pupil attendance zones, and the companion case, *North Carolina State Board of Education* v. *Swann,* in 1971,[34] where the Court struck down a State prohibition on busing; and, on the other hand, *Milliken* v. *Bradley,* in 1974,[35] where the Court drew significant limitations on the *Swann* doctrine in refusing to approve a plan for wholesale busing between predominantly black Detroit schools and those in basically white suburbs. The lower court, in *Milliken* v. *Bradley,* had ordered a metropolitan area desegregation plan, covering both Detroit and fifty-three suburban school districts; and it was the multi-district remedy, applied on a general basis and requiring the busing between city and suburbs, that the Supreme Court found objectionable, ruling that a desegregation plan might normally embrace only districts that had violated the ban against intentional segregation. The path to constitutional justice in pursuit of the Fourteenth Amendment's equal protection principle, as authoritatively reinterpreted, in its modern-day form, in the Court's 'general principle' ruling of 1954 has thus been highly pragmatic; and it has involved, in consequence, making an ally of time and 'hastening slowly', and it has also involved a certain amount of evident, judicially-tolerated and encouraged, trial-and-error, sometimes relatively clumsy and hit-or-miss, social experimentation. Could it have been otherwise, granted the obvious limitations of judicial expertise in applied sociological jurisprudence? Could and should the Courts, on this basis, have left the community policy-making involved to the other, popularly-elected, executive and legislative, institutions of government? On all the evidence of the 1950s and the early 1960s, probably not; for in the absence of any clear willingness by executive-legislative authority, federal or State, to become involved, in socially constructive ways, in that particular time era there would probably, in the absence of judicial activism, have been a gap in effective community policy-making, of whatever form. By the mid-1960s, the federal Presidential and Congressional activism that produced the Federal Civil Rights Act of 1965, might have been intellectually capable and politically willing to take up the challenge of directing and controlling integration in public education; but by that time the Court was fully engaged in the process, and it hardly seemed to make sense, and would hardly have been politically possible, anyway, for the Court to disengage itself at that late stage from the Court-based process long since undertaken and already partly achieved in operational and concrete terms. For purely negative, obstructionist or blocking actions by State authority – as, for example, the Governor of Arkansas' action, in 1957, in ordering out the State National Guard to the Little Rock Central High School grounds and placing the school 'off limits' to

Negro children, in the attempt to defeat a local School Board-approved plan for a staged desegregation of the school system that would be completed, in successive steps, from 1957 to 1963 – the Supreme Court would lend its full cooperation and support to the federal Government, as it demonstrated in its decision in *Cooper* v. *Aaron* in 1958.[36] That decision stands as the leading case on the affirmative duty of cooperation, in a federal system, between State and federal authorities in implementation of federal policies under the Constitution. The Supreme Court thereby added a federal principle – the affirmative duty of cooperation by the States, in deference to federal comity – to the armoury of constitutional weapons available to secure and enforce the Fourteenth Amendment's equal protection imperative.[37]

3. CONSTITUTIONAL EQUALITY: THE 'OPEN SOCIETY' AND 'AFFIRMATIVE ACTION'

We have already in the context of the Courts and the Electoral Processes, and in particular the U.S. Supreme Court decision in *United Jewish Organisation* v. *Carey,* in 1977,[38] touched on the issue of 'affirmative action', mounted by governmental authority in favour of minority group interests. 'Affirmative action', sometimes called 'reverse discrimination', denotes, among other things, quota programmes designed to favour specific racial, ethnic, or even sexual groups, and such quota programmes immediately raise constitutional questions concerning the claims of persons disregarded by such programmes or excluded from job or similar opportunities because of the demands of the new programmes. In *De Funis* v. *Odegaard,* in 1974,[39] what was involved was the exclusion of a white applicant for admission to the Law School of the University of Washington, in favour of intellectually less qualified black applicants admitted under a general law school admission programme which chose minority applicants to fill a set minority quota even if they fell short of general admission standards and displaced white candidates who had met those same general admission standards. The Supreme Court, in the *De Funis* case, avoided deciding on the substantive law issue of the meaning of the Fourteenth Amendment equal protection guarantee in relation to affirmative action, reverse discrimination programmes. Instead, it based its decision on preliminary, procedural, adjectival law grounds: the petitioner was in the final term of Law School by the time the case was argued in the Supreme Court and the University had stated that it would not cancel his Law School registration (gained as a result of lower court proceedings) whatever the outcome of the Supreme Court proceedings on the substantive law issue. The matter, the Supreme Court majority correctly reasoned, in full accord with its earlier jurisprudence and the Brandeis principle of deciding on non-constitutional grounds where possible, had become moot. Mr. Justice Douglas, the long-surviving judicial liberal from the Roosevelt era, reasoning in full accord with the liberal 'Open Society' values which he had been maintaining on the Supreme Court, now, for more than thirty years, dissented, in a vigorous opinion that eschewed the narrower procedural grounds of decision applied by the Court majority and went straight to the legal merits; the – 'consideration of race as a measure of an applicant's qualification normally introduces a capricious and irrelevant factor working an invidious discrimination', the Constitution in Justice Douglas' view conferring no right of racial preference either. In *McDonald* v. *Santa Fe Trail Transportation Co.,* in 1976,[40] the Supreme Court concluded, without difficulty, in a case involving discharge of two white employees of a company because of accusations of theft of company property, where a similarly accused black employee had not been discharged, that the Fourteenth Amendment equal protection guarantees, as a matter of history as well as language, were never understood or intended to apply to the protection solely of non-whites. As Mr. Justice Marshall, for the Court, noted, unlikely as it might have appeared in the 1860s that white citizens would encounter substantial racial discrimination – 'Congress was intent upon establishing in the federal law a broader principle than would have been necessary simply to meet the particular and immediate plight of the newly freed Negro slaves'. The *Santa Fe* case thus disposed of one troubling incident of the Fourteenth Amendment equal protection debate and established its application, universally, without regard to race or colour; but it still left unresolved the problem pointed to by Mr. Justice Douglas in his dissent in *De Funis,* namely the latter-day dilemma of American liberals as to whether the Bill of Rights as a whole and the Fourteenth Amendment in particular represented 'Open Society' values, involving the removal of clogs in the legal and general community processes constituting barriers to political, social and economic mobility on account of race or colour, and no more than that; or whether, in fact, the Fourteenth Amendment was broad enough in constitutional scope to include also affirmative action programmes that might involve creating legal barriers to some particular community groups or even the majority, on account of race or colour, as the price of legally advancing some other groups. For most of their constitutional history, indeed, the Bill of Rights and Fourteenth Amendment guarantees had been interpreted according to classical liberal, 'Open Society' principles, corresponding to and reflecting the ethic and also the political and social imperatives of the dominant legal *élites* who had been interpreting and applying them from within the Supreme Court. The 'Open Society' values are predicated, for their successful political operation, upon the existence of political parties and political and social pressure groups with the necessary professional sophistication and technical legal skills to compete successfully in the struggle in what Holmes called 'the market place of ideas', with other countervailing parties or pressure groups. The 'Open Society' values certainly promote and assist upward vertical mobility for the hard-working and ambitious and confident social groups: the relation to the 'Protestant ethic', as identified by Max Weber, is clear enough, as it is also to the general Judao-Christian intellectual tradition in American law. Does successful utilisation of 'Open Society' values require, however, a certain ruthlessly combative, aggressive social disposition, and does it maximise, thereby, the opportunities for the economically or educationally privileged? Certainly, minority religious groups like the American Jewish community, and minority racial groups like the Germans, the Scandinavians, and perhaps also the Irish and the Italians, have been able to work within the rules of the game, as so established, and to cross the various hurdles to their political, social, and economic advance. More recently politically-conscious ethnic-cultural minority groups, however, like the Mexican-Americans and the Negroes, have not had the same obvious success. The political issue now raised, with its major constitutional implications, is whether there should not now be – however belated it may seem – positive governmental intervention, by way of 'reverse discrimination' programmes, to redress an evident extreme imbalance in social and economic opportunity and access, therefore, to constitutional values, for these specially disadvantaged ethnic-cultural minority groups. The conflict – to some extent as with the conflict years before over Substantive Due Process 'liberty of contract' under the Fourteenth Amendment – is also a conflict between a constitutional right in the abstract, and the existence of that right in the concrete which might imply a very substantially augmented social, economic, or educational base as a pre-condition to effective user of the right. It is perhaps not surprising that the first legal confrontations over the issue, in the challenge to the constitutionality of the *numerus clausus*-type, affirmative quotas provided for members of educationally-disadvantaged minorities seeking preferred admission to University professional schools, Law and Medicine in particular, were long drawn-out and bitter, and that they divided more traditional 'establishment' liberal majorities that had been put together, in the past, from coalitions between disparate ethnic-cultural groups and political associations that had been able, themselves, to achieve community influence and power under the 'Open Society'-based rules of the game. It is also not surprising that the attempts at judicial resolution of the value dilemma involved, have not been altogether happy or intellectually persuasive, in constitutional-legal terms. The dialectical process of community test-

ing and probing of alternative, competing policies under the constitutional equal protection formula, had simply not advanced far enough for a
completely satisfactory judicial synthesis to be obtained and worked out
by the late 1970s, when the leading case arrived for decision and could
not, it was thought, be postoponed any further on procedural grounds as
had been done with *De Funis* in 1974.[41] The Supreme Court decision in
Regents of the University of California v. *Bakke,* in 1978,[42] in the actual
voting split within the Court's ranks and also in the different constitutional grounds filed in the different judicial opinions in support of the
votes, reveals a case that, in the Supreme Court's own terms, was probably not yet ripe for final judicial decision, no clear and sufficient community consensus evidently having as yet emerged as to the Fourteenth
Amendment equal protection clause and as to whether a new, more
activist meaning and content should not now be given to it in response to
new community awareness of rather unpleasant societal facts – here the
specially disadvantaged political, social, and economic position of certain
ethnic-cultural and racial minorities, and their failure to achieve relative
progress in comparison to all other community groups. In the *Bakke*
case, the contest was over the University of California at Davis, Medical
School's reservation of a specific quota of places its first year class to
minority students, pursuant to the University's special programme to aid
black students. The quota plan was challenged on Fourteenth Amendment equal protection clause grounds, on the argument that race could
not properly be used as a criterion of admission and that racially prefer-
ential quotas could not be established. Prominent Jewish community
organisations, responding to the Jewish community's own experience, in
earlier years, with *numerus clausus*-style negative quotas and exclusiona-
ry policies generally based on religion or race, in academic admissions,
joined in filing briefs in support of the challenge to the constitutionality
of the University of California programme. The Supreme Court, by
majority, upheld the challenge, but it was a majority which reflected the
major philosophical conflicts, the decision being rendered by a five-to-
four vote, only with no single, clear ground of majority decision or *ratio
decidendi* for the case. Four of the five majority judges decided against
the constitutionality of the University admissions programme on statutory construction grounds related to the Federal Civil Rights Act of 1965.
The four minority judges contended that the University admissions programme – reserving sixteen out of one hundred places in the First Year
class of the University Medical School for blacks and members of other
minority groups – violated neither the Federal Civil Rights Act nor the
Constitution. The ninth judge, Mr. Justice Powell, who tilted the balance
on a Court otherwise evenly divided, four-four, agreed with the first
group of four judges that the University admissions programme, with its

inflexible provision of sixteen places for minority groups, was invalid, and thus decided the instant case that way; but he also went on to agree with the second group of four judges that race might be taken into account for purposes of admission criteria. The case was decided, but the philosophical dilemma for American liberals and for American constitutionalism generally remained.

It is interesting to compare the experience under the post-independence Indian Constitution, as a modern legal document and one devised for a plural society with vast differences in social status, education, and economic wealth and opportunity as between different communities and classes. The constitutional text itself manifests the basic constitutional antinomy, already referred to in the American context, between the older, liberal, 'Open Society' values, and the more contemporary 'affirmative action' thinking on constitutional equality. Article 14 (equality before the law), Article 15 (prohibition of discrimination on grounds of religion, race, caste, sex, or place of birth), Article 16 (1) and (2) (equality of opportunity in matters of public employment), and Article 29 (2) (protection against denial of admission to educational institutions maintained out of State funds, on grounds only of religion, race, caste, language), reflect, very much, the classical liberal, 'Anglo-Saxon' (British and American) attitudes on constitutional equality. However, these provisions are balanced by Article 15 (4), specially inserted in the Constitution by the Constitution (First Amendment) Act of 1951:

Article 15 (4):
'Nothing in this article or in clause (2) of article 29 shall prevent the State from making any special provision for the advancement of any socially and educationally backward classes of citizens or for the Scheduled Castes and the Scheduled Tribes.'

There is also the balance provided by Article 16 (4) of the Constitution, which specifically authorises the state to make

- 'any provision for the reservation of appointments or posts in favour of any backward class of citizens which, in the opinion of the State, is not adequately represented in the services under the State.'

Again, the Directive Principles of State Policy (Articles 36 to 51), reflecting the newer, social democratic constitutional thinking rather than the older, *laissez-faire* liberal values, create an affirmative duty on the part of the state, in terms of Article 46, to –

'promote with special care the educational and economic interests of the weaker sections of the people, and, in particular, of the Scheduled Castes and the Scheduled Tribes, and [to] protect them from social injustice and all forms of exploitation.'

Article 15 (4) had been inserted into the Indian Constitution by way of constitutional amendment in 1951, in order to 'correct' a very early Supreme Court of India decision, in *State of Madras* v. *Champakam Dorairajan,* in 1951,[43] to the effect that Article 46, as a Directive Principle, could not overcome Article 29 (2), a Fundamental Right; and that the reservation of seats on communal grounds (in purported reliance on Article 46), therefore violated Article 29 (2) and was unconstitutional. The patent conflict between Article 16 (1) and (2) of the Constitution, and Article 16 (4), could not, however, be disposed of on such intrinsically technical legal arguments. In *State of Kerala* v. *N.M. Thomas,* in 1976,[44] the Supreme Court of India had to pass upon a State of Kerala plan designed to favour Scheduled Castes and Scheduled Tribes employees by exempting them from the obligation of passing the regular departmental tests required for promotion within the civil service – here, promotion from lower division clerk to upper division clerk. The constitutional challenge to the State of Kerala plan was based upon Article 16 (1):

> Article 16 (1):
> 'There shall be equality of opportunity for all citizens in matters relating to employment or appointment to any office under the State.'

It was contended that Article 16 (4), with its provision allowing States to make –

> 'any provision for the reservation of appointments or posts in favour of any backward class of citizens which, in the opinion of the State, is not adequately represented in the services under the State,'

simply did not apply. Within the Supreme Court of India majority which upheld the constitutinality of the State of Kerala plan, vestiges of the original philosophical contradiction between the liberal, 'Open Society', and more contemporary, social democratic values, still remained, however. While one majority judge, Mr. Justice Beg, justified the Kerala plan as a conditional or partial State reservation in favour of backward classes under Article 16 (4), the four other majority judges preferred to uphold the Kerala plan directly under Article 16 (1) as a valid protective discrimination, designed to ensure 'equality of opportunity for all citizens in matters relating to employment or appointment to any office under the State' – as mandated, in terms, by Article 16 (1), and not being hit by Article 16 (2).[45] By basing their votes upon Article 16 (1), these four majority judges thus avoided any necessity for ruling on any notional conflict that might exist between the two quite different approaches to constitutional equality represented in Article 16 (1) and Article 16 (4) respectively. The most direct approach to the problem, of course, would be the solution, only partly achieved in the case of the Indian Constitution because of the inherent contradictions – within the Fundamental Rights themselves, and also reflected in the antinomy between the Fundamental Rights as a whole and the Directive Principles of State Policy[46] – of resolving the philosophical dilemma over constitutional equal protection and its contemporary meaning and application, through the Constituent Processes, rather than the judicial processes, by way of a constitutional amendment, in reasonably explicit and unequivocal terms, setting out the relevant contemporary community values. If the implication be affirmative community responsibility of redressing, by legal means, marked imbalances existing between different races, classes, or groups within the community, in terms of access to political, social and economic rights under the Constitution, then there are no particular constitutional drafting or similar technical problems involved – only problems of community value choice and producing the requisite community consensus.

NOTES

1. Decision of 25 February 1975, 39 B Verf GE 1 (1975) (First Senate).
2. Wiltraud Rupp von Brünneck and Helmut Simon, who filed a joint dissenting opinion.
3. *Roe* v. *Wade,* 410 U.S. 113 (1973).
4. 381 U.S. 479 (1965).
5. *Ibid.*
6. 410 U.S. 113 (1973). And see, generally, Donald P. Kommers, 'Abortion and Constitution: United States and West Germany', 25 *American Journal of Comparative Law* 255 (1977).
7. 410 U.S. 113 (1973).
8. *Ibid.*
9. *Ibid.*
10. *Ibid.*
11. *Ibid.*
12. *Ibid.*
13. *Conseil constitutionnel,* Decision of 15 January 1975 (Interruption volontaire de grossesse); *Les Grandes Décisions du Conseil constitutionnel* (L. Favoreu and L. Philip, eds., 1975), p. 357.
14. *Ibid.,* at p. 359.
15. *Ibid.,* at p. 360.
16. *Ibid.*
17. 347 U.S. 483 (1954). The discussion that follows draws, in part, on the author's early, historically-based study, 'An end to racial discrimination in the United States?', 32 *Canadian Bar Review* 545 (1954).
18. 163 U.S. 537 (1896).
19. 17 Wall. 445 (1873).
20. 16 Wall. 36 (1873).

21. 16 Wall. 36, at 82 (1873).
22. 109 U.S. 3 (1883).
23. 163 U.S. 537 (1896).
24. *Ibid.*, at 544.
25. *Ibid.*, at 551.
26. 347 U.S. 483 (1954).
27. 245 U.S. 60 (1917).
28. 334 U.S. 1 (1948).
29. 347 U.S. 483 (1954).
30. *Ibid.*
31. *Brown* v. *Board of Education,* 349 U.S. 294 (1955).
32. 349 U.S. 294, 301 (1955).
33. 402 U.S. 1 (1971).
34. 402 U.S. 43 (1971).
35. 418 U.S. 717 (1974).
36. 358 U.S. 1 (1958).
37. See the author's discussion, 'Federalism and the Principle of Federal Comity', in *Comparative Federalism. States' Rights and National Power* (2nd ed., 1965), p. 78 *et seq.* The Links to the German constitutional concept of the *Bundestreue* are clear.
38. 430 U.S. 144 (1977). And see, generally, Chester Antieau, 'The Jurisprudence of Interests and Adjudication of Equal Protection controversies', 57 *University of Detroit Journal of Urban Law* 831 (1980); Julius Stone, 'Justice in the slough of Equality', 29 *Hastings Law Journal* 995, 1009 (1978).
39. 416 U.S. 312 (1974).
40. 427 U.S. 273 (1976).
41. 416 U.S. 312 (1974).
42. 438 U.S. 265 (1978). And see, generally, Julius Stone, 'Equal Protection in special Admissions Programmes: forward from *Bakke*', 6 *Hastings Constitutional Law Quarterly* 719 (1979); Julius Stone, 'Equal Protection and the Search for Justice', 22 *Arizona Law Review* 1 (1980); Chester Antieau, *op. cit.,* 57 *University of Detroit Journal of Urban Law* 831 (1980).
43. A.I.R. *1951* SC 224. And see S.P. Sathe, *Fundamental Rights and Amendment of the Indian Constitution* (1968), at 8; S.N. Ray, *Judicial Review and Fundamental Rights* (1974), at 119-120, 128.
44. A.I.R. *1976* SC 490. And see the earlier study, M. Galanter, 'Protective Discrimination for Backward Classes in India', 3 *Journal of the Indian Law Institute* 39 (1961).
45. A.I.R. *1976* SC 490.
46. S. Sundara Rami Reddy, 'Fundamentalness of Fundamental Rights and Directive Principles in the Indian Constitution', 22 *Journal of the Indian Law Institute* 399 (1980).

CHAPTER XII

JUDICIAL LAW-MAKING FOR SOCIETIES IN TRANSITION

1. THE JUDICIAL PROCESS: A 'STRICT AND COMPLETE LEGALISM', OR JUDICIAL POLICY-MAKING?

When the present author was publishing *Judicial Review* in its first edition, in 1956.[1] a distinguished and venerable English jurist who had read the manuscript in draft form wrote that the notion that judges – here, constitutional judges – made law in their decisions was 'dangerously heretical and shocking'. Outside the United States, at that time period, what the American Legal Realists had called the 'basic legal myth' still persisted: that the judicial process was a purely mechanical, value-neutral exercise that reduced to the application, to constitutional charter or statutory text, of pre-ordained 'logical' rules of construction, and no more, with objectively verifiable and predictable results in terms of the final Court decision. A great task of the legal scholar writing about final Courts and their decisions, therefore, consisted in demonstrating the free, discretionary element inherent in judicial, as in other forms of community decision-making; of identifying, on a properly scientific-empirical basis, the value elements present in the actual decisions, and also in the supporting, concurring and dissenting judical opinions, of the Court or Courts selected for research and study; and, finally, of demonstrating the relationship between Court and changing Society, and the extent to which Court decisions were influenced or determined by broader societal developments or, in their turn, themselves helped to shape and direct popular opinions and attitudes and practices in the community at large.

Today, it is hardly necessary to canvass the question whether judges can and do make law in their decisions. The weight of academic writing, outside as well as inside the United States, on the indeterminacy of the judicial process as a whole, and the fallacies of the logical form in judicial and general legal reasoning – in particular, the pioneer works of Julius Stone which inspired a whole school of thinking on the judicial process and judicial decision-making in the Commonwealth Countries – has changed the question from the factual one – whether judges make law –

to a normative one. It is no longer, therefore, a question of *whether* judges make law, but on what basis they do it and according to what values. So much have the American Legal Realist lessons been 'received' outside the United States! The legal scholar today is also likely to be concerned with questions of the constitutional consequences of judicial law-making for the other, coordinate, popularly-elected, executive-legislative institutions of government; and for the processes and practices of judicial appointments at the final Court level. There is a shift, here - in line with the general trends in contemporary democratic constitutionalism throughout the World to a new, participatory democracy – towards, issues of political and constitutional legitimacy, and whether it is right and proper in democratic terms for non-elected officials – as judges have generally tended to be – to exercise wide and constitutionally largely uninhibited, discretionary powers of the sort that the scholars and other commentators had demonstrated them to be doing in their decisions. Judicial values, or, if you wish, judicial preferences and prejudices on great issues of social and economic policy choice that divide the contemporary community, insofar as 'inarticulate major premises' to judicial decision-making and opinion-writing, become a legitimate subject of public-political examination and enquiry, and if need be public-political debate and criticism, of a sort that would hardly have been thought admissible or tolerated by the judges in that earlier era of postulated judicial neutrality on great societal issues and conceived absolute separation of the Courts from politics and the political aspects of community decision-making on such issues.

One may suggest, of course, that the gap between the essentially static, mechanical, 'logical', positivist conception of the judicial process, and the much more dynamic, instrumental, value-oriented approaches now prevalent has never been as great as all that; and that, rather than representing a jurisprudential dichotomy, the two different positions on the judicial process are better represented as points on a continuum of judicial decision-making. There is no doubt, however, of the decline in the popularity of the positivist conception of the judicial office and in its active practice by the judges themselves. For one thing, it is an intellectually very demanding judicial art form, and hard to do well and also to apply consistently over a range of cases: the all too frequent and evident gap between what the judges actually did in deciding cases (in terms of the end-results), and what they said they were doing (applying 'a strict and complete legalism') – was one of the reasons for the popular success of the Legal Realists' teaching as to the 'basic legal myth'. For another thing, though, the Positivist approach may prove to be rather tiring and boring for final Court judges recruited, as they so largely have been, from the best intellectual talent in professional legal or public life. It is much more pleasant, today, to allow oneself to succumb to all the delights of judicial policy-making on great issues of public controversy. Here, indeed, the judicial philosopher can really indulge his fancies to play philosopher-king! There are some judges – some rare judges – who still hew to the determinedly neutral and non-political, 'logical' appoach to the judicial process and judicial interpretation, and who manage to develop it with some intellectual style and consistency, and also to maintain it, with some civil courage, against the increasingly captious political attacks that we have come to expect with the increasingly sophisticated company of legal critics and scholars who have developed in the wake of judicial policy-making. Sir Gerard Fitzmaurice, the British judge of the International Court of Justice, who master-minded the Opinion of Court in *South West Africa, Second Phase* in 1966. [2] decided by a narrow, eight-to-seven vote on the second, tie-breaking vote of the President, Sir Percy Spender, is an example of a modern master of the 'classical', 'logical' approach to decision-making. Of Sir Gerald's conscious political neutrality, in value terms, there is no doubt among those who knew him and who studied his judicial opinions over a period of years, for these reflected the meticulous attention to past judicial authority and the emphasis on the 'dry light of reason' that had always characterised the English equity Bar. Sir Gerald Fitzmaurice had refined these particular legal skills during his service as British Foreign Ministry Legal Adviser, prior to his election to the Court, when the divorcement between strict law, which was the province of the Legal Adviser, and policy, which was supposed to be the exclusive domain of the Minister and political head of the Department, was officially respected and celebrated. But the political price that the International Court of Justice had to pay for yielding to Judge Fitzmaurice's positivist persuasiveness in *South West Africa, Second Phase* in 1966, was a very heavy one for the exercise in logic and not in life therein involved. In fact, it was considered too heavy a price to pay, and one unacceptable in relation to the Court's long-range health and future as a main United Nations institution. Granted a second chance only five years later, in *Namibia* in 1971, [3] the Court (with some changes in its membership, from the 1966 and 1969 elections of judges, which had been induced in political reaction to that 1966 decision), deserted Judge Fitzmaurice almost to the man and left him to file a lonely dissent and lament for a positivist judicial position now lost.

2. THE NATURE OF CONSTITUTIONAL COURTS AND CONSTITUTIONAL JUDGES

We have noted some long-range tendencies present in Western and 'received' Western constitutional-legal systems, where some form of constitutonal review operates. First, to have it exercised by a specialist, constitutional tribunal, either created, *de jure,* under the constitutional charter, or else becoming that way, *de facto,* through Court preference and encouragement in the selection and allocation of cases coming to the Court for decision. Second, in judicial recruitment for such specialist constitutional tribunals, to look increasingly for the man (and today, also, the woman) of affairs, with a broad political or public experience, rather than the narrow legal technician who has spent all his life arguing legal cases. Third, in the devising or practical operation of constitutional processes for the appointment of judges to such specialist constitutional tribunals, to opt where at all possible for a short, preferably defined and non-renewable, term-of-years, rather than the longer and largely indefinite judicial time periods prevalent with some older courts exercising constitutional review. The *second* and *third* of these long-range constitutional trends are themselves the consequence, in considerable part, of the *first* constitutional trend towards specialist constitutional tribunals, and away from the old, multi-purpose, multi-jurisdictional Supreme Court of yesterday. Much of the contemporary constitutional debate and discussion as to the constitutional 'legitimacy' of Courts and judges exercising constitutional review has little direct relevance to those comprehensive-jurisdiction Supreme Courts which cover private law, criminal law, administrative and labour law and other matters, in addition to constitutional law: there is a risk of distorting the *rôle* of such Supreme Courts, at the apex of the general legal pyramid, if their internal organisation and procedures and practices are subordinated to the special constitutional-institutional arrangements – covering judicial appointments, for example – now thought appropriate and relevant for specialist constitutional tribunals. One of the more intriguing questions thrown up, indeed, by the contemporary long-range trend towards specialist constitutional tribunals, for example, is whether the function of constitutional review needs to be exercised by a court *stricto sensu,* or even by a court at all; and whether the persons actually exercising such constitutional review need to be judges or even lawyers or legally-trained persons. The character of the French *Conseil constitutionnel* and its evident operational success, is a living demonstration of the proposition that the high policy choices that are at the core of constitutional review are not intrinsically legal in the traditional sense of the word, and that they can, in fact, be fairly readily separated from the adjectival law, processual elements inherent in the

normal Court proceeding without any apparent damage to or impairment
of the tribunal's comprehension and resolution of the policy problem.
The *Conseil* itself, of course, over the years since its establishment, has
shown a tendency to develop the pragmatic skills of timing, and definition of issue, and establishment of the parameters for application of its
decision, that characterise some of the more experienced constitutional
tribunals that are in fact courts, and thus to 'judicialise' itself in the
process. As for the members of such specialist constitutional tribunals, it
is a fact that some of the intellectually most impressive and operationally
effective judges on constitutional courts have been persons with very little in the way of formal legal education or experience in professional legal
practice: one thinks, in this sense, of the two mutually contesting liberals
of the Roosevelt-appointed bench of the U.S. Supreme Court, Hugo
Black and Robert H. Jackson, whose experience in the give-and-take of
other, more direct community policy-making arenas far out-weighed any
deficiencies or gaps in their strictly legal formation. With the *Conseil
constitutionnel,* over its first two decades of service under the Constitution of 1958, according to the surveys made by Favoreu and Philip, out
of thirty-one members who had served during that time period, twenty-
two had connections with the legal World, either as members of the
Conseil d'Etat (administrative law Supreme Court) and the *Cour de cassation* (private law Supreme Court), or as barristers, legal advisers, professors of law, and professor of political science; while eight of these had
the basic undergraduate law degree, eight some post-graduate legal degree, and four the admission to the status of *agrégé* (teacher) of law.
Beyond that, ten were graduates of the prestigeful *Ecole des Sciences politiques.* A 'bench' selected as a typical cross-section of the *Conseil*
throughout its first two decades – that from 1968 to 1971 – shewed,
among its nine members, three law professors, one member of the *Conseil d'Etat,* one member of the *Cour de cassation,* and four former deputies of the National Assembly or Government Ministers. From being a
tribunal deliberately exempted from any obligation to seek prior judicial
training and experience or formal education or professional practice in
law, for purposes of the recruitment of its members, the *Conseil constitutionnel,* in the actual patterns of appointment over the years, demonstrates a certain consistent respect for legal accomplishments, at least
those normally lending themselves to informed, policy judgments in relation to law. Correlatively, the courts, *stricto sensu,* among the specialist
constitutional tribunals shew, more and more, both in their formal rules
as to judicial recruitment and, even more important, in the actual
appointment practices, a tendency to approach the *Conseil constitutionnel* in liberating themselves from too much deference and respect for
strictly technical-legal qualifications, acquired in past judicial service or

in the professional practice of law.

Within the constitutional tribunals, both the *de jure* and the *de facto,* there has been some experimentation with special Senates or Chambers or panels, as a device, variously, for allowing intra-Court specialisation or for lightening the over-all Court work-load by dividing the burden up and allocating it between the different Court sections. On the second point, the *rationale* seems doubtful, and one wonders if the same results might not be achieved more easily, and with more economy as to actual judicial numbers, by the Court as a whole's assuming more discretionary control over its own business and exercising its undoubted inherent right *not* to receive cases not raising substantial issues or else capable of being adequately dealt with elsewhere. Beyond that, there is always a danger, with a plural-panel system within a Court, that in the selection of the actual membership of those panels, the power (usually exercised by the Chief Justice – unless the membership is fixed in advance, in the Constitution or Court statute) may be used on a politically discretionary basis, with potential influence on the outcome of pending cases if the choice of the panel is oriented towards producing particular, long-range policy trends. Some would argue that such a situation is not undesirable in itself and can be a useful way in which the Court, through its Chief Justice, can 'correct', relatively unobstrusively and harmlessly, certain trends in past Court jurisprudence that are considered, with the latter-day judgment of history, to be either errors in judicial interpretation, conventionally applied, or else simply embarrassing in more contemporary political terms – what Charles Evans Hughes, referring to the *Dred Scott* decision of the U.S. Supreme Court,[4] had called one of its great, 'self-inflicted wounds'.[5] We have seen the two antonyms of the plural-panel system within a special constitutional tribunal in the West German Federal Constitutional Court with its two autonomous Senates, each with its own fixed membership and fixed jurisdiction, and the Indian Supreme Court where the Chief Justice had the power, and exercised it in full political consciousness and freedom, to compose the membership of the particular bench, being normally less than the somewhat unwieldly, large membership of the *plenum* or full Court, designated to hear and decide a case, in the absence of a direction by the Chief Justice that it should be dealt with by the *plenum.* The Japanese Supreme Court, with its Grand and Petty Benches, represents a practical way of accommodating the old, multi-purpose, multi-jurisdictional model of a Supreme Court to conceived contemporary constitutional imperatives of Court specialisation for constitutional cases at least, without having to go to the trouble of effecting a fundamental reform of principles of Court jusrisdiction by formal constitutional amendment or amendment of the Court statute. The case for doing by constitutional indirection what can always be done by the front-door, does not seem especially compelling, however.

As for the membership of constitutinal tribunals, the factor, already referred to, of whether the tribunal concerned is indeed specialised, *de jure* or *de facto,* or whether it still retains vestigial, multi-purpose, multi-jurisdictional responsibilities, as a general Supreme Court for all seasons, has its own relevance. In the latter case, as we have noted, there will be political pressures and also obligations to appoint people with some high technical legal training, competence and experience – qualities which, with the specialist constitutional tribunal, seem increasingly subordinated to policy skills, and this with increasing public acceptance or approval of the change of direction involved. What is striking, however, is the substantial consensus among contemporary constitution-makers, and also executive decision-makers exercising a consitution-granted power to nominate or appoint judges to constitutional tribunals, that enough is enough in terms of years of judicial service and that, at a certain point not too far removed from the original date of appointment, there should be a certain 'sunset law' applied. With the West German Court it is a single, non-renewable, twelve-year term, after the earlier experimentation with both life and also renewable eight-year terms (which latter were generally renewed once or even twice, if the incumbent desired it); with the *Conseil constitutionnel* it is a single, non-renewable, nine-year term. By special historical accidents attaching to their legal traditions – the respect accorded age and professional seniority, which has meant that judges have not normally been appointed to the Supreme Court before attaining a 'ripe' age, plus a fairly early, imposed, mandatory retirement age (sixty-five in the case of India, and seventy in the case of Japan), the situation has been achieved, *de facto,* where a Supreme Court judge in either India or Japan will not serve any longer than his West German or French counterpart and normally, indeed, for a very much less term. The American Supreme Court rules and practice as to judicial appointments which have seen jurists like the great early judge and member of Chief Justice John Marshall's Court, Joseph Story, appointed to the Court at the age of thirty-two, or like the crusading 'New Dealer', William O. Douglas, appointed at age forty, with eligibility to serve for life, meant, in the two cases, judicial terms of thirty-four and thirty-six years respectively. The great early Chief Justice, John Marshall, served for thirty-four years; the arch-conservatives of the 'Gilded Age' of American constitutionalism, Stepehn J. Field and Joseph P. Bradley, served, towards the close of the 19th century, for thirty-four and twenty-two years respectively. The 'Four Horsemen', who intransigently held up President Franklin Roosevelt's 'New Deal' reform measures throughout his first, four-year Presidential term from 1933 until after his re-election in 1937, had, on all the evidence, tarried too long on the Court and long outlived their own constitutional era: the intellectually strongest of them, Sutherland, lasted from 1922 to 1938, Van Devanter from 1910 to 1937, McReynolds from 1914 to 1941, and Butler from 1922 to 1939. They were all carry-over appointments from much earlier Presidents with much earlier constitutional and general political philosophies: President Taft in the case of Van Devanter, President Harding in the cases of Sutherland and Butler, President Wilson with the politically aberrant (as it turned out) choice of McReynolds. President Franklin Roosevelt was so determined not to have his successors frustrated, as he had been, by a politically conservative, 'stonewalling' Court majority, that he chose his own judges with a certain long view of history, and five or six different Presidencies later several of his judicial nominees were still serving on the Court, Black lasting thirty-four years until near the end of the first Nixon term as President, and Douglas lasting into the Gerald Ford Presidency. Even allowing for the fact that the Supreme Court is understood to act as a certain brake on executive and legislative power, the modern conception of the Court as a community policy-making institution, coordinate with – if not exactly equal in the range and depth of its decision-making competence – those other institutions, suggests a certain constitutional merit in the renewal of the Court's membership at certain intervals in time. The West German judges, with their single, non-renewable twelve-year term, may, serve, at maximum, for three times the stipulated term of the lower federal House or *Bundestag;* the French *Conseil constitutionnel* members, with a non-renewable nine-year term, will serve, at maximum, two years longer than the President of the the Republic who is himself eligible for re-election. The West German Court, the French *Conseil constitutionnel,* and for that matter the International Court of Justice, in staggering the election system so that a part, only, of the tribunal will retire at any time, balance continuity and also turn-over of personnel as constitutional principles governing judicial selections. Both the *Conseil constitutionnel* and the International Court agree, as a norm for judicial elections and judicial tenure, on the principle of one-third of the tribunal retiring every three years, with the judicial term itself as nine years. The compulsory retirement for age rule – applied in India (at sixty-five), West Germany (at sixty-eight), Japan (at seventy), Canada (at seventy-five) – seems out of touch with contemporary constitutional trends towards outlawing discrimination or differentiation on the basis of age alone, as an unconstitutional denial of equality before the law and equal protection of the laws. Where it is recorded as a rule in the Court statute only, it may be unconstitutional on the face of it; where it is included in the constitutional charter itself, it may fall within the category of 'unconstitutional' constitutional norms already referred to. Where the rules governing judicial appointment include a specific and limited term-of-years that is non-renewable, as in the case of West Germany, the superimposition on that of an additional requirement that a judge retire at a certain age (sixty-eight, in West Germany) even though he may still have some time in the regular electoral term-of-years still to run, seems quite unnecessary, and also objectionable in general constitutional terms. Presumably the executive legislative forces, in presenting nominees for judicial posts or candidates for judicial election, will weigh the age factor – relative youth or relative age – in deciding on their choices.

The issue, within a Court, as to what to do with the choice of its presiding officer – designated President or Chief Justice as the case may be – is in part determined by general rules and practice as to length of the judicial term. Presumably, if there is a fairly short judicial term of office, *de jure* or *de facto,* then this will affect the presiding officer equally with the other, associate members or judges. While there are considerable advantages, in terms of continuity and long-range development of a tribunal's jurisprudence, particularly in its earlier, formative years in having a strong, long-serving Chief Justice, as with John Marshall, the fourth Chief Justice of the U.S. Supreme Court, it has a negative side in that it may emphasise, too much, the legal *status quo* and stifle new thinking on constitutional law. Except for the U.S. and the Canadian Supreme Courts, however, this is hardly a practical problem, granted that, with the other tribunals surveyed, the presiding officer's term will be, either *de jure* or *de facto,* no more, at most, than twelve years and, on average, perhaps half that time. The only real controversy that has surfaced, publicly, has been over the question whether the presiding officer or Chief Justice should be promoted from within the tribunal on the death or retirement of the incumbent, or whether one should reach outside the tribunal's ranks for a new appointment; and, if the principle of promotion from within the tribunal's own ranks be accepted, whether the post should automatically devolve to the next in line, in seniority, through number of years of service on the Court, or whether the executive should feel free to exercise a complete discretion and choose a more junior serving member of the tribunal. In several national legal systems in recent years – in Canada, and in India at least twice in the 1970s, the dilemma of choice of the presiding officer, and the resultant selection, have caused evident ill-feeling within the ranks of the tribunal concerned and some public comment. There are instances, of course, where feelings within a tribunal run high and it is closely divided, in its own ranks, in policy terms, where it makes sense to reach outside the ranks for a fresh personality. The U.S. Supreme Court, in modern times – the succession of Harlan F. Stone to the Chief Justiceship in 1941 excepted – has seen its Chief Justice appointed from outside, the Presidential choice of the Chief Justice being dictated, understandably enough, by the desire of the President to leave his own personal imprint on constitutional history by naming someone in his own conceived political-philosophical image to the highest, most authoritative, and most influential legal post for these purposes. Outside the U.S. Supreme Court, the potentially pivotal *rôle* of the Chief Justice in influencing constitutional-legal development has not been so fully admitted, and the conflicts over choice have tended to concern the promotion issue. The case for automatic promotion of the next-in-line, in seniority of service within the Court, is that it is the most objective choice of all since eliminating any question of executive discretion or political preference and discouraging, at the same time, any judicial 'grandstanding' or playing to the gallery in the expectation of earning, thereby, an earlier promotion to the head post. But, in being automatic and taking no account of relative judicial intellect and imagination, energy, and civil courage, it may encourage judicial somnolence where, particularly in eras of transition in society, the wit and courage to attempt breakthroughs in legal doctrine may be needed and can be facilitated, certainly, by a wise executive preferring of an intellectually more gifted candidate with less actual Court seniority. Prime Minister Indira Gandhi, as someone who always displayed a certain cool realism as to the political base of the community decision-making processes, did not, until very late in the day, recognise the political importance of the federal executive power of deciding judicial appointments at the Supreme Court level, and that the Chief Justice, in this sense, was more than *primus inter pares* in view of the developed federal executive practice of consulting with the Chief Justice and taking his advice on the appointment of Associate Justices, and also the Chief Justice's practice of using his own discretion very fully in the formation of Court panels for hearing of cases and their decision. When Prime Minister Gandhi finally decided to make her own preferred choices for the Chief Justiceship and to by-pass the 'automatic promotion' principle, as she did on the two successive occasions in the early and mid-1970s, it ran in the face of several decades of practice the other way and created a political storm, though it was no more, in fact, than American Presidents had been doing right from the beginnings of the U.S. Supreme Court. On one point, however, there is unanimity in the practice of the different tribunals we have discussed: the choice of the presiding officer or Chief Justice is never left, either *de jure* or *de facto,* to the members of the tribunal concerned, and there hardly seems evidence even of informal consultation with them, on the part of the executive, prior to the choice being announced and legally made.

3. THE *RÔLE* OF THE CONSTITUTIONAL CHARTER AND THE RULES OF CONSTRUCTION

What we have observed, in surveying the sweep of Court jurisprudence in a number of different problems, over a certain period of time, is that the same problems tend to recur in all societies, and that the judicially-found solutions are often remarkably similar in spite of the seeming disparateness of the constitutional charters involved. The first point, the recurrence of the same problems in a number of different societies, is hardly surprising. They are all post-industrial societies, or else newly-independent countries, like India, that are moving very rapidly through the various stages of economic growth towards large-scale industrialisation, with the predictable sociological consequences of mass urbanisation, movement of population, dislocation of traditional folk-ways, extreme imbalances in terms of wealth and well-being and social opportunity, strains on community health and social services and the like. The tensions between classical, liberal economic principles that favoured entrepreneurial activity, and the newer social democratic principles that were more concerned with the social consequences of such entrepreneurial activity, if unrestrained in community terms, were more or less inevitable in all the societies we have looked at: the post-independence Indian constitution-makers, with political prescience, recognised the conflict and consecrated it, as a constitutional antinomy, in the constitutional charter text itself by the successive provisions, in Part III, of the Fundamental Rights (with their certain 'classical' constitutional orientation), and, in Part IV, of the Directive Principles of State Policy with their determined opening, in terms, to social democracy. Chief Justice Gajendragadkar, who had a feeling for ultimate, ordering legal principles, expressed it very well, after his retirement as Chief Justice, in saying that the Fundamental Rights, important though they were, were in a very real sense static, whereas the Directive Principles had a dynamic quality and were designed to promote a transition to welfare state principles.[6] In its earlier jurisprudence, the Supreme Court of India, responding to the express stipulation, in Article 37, that the Directive Principles 'shall not be enforceable by any court', ruled that the Directive Principles had to conform to the Fundamental Rights sections of the Constitution and were subsidiary to them in cases of conflict between the two. These essentially conservative judicial interpretations, restricting the social democratic openings provided by the Directive Principles, led on to the serried battles of the 1950s and 1960s between the Supreme Court and executive-legislative power at the federal level, over the attempts by the federal Government to advance the social and economic interests of the backward classes of citizens and to redistribute land and wealth more generally in the cause of social justice. This produced that extraordinary sequence of political-legal events, that we have already seen, of Governmental legislative action; followed by Court response; then Government counter-response through use of the constitutional amending power to 'correct' the Court decision; followed by still further Court decision negativing or frustrating the Governmental 'corrective' action. At the purely doctrinal-legal level, the constituional antinomy between Fundamental Rights and Directive Principles was resolved, as a matter of constitutional construction, by the judicially developed canon of 'harmonious construction' – put forth in the *Quareshi* case,[7] and in the *Kerala Education Bill* Advisory Opinion ruling,[8] both rendered in 1958 – under which, the Court held, the attempt would be made to give effect to both Fundamental Rights and Directive Principles as much as possible, though not in such a way as to make the Fundamental Rights a 'mere rope of sand'.[9] Yet it is difficult to avoid the conclusion, in examining the Indian Supreme Court jurisprudence in the economic and property cases that the actual textual provisions, constitutional or statutory as the case may be, were subordinate to ultimate judicial conceptions of policy, and that the constitutional texts served largely as vehicles for conveying judicial decisions already arrived at on other, non-textual grounds;[10] and that, in this sense, the same battles between judicial power and executive-legislative power would have occurred, and no doubt been resolved the same way, with or without the presence, in the Constitution itself, of the constitutional antinomy between Fundamental Rights and Directive Principles. The Indian jurisprudence in this general area, in the competition and conflict of the different societal interests involved, and in the actual resolution of such conflicts by the judges, approximates to a very substantial extent to U.S. and Canadian jurisprudence in this same general area, in spite of the patent, major differences in the respective constitutional charters and the particular constitutional Articles invoked by the respective Supreme Courts in rationalisation of their decisions.

The constitutional charters differ very much as to their texts, which reflect the vagaries and varieties of constitutional drafting current at the time of their adoption, and present among the people – national constituent assembly, committee of local notables, foreign Colonial Office drafting committee – legally charged with their elaboration. I have elsewhere suggested[11] that the short, lapidarian texts, cast in general principles, and in clear literary expression – the Constitution of the United States, many of the French Charters from the Revolution onwards – are more likely to stand the test of time, and to be understood and supported by the people to whom they are addressed, than the prolix, pedantic texts that so many parent, Imperial states seem to have willed to their former possessions overseas, on decolonisation and independence. As Chief Justice Marshall had said, in *McCulloch* v. *Maryland* in 1819,[12] 'We must never forget tha it is a *constitution* we are expounding'. The same injunction might well be addressed to constitution-makers – that it is, indeed, a constitutional charter intended to endure, if not for the ages at least for some considerable period of time; and that it is not intended, like statutes or municipal ordinances, to be addressed to too many, low-level and specific and frequently purely transitory, problems, or to be eleaborated in corresponding exhaustive detail. Too long a charter, with too many Articles, invites the search for the internal contradictions or verbal conflicts which are, almost certainly, there in spite of the best efforts of the original drafters; and compels, in the end, a form of selective judicial interpretation in which one or two constitutional charter Articles only, or even particular clauses within those Articles, will be called on by the judges to do all of the work and carry the burden, in constitutional construction, that the constitutional drafters clearly intended to allocate, as to certain categories of social problems, to other, more specific and detailed sections of the Constitution. This phenomenon of selective judicial interpretation of constitutional charters can be observed, also, in the case of the short, lapidarian texts. It was no doubt inevitable that the great battles over economic and property interests and their regulation by law should be transferred, in the late 19th and early 20th century United States, from the executive and legislative arenas of government to the judicial arena; but it was by no means inevitable, as a matter simply of the ordinary meaning of words in the constitutional charter and their history, that the constitutional 'Due Process' clause should be made to serve as the constitutional textual field of battle, rather than a number of seemingly more obvious and more immediately available, alternative constitutional sections. The element of the purely accidental and capricious in the history of judicial interpretation, begins to emerge, here. But, in the end, are the differences in textual provisions, and thus the differences in the relative length and specificity of particular constitutional charters taken as a whole, really significant and determinative in their subsequent history of judicial interpretation? The distinguished American scholars, Lasswell and McDougal,[13] in their venture in elaboration of scientific models for comparative study and analysis of different legal systems and approaches to law, at the national and the international levels, attempted to reduce the disparate legal systems to eight main categories or classifications – what they called 'base values'; and though their models, when first published, may have seemed to many as overly ambitious, in the present era when Courts liberate themselves increasingly from constitutional texts and their logical exegesis, in favour of much more avowedly 'free-law-finding' approaches, the comparative analysis of judicial behaviour in community problem-solving tends to demonstrate, more and more, that constitutional judges are thinking in terms of such larger legal categories and deciding accordingly, and that the patterns of judicial analysis and decision-making accord across national frontiers in spite of the vast, surface differences in the constitutional texts with which the judges have been charged.

The rules of construction – the older, 'ordinary rules' of construction, and the newer, more instrumental ones, have had their part to play, of course. In the period when the 'logical' approach to constitutional interpretation was still dominant – and still being exercised by many judges with exemplary skill and proper intellectual detachment from the exigent political here-and-now – the great American constitutionalist, Walter Dodd,[14] endeavoured to break up and classify the provisions in a constitutional charter into different categories according to the manner of their formulation, and to identity different modes of interpretation appropriate to each of them. Some constitutional provisions, according to Dodd, were obviously *narrow and definite,* presenting objective standards capable of application by a Court without any great discretion – identifying, here, provisions as to the form of legislative action, special types of oaths of office, definite mathematical standards ('two-thirds majority') and the like. Other constitutional provisions were *broad in character but still definite,* and still presenting an objective standard by which to test legislation – for example, the Contract Clause (Article I (10) (1)) of the U.S. Constitution stipulating that no State shall make any law 'impairing the obligation of contracts'. From there one moved on to constitutional provisions *narrow in character but indefinite,* and not presenting an objective standard by which to test legislation – for example, the provision in some State constitutions that no Bill should contain more than one 'subject': but what was a 'subject'? Finally, Dodd identified constitutional provisions both *broad in scope and indefinite in character,* neither limiting themselves to the control of definite types of legislative action nor presenting an objective standard by which to test legislation, and the textbook example of such a category would be, of course, 'Due Process' under the U.S. Constitution, which, as judicially interpreted, opened the flood-gates to a judicially-activist striking down of social legislation. One might quarrel with 'Due Process' as an illustrative example of this category since,it might be argued, on the basis both of its actual words and also its legislative history (English and American) it had a reasonably precise and limited, procedural (non-substantive) connotation, and was simply used or misused by judicial majorities as a textual vehicle for their own particular, substantive policies. But the category itself – what Julius Stone called the 'legal category of indeterminate reference'[15] – clearly exists within every legal system and has application to every branch of law, public and private. Approached systematically enough and early enough, it might have been possible to introduce more order and coherence, and certainly more predictability in strictly logical terms, into the processes of judicial interpretation by using categories such as these and recognising that, for certain types of constitutional provisions, the species of strict, logical interpretation, making use of the 'ordinary rules' of construction, not merely has meaning and is capable of being objectively and consistently applied; but probably ought (according to the ordinary constitutional 'rules of the game' and the necessary balance between the judiciary and the other, popularly-elected, executive-legislative institutions of government), to be so applied. This would involve, as correlative, the proposition that for other categories of constitutional provisions, normally those incorporating standards or involving some species of judicial evaluation, the 'ordinary rules' of construction tend to break down or to provide no objectively verifiable answer; and that the judge, in such cases, must proceed to a 'policy'-style decision and acknowledge it as such in his opinion, or else return the problem altogether to the executive-legislative institutions of government for avowedly 'political' decision in those political arenas. It is, I think, a little too late in the day, now, to expect the adoption of such a disciplined, gradualist or staged, escalation by judges, in the process of judicial interpretation, from the painstakingly 'logical' interpretation of the narrower and more definite constitutional provisions to the freer, 'policy' approach to the broader and more open-ended sections of a charter, too many judges preferring today to make the leap from constitutional text to policy, more or less right away and without intermediate steps. Every legal system, whether Common Law or Civil Law in base, and whether public law or private law in the application, has its categories of rules of interpretation, with ascending orders of freedom in the discretion accorded to the judge under them: as Gény had identified in relation to Civil Law, private law, Code interpretation, the Grammatical interpretation, with its extreme deference to the text of the Code and the exegetical rules, shades off into Logical interpretation and the use of history, and when these break down one may move into 'teleological' (purposive, goal-oriented) interpretation, which opens the door to what Gény called 'la libre recherche scientifique'[16] and ultimate free-law-finding.

4. THE SPECIAL COMPETENCE OF CONSTITUTIONAL COURTS

The examination of the particular fields or areas of application of judicial interpretation, on a comparative basis through space and time as between different legal systems and different time periods, leads inescapably to certain conclusions as to what judges do very well and what they tend, by comparison, to do very badly. Certainly, the verdict of history, in comparative law terms, is sometimes very harsh, – that the Courts have performed inexcusably, both technically, in terms of the relation of their decisions to constitutional text and constitutional history, and also in substantive, policy terms. On the issue of the technical performance, *qua* Court, in the 'economic' cases, there can be little quarrel: over a number of different legal systems, the judicial performance indicates a fairly systematic and deliberate misreading or misinterpretation in the pursuit of specific policy goals favoured by the judges and opposed to those of the executive-legislative majorities who had sponsored the measures the judges were ruling on. In substantive, policy terms, in these 'economic' cases, the debate may be historically more open: certainly, though the Court majority in the 'Gilded Age' of American capitalism, frustrated particular legislative majorities, usually at the local, State level, it did not seriously get in the way of the national will as expressed through the Presidency and Congress until President Franklin Roosevelt's first term from 1933 to 1937, and it gave way immediately on his triumphant re-election. The conscious judicial diffidence or somnolence on race relations, in spite of the historical intent and the clear choice of language, of the post-Civil War Reconstruction Amendments, exactly corresponded to the national mood as expressed through the Presidency and the Congress, and indeed the Court was much quicker than those other two, popularly-elected organs of government, in changing its mind from the early 1950s onwards, and much more determined, then, in returning to the original spirit of the Reconstruction and to readapt it, creatively, to contemporary societal conditions. But whatever our historical verdict as to past jurisprudence in the United States, Canada, India and elsewhere, on economic and property cases, the conclusion for contemporary purposes would seem powerful. Judges tend, unconsciously, to reflect too much the special interests of their largely private clients and would be well advised, in the future, to exercise judicial self-restraint and to consider very, very carefully before rushing in to strike down government regulation, in the larger, community interest, of economic and property interests. On social policy, one might go even further and suggest that the past judicial interventions have often been awkward and self-conscious, particularly in relation to issues of public morality, and that, if anything, they reveal the cultural limitations inherent in legal education and professional legal experience and service on the bench.

Where the judges were, perhaps, far too slow to begin and to intervene positively in the larger community interest, but where, once they had summoned up the civil courage to cross the threshold, they performed with flair and imagination, is in the area of the political processes. That Presumption of Constitutionality in favour of executive and legislative action, developed by the post-1937, 'Roosevelt' Supreme Court as a conscious reversal of conservative, obstructionist tactics deliberately maintained by the 'Old Court' majority over a considerable period of years, is predicated upon the representativeness, in democratic constitutional terms, of those other, coordinate institutions of government. Judicial deference to the executive-legislative will stem from the notion that it is undemocratic for non-elected judges to seek to impose their own will, and their own preferred judicial policies, upon the popularly-elected institutions. It all breaks down, however, as constitutional theory, if those other, coordinate institutions of government are not really representative, either because the constitutional-electoral laws are not applied in *bona fide* fashion; or if the electoral processes exclude, either *de jure* or *de facto,* significant voting groups; or if the constitutional-electoral laws only take on meaning in the context of the practice of the political parties which may themselves, perhaps, be unregulated and uncontrolled in constitutional terms. The modern constitutional thinking in this area, bound up in Mr. Justice Harlan Stone's 'political process' concept, elaborated and extended as it was by Judge Gerhard Leibholz's conception of 'equality before the law' as applied, particularly, to the electoral processes and to the contemporary political reality of the 'political parties'-state, stems from the period just before the Second World War, and finds constitutional expression in the Bonn Constitution of 1949 and in West German and, later, American constitutional jurisprudence as developed by the Courts. It involves acceptance by the Courts of an affirmative obligation to keep the political and electoral processes free and unobstructed, by removing legal or other clogs that effectively militate against the full expression of the public will, and by intervening actively to secure the democratic character of the political parties' membership rules and internal voting practices as to the selection and endorsement of party candidates in the general elections; and it also extends to the Courts' positively promoting that free flow of information and ideas, through the press and other media, that is indispensable to the exercise of an informed judgment in the casting of one's vote in the general elections and in participating in the political processes generally. This aspect of constitutional law is still evolving, such is its importance and interest today, but it already includes quite sophisticated jurisprudence – in West Germany, the United States and other countries – on the compatibility of various types of electoral systems with the principles of democratic constitutionalism, and the possibilities and limits of public, governmental financing of political parties. The refusal of the Courts, before the 1950s, to intervene in this category of constitutional problem, on the argument that it was a non-justiciable 'political question' that was either potentially too embarrassing, politically, for the Courts or else too complex and technically difficult to be comprehended and resolved intelligently by the Courts, seems, in retrospect, to have been a major policy error. In any case, it is accepted, today, that Courts can, and should, intervene in this type of case, to establish the general legal parameters of permissible and impermissible electoral conduct and party political practice bearing on elections, and that the technical skills necessary to a fruitful judicial examination can be fairly easily and readily mastered. We speak here, of course, of general codes of electoral and party political conduct: it is not suggested that the final Supreme Courts or specialist constitutional tribunals should act as, in effect, courts of disputed electoral returns to hear and resolve individual cases of alleged fraud or irregularity not involving general constitutional principles; although the *Conseil constitutionnel* in France has seemed able to fulfil such a limited, electoral review function[17] easily and elegantly at the same time as its larger, constitutional-electoral policy questions. *A fortiori,* however, it would seem an error of political judgment for the Courts to allow themselves to become embroiled in partisan politically-motivated electoral battles, revolving around one constituency only, of the sort that saw the Opposition political forces in India fight a deliberate guerrilla war, in the Courts, in the early 1970s, to try to take away Prime Minister Indira Gandhi's individual Parliamentary seat by impugning her election in the preceding general elections.[18]

What has been said in relation to the special competence (and special obligations) of Supreme Courts in relation to the political and electoral processes applies, even more strongly, in regard to minority groups, especially those of an ethnic-cultural character – what Mr. Justice Harlan Stone, in the *Carolene Products* case, in 1938,[19] called 'discrete and insular minorities'. Among these are native aboriginal or autochthonous peoples who in certain countries – the United States and Canada, for example – may have no representation, or, at best, a less than complete and effective representation – in the ordinary political processes (including here the electoral systems). The Courts, in such cases, would seem to have a special duty to scrutinise very closely any executive or legislative dispositions pourporting to deal with their rights, and not to apply the normal presumption of constitutionality in favour of such governmental dispositions unless and until it be demonstrated, beyond reasonable doubt, that the aboriginal peoples concerned have freely consented thereto, and that that consent was *bona fide* and properly informed. This, of course – the affirmative judicial policy of favouring minorities not effectively represented in the ordinary political processes – would be the principal *raison d'être* and justification of the U.S. Supreme Court's positive intervention, in applied judicial activism, in public education cases from the early 1950s onwards, as a means of promoting effective integration of black children into the general educational system, even though it involved the Court in three decades of exhaustingly painstaking and time-consuming supervision of the public schools and required the judges to experiment with particular techniques of social control – school busing, as the most obvious example – that ran well beyond the capacities of traditional legal training and judicial expertise. The executive and legislative arms of government could no doubt have done it all far more effectively, and scientifically in social science terms; but they were unwilling to act, at all, in fulfilment of their constitutional mandate, until very late in the day, and the Courts chose to fill the resultant gap in community decision-making on an urgent social problem and so to make the political-social processes operate.

5. JUDICIAL SELF-RESTRAINT AND 'POLITICAL QUESTIONS'

The doctrine of 'political questions', which proclaims the non-justiciability of certain categories of constitutional questions, appears, in comparative law, historically-based study, to have had a number of different origins and justifications. It has been, first of all, related to an alleged technical difficulty of certain subjects which are, on that basis, argued to be beyond the special competence, *qua* Court, of constitutional tribunals: this argument, as we have seen in the election cases, may at a certain point be rejected by the judges themselves on the score that any extra technical skills can, by now, with increased judicial sophistication, be acquired easily enough, or else that the particular problem to be solved is so intrinsically important in itself (with no other, coordinate institution of government able or willing to try to solve it, instead) that the case for judicial intervention far outweighs any incidental inconveniences or embarrassments for the judges.

A second explanation and justification for the 'political questions' doctrine and its application by the Courts to render a particular issue non-justiciable has to do with separation-of-powers style considerations going to the respect and deference that the Courts owe to the other, coordinate, popularly-elected, executive and legislative institutions of government. Except where the issue raised goes to the *bona fide* character of the constitution of such coordinate, executive and legislative institutions, and therefore to their claim to representative status which is the foundation of all democratic constitutionalism, the 'political questions' doctrine is here at its strongest. The Courts' claims to intervene are clearly weakest of all when they involve a purported review of the constituent (constitutional amending) processes when there is no issue of the *bona fide* operation of those processes and where, in any case, they include participatory democracy and consultation of the people or their elected representatives in some form. The Indian Supreme Court's passing on the substantive content of constitutional amendment projects seems questionable in this regard; some of the 'Watergate' era rulings of the U.S. Supreme Court on the scope of federal executive, Presidential power, seem to go somewhat beyond the necessities of the particular case and to involve an over-hasty, too sweeping judicial intrusion into the powers and privileges of a coordinate, popularly-elected institution of government. Judges, where they are not themselves elected, would seem to have a certain duty to be sparing in their review of the conduct and operation of the other, elected institutions of government, where the direct, electoral review by popular vote is available in timely fashion or some other, special constitutional remedy – impeachment, for example – has been provided, and where no legal impediment has been sought to be created by executive-legislative authority to its effective expression. Inter-institutional disputes, West German fashion, between executive and legislature, or between a central, federal government and local, regional authorities, offer certain attractions in terms of third-party, judicial arbitrament, especially where those other instituions themselves volunteer to seek the Courts' arbitrament; but the Courts have an obligation, in such instances, to ensure that the conflict is real and not factitious and, for example, in supposedly federal-local, inter-governmental conflicts, to lift away the veil, if need be, just to be sure that it is not simply some private, non-governmental special interest or pressure group invoking federalism and 'States' Rights' as a means of defeating governmental intervention by way of legal regulation in the larger, community interest. The executive, operating in its foreign affairs jurisdiction, and also in the name of constitutional emergency, has traditionally claimed immunity from Court review, and those executive claims are, on constitutional separation-of-powers and inter-institutional, 'comity' grounds, very hard to reject, even though the claim to the existence of an 'emergency' justifying recourse by the executive to extraordinary constitutional powers, beyond the legal jurisdiction of the Courts to review and correct, may be factually doubtful or contestable in the particular instance in which it is invoked. Perhaps the judicial remedy, here – outside the ordinary political processes and the regular electoral processes – lies only after the event, although even that has not been admitted as a domain of legitimate Court activity. *Salus populi suprema lex,* as expressed, variously, in the concepts of 'political question', *Acte de Gouvernement,* and *Staatsraison,* here goes to the postulated foundations of the state, the *Grundnorm,* and is, by definition, a pre-legal, meta-legal, political fact and non-reviewable, as such, by the Courts.

The most indefinite or amorphous aspect of the 'political questions' category relates to issues that are simply considered by the judges – usually on good and sufficient, purely subjective, pragmatic grounds – to be too hot, politically, for the judges to handle without the risk of themselves becoming embroiled in partisan political controversy. Sometimes this type of burning political issue ends up before the Courts because the other, popularly-elected institutions of government have been too prudent and realistic to run the risk of trying to resolve it themselves, and so they have been happy to pass it on to someone else. There may be certain urgent issues, like race relations in the 1950s, that are ripe for community problem-solving and urgently need some community intervention – by the Courts, if need be, if the other, coordinte institutions default. No one can quarrel with the Courts' initiatives in such cases, particularly where, as with minority questions, they involve, also, other affirmative, 'political process' grounds for Court intervention.

But many other types of community conflicts raise no such 'political process' questions. They are simply burning social conflicts on which, as yet, no discernible, reasonable societal consensus has emerged. In such cases, it may make sense to do as the other, coordinate, executive-legislative institutions have seemed to do, and try to make an ally of time and wait on a sufficient community consensus to emerge before acting. Courts have sometimes, in the past, seemed overly anxious, – unnecessarily anxious, – to rush in to certain types of social controversies where Angels (and executive-legislative authority) prudently choose not to tread. The public morality cluster of cases, the 'right-to-life'/'right-to-choice' legalised abortion controversy – seem examples of this, and yet judges, in this general area, having little in the way of constituional text prescriptions to guide them, seem left with their own personal policy preferences or prejudices, and not much more, to guide them to a wise decision. The limitations of judicial expertise are apparent, here, simply because technical-legal expertise has almost nothing to offer here. Is it not better for the judges to leave these issues for resolution by the ordinary political processes and the popularly elected institutions of government, and, if need be, by the constituent processes and the constitutional amending power?

If the judges wish to avoid such questions and to leave them to executive-legislative authority or to the people, then all the developed techniques of judicial self-restraint are available to them for that purpose. We have referred to these already: the judicial insistence on a proper case/controversy, and of a genuine and substantial constitutional 'interest' (beyond that of other, normal taxpayers) before a petitioner will be allowed to raise the constitutional issue; the judicial deciding on the lesser, non-constitutional grounds, where these are available in a particular case; the judicial refusal to proceed when an issue is, or has become, 'moot' in the particular case, because the original cause of action has disappeared. All these preliminary, procedural, adjectival law, grounds were originally developed, over the years, as rules of judicial prudence to allow judges to immunise their Courts from involvement in great political *causes célèbres* in which there was no obvious and immediate need for Court involvement, and no other, overriding public interest crying out for Court intervention nevertheless. The argument for judicial prudence rests, it is clear, on the conception of the Courts as a purely dependent, non-elected institution of government and it has greatest weight and persuasiveness when the judges are purely appointed officials without any direct public involvement in their selection processes. On the other hand, if the judges are themselves elected (albeit indirectly, as with the West German Federal Constitutional Court, and the International Court of Justice), or if there is some other public involvement in their appointment processes (as with the U.S. Senate's ratification of Presidential nominees to the U.S. Supreme Court), then the judges so chosen begin to acquire their own form of mandate, in their own right, to make community policy on burning social issues, and become constitutionally legitimated in its exercise. The judges may therefore feel constitutionally justified in refusing to treat such burning social issues as 'political questions' beyond their jurisdiction as Courts, and opt to intervene in spite of all the political hazards on the way. It would still seem useful, however, to recall Mr. Justice Frankfurter's wise reminder that – 'Only fragments of a social problem are seen through the narrow windows of a litigation'; [19a] and that the judges, therefore, are not necessarily the best equipped, in relation to executive and legislative authority, to undertake the prime responsibility for community problem-solving on great social issues, at least where other 'political process'-style arguments are not present too.

6. THE HISTORICAL RELATIVISM OF JUDICIAL REVIEW, AND ITS FUTURE

After the popularity of judicial review in the immediate post-World War II era, and the enthusiasm with which it was adopted either in new acts of constitution-making for new socieites or the renewal of old constitutional charters in older societies in search of modernisation and up-dating of their constitutional institutions and practices, there has been something of a reaction in recent years. Judicial review, 'export variety', was the product of the United States in the full political confidence and constitutional optimism of War's end in Europe and Asia in 1945; and something of the enormous prestige and authority of the United States Supreme Court of that particular time period, as a liberal activist tribunal boldly remaking society in a better and braver image carried over to other countries, including the recently defeated Axis powers, Germany and Japan. How much the 'reception' of American constitutional institutions and practices, including judicial review, in those countries, owed to the political pressures of American Military Occupation officials who might have sought to include it as a condition of restoration of self-government and return of legal sovereignty, is still debatable; though there is enough firm evidence, in the case of both countries, and enough early, Weimar Republic practice (embryonic though it was) in the case of West Germany at least, to suggest that the opting for judicial review in the new, post-War constitutional system was a local decision and a positive one. There is no doubt that the 'reception', in both cases, was a highly successful one, for the opportunity was taken at the same time of streamlining and modernising some of its incidents in the light of the lessons to be learnt from trial-and-error American experience – particularly as to access to the courts and as to responsibility and accountability of the judges themselves.

Some of the contemporary doubts about judicial review stem from changes in general constitutional thinking over the years since 1945, and also the long-range trends, in contemporary constitutionalism, towards participatory democracy and towards responsibility or at least accountability of officials who exercise broad discretionary powers, to the popularly-elected institutions of government or to the people. While it is doubtful if the highly cumbersome and complicated post-War Japanese system for the popular recall of judges – hardly used as it has been – represents a constitutionally effective or satisfying response to these new constitutional imperatives, there is no doubt as to the trend, manifested in various latter-day constitutional charters or Court Statutes, towards the election of judges (the West German Court, the International Court), and election for a limited term-of-years only (the West German Court, the International Court, the French *Conseil constitutionnel*), with such limited term-of-years being non-renewable (the West German Court, the *Conseil constitutionnel*). All this reflects, in measure, the view that the older tradition of life-time appointments of judges (the United States Supreme Court) or life-time appointments defeasible by mandatory retirement on attaining a stipulated 'old' age (the Canadian, Indian, and Japanese Supreme Courts), while undoubtedly producing its stated objective of judicial independence from outside political or public pressures, may also conduce to judicial arrogance or irresponsibility in relation to the foreseeable practical consequences of particular Court decisions when they have to be implemented, eventually, at the executive-administrative level of government. Contemporary constitutional thinking is also moving away from conceding or tolerating constitutional decision-making in non-elected officials, whether their title to office be hereditary, as with the Head-of-State in Great Britain; or purely appointive, as with the Canadian Senate. When such non-elected officials have, by the historical accidents of old constitutional charters or their practice, been granted, *de jure,* broad discretionary powers, a constitutional custom or convention begins to emerge, *de facto,* in modern times, that those discretionary powers be never exercised, and so they will lapse, in time, through constitutional desuetude. This has happened with the office of Head-of-State in Canada, a constitutional institution 'received' from Great Britain and patterned on the British Crown, and which has become essentially titular or nominal; and it is so, essentially, with the purely appointive Canadian Senate which resembles, in modern times, the British House of Lords. This same constitutional thinking carries over to a constitutional judiciary where the judges' title to office derives from executive appointment only. It merges with contemporary constitutionalism's reaction against *élitism,* of any form. Judicial review, above all, is *élitist* in character where, under the newer, frankly policy-making approach to decision, the judges may seek to define the public interest or to set community goals through their decisions. The challenge to *élitism,* judicial or other, is that it does not meet contemporary constitutional requirements; that it is increasingly ill-adapted to the needs of the post-industrial society which, with the goal of mass education attained, seeks to promote personal initiative and to guarantee independence in making up one's own mind, and then to encourage acceptance of personal responsibility for the particular social choice one has made. The argument, here, is not against judicial review, as such, or even against judicial policy-making in the exercise of judicial review, but against the judges seeking to become overly directive or controlling in developing social policy, outside the areas of the Courts' special competence to safeguard the integrity of the political processes and to ensure that minorities excluded, *de jure* or *de facto,* from the ordinary political processes, are, indeed, properly consulted and are also able effectively to participate in community decision-making that touches on or adversely affects their own special interests. Outside the areas of their special competence, *qua* Court, the judges of special constitutional tribunsls – like other constitutional-governmental *élites,* executive and legislative – may need to redefine their relation to society in the new era of participatory democracy, when the people, having become emancipated in educational and economic terms, are increasingly demanding the right to exercise their own personal, social choices, without too much governmental paternalism, judicial or other.

When the question of including a constitutionally-entrenched Charter of Rights and Freedoms in the Canadian constitutional 'patriation' project of 1982 was being debated in the several years preceding its actual legal adoption, the scholarly social-democratic Premier of the Province of Saskatchewan, Allan Blakeney, expressed grave reserves about the potentially greatly-expanded *rôle* of the Canadian Supreme Court in the practical application and development of the new Charter of Rights. He was thinking back, of course, as a social-democrat, to the politically unhappy history of judicial review under the conservative, 'Old Court' majority within the United States Supreme Court, up to the President Roosevelt-inspired 'Court Revolution' of 1937. That criticism, which was widely shared at the time if not in the end persuasive against the adoption of the new Charter and the correctly forecast vast increase in the Supreme Court's business, reflected a lot of thinking among constitutional jurists as to the historical relativism of judicial review, in both spatial and temporal terms. Is it an intrinsically Western, *Eurocentrist* institution that has been crucially interrelated with, and dependent for its successful operation upon, the special constitutional 'rules of the game' operating in Western, Western European-derived society, and incapable, therefore, of easy export to other, non-Western societies with different cultural patterns and attitudes on Law in Society? Is it also, as an institution, rooted in the particular time era in which it evolved in Western society, and in the particular social and economic ideology – *laissez-faire* – dominant at that time in Western society as a whole? It was the suspicion of just such a static relationship between judicial review as an institution, and a society now past – which seemed amply confirmed by the history of judicial interventionism, in behalf of conservative policies and in favour of private special interest and pressure groups that had already lost out in the ordinary democratic political processes, in the United States and elsewhere – that lay behind the various public criticisms of the new Charter of Rights and the envisaged new activist *rôle* for the Supreme Court, under the Canadian constitutional 'patriation' project of 1982.

Some contemporary criticisms of judicial review in the United States seem attributable, ultimately, to the initial, post-1937, confusion of American constitutional liberals over the correct lessons to be drawn from the 'Court Revolution' of that year and the political overthrow of the 'Old Court' majority. The ambivalence in the constitutional-liberal heritage, from Holmes and Brandeis, was not fully perceived; or, if it was perceived, the wise, institutionally-based objection to the 'Old Court' majority that it was eschewing its obligations of judicial self-restraint *vis-à-vis* executive-legislative majorities and wilfully substituting its own preferred policies (whatever their content) for the policies determined by the people's elected representatives, was lost in favour of the politically somewhat more direct, but constitutionally more simplistic, objection that the 'Old Court' majority was applying conservative instead of liberal, policies in its decisions. Constitutional liberals who embraced the cause of judicial activism because it meant, after 1937, liberal judicial activism, could hardly object – except on a straight contest over the values themselves – if a latter-day Court, the Burger Court of the 1970s and early 1980s, for example, tried to reverse the liberal trend in various areas by applying neo-conservative values, apparently with a sufficiency of public support behind such reversal in majority Court attitudes. Any latter-day informed reactions against the Court, after the enthusiasm displayed by constitutional liberals in the 1950s and the 1960s, have a technical aspect also. A Congress long dormant on civil rights after the first, short-lived activism of the post-Civil War era, demonstrated, by its legislative interventions from the mid-1960s onwards, how, with the support and encouragement of the Presidency, also become newly activist on civil rights, it could move affirmatively and effectively to implement the constitutional equality principle in all aspects of race relations, and this more efficiently and comprehensively than the Court. For of course Congress and the Presidency, in comparison to the Court, have virtually unlimited financial resources and technical skills available in aid of their community problem-solving initiatives, when they choose to take such initiatives.

On the International Court of Justice, the decline of the Court's business – at least in its contentious jurisdiction – since the mid-1960s, has been striking and startling, and seems due to the two politically somewhat contradictory reasons: the disillusionment, by the 'new', newly-decolonised, Afro-Asian countries with what they felt was a 'European', 'white man's' tribunal that had rendered the eight-to-seven decision in *South West Africa. Second Phase* in 1966,[20] that seemed to want uphold *Apartheid* and racial discrimination by its refusal to decide the substantive issue involved; and the correlative fear by the older, Western, or 'European' states party to the Court's Statute, that the Court would become swamped with non-Western, non-'European' judges as the 'new' countries increasingly exercised their legal voting rights in the periodic elections of judges to the Court by the U.N. General Assembly and Security Council – an irritation that was partly manifested in the reaction by some Western European Foreign Ministries, traditionally supportive of the International Court and the principle of adjudication of international disputes, to some of the special opinions filed by the other, non-Western European judges in *North Sea Continental Shelf* in 1969,[21] a dispute that happened to be limited to three members of the old, Western European, 'special legal community' that had dominated the present International Court's predecessor, the old Permanent Court of International Justice of the between-the-two-World-Wars period. The objection of ethnic-cultural relativism – of a too exclusively Western European, *Eurocentrist* character of the present International Court is easily enough disposed of. Insofar as it may have existed and been reflected in the composition of the eight-judge majority in the eight-to-seven *South West Africa* decision of 1966, it is by now past history. The Court itself profited from the United Nations Security Council's timely initiative, with the request for Advisory Opinion in *Namibia* in 1971,[22] to retrace its steps from *South West Africa* in 1966, and by a ruling, rendered by overwhelming judicial majority, on the substantive legal issue, to outlaw *Apartheid* in contemporary International Law terms. Any reluctance on the part of Western states to resort to the Court, in the future, for resolution of disputes to which they are themselves parties – if it should be based on fear of a new, non-Western majority on the International Court reflecting, more or less exactly, the new, more nearly universal United Nations – would represent a failure to adjust constructively to the general 'winds of change' in the World Community since the wave of admission of 'new' states, in the wake of decolonisation and independence from the 1950s onwards that far more than doubled the United Nations membership in the space of several decades. In any case, the political organs of the United Nations – the General Assembly, the Security Council, and also other U.N. organs and specialized agencies so authorised by the General Assembly, have the right, under Article 96 of the United Nations Charter, to approach the Court directly for Advisory Opinion ruling on any legal question; and this right of initiative, which was at the origin of the *Namibia* process in 1971, should help to fill awkward gaps in the Court's actual work-load, as its representativeness in ethnic-cultural and also legal-systemic terms is clearly demonstrated to General Assembly majorities.

The truth that Jeremy Bentham noted that Law is not made by Judge alone, but by Judge and Company,[23] referring here to all the other actors in the community law-making processes, holds true for the United Nations special legal community, as for the various national legal communities. One of the points to be observed in connection with *Namibia, 1971,*[24] and also noted in some later International Court jurisprudence – for example, in *Aegean Sea Continental Shelf*[25] (Judge Lachs' Separate Opinion), – was that all main United Nations institutions – General Assembly, Security Council, Secretary-General, and International Court, contributed to the international legal problem-solving, coordinating and complementing their individual efforts, wherever possible, in the 'progressive development of international law'. This essentially cooperative approach to decision-making in which the main governmental institutions respect each others' constitutional special competence but also expect reciprocal support in what becomes, in the end, a collective, stage by stage approach to fundamental legal change, has lessons to offer, also, to national legal systems. These lessons have to do, in particular, with the un-wisdom of Courts doing today, as they so often did in the past: that is, setting themselves on a collision course with the executive-legislative institutions of government, thereby producing a 'carnival of unconstitutioinality' and a major gap in effective community problem-solving when all the avenues for inter-institutional coordination and cooperation have not been fully tested and utilised in what is, after all, a common societal problem affecting all institutions of government equally and also the people.

7. SOCIETIES IN TRANSITION AND JUDICIAL REVIEW

The comparative lawyer, aware that legal rules and even legal institutions and processes, cannot be divorced from underlying societal conditions with which they exist in symbiotic relation, is aware of the double hazard of his profession. If the study of law, today, is and must be, in social science terms, an exercise in sociological jurisprudence, then comparative law, *qua* social science, involves, really, comparative sociological jurisprudence,[26] One has special obligations of prudence, therefore, in seeking to borrow from one national legal system to another, or to establish hypotheses based upon the empirical experience of one national legal system alone as sounding generalisations good for all seasons and for all countries.

The comments upon and the critiques of ethnocentricity in the institution of judicial reveiw – that it is rooted in Western liberal constitutional legal thought-ways and practice (Eurocentrism) – have this substantial element of truth in them, that judicial review exercised its greatest evident political success and public acceptance and support in the political heyday of Western society when the range and depth of national consensus as to present and future community goals was at its greatest. Even in the race relations area, when the U.S. Supreme Court reversed half a century and more of jurisprudence, from the early 1950s onwards into the civil libertarian activism of the Warren Court, although there was considerable regional or locally-based dissent which expressed itself publicly in the political arenas of government, the Court could argue that it was legislating for a new, libertarian consensus on race relations and racial equality, now in process of emergence as community conscience at the national level and including, necessarily, scope for regional divergence which it was the Court's right and duty to incorporate in, and if need be subordinate to, the larger national will. In sociological jurisprudence terms involving what Roscoe Pound,[27] following the German jurist Josef Kohler,[28] identified as 'civilisation-areas' with their own appropriate jural postulates, in the area of race relations by the 1950s the relevant geographical unit within the United States for purposes of judicial law-making was the larger, *national* civilisation-area with its larger, *national* goal values reflected in the emerging new national consensus.

In Max Weber's analysis of Law in relation to Economy and Society,[29] the logico-formal rationality which he regarded as the expression of the Western liberal capitalist society at its *apogée* of development, was reflected in the drives for systematic legal codification and the rule-bound, detached objectivity of the professional, University-trained, legal *élite* – the legal *honoratiores* in Weber's own term – who applied the legal codes and charters that had been so developed, to general societal decision-making, judicial and other. Weber himself clearly sensed the inevitability of conflict between such logico-formal rationality as the main criterion of excellence in law, and conceptions of substantive justice, if the foundations of the Western liberal capitalist society should ever seem seriously threatened as they have been, of course, in the post-World War II era – in purely internal terms, by the very difficult transition, in very many Western societies, from the industrial to the post-industrial society; and in external terms by the emergence of the new political forces unleashed in the World Community by decolonisation and independence on a World-wide scale, and by the challenge that these forces have posed not merely at the political level, in the United Nations General Assembly, but also at the economic level in the demands for a New International Economic Order and new approaches to the international monetary and trading systems. The older national consensus may begin to crumble in a crisis of national confidence as to long-range national goals, at home and abroad. The judges, as legal *honoratiores,* seem ill-equipped to handle the problems of devising and imposing national consensus in a society undergoing large-scale transition, involving a much larger than usual division and doubt as to legal values. The postulated principle of judicial 'neutrality' or judicial 'independence' on great issues of social choice still unresolved, becomes strained under these circumstances; and the techniques of judicial self-restraint, and deliberate political disengagement by the judges through the various recognised techniques of avoiding the substantive legal issues on procedural grounds, commend themselves increasingly, on pragmatic grounds as a relief from the judicial decision-making burden. The parallel tendency, which we have noted elsewhere, to retreat into oneself in ethnic-cultural terms and thus try at least to reduce, if not remove, the problem of value-conflicts or dissonance, also offers itself: the International Court of Justice's quest for value-homogeneity through toleration of the formation of special, numerically-limited 'regional' panels, whose judicial membership will reflect special, 'regional' clusters of values and no more, and be selected by the parties themselves, reflects just such a tendency. It should certainly facilitate the task of achieving judicial consensus in the instant case, granted the 'regional' (geographical, ethnic-cultural, legal-systemic) factors that determined the choice of the membership of the limited Court panel involved. But it raises the larger issue, beyond the instant case so disposed of, of the relevance of any such disposition, *qua* Court jurisprudence, for the larger World Community outside the special 'region' directly involved. The objection is much the same as that raised against the continued relevance, today, of the jurisprudence of that old, between-the-two-World-Wars, Permanent Court of International Justice whose decisions were the product, essentially, of a limited Western European [in Stammler's terms][30] 'special legal community' group of judges, in cases arising from that same 'special legal community' client-states. The ethnic-cultural and value base is simply too narrow, it is contended, in a new, pluralistic World Community for too much automatic legal respect or legal deference to be accorded, today, to such jurisprudence from yesterday.

If value homogeneity in 'regional' (geographical, ethnic-cultural, legal-systemic) terms may thus establish certain limits of relevance to the exportability, and also the 'reception' abroad, of the jurisprudence of particular national tribunals, or even of some particular 'regional' supra-national tribunals like the High Court of Justice of the European Communities or the European Court of Human Rights that are characterised by a sufficiency of legal consensus within their own regional 'special legal communites', what are the consequences for legal eclesticism and borrowing from one national legal system to another where not merely are the national 'special legal communities' involved disparate in 'regional' terms but where the societies concerned are manifestly at different stages of social and economic development? The temporal factor, in other words, is different! The answer may be that the problem in making significant 'receptions' from the legal institutions and practice of the one society to the other, is at least sensibly reduced if one takes the trouble to study the society that one is seeking to borrow from to try to determine if it is at a more or less equivalent stage of political or other development. It is intriguing, in this special context, to note that, after the first three decades of constitutional jurisprudence of the Indian Supreme Court when the Court majoirty seemed to have been preoccupied in limiting and if not downright frustrating, community decision-making on social and economic problms as practised by legislative majorities at the federal and also the State level, younger Indian scholars[31] now seem to be looking to the Indian Supreme Court to assume some of the pioneering, trail-blazing *rôle* essayed by the United States Supreme Court in race relations from the 1950s when, for various reasons, Congress and the Presidency, the two main community policy-making institutions under the Constitution, were somnolent or deliberately avoiding the issue and remained so until the middle 1960s. If the Supreme Court could fill the gap in community policy-making, then, in the United States, why not, now, in India where special political problems seem to attend the formation of a sufficient legislative consensus to produce further legislature-based action on a number of burning issues of social policy? The political risks for the Court would be considerable, of course, unless it could be sure it was acting in furtherance of an emerging national consensus (as in the United States in the 1950s) which it could correctly discern and also inform and assist by its course of decisions. Now, however, that the federal executive in India seems to have finally concluded that the Supreme Court is, indeed, one among a number of community policy-making institutions at the federal level, and to be no longer reticent about using the federal executive appointment power as to Supreme Court judges to try consciously to shape and influence the long-range jurisprudence of the Court (as with the exercise of the judicial appointing or electing power in other legal systems, national and international), the way is at least opened, intellectually, for a coordinate, 'judge and company' approach to major community problem-solving, involving affirmative cooperation and mutual support between all the main decision-making institutions. For Indian, not less than for other, 'older' constitutional societies, Western and non-Western, the large problems of judicial value choice, and resolution of political and constitutional antinomies in a period of large-scale and rapid transition in society, will remain. These will necessarily involve the judicial skills of establishing priorities as to constitutional change and for judicial law-making in support thereof, by setting up some sort of hierarchy of social problems according to their relative degree of importance or urgency; of knowing when to act, and when not to act, as judicial law-maker; and of recognising that the scientific approach to judicial policy-making requires mastering the techniques of judicial self-restraint and self-denial as well as the more obvious ones of judicial activism in support of desirable community goals.

NOTES

1. *Judicial Review in the English-Speaking World* (1st ed., 1956; 4th ed., 1969). And compare Henry J. Abraham, *The Judicial Process* (1962); Walter F. Murphy and C. Herman Pritchett, *Courts, Judges and Politics* (3rd ed., 1979); M. Cappelletti, *Judicial Review in the Contemporary World* (1971).
2. I.C.J. Reports 1966, p. 6.
3. *Legal Consequences for States of the Continued Presence of South Africa in Namibia (South West Africa) notwithstanding Security Council Resolution 276 (1970), Advisory Opinion*, I.C.J. Reports 1971, p. 16.
4. *Scott v. Sanford,* 19 Howard 393 (1857).
5. Charles Evans Hughes, *The Supreme Court of the United States* (1928), pp. 50-51.

300

6. P.B. Gajendragadkar, *The Indian Parliament and the Fundamental Rights* (1972), p. 35 *et seq.;* S.N. Ray, *Judicial Review and Fundamental Rights* (1974), pp. 123-124.
7. *M.H. Quareshi* v. *State of Bihar,* A.I.R. *1958* S.C. 731.
8. A.I.R. *1958* S.C. 956.
9. *State of Madras* v. *Champakam Dorairajan,* A.I.R. *1951* S.C. 226, 228. And see also M.P. Jain, *Indian Constitutional Law* (1962), pp. 505-507.
10. S.P. Sathe, *Fundamental Rights and Amendment of the Indian Constitution* (1968), p. 43 *et seq.*
11. *Constitution-Making. Principles, Process, Practice* (1981), p. 57 *et seq.*
12. 4 Wheaton 316 (1819).
13. M.S. McDougal and H.D. Lasswell, 'The identification and appraisal of diverse systems of public order', 53 *American Journal of International Law* 1 (1959); M.S. McDougal and Associates, *Studies in World Public Order* (1960).
14. Walter F. Dodd, *State Government* (1928), pp. 130-137; Walter F. Dodd, *Constitutional Law* (4th ed., 1949), p. 77 *et seq.*
15. Julius Stone, *The Province and Function of Law* (1946), p. 185.
16. F. Gény, *Méthode d'Interprétation* (1899); F. Gény, *Science et Technique en Droit Privé Positif* (4 vols.) (1913-1924).
17. F. Luchaire, *Le Conseil constitutionnel* (1980), p. 295 *et seq.;* L. Favoreu and L. Philip, *Le Conseil constitutionnel* (1978), p. 47 *et seq.*
18. *Indira Nehru Gandhi* v. *Raj Narain,* A.I.R. *1975* S.C. 2299 (the Indian Supreme Court here overruling a lower Court's purported invalidation of Madame Gandhi's election as a Member of Parliament).
19. per Stone J., for the Court, *U.S.* v. *Carolene Products Co.,* 304 U.S. 144 (1938).
19a. *Sherrer* v. *Sherrer,* 334 U.S. 343, 365-366 (1948), (per Frankfurter J., dissenting).
20. I.C.J. Reports 1966, p. 6.
21. I.C.J. Reports 1969, p. 3.
22. I.C.J. Reports 1971, p. 16.
23. See P.A. Freund, *On understanding the Supreme Court* (1949), pp. 77-78.
24. I.C.J. Reports 1971, p. 16.
25. *Aegean Sea Continental Shelf, Interim Protection, Order of 11 September 1976.* I.C.J. Reports 1976, p. 3, pp. 20-21 (Separate Opinion of Judge Lachs).
26. See, for example, E. McWhinney, 'Toward the scientific study of values in Comparative Law research', in *XXth Century Comparative and Conflicts Law. Legal Essays in honour of Hessel E. Yntema* (K.H. Nadelmann, A.T. Von Mehren, J.N. Hazard, eds.) (1961), p. 29; Konrad Zweigert, 'Zur Lehre von den Rechtskreisen', *ibid.,* p. 42; Rudolf B. Schlesinger, 'The Common Core of Legal Systems: an emerging subject of Comparative study', *ibid.,* p. 65; John R. Schmidhauser, 'The circulation of Judicial Elites', in *Does Who Govern Matter? Elite Circulation in Contemporary Societies* (M.M. Czudnowski, ed., 1982).
27. Roscoe Pound, 'Scope and purpose of sociological jurisprudence', 24 *Harvard Law Review* 591 (1911); Roscoe Pound, *Social Control through Law* (1942). And see generally Julius Stone, *The Province and Function of Law* (1946), p. 355 *et seq.*
28. Josef Kohler, *Lehrbuch der Rechtsphilosophie* (1909).
29. Max Weber, *Wirtschaft und Gesellschaft* (2nd ed., 1925).
30. Rudolf Stammler, *Lehre von dem richtigen Recht* (1902); Julius Stone, *The Province and Function of Law* (1946), p. 317 *et seq.*
31. Upendra Baxi, *The Indian Supreme Court and Politics* (1980).

INDEX

302

Civil War (U.S.A.) 253–7
Codetermination in industry, W. Germany 238–9
Codification, legal 2
Collegiality, Court xii, 23–5, 34, 104–6
Comité constitutionnel (France) 19
Comity, federal 173, 261
Common Law xi, 23, 27, 36, 51, 213–4, 283
Communist Party case (W. Germany) 195
'Complaint', constitutional 12, 130, 207
Concordat case (W. Germany) 154–6
Concrete norm control 11–12, 15–18
Concurring opinions 24–5
Confirmation, judicial 290
Conseil constitutionnel (France) xv, 19–20, 50–1, 72–3, 138–40, 147–9, 157–60, 183–4, 240–2, 251–3, 272–4, 286
Conseil d'Etat 273
Constituent Assembly 117–8
Constituent processes 133–43
Constitutional construction 91–4, 94–9, 279 et seq.
Constitutional courts, de facto 27, 272, 283–7
Constitutional courts, de jure 28, 272
Constitutional review xiv, 1, 18–20
Corsica (Conseil constitutionnel) 183–4
Coty, René 55

Das, Justice (India) 95–6
Decentralisation, constitutional 183–4
de Gaulle, Charles 83, 118–9, 138, 240
Direct election, President (Conseil constitutionnel) 138–40
Directive Principles of State Policy (India) 226–7, 265–7, 279–80
'Discrete and insular minorities' 166–8, 286
Disqualification, judicial 39, 198
Dissenting opinions 24, 37, 41, 99
'Dissolution' case (India) 182–3
Dissolution case (Japan) 146–7
Dissolution of legislature (W. Germany) 147
Douglas, Justice (U.S.A.) xii, 52, 70, 75, 97, 101, 190, 249, 262, 275–6
Due Process, Procedural 95–6, 215–6, 225–6
Due Process, Substantive 165, 216–21, 225–6, 235, 281
Duff, Chief Justice (Canada) 52, 97

Economic and property interests 135–6, 176–7, 211 et seq., 234–7, 284
Education, equality 257–61
Education, segregation by race 257–8
Election of judges 94
Elections, constitutional equality principle 168–9, 194 et seq., 203 et seq.
Electoral processes 13, 149–50, 159–60, 166, 187 et seq., 203 et seq., 285
Elias, Judge-President (ICJ) 85
Emergency, constitutional 122–3, 137, 149–50, 288
'Emergency' doctrine, Canada 236
Equal protection of the laws 254 et seq.
Equality, constitutional 183–4, 203–8, 253–61, 265–7
Equilibrium, constitutional 143–51
Ethnic-cultural minorities 247 et seq., 253 et seq., 261 et seq.
'Eurocentrism', legal 31, 68, 94, 293, 294–6
European Communities case (Conseil constitutionnel) 158–60
European Defence Community litigation (W. Germany) 16, 28–9, 71, 102–4, 128, 153
Executive power 124, 133 et seq.

Fazl Ali, Justice (India) 6, 95–6
Federalism 168 et seq., 188, 234
Field, Justice (U.S.A.) 217–8
Fifth Republic (France) 239–40
Fitzmaurice, Judge (ICJ) 93–5, 108, 271
Foreign affairs 151 et seq.
Fourth Republic (France) 50–1, 89
France, constitution 19–20, 36, 50–1, 87, 115–6, 147–9, 207–8
France, Courts xv, 27, 50–1
Frank, Jerome xi
Frankfurter, Justice (U.S.A.) xii, 6, 37, 70, 74, 101, 165, 189, 259, 290
Frey, Roger (Conseil constitutionnel) 83, 242
Friedrich, Carl J. 7, 170
Friesenhahn, Judge (W. Germany) 71
Fundamental Rights (India) 95–6, 135–8

Gajendragadkar, Chief Justice (India) 79, 135, 279
Gandhi, Indira 30, 35, 78–9, 88, 136–8, 149–50, 233–4, 278, 286
Gény, F. 283